Intelligent Cities

Enabling Tools and Technology

Intelligent Cities

Enabling Tools and Technology

Pethuru Raj
Anupama C. Raman

CRC Press
Taylor & Francis Group
Boca Raton   London   New York

CRC Press is an imprint of the
Taylor & Francis Group, an **informa** business

AN AUERBACH BOOK

CRC Press
Taylor & Francis Group
6000 Broken Sound Parkway NW, Suite 300
Boca Raton, FL 33487-2742

First issued in paperback 2022

ISBN-13: 978-1-482-29997-7 (hbk)
ISBN-13: 978-1-03-234014-2 (pbk)
DOI: 10.1201/b18561

Publisher's Note

The publisher has gone to great lengths to ensure the quality of this reprint but points out that some imperfections in the original copies may be apparent.

Library of Congress Cataloging-in-Publication Data

Raj, Pethuru.
    Intelligent cities : enabling tools and technology / Pethuru Raj and Anupama C. Raman.
        pages cm
    Includes bibliographical references and index.
    ISBN 978-1-4822-9997-7 (hardcover : alk. paper) 1. Municipal engineering--Data processing. 2. Intelligent control systems. 3. Community development, Urban. I. Raman, Anupama C. II. Title.

    TD159.3.R35 2015
    628.0285--dc23
                                        2015006880

Visit the Taylor & Francis Web site at
http://www.taylorandfrancis.com

and the CRC Press Web site at
http://www.crcpress.com

Contents

Foreword

The information technology (IT) field hitherto has been the biggest enabler of worldwide businesses by automating, accelerating, and augmenting business processes. Now, as a result of the innate potentials of IT through a bevy of wonderful and decisive advancements in the form of fresh pioneering technologies, corporations are steadily and smartly leveraging its power across multiple industry verticals to increase their competence in facing all kinds of challenges (social, business, technology, etc.). Of late, IT is making pragmatic contributions toward empowering people to perform their day-to-day activities efficiently. This in turn has led to the emergence of several types of smart environments such as smart homes, hotels, hospitals, and so on. Technologies immensely gain both market and intellectual shares because of their people-centricity. All of these have led directly and indirectly to the formation of the overarching concept of intelligent cities to fulfill the varying expectations of their residents.

According to the latest surveys by leading market research organizations, by 2020, 75% of the world's population will be living in cities. But cities across the world are facing a variety of problems, such as aging infrastructures, unprecedented urbanization, environmental sustainability, and declining city budgets. There is a continued insistence on next-generation service delivery systems. Here, too, IT is being positioned as the savior of our struggling cities. The need of the hour for cities is to devise viable IT-inspired techniques and tools that will help them overcome internal concerns and deliver more with limited resources. IT is being touted as the strategically sound mechanism for facilitating the long-term goals of providing enhanced care, comfort, choice, and convenience for people living in cities. In short, as digital enterprises wade through a host of digital technologies, the long-standing goal of digital living will soon see fruition with the convergence and cluster of digitization, distribution, federation, industrialization, commoditization, and consumerization technologies. Concerted efforts are under way by different stakeholders, such as product vendors, original equipment manufacturers, system integrators, cloud brokers, research labs, government agencies, independent software vendors, and end-users across the globe to formulate and firm up the pragmatic vision of smart or intelligent cities—efforts that comprise smart systems and networks, intelligent grids, healthcare systems, retail, and governance.

In this book, the authors have presented a large number of right and relevant details on realizing and sustaining intelligent cities (the system of systems) across the world. The book has specifically focused on the following three aspects:

1. *Enabling Technologies.* The chapters that consider these are specifically crafted to explicate the recent arrival and acceptance of several proven and promising technologies, toolsets, and tips for efficiently transitioning our cities to be smart as well as for freshly establishing smart cities. Some of the key technologies covered are cloud, mobile, and high-performance big data analytics. The book has sufficient details on each of these technologies and how they converge and collaborate with one another for building next-generation intelligent cities.

2. *IT Platforms and Products.* Having realized the mind and market shares for intelligent cities, product specialists have come out with a number of intelligent city–specific solutions and services that simplify and streamline the process of constructing intelligent cities from the ground up.

3. *Business and Technical Use Cases.* Intelligent cities are a growing collection of several modules ranging from intelligent grid, transportation, home, utility, healthcare, and public

safety systems. The book has lucidly provided all the information for realizing these modules that help in building intelligent cities of the future.

I am sure this book will be informative and inspiring for readers, especially business executives, technical experts, solution architects, city planners and consultants, and government officials. The book has been designed and developed to be comprehensive and compact in explaining the nitty-gritty of promising smart city technologies, IT solutions, and use cases.

Sandesh Bhat
Vice President, India Software Labs, IBM

Preface

The transformative power of information technologies (IT) enables it to penetrate beneficially and bountifully into every tangible domain these days. For a significant time, IT has been the biggest enabler of business operations. Of late, there has been a paradigm shift. In addition to business enablement, IT is being touted as the best way for people empowerment through the perfect formulation and provision of sophisticated and situation-aware services (information, transaction, physical, etc.). IT has been granted the glowing and grandiose role of precisely understanding people's needs (personal as well as professional) and delivering them unobtrusively in time in the years ahead. This has led to the penetration of IT in all facets of our everyday lives, such as establishing and sustaining technology-inspired environments, such as smart homes, hospitals, and hotels, and for guaranteeing enhanced care, comfort, choice, and convenience for their occupants and owners.

Intelligent city is a new buzzword that is creating waves across the globe and is a kind of seamless and spontaneous convergence of several life-critical modules, such as smart government, retail, energy, healthcare, transport, utilities, and traffic. The emergence of highly promising and potent technologies has enabled the transition of ordinary objects into smart artifacts, provided deeper and wider connectivity of digitized entities, and devised systems that can empower people toward the concept of building connected cities. These technologies have also ensured and revolutionized the following aspects of our everyday lives: the service enablement of every important thing in our midst to be innately integrated and intelligent; IT infrastructure optimization through the pervasive cloud concepts; and the simplified and streamlined transition of data to information and to knowledge to bring forth actionable insights for a variety of systems to become activated, accelerated, and automated. IT has, in short, enabled people to make informed decisions with the help of ubiquitous access of information and services on the move, capturing various views and voices of people being expressed through various social sites, knowledge engineering, and enhancement.

The proliferation of diminutive yet smart sensors, multifaceted machines, humanoid robots, adaptive actuators, multitenant applications and services, converged platforms, slim wearable devices and sleek smart phones, and so on and the versatile technologies for the formation of ad hoc networks of these indispensable devices have enabled the quick realization of intelligent cities. The aim of this book is to explain the various aspects, especially the implementation technologies, facilitating tools, and pragmatic techniques, of intelligent cities. Further, salient use cases of intelligent cities, such as smart homes, buildings, transports, healthcare systems, and airports, are provided.

Chapter 1, "Envisioning Intelligent Cities," explains the principal technologies, absorbing use cases, and the leading platform solutions for implementing intelligent cities. Chapter 2, "Mobile Technologies and Applications for Intelligent Cities," details the various types of mobile device technologies, platforms, and use cases for intelligent cities. Mobile devices and technologies have revolutionized the lives of people across the world. A plethora of mobile applications have found their way into the everyday lives of people to simplify various tasks. Chapter 3, "The Role and Relevance of Software-Defined Cloud Infrastructures," vividly illustrates the cloud journey in substantially raising the utilization level of expensive IT infrastructures (computing, storage, and network) as clouds are being positioned as the core, central, and cognitive platform for hosting all kinds of intelligent city applications and data. Chapter 4, "Big Data Analytics for Real-Time City Insights," describes the significance of automated transition of data to information and to knowledge that can be easily disseminated to different and distributed smart city systems and services to accomplish the right and relevant automation and augmentation in time. Chapter 5, "The Internet of Things for Connected and Cognitive Cities," explains how various entities receive the intelligence in time through device instrumentation and interconnectivity. The concept of cyber physical system (CPS) is discussed in this chapter to demonstrate how the physical world is integrated with the remote virtual world to bring in scores of next-generation integrated and orchestrated applications for people. Pioneering developments are occurring in the actions and reactions of machines as a result of their capacity to communicate with one another in their vicinity and with others over any network. All of these purposeful integrations result in hitherto unforeseen people-centric and path-breaking applications.

Chapter 6, "Social Media Analytics for People Empowerment," describes two different perspectives about the usage of social media analytics: use of social media analytics for boosting business of organizations that in turn will contribute to the emergence and sustenance of intelligent cities and use of social media analytics in intelligent cities to track and understand the sentiments of residents that will contribute to the development of resident-friendly governments in cities across the world. Chapter 7, "Intelligent Cities: Strategy-Making and Governance," sheds more light on the power of IT integration as the key aspect of intelligent cities. Cities across the world are classified into two different levels of IT maturity: digital cities and ubiquitous or intelligent cities. The various IT aspects of these two types of cities are elucidated in detail in this chapter.

Chapter 8, "Smart Homes and Buildings," delineates the role of various technologies, standards, protocols, and tools in readily and rewardingly envisioning and establishing flexible homes and buildings of the future. Chapter 9, "Smart Energy, Utility, and Transport," mainly discusses the importance of bringing technology-enabled intelligence to energy preservation, utility monitoring, management, and analytics, as well as in everyday traffic management, whose quality has been declining day by day. There are several techniques to reduce power consumption substantially, thereby attaining the goal of environmental sustainability. Other related aspects are given sufficient attention in this chapter as well. Chapter 10, "Intelligent

Airports," focuses on developing smart airports to increase air traffic efficiency. The aviation industry has always been a forerunner in the field of technological innovation and its application for the benefits of air travel passengers. Airports are continuously evolving to cater to the ever increasing and ever changing demands of air travel passengers. This chapter explains the rich technology-enabled airports of future cities that will fulfill the expectations of air travel passengers and provide an enhanced travel experience.

Chapter 11, "Next-Generation Healthcare Systems," elucidates the tips and tools for enabling healthcare to be smart in its offerings and operations. Healthcare service providers across the world are under tremendous pressure to eliminate their aging infrastructure and improve the quality of services offered to patients. The healthcare-related service offerings of cloud service providers have proved to be a boon for healthcare service providers in enabling them to use cutting-edge technological tools and infrastructure. Use of big data analytics in healthcare provides valuable insights that can be used to improve the quality of services offered to patients. This chapter describes the different use cases for cloud services and big data analytics in the healthcare sector.

The final chapter, "Security Management of Intelligent Cities," is devoted to the security and privacy implications of technology adoption for devising and implementing intelligent cities. IT is the key enabler of intelligent cities, and its components can be subjected to various types of threats and vulnerabilities that can compromise the security of the entire city. This chapter explains the various security requirements of intelligent cities and the threats and vulnerabilities of the various components that form the basis of the intelligent city framework: cloud, big data, Internet of Things, and mobile technologies.

Please note that throughout the book, the terms "smart city" and "intelligent city" are used interchangeably unless specifically noted.

Disclaimer: This book and its contents are intended to convey the views of the authors and not any organization.

Acknowledgments

I express my sincere gratitude to John Wyzalek, senior acquisitions editor, for immensely helping us from the conceptualization to the completion stage of this book. The reviewing and publishing teams at CRC Press have been very prompt during this book project, for which I am very thankful. I wholeheartedly acknowledge the fruitful suggestions and pragmatic contributions of my coauthor, Anupama Raman.

I thank my supervisors—Prof. Ponnammal Natarajan, Anna University, Chennai; Prof. Priti Shankar (late), Computer Science and Automation (CSA) Department, Indian Institute of Science (IISc), Bangalore; Prof. Naohiro Ishii, Department of Intelligence and Computer Science, Nagoya Institute of Technology; and Prof. Kazuo Iwama, School of Informatics, Kyoto University, Japan—for shaping my research life. I express my heartfelt gratitude to Thomas Erl, the world's top-selling service-oriented architecture (SOA) author, for giving me a number of memorable opportunities to write book chapters for his exemplary books. I thank the IBM managers for extending their moral support.

At this point of time, I recollect and reflect on the selfless sacrifices made by my parents in shaping me to this level. I expressly thank my wife, Sweetlin Reena, and sons, Darren Samuel and Darresh Bernie, for their perseverance as I took on the tremendous and tedious challenge of putting the book together. I thank Pastor George, the Shalom Church, Naganathapura, Bangalore, for his earnest prayers. I thank all the readers for their overwhelming support for my previous book. I give all the glory and honor to my Lord and Savior Jesus Christ for His grace and guidance.

Pethuru Raj

At the outset, I would like to express my heartfelt thanks to John Wyzalek, senior acquisitions editor, for helping us at each stage toward the completion of this book. I also express my sincere thanks to the reviewing and publishing teams of CRC Press. I extend my wholehearted thanks to my coauthor, Pethuru Raj, for his constant support, guidance, and insights that helped me in crafting various chapters of this book.

I thank IBM management for their wholehearted support in the successful completion of this book project. I also sincerely acknowledge the sacrifices of my parents that made me what I am today. I extend a special note of thanks to my husband, R. Murali Krishnan, and daughter, Aparna, for their constant support and motivation. I also acknowledge the support given to me by my parents-in-law, my sisters, and their families. I thank all my friends who have constantly helped and supported me to complete the book successfully.

A final note of thanks to Sandesh Bhat, VP, India Software Labs, IBM, who wrote the Foreword of this book.

Anupama Raman

1

ENVISIONING INTELLIGENT CITIES

Abstract

As a result of the unceasing adoption and adaptation of newer technologies in the information technology (IT) space, the most perplexing yet pioneering IT-enabled digital living is being prescribed for every individual that will be cognitively constructive and contribute to his or her personal as well as professional life. Increasingly, every common, casual, and even cheap object in our daily environments is being readied to become smart in its operations and offerings through a host of edge technologies. All kinds of everyday devices (consumer electronics, handhelds, mobiles, wearables, portables, implantables, gadgets, etc.) in our midst are systematically empowered to be intelligent in their actions and reactions through a bevy of smartness-filled instrumentation and interconnectivity processes and platforms. Enabling a seamless and spontaneous integration with remotely hosted software applications and data goes a long way in transforming all sorts of physical systems to be cognitive in their sensing, interpretation, knowledge extraction, decision making, and actuation capabilities. All the unique and universal innovations and improvisations in the information and communication technologies (ICTs) space collectively lead to a variety of smarter environments such as smarter homes, offices, manufacturing, hospitals, retail establishments, governments, and so on. Smart cities are the overarching concept of a number of the aforementioned smart environments. Establishing and sustaining intelligent cities is one prominent derivative of the praiseworthy advancements in the flourishing ICT space. In this chapter, we delve deeper and describe in detail the various insights associated with smart cities.

1

1.1 Introduction

The information technology (IT) landscape is continuously captivating owing to the faster maturity of newer and nimbler technologies that open up fresh possibilities and hitherto unforeseen opportunities. In particular, manifold new-generation applications and services are being developed and delivered as a result of the unprecedented stability of upheaving and transformative technologies. For example, we extensively read about enterprise (transactional and analytical), embedded, social, mobile, and cloud applications in the recent past. Converged platforms and infrastructures are being built to streamline application design and development (from the ground up or assembling), deployment, management, integration, and delivery requirements. In other words, a paradigm shift has occurred. IT has been the prime enabler of worldwide businesses and today is being prescribed as a viable, venerable, and value-adding mechanism for empowering individuals. With self-, surroundings-, and situation-aware technologies emerging and evolving, scores of context-sensitive services could be readily built and deployed to enhance human care, choice, convenience, and comfort substantially.

1.2 Unfolding the Smarter Planet Vision

In the recent past, a horde of automation and acceleration technologies in the IT domain have been positioned to ensure a productive journey toward the realization of revolutionary, real-time, and real-world people-centric applications. The well-known and recognized accomplishments hitherto unheard of include software-defined cloud environments, cognitive computing, ambient communication, ubiquitous sensing, vision and perception, predictive and prescriptive analytics based on big data, knowledge engineering, social networking sites, ad hoc networking, mobility, smart spaces, and digital societies. The future too seems to be very bright and endowed with numerous pragmatic breakthroughs. Situation-aware edge technologies (tags, stickers, codes, chips, labels, sensors, microcontrollers, smart dust, light-emitting diode [LED] lights, motes, speckles, etc.) carrying our personal profiles and preferences digitally will map, merge, and mingle with other entities and elements in our locations (personal and professional) to effortlessly, precisely, and perfectly understand people's needs and fulfill them deftly and dynamically in time in synchronization with IT.

The commonly found artifacts and articles in our midst can be digitally empowered to be smart in their outlooks. This purpose-specific transition is achieved mainly by two matured processes. The first consists of internally embedding multifaceted functional modules into any tangible objects (mechanical, electrical, electronics, etc.) using nanoscale technologies and adeptly instrumenting new-generation devices to be distinct in their characteristics. The second consists of externally attaching diminutive, disappearing, and disposable computers, communicators, sensors, and actuators. The idea is ultimately to enable every physical thing to be interconnected; interactive; and finally, intelligent. For example, our coffee cups, dinner plates, tables, tools, terminals, tangibles, and tablets, and clothes will be skillfully empowered to be smart in their interactions with other products in the vicinity and even with human beings. Eventually all sorts of physical day-to-day items will be smoothly transitioned into smart and sentient digital entities. Hence future generations will no doubt experience and realize completely new technology-sponsored and flourished digital living. The impact of IT in our lives becomes bigger, deeper, yet more relaxed and unobtrusive with time.

Technologies for enabling minimization, interconnectivity, services, federation, virtualization, perception, analytics and actuation, and so on are fast maturing toward producing affordable, connected, dependable, people-aware, and context-sensitive systems and services. In a nutshell, technologies are increasingly penetrative, participative, and productive. Technology-driven integration among digitalized objects at the ground (physical) level with scores of Web, social, embedded, and enterprise software applications at the cyber level will pour out a stream of futuristic, adaptive, and knowledge-filled and mission-critical applications. That is, IT roles and responsibilities are bound to thrive substantially in peoples' lives. Already machines are talking to one another locally as well as remotely. Services hosted across geographically distributed cloud infrastructures are interacting with one another in an ad hoc manner according to evolving needs to conceive, compose, and provide sophisticated facilities, features, and functionalities. As the Internet of Things (IoT) idea unfolds and expands, casual and cheap items are being endowed to join in mainstream computing. Business ventures, investors, and entrepreneurs are hence strategizing to embrace competent technologies to keep the edge earned intact, and IT is gradually yet happily moving toward the originally envisaged human empowerment.

All of these delightful transformations, optimizations, simplifications, and so on will result in smarter spaces. In other words, peoples' care, choice, convenience, and comfort levels will reach greater heights in the days to come. The main purpose of this chapter is to describe the key drivers and trends, the principal benefits to governments and their constituents, the eruption of versatile and value-adding technologies, and the prickling challenges ahead. We dig deeper and extract the essential details about the rapidly emerging idea of smart cities.

1.3 The Need for Intelligent Cities

Cities are emerging as the principal drivers for the overall growth of nations across the world. They are the primary innovation hubs and provide plentiful opportunities for various stakeholders including immigrants, skilled workers, innovators, investors, local governments, and entrepreneurs. Highly visible establishments such as universities and research labs, coupled with clusters of industries and knowledge workers with higher education, industry experience, and technology expertise pouring into cities, augur well for the increasing relevance of cities for their occupants. Businesses and commercial establishments are more concentrated in cities, empowering them to be the chief job creators and wealth generators for their inhabitants.

Cities are bound to become the most appropriate building blocks and the key focus area for nations in the years to unfold. Our cities are slated to become lovable, livable, and sustainable because of the smart leverage and immense contributions of highly robust and resilient technologies. The cities of the future are going to be elegantly and extremely connected and cognizant, grandly synchronized and IT enabled, and software intensive. All kinds of city resources are being optimally shared across. City infrastructures are being well planned, executed, shared, and maintained while taking into account the changing equations of peoples' expectations. Above all, the cities around the world ought to be greatly people-centric, converged, sensitive and responsive (S & R) for any eventualities, deftly anticipative and active, green, exemplarily exquisite, service-oriented, event-driven, and so on. Accordingly, newer and nimbler techniques, tips, and tools explicitly provide a stimulating and sustainable foundation for knowledge generation, corroboration, correlation, and dissemination. Thus the concept of knowledge incubation is to become a common entity by ingeniously leveraging all the significant and astute developments in the analytics space for cities to be increasingly knowledge-inspired and inclined. The fast-maturing domain of big data analytics comes in handy in realizing knowledge cities across the globe.

Clouds will become the central and core IT infrastructure for hosting, managing, and delivering people-centric city services, applications, and data. More unified IT platforms will be in place to facilitate the formation and maintenance of smart cities. The transition to service-oriented architecture (SOA) and event-driven architecture (EDA) helps the prosperity of cities in many ways. That is, besides the much-applauded cloud enablement, service enablement is going to be a game-changer for cities of the future to be intrinsically extensible and sustainable. The accessibility, simplicity, and, consumability of city services are being quickly and easily facilitated through a growing array of intuitive and natural interfaces. Service implementation platforms will become pervasive and persuasive too for simplifying and streamlining smart city implementations and enhancements. National leaders, government officials, public servants, and bureaucrats will eventually show greater interest in formulating and forming the right and relevant policies, powerful processes, and pragmatic practices as a vital precursor toward intelligent cities. The next-generation cities will be hugely endowed with competent and cognitive social, physical, and cyber infrastructures. Ultimately people will be smartest in their deeds, deals, and decisions ably assisted by a growing array of networked and multifaceted devices. The city government will become transparent, auditable, responsible, and accountable. The service delivery mechanism will go through a series of reformations and recognitions, insightfully benefiting people. All kinds of wastage, pilferage, slippage, and shrinkages can be fully identified in time and avoided so that human productivity and system efficiency can be increased considerably.

1.4 City-Specific Challenges

Numerous critical and crucial issues are noticeably plaguing cities worldwide these days. Large and mega cities are beset with scores of problems as a result of rapid and unbridled urbanization. That is, the consistent shrinkage of various livelihood resources, the continued growth in the urban population due to the spike in peoples' migration to cities primarily in search of jobs, and so on complicate the already overloaded and overcrowded cities. Other noteworthy trends include global warming, a lack of or poor city infrastructures, a decline in the safety and security of people and property, a slide in seamless transport, a growing scarcity of energy and clean water, and so forth. The unfortunate result is the sharp decline in and dissatisfaction with the quality of city dwellers' lives. Another factor is that the receding and recessionary world economy puts more stress and strictures on declining and deteriorating cities. As city budgets are being slashed everywhere, the mantra of "more with less" gains prominence and hence there is a clarion call for a flurry of activities such as rationalization, simplification, optimization, standardization, automation, and so on through an apt adoption and adaptation of IT. Well-known challenges for our cities include the following:

- Environmental sustainability and ecological degradation. Global warming and climate change are occurring as a result of the enormous outflow of greenhouse gases such as carbon dioxide and methane.
- Teeming population and at the same time scarcity of resources.
- Rapid urbanization, exposing the infrastructural weaknesses and insufficiency.

1.4.1 Trickling Urbanization Challenges

It has been said that the world is no longer a comity of nations but is being visualized as a dynamic collection of cities. Cities are bound to play a vital role in strengthening and shaping up human society in the years ahead. Urbanization is happening rapidly as people migrate in large numbers to urbanized areas to find suitable jobs and to sustain their livelihoods. Governments are encouraging and enabling both private and public sectors to set up innumerable industry clusters in city outskirts. Cities are given prime importance in formulating and framing of policies, developmental roadmaps, and processes. It is estimated that by 2050, 70% of the total world population will live in cities. An IBM white paper reports that city planning officials are faced with critical decisions of how to deal with these swelling city populations. Large-scale population centers and countries such as China and India are expected to have more people in their cities. Because of the uncertainty in the global economy, the resource crunch is being premised as the huge barrier for cities to grow their infrastructures to accommodate the growing population. Fresh cities are being carefully designed and developed to enhance the quality of life considerably.

Global urbanization is one of the key challenges of the 21st century. The number of people living in cities is increasing rapidly: Since 2007, more people have been living in urban areas than in rural areas, consuming 75% of global energy production. The United Nations has estimated that by 2030, nearly 60% of the world population will be living in an urban environment. In 1900, this figure was only 13%. The increasing degree of urbanization affects not only industrialized nations (80% by 2030), but in particular the developing countries (55% by 2030). Cities, which cover only a small portion of the planet's surface area, consume more than three quarters of all energy produced and are responsible for 80% of CO_2 emissions.

Having understood the mandated transformation for worldwide cities, those who are in charge and control of cities are seriously strategizing and brainstorming to finalize workable ways and means of steadily embracing the sparkling concept of smart city. Standards-compliant technical solutions and deployment architectures are being prepared to painstakingly build an intelligent digital nervous system supporting all sorts of existing and emerging urban operations. The pace of digitalization is picking up quickly; the interconnectivity among distributed, diverse, and decentralized systems is being established and preserved; the goal of service enablement of every participating and contributing system module is being speeded up to enhance interoperability in the midst of diversity; virtualization/

containerization (overwhelmingly through the Docker solution) is being accelerated for the portability factor; and fruitful integration with social sites is being carried out to readily understand peoples' concerns, comments, compliments, curiosities, and so on.

1.5 The Vast Potentials of Smart Cities

At the same time, cities also open up fresh opportunities for individuals, innovators, and institutions to contemplate and do different things for the betterment of societies and communities. Cities need to change their structure and behavior remarkably to cogently fit with the distinctly identified and articulated ideals of the smarter world, the vision being proclaimed and pursued vigorously and rigorously by leading IT companies today. This incredible and long-term notion of the smarter world is being presented as the next logical move by worldwide technology creators and service providers to be relevant in their long and arduous journey. There are several key drivers and motivators for the surging popularity of this game-changing concept as a series of decisive developments and advancements in the form of a growing community of realization technologies being unfolded to simplify the hitherto unknown path toward the challenging transformation. Smart cities, as a noticeable component of the smarter world, occupy a substantial and venerable position in the journey.

1.6 City Transformation Strategy

Worldwide cities yearn for remarkable and resilient transformations in two major aspects: city operation model and information leverage. Another vital point not to be taken lightly is to sharply enhance the user experience of city services. The following five factors are overwhelmingly accepted as promoting the desired city renovation.

- Infrastructure optimization
- Technology adaptation and adoption
- Process excellence
- Architecture assimilation
- Making sense of data and leveraging it for city efficiency

1.6.1 Infrastructure Optimization

The overwhelming adoption of infrastructure consolidation, convergence, centralization, federation, automation, and sharing methods clearly indicates that the much-maligned infrastructure landscape is bound to be supple and smart in the days to follow. Compute, communication, and storage infrastructures are going through a bevy of exemplary transitions. Hardware infrastructures are turned and tuned to be network discoverable and accessible, loosely coupled yet cohesive, programmable, and remotely manageable in a virtual space. In the recent past, we heard and read more about software-defined environments (SDEs), that is, things are moving in the direction of complete and comprehensive virtualization of every tangible element. It started with server virtualization and now we are heading toward storage, network, desktop, service, application, data, operating system (OS) virtualization (alternatively termed as containerization), and so on. Several buzzwords thus emerged in the IT industry: software-defined infrastructure (SDI), software-defined networking (SDN), software-defined storage (SDS), and so on. First there were data centers (DCs), then cloud centers, and now software-defined cloud centers (SDCCs). We discuss the raging cloud paradigm in great detail in this and subsequent chapters.

1.6.2 System Infrastructure

Hardware infrastructures include servers, storage, network solutions, specific appliances, and so on. Software infrastructure solutions are plentiful, as listed here.

- *Application and data infrastructure*—Development, execution, and management platforms and containers, databases, cubes, marts, and warehouses, and so on.
- *Middleware and management infrastructure*—This includes integration hubs, buses, backbones, engines and fabrics, messaging brokers, etc. With the intensifying complexity of IT space resulting from the uninhibited complicity and heterogeneity of technologies, products, programming languages, design approaches, protocols, data formats, and so on, the importance of introspective and insightful middleware solutions increases considerably.

Infrastructures are becoming lean, mean, and green. Further, with IT agility becoming operationalized as IT infrastructures are optimized and organized by leveraging cloud principles, the goal of increasing business agility is steadily approaching reality. Considering the greater and impressive role of infrastructures for cities of the future, rationalization, simplification, automation, orchestration, and so on are the chief techniques to enable IT to be cognitively city-friendly. Precisely speaking, the cloud paradigm represents IT industrialization, standardization, and commoditization.

1.6.3 The Adoption of Versatile Technologies

It is a fact that a number of noteworthy transitions and trends are occurring in the IT field. At the fundamental and foundational level, a variety of nimbler technologies are emerging to bring desirable transformations in data capture, representation, transmission, enrichment, storage, processing, analysis, mining, visualization, and virtualization tasks.

- *Digitalization is spreading quickly*—With the enhanced and enticed maturity and stability of smartness-enabling technologies, platforms, and processes, every tangible object is set to become smart in its actions and reactions. "Dumb" and fixed objects in our midst are being consciously readied to join in mainstream computing. Ordinary articles become extraordinary artifacts to be computational, communicative, sensitive, responsive, perceptive, and so on. Besides the decisive miniaturization technologies such as nanotechnology, microelectromechanical systems, and so on, more powerful edge technologies such as pads, stickers, labels, tags, cards, chips, speckles, and nanoscale materials are powering up collectively the goal of transitioning physical items into digital ones. In short, the key drivers for the impending smarter world are computing, communication, sensing, vision, fusion, perception, knowledge-engineering, interfacing, and actuation technologies. That is, self-, situation-, and surroundings-aware technologies are emerging and evolving rapidly.
- *Digitalization toward sentient and smart materials*—Attaching scores of edge technologies (invisible, calm, infinitesimal and disposable sensors and actuators, stickers, tags, labels, motes,

dots, specks, etc.) with common objects results in the accumulation of digital objects that can be registered, discovered, service-enabled, integrated, orchestrated, and so on. Digital technologies enable an effective and sustainable development of different types of city services for residents, visitors, and businesses. Digital technology contributes much toward seamless public transport, travel (carpooling and sharing), road maintenance, traffic, parking, energy, waste disposal, street lighting, and urban furniture. Technologies also play an essential role in building relations with the local population, encouraging tourism and culture and developing the area's appeal for businesses, companies, and shops.

- *Consumerization (extended device landscape)*—There is a huge market for trendy and handy, slim and sleek mobile, wearable, implantable, and portable devices. These are instrumented in such a way as to be spontaneously interconnected to exhibit intelligent behaviors. The device landscape is embracing a bevy of miniaturization technologies to be slim and sleek, yet smart in their operations, outlooks, and outputs. Smartphones and wearables are ubiquitous these days and play a very substantial and influential role in people's lives.

- *Extreme and deeper connectivity* is another well-known phenomenon to establish and sustain ad hoc connectivity among different and distributed devices at the ground level and with remote, off-premise, on-demand, and online applications.

- *Cyber physical systems (CPSs)*—Embedded systems are becoming networked; physical systems cyber-enabled; machines integrated with one another as well as with cloud-based services and data; things are Internet worked, and so on as a result of solid improvements in extreme and deeper connectivity and networking standards, technologies, platforms, and appliances.

- *Commoditization and industrialization*—IT infrastructures are being commoditized and system components produced in massive volumes to enable selection, assembly, and configuration toward full-fledged systems (software and hardware).

- *Infrastructure optimization*—Clouds, the core and central IT infrastructures, are the next-generation infrastructures to be consolidated, converged, centralized yet federated, virtual-ized, automated, and shared. All kinds of smart city appli-cations, data, platforms, and infrastructures will be in cloud environments. The centrality and criticality of clouds are bound to play a vital and value-adding role for future smart cities. Clouds are programmable, consolidated, converged, adaptive, automated, shared, quality of service-enabling, green, and lean infrastructures.

- *Middleware solutions*—include intermediation, aggregation, dis-semination, arbitration, enrichment, collaboration, delivery, management, governance, brokering, identity and security.
- *New kinds of data-driven insights* (big and fast data analytics).
- *New kinds of databases* (analytical, clustered, parallel and dis-tributed SQL databases, NoSQL, and NewSAL databases).

Disruptive and transformative technologies with the smart syn-chronization of a galaxy of information and communication tech-nologies will emerge to realize revolutionary applications and to accomplish hitherto unheard of social networking and digital knowl-edge societies. Auto-identification tags carrying our personal pro-files and preferences digitally, will map, mix, merge, and mingle with others in realizing new human aspirations. Our daily tools and products can be converted into smart products by attaching ultrasmall computers. For example, our coffee cups, dinner plates, tablets, and clothes will be empowered to act smart in their opera-tions and interactions with other products in the vicinity or even with human beings. Finally all the tangible and appropriate objects, materials, and articles will be transitioned into smart and sentient digital artifacts. This will result in the era of IoT in the years to come. Hence future generations no doubt will experience and real-ize complete and compact technology-enabled living. The impact of IT in our lives becomes bigger, deeper, yet more relaxed and unob-trusive with time.

1.6.4 The Assimilation of Architectures

A family of futuristic and flexible architectural paradigms, patterns, and principles such as service-oriented architecture (SOA), event-driven architecture (EDA), model-driven architecture (MDA), and so on are evolving to be a greater enabler of futuristic systems. Architectural patterns are a kind of complexity-mitigation technique. With multiplicity and heterogeneity-imposed complexity on the rise, architectures are bound to play a stellar role in moderating the unbridled complexity. The veritable trend is that with the stability and maturity of the service paradigm, everything is being presented as a service providing, brokering, and consumer entity. Data, applications, platforms, and even infrastructures are being consciously codified and comingled as publicly discoverable, remotely accessible, autonomous, highly available, usable, reusable, and composable services. With the unparalleled popularity of the service-orientation paradigm, the vision of "Everything is a service" is becoming a reality. Service enablement delicately hides the implementation and operational complexities of all kinds of IT resources and exposes only the functionality and capability of those resources in the form of public interfaces to be dynamically found and bound. Everything is given its functional interface so that other systems and services can find, bind, and leverage the distinct capabilities and competencies of one another.

1.6.5 Services Are Everywhere

The concept of service enablement has penetrated deeper as well as broader. That means every tangible thing is being service enabled. The idea is to just expose its distinct functionality through standardized interfaces rather than the thing itself. That is, the objective of making everything a service is slowly yet steadily seeing the light. The future definitely belongs to a growing collection of adaptive and ambient services as every concrete object in our everyday environment is being explicitly expressed and exposed as a self-describing and autonomous service. This strategic shift is being realized as a result of the unprecedented maturity and stability of the service paradigm principles. This kind of service exposition capability helps every tangible item in our midst to hide behind one or more network-accessible service interfaces. The new concept of interface and implementation segregation goes a long way in conveniently abstracting and dismantling all kinds of differences and deficiencies to facilitate automated and unambiguous identification, assemblage, and utilization of any local as well as remote services. This service-enablement capability enables every tangible thing to join in mainstream computing. In a way, everything can be a service-providing, requesting, and brokering entity.

Such a tectonic transition empowers every service (thing) to dynamically find, understand, bind, and leverage the unique capabilities of services (things) over any network. Such syntactically and semantically correct interactions strengthen the foundation for bringing better and bigger services. As we all know, services are instinctively powerful to be reusable and composable to craft smart and sophisticated service-oriented applications and processes. Another important revelation is that the connectivity capability becomes deeper and extreme. Diminutive, distributed, decentralized, and diverse devices and digitalized objects are increasingly intertwined with one another to make them aware and active. Devices and smart objects are being produced quickly through a host of substantiated methods and they are more tuned to context-awareness and people-centricity.

1.6.6 Devices Are Connected and Cyber-Enabled for People-Centric Services

Leading market analysts and research groups predict that by 2020, there will be more than 50 billion connected devices in the world. That is, all kinds of electronic devices in our working and living places are being empowered to connect with one another in the vicinity as well as with any remote devices. These devices are further enabled to connect and communicate with all sorts of personal and professional software applications and services that could be online, on-demand, off-premise, remotely hosted, managed and maintained in cloud platforms, and so on. In a nutshell, diverse, distributed, and decentralized devices, data sources, and applications are expected to dynamically find, deftly bind, and decisively leverage one another to derive and deliver highly smart and sophisticated services to people in the years to come.

The unique capabilities originating and flourishing with these technology-driven connectivity machinations could provide a stimulating and sustainable foundation for conceptualizing and concretizing a variety of people-centric and path-breaking services and applications in the future. Everyday gadgets and gizmos are appropriately being empowered to manifest distinct computational, communicative, collaborative, and cognitive capabilities in their actions and reactions through two major noteworthy transformations, as stated previously. The first is seamlessly embedding a number of powerful and purpose-specific yet highly miniaturized modules internally into devices to bring in the much-needed smartness in the devices' actions and reactions. The second is establishing a scintillating integration with other machines in the vicinity and with any personal or professional applications in enterprise, Web, and cloud servers indirectly via device middleware solutions. The communication could be wireless or wired for local interactions and the open, public, and inexpensive Internet is the communication infrastructure for remote associations.

Numerous well-written and widely circulated articles and articulations about the fast-emerging and evolving field of machine-to-machine (M2M) communication have appeared in national as well as international publications. The spontaneous integration among disparate machines is acquiring a significant intellectual and market share these days as such a linkage can bring forth a series of innovations and improvisations in each and every industry segment. Increasingly a variety of personal as well as professional devices are becoming intricately yet intimately linked to a growing array of cyber applications, sensor and actuation networks, policy and knowledge bases, social network sites, and data sources in cloud servers and storages. With these prospective and positive trends emanating and evolving rapidly, there is a fruitful possibility and opportunity for speedy conceptualization of services for hitherto unexplored territories. Further, not only new service design and development, but also assembly with existing services to elegantly compose advanced and adaptive applications is bound to become pervasive. Individuals, innovators, and institutions could gain experience in dynamically composing a bevy of sophisticated services and applications across industry segments at the speed of business.

1.6.7 Process Excellence

Processes have been the preferred engine for activating and sustaining the IT domain. There are sophisticated algorithms and methods to bring in a stream of innovations in realizing highly synchronized, slim, and smart processes that directly impact all kinds of business offerings and IT operations. The process engineering and enhancement field is ceaselessly on the right track by inscribing fresh process consolidation and orchestration, process innovation, control, reengineering, process governance, and management mechanisms.

1.6.7.1 Monitoring and Management of City Processes Today people subscribe to and consume an increasing collection of city services and participate in multiple processes that interact with various city departments and service providers. Hence it is vital for the city to monitor the performance of its services and gain consumers' feelings, preferences, concerns, and deficiencies to bring in necessary rectifications in the subsequent versions of city services [1]. Multiple dimensions of city processes can be monitored and measured in real-time, including

- Lifestyle processes of the city population
- Performance of each department to fulfil its services to its people and businesses without getting into the operational details of each department
- Public sentiment
- Response and feedback of the constituents

Understanding public sentiment could reveal the lacunae in the system design and acting on them can help system designers and architects understand the root causes. This will remarkably improve the multifaceted management of the city, create more fruitful synergies, and help identify new and evolving needs.

1.6.7.2 Process Management This is the centerpiece of a people-centric platform as it orchestrates multiple processes around a person and integrates services across departments. It has the ability to manage "clusters of services" and this function allows multiple services to function together to run a government program seamlessly. For example, a government program to manage chronic disease in a population is a cluster of services. As the resident uses the various schemes and services in the governance area, the process management component will track the utilization, quality of services, and outcome of these services. The process management capability ultimately dawns on intelligent ways to conceive and deliver smart services to residents.

1.6.8 Make Sense Out of Data for Big Insights

Insights-driven cities are a most welcome development for the future of this world. Data become big data as they are being produced, gathered, and processed in multiple structures (structured, semistructured, and nonstructured) at differing velocities and a large scale. Machine-generated data are far larger than human-generated data. The data volume, velocity, and variety are seeing a remarkable climb. With innumerable devices, tags, stickers, sensors, appliances, machines, instruments, gadgets, and so on becoming fervently deployed in distributed and decentralized fashion in important locations such as homes, hospitals, hotels, and so on, tasks such as data collection, classification, fusion, transition to information and knowledge, and dissemination to authorized users and agents need to be accomplished in real time using a series of greatly sophisticated and dependable technologies.

Big data is quite a recent phenomenon capturing the imaginations of many. Data generation, capture, transmission, storage, processing, analyzing, and mining have been an important factor among worldwide organizations for enhancing business opportunities, productivity, and value. Now with the multiplicity of many data sources, the traditional analytics space is going through a stream of delightful transformations to be better prepared for capturing and capitalizing big data (greater data volume, variety, velocity, variability, etc.). Big data analytics assumes a greater significance and success in promptly realizing needs and reaching out to people in unique ways. Smart city services will be more knowledge encapsulated, context aware, and relevant for people. Real-time analysis results in a ready realization toward producing actionable insights in time with the emergence and escalation of converged, centralized, automated, shared, optimized, virtualized, and even federated cloud infrastructures.

1.7 The Key Trends in IT toward Smart Cities

1.7.1 The Shift toward People IT

A bevy of pioneering technologies (service computing, cloud, big data, analytics, mobility, extreme connectivity, etc.) are emerging and evolving rapidly toward the compact fulfillment and the sustenance of the IBM smarter planet vision. The essence of the ensuing era is that every tangible thing in our environments (personal, social, and professional) is destined to become systematically digitalized, service enabled, and interconnected in the immediate vicinity as well as with cloud applications and services to be smart in its actions and reactions. This strictly technology-sponsored empowerment will result in a series of hitherto unforeseen, people-centric, and sophisticated services for humans. Besides a cornucopia of informational, transactional, and knowledge services, a new set of path-breaking services such as context-aware and insights-driven physical services will also be conceived dynamically and delivered to the right people, at the right time and place unobtrusively to enhance the quality of life significantly in this extremely networked world. That is, technologies are coming closer to people to make them the smartest in all their everyday deeds and decisions.

Having contributed to the unprecedented uplift of business-operation productivity and for composable businesses, IT is turning toward human productivity. We have been experiencing several noteworthy advancements in the IT landscape. Therefore the shift toward human empowerment is on the right track. That is, not only business services and applications, but also conceptualization, best-of-breed implementations, and maintenance of people-centric and physical services will become available. Best practices, patterns, platforms, processes, and products are being unearthed and built to smooth the route toward the envisioned people-centric IT.

1.7.2 The Era of Smart Computing

What will human life on this planet be like around the year 2025? What kind of lasting impacts, cultural changes, and perceptible shifts will be achieved in human society as a result of the consistent innovations, evolutions, and inventions in information, communication, sensing, vision, perception, knowledge engineering, dissemination, and actuation technologies? Today this has become a dominant and lingering question among leading researchers, luminaries, specialists, and scientists. Many vouch for a comprehensive turnaround in our social, personal, and professional lives owing to a dazzling array of technological sophistications, creativities, and novelties. Presumably computing, communication, perception, and actuation will be everywhere, all the time. The days of ambient intelligence (AmI) are not far away with the speed and astuteness with which scores of implementation technologies are being developed and sustained.

It is also presumed and proclaimed that the ensuing era will be a fully knowledge-driven society. Databases will pave the way for knowledge bases and there will be specialized engines for producing and maintaining self-managing systems. Knowledge systems and networks are readied for autonomic communication. Cognition-enabled machines and expert systems will become our casual and compact companions. A growing array of smarter systems will surround, support, and sustain us in our classrooms, homes, offices, hotels, coffee houses, airport lounges, gyms, restaurants, meeting places, and other vital junctions in large numbers. They will seamlessly connect, collaborate, corroborate, and correlate to understand our mental, social, and physical needs and deliver them in a highly unobtrusive, secure, and relaxed fashion. That is, the right information and appropriate services will be conceived, constructed, and delivered to the right person, at the right time and at the right place. Extensively smart furniture, sensors, and artifacts will become the major contributors to this tectonic and tranquil modernization and migration.

1.7.3 Smarter Environments

Our living, relaxing, and working environment is envisioned as filled with a variety of electronics including environment monitoring sensors, actuators, monitors, controllers, processors, tags, labels, stickers, dots, motes, stickers, projectors, displays, cameras, computers, communicators, appliances, gateways, high-definition IP TVs, and so on. Apart from these, all the physical and concrete items, articles, furniture, and packages will become empowered with computation and communication-enabled components by attachment of specially made electronics onto them. Whenever we walk into such kinds of empowered and augmented environments illuminated with a legion of digitized objects, the devices we carry and even our e-clothes will enter into a calm yet logical collaboration mode and form wireless ad hoc networks with the inhabitants in that environment. For example, if someone wants to print a document from his or her smartphone or tablet and enters into a room where a printer is situated, then the smartphone will begin a conversation with the printer automatically and send the document to be printed.

Thus, in that era, our everyday places will be made informative, interactive, intuitive, and inspiring by embedding intelligence and autonomy into their constituents (audio/video systems, cameras, information and Web appliances, consumer and household electronics, and other electronic gadgets besides digitally augmented walls, floors, windows, doors, ceilings, and any other physical objects and artifacts). Unobtrusive computers, communicators, sensors, and robots will be instructing, instigating, alerting, and facilitating decision making in a smart way, apart from accomplishing all kinds of everyday tasks proactively for human beings. Humanized robots will be extensively used to fulfill our daily physical chores. That is, computers in different sizes, looks, capabilities, interfaces, and prices will be fitted, glued, implanted, and inserted everywhere to be coordinative, calculative, and coherent yet invisible for discerning human minds. In short, the IoT technologies, in sync with cloud infrastructures, analytics, and social and mobile computing, will result in people-centric smarter environments.

1.7.4 The Need for Cloud-Enablement

Infrastructure optimization is the gist of cloud computing. It is all about transforming traditional data centers and server farms to become virtualized, automated, and shared environments so that moving on-premise computer resources (applications, platforms, and hardware resources such as compute, memory, storage, network, etc.) to cloud centers comprises a strategic business decision. Cloud environments are agile, optimized, and software-defined through smartly applying a host of technological advancements.

Cloud hosts online and on-demand applications that can be accessed remotely over a network using multiple input/output devices. This is analogous to centralized and federated electricity generation utilities by government or private individuals through which people can access the required electricity for a small fee based on the amount or duration of power usage. In a similar way, the total compute facility as a coherent pool of virtualized and managed servers (bare metal as well as virtual machines [VMs]) is being put up in a central location to be monitored, managed, and maintained by those with data center administration certifications and capabilities. And any user (individual as well as institution) can subscribe to the relevant and right amount of compute/storage/network facilities at any point in time. That is, it is all about the utility-like resources that inherently support the plug-and-play paradigm. All sorts of infrastructural and usage complexities are displaced and delegated into highly experienced hands. The resounding success is due not only to the extra abstraction obtained through this cloud paradigm but also to the fact that even the average person with an Internet connectivity can easily find and access the growing list of cloud services, applications, data, and other resources immediately.

In a single stroke, the much-discoursed and deliberated cloud paradigm brings to the table an altogether different business, pricing, delivery, and usage model, which deviates significantly from the conventional model. Institutions and innovators, among others, can make use of cloud resources in innumerable ways. All kinds of ICT infrastructures (compute, storage, and network) are being cloud enabled to be subscribed to and used by anyone, anywhere, anytime, on any device. Increasingly IT development, deployment, and enhancement tasks are being slowly yet steadily shifted to large-scale cloud centers that are empowered with all kinds of software engineering frameworks, integrated development environments, testing suites, software containers, integration middleware, and delivery platforms. In a nutshell, cloud is the most sought-after, hot, and happening place.

Services and data made available in the cloud can be more ubiquitously accessed, often at much lower cost. This in turn increases their value by creating opportunities for enhanced orchestration, integration, and analysis on a shared common platform. At its heart, cloud computing is a new operational and business model for IT hosting.

1.7.5 A Few Smart City Use Cases

Any smart city is being aptly presented and proclaimed as a system of systems to emphasize clearly the rising and unbridled complexity of multiple systems collaborating and contributing together in a purposeful manner to fulfill varying needs of cities. Typically a city comprises several modules such as homes, villas and apartments, financial services buildings, multispecialty hospitals, hotels, corporate offices, various types of infrastructures (communication, cyber, social, physical, etc.), educational campuses, shopping malls, entertainment plazas and restaurants, bus and train stations, airports, resorts, spas and casinos, and so on. Considering the growth patterns of cities worldwide, IT solutions providers have brought forth highly competent solutions for different modules such as home networking systems, building automation solutions, energy management software, and so on. There are integrated and insights-driven platforms for managing the different aspects of cities; that is, the centralized monitoring and management of distributed and different environments has become the crucial tenet and testament of city planning and management. Thus IT has become an inseparable part of daily life these days.

1.7.5.1 Smart Homes Newer types of electronic devices are being placed inside and outside homes. Typically there are hundreds of microcontrollers in any advanced home today. Besides all kinds of household goods, all fixed, mechanical, and electrical articles in a home environment are being digitalized. This digitalization-enabled paradigm shift leads to their becoming linked with one another directly (peer-to-peer) or indirectly through an integration and orchestration middleware (hubs and buses). The reason for envisaging this connectivity is the irrefutable fact that anything capable of interacting with others in the neighborhood or through a network could demonstrate intelligence in its behavior.

With network connectivity and application-level integration, next-generation and premium services can be developed and delivered to a customer's delight. For example, say someone is coming to your home and you are keenly watching your preferred TV programs. The security camera outside your home could capture the image of the person standing outside and the image can be flashed on the TV screen so that you can see and orally command the door of your home to open or not. The connectedness lays a versatile foundation for conceptualization of people-centric services (Figure 1.1). A few interesting smart home use cases are now presented.

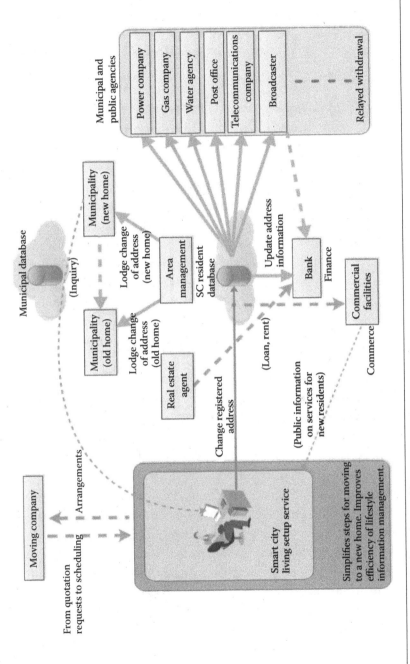

Figure 1.1 A connected and complex smart home use case.

1.7.5.2 Security and Surveillance   This is a leading use case for smart homes. Physical security and safety are important factors for next-generation homes, and effective security and surveillance solutions are available. With the unprecedented rise in cloud space, more generic as well as specific use cases will be unearthed and articulated in the days to come.

1.7.5.3 Remote Asset Management   There ought to be several electricity-gulping systems in any smart home. There are remote management solutions allowing residents to remotely operate home-bound devices to save energy costs. For example, adjusting HVAC and lighting in homes remotely is a well-known use for smart homes. Similarly, other important possessions in a smart home can be adjusted remotely toward their effective and efficient functioning. If a new product is being bought and if there is a problem with it, then the post-sale support team for the product can remotely tele-diagnose the problem and provide an appropriate solution to the product owner or do a remote repair. If a physical visit is needed, then the repair team could understand which components need to be replaced or repaired and accordingly arrive with all the right tools and components in hand to attend to the problem in a single trip.

1.7.5.4 Connected Goods   As mentioned previously, household items and kitchen appliances are increasingly connected with one another as well as with remote cloud services. Today solutions and services abound for connected refrigerators that proactively monitor their inventory. Sitting in his or her office, a homeowner can see what is lacking inside a refrigerator through his or her smartphone and on the way back home could buy the needed goods. A parent can understand how much milk and orange juice is available for the children. Similarly connected washing machines can determine if the user is over- or underutilizing detergent. Further, e-shirts can talk to the washing machine to decide the optimal washing, rinsing, and spinning needs for those items. Connected ovens can notify family members via a text message when chocolate chip cookies are fully ready. The recipe details can be automatically downloaded by ovens from cloud-based services to come out with delicious meals. Similarly, other appliances, microwave ovens, juicers, mixers, coffee makers, toasters, and so on operate collaboratively to offer several unique experiences to the occupants of a home.

1.7.5.5 Connected Consumer Electronics The range of consumer electronics solutions is truly phenomenal. Computers, communication gateways, security appliances, medical instruments, printers and scanners, cameras (still as well as running images), game consoles, TVs, video players, personal handsets, and so on are increasingly connected with one another as well as with off-premise cloud servers. The growing connectivity enables next-generation devices individually as well as collectively to conceive newer and premium services for people in the days to follow.

These intelligently instrumented, fixed yet interconnected, service-oriented and cloud-enabled electronics in synchronization with consumer goods will bring about a stream of enhanced choice, care, convenience, and comfort. Smart cars are becoming closely aligned with human requisites these days. The prospective integration of vehicles with smart home solutions and services will facilitate more sophisticated benefits for consumers. There are in-vehicle infotainment solutions along with eye-catching dashboards in automobiles wirelessly interacting with home-bound devices at vehicular speed to implement delightful services for car users. Further, cloud-connected smart vehicles are capable of orchestrating multiple tasks dynamically. Thus physical systems in collaboration with cyber applications can gain a variety of distinct capabilities and competencies dynamically to be cognitive and context-aware in their actions.

With the maturity of miniaturization, edge, and digital technologies, every tangible object is digitalized toward local as well as remote connectivity. Thus connected consumer and household goods and electronics in association with connected vehicles on the road can breed delightful innovations in large measure. For example, the data collected from a security/surveillance camera will be able to determine proactively if the person parking his car in your parking slot is your son or not. If so, the energy management system will turn on the air conditioning in the house and some interior and exterior lights. If not, the energy management solution will turn on exterior security lighting and notify your smartphone that an unidentified visitor is in your parking place. Data generated, captured, and transmitted instantly by these connected entities can be duly transformed into actionable information by analytical, knowledge engineering and expert systems for actuators as well as practitioners to do their tasks perfectly and precisely in time. Thus the era of knowledge-based process automation is being activated with knowledge emanating from interconnected entities.

It is anticipated that as with smartphone service stores today, there will be smart home services stores aplenty. Resident in sensors and device clouds, these stores can be accessed and used by various smart home embedded systems to realize hitherto uncharted applications for homeowners and occupants. We expect various original equipment manufacturers (OEMs), cloud service providers (CSPs), standard bodies, telecommunication and IT services providers, application developers, and so on, to work together to power up smarter homes of the future. Users can buy those services or subscribe to other services. It is a hybrid world altogether. At all levels, the required intelligence is incorporated. Next-generation devices will be innately intelligent, integration with cloud-based services could enhance any service-enabled electronics with relevant insights, and connectedness with nearby as well as faraway devices will also contribute to intelligent behavior.

Wireless broadband communication, ambient, agile, and adaptive sensors and actuators, smart heating, lighting, ventilation and air control systems, sophisticated energy-efficient and connectable edutainment infotainment electronics, home security appliances, kitchen utensils, and so on will be ubiquitously and prominently utilized in home environments of the future to sufficiently enhance the quality of life. Digital electronics, technology-enabled and gripped spaces, the information superhighway, the Internet of services things, and energy all individually contribute to the goals of smarter homes. Sophistication and smartness are the decisive trends in home ICT. The powerful arrival of cloud technology works in sync with smart home technologies and methodologies to lead to smarter homes.

1.7.5.6 Other Potential Uses Figures 1.2 and 1.3 illustrate two interesting use cases for a smart city. We will come across many more inspiring ones.

A variety of incredible and strategically sound results can be achieved with the smart adoption of these technologies. For example, in the energy domain, the pulsating smart electric grid idea is quickly proliferating to enhance energy saving. The Internet of Energy (IoE) is

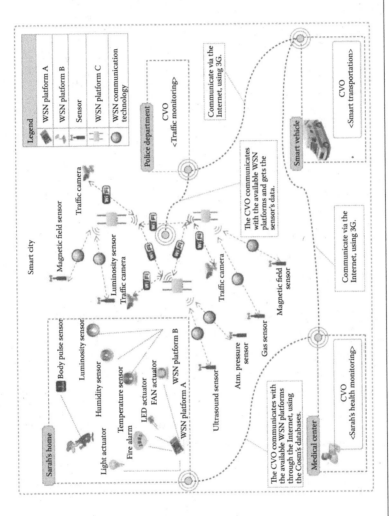

Figure 1.2 A citywide use case covering smart traffic, home, hospital, and police department.

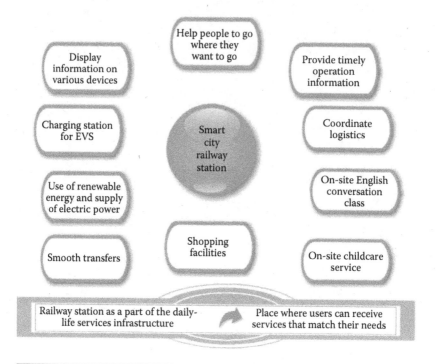

Figure 1.3   The various services of a smart city railway station.

a new topic of deeper study and research for energy efficiency among students, scholars, and scientists across the globe. Other prominent applications include the establishment and sustenance of smarter environments such as smarter homes, hotels, offices, cars, and so on. For example, smarter buildings are an indispensable constituent of smart cities. The use cases include the following:

- *Building automation system*—Automatic management of various electrical as well as electronic systems inside and outside buildings.
- *Energy management system*—Switching off unutilized power-consuming entities using presence sensors for reduced electricity consumption and less heat dissipation to our fragile and warming environment.
- *Security and safety of people and properties.*
- *Remote operations and management* of all kinds of devices, information appliances, kitchenware, consumer electronics, medical instruments, and so on.

- *Ambient assisted living (AAL)*—Providing all kinds of care and facilities for those who are living alone, debilitated, bedridden, and diseased.
- *Smart bus/train stations and ports*—Figure 1.3 clearly illuminates how smart stations can be achieved with technological advancements and adoption.
- *Smart traffic*—This is an important use case for future IT-enabled cities.

Similarly there are a number of technology-sponsored benefits to people living in cities. We discuss these further in the subsequent chapters. Further, an increasing array of optimization techniques and tips is bound to emerge and evolve to bring in bigger and better things for human society. Digital living is the ultimate result.

1.8 Smart City Infrastructure and Platform Solutions

As national as well as local governments are keen to make their cities intelligent and people-friendly, there is a huge market for integrated smart city solutions across the world. Several cities are already undergoing the relevant and right changes through well-intended smart city initiatives being facilitated by leading product vendors and consulting organizations. There are worldwide confluences to discuss the nitty-gritty associated with the establishment and sustenance of smart cities. In this section, we consider the ICT infrastructures and smart city solutions.

1.8.1 Smart City Infrastructures

There is no doubt that cloud-enabled ICT infrastructures are the most appropriate for next-generation cities. We dwell at length about cloud compute, storage, and network infrastructures in the subsequent chapters. A marketing report by Alcatel-Lucent [2] has portrayed a four-stage approach for setting up smart city infrastructures.

- *An IP network infrastructure*—The infrastructure for the single Internet Protocol (IP) network must be considered during the planning stage and, for maximum impact, should be a part of the master development plan. Fiber optics should be installed as an integral element of each building during construction so that it can be used to control all other utilities with the addition of active components such as switches and routers.

- *Converged communication*—The network infrastructure lights up core services for the city, delivering telephony, broadband Internet access, and video-on-demand (VoD) over a single network to enable smart homes, hotels, and businesses.

- *Infrastructure and platform software solutions*—Empowering every tangible thing to behave intelligently is the ultimate vision. A variety of software solutions (environment management systems, mobility and transport systems, smart buildings, and smart energy grids) need to be identified and introduced. Infrastructure and platform solutions in the form of software are the real differentiators for next-generation environments to be user-friendly. Smart sensors are capable of automatically controlling pollution, lighting, cleaning, and waste optimizing carbon footprints, and of reducing energy bills.

- *Cognitive services to citizens*—Once infrastructure and platform software are ready, then both technically competent application developers in association with end-users can create a plethora of people-centric applications to be provided as a network from local as well as remote cloud environments. Finally, services and applications are introduced for information sharing, healthcare (remote medical care and ambient assisted living), education, entertainment, culture (museum, cultural activities), and commerce and exchange (micro-payment and micro-commerce). In addition, the community is made safe by closed circuit television integrated with a communications system. With these services, individuals can use Wi-Fi at Internet cafes or portals in shopping malls or civic buildings for information or transactions. During a day in the city, a resident or visitor can buy movie tickets, pay for parking, place a bet, vote for a political representative, use a telemedicine facility, call an intelligent transportation system, or just order a pizza online.

Thus a city-wide ambient, adaptive, and unified communication network is the base infrastructure to have connected cities wherein people find, bind, interact, participate, and collaborate with one another in realizing their unique necessities (temporal, spatial, physical, mental, etc.). Many new capabilities can be meticulously added to serve peoples' needs in time.

1.8.2 Leading Smart City Platforms

A city needs to use the IT advancements effectively to deliver multipurpose services and actionable intelligence to its constituents. The goal of anytime, anywhere, any device, any network, any media, and any application access can be accomplished through the smart leverage of IT. As mentioned previously, IT is to be the biggest enabler of next-generation cities. All kinds of city resources are being minutely monitored and optimally shared through IT in a well-organized, responsible, and transparent manner. IT is able to formulate premium services proactively to delight city people. The recent city analytics systems go a long way in empowering city designers and bureaucrats to come out with personalized services to people. Thus all value-adding and decision-enabling city data being captured in a systematic fashion are the fountainhead to conceive and concretize hitherto unheard of services to ensure enhanced safety, security, and smartness to every resident.

Having a single window system for all city services is the foremost requirement to facilitate their seamless and spontaneous usage by all the stakeholders across the city. The service delivery platform (SDP) has to be sophisticated and adaptive enough to meet the varying expectations of people stylishly. Thus any smart city IT solution needs to be a highly integrated and configurable one. In this section, we discuss a few leading smart city platforms.

1.8.2.1 IBM Intelligent Operations Center

This highly synchronized solution from IBM [3] intrinsically integrates and uses data from multiple sources and makes sense of it using a single and simple interface. The knowledge gained through purpose-specific and generic processing steps gets seamlessly disseminated to those concerned in time so that appropriate countermeasures could be calculatedly considered and performed. This solution decimates all kinds of data diversity and handles the constricting disarray with complete ease. The exponential growth of multistructured data in the recent past with the addition of multiple data sources is also being tackled effectively by this classic platform solution. The real beauty is that the IBM Intelligent Operations Center comes with a unified interface to all systems of an enterprise or city to make them accessible and usable without being overwhelmed. The real simplicity lies in the easy consumability of the solution's functionality and facility so city administrators and officials could leverage this exemplary platform for automating, accelerating, and augmenting city operations and offerings to the city residents' liking.

A flexible rules-based data flow transforms large quantities of polystructured data into a structured format that can be used by analytical systems for report generation and key performance indicators (KPIs). IBM Intelligent Operations Center is capable of handling events and emits dependable insights getting extracted out of all discrete as well as continuous streams. It also provides a Web-based and easy-to-configure interface that is specific to the user's role and needs so that everyone in the organization can see and collaborate on the same data in their own way. The innate ability to collaborate allows synchronization of effort, audit trails, collaboration, and group decision making. It also can help to synchronize and analyze efforts among sectors and agencies as they occur and give decision makers and executives consolidated, corroborated, and correlated information that helps them anticipate what is in the offing and act proactively and preemptively rather than react to problems.

The IBM Intelligent Operations Center provides a unified view of city agencies and other complex infrastructures. It enables a city to monitor its services and operations to facilitate insightful decision making. This approach helps provide effective event response management and coordination from operational to critical events. The IBM Intelligent Operations Center processes data feeds and event information from individual departments to help improve the operational efficiency of a city and other complex infrastructures. It provides an executive dashboard to depict the overall status of a city's operations. The dashboard spans individual agency-specific solution areas and enables drill-down capability in each underlying agency or department, for example, water management, public safety, and traffic management. By taking advantage of the power of advanced analytics, asset management, and collaboration tools, the IBM Intelligent

Operations Center delivers the ability to gain insight into an environment through centralized information. This offers integrated data visualization, real-time collaboration, and deep analytics that can help city agencies prepare for problems, coordinate and manage response efforts, and enhance the ongoing efficiency of city operations.

The capabilities of the IBM Intelligent Operations Center include

- Incident reporting and tracking
- Situational awareness and reporting
- Support for creating and using standard operating procedures (SOPs)
- Real-time collaboration
- Resource and critical asset management
- Assessing and displaying KPIs
- The ability to open standard connection points to existing and future systems
- An easy-to-use interface that is designed with multiple types of users in mind, from senior managers to daily operators

Executive dashboard capabilities give decision makers a near-real-time, unified view of operations so they can see what people and resources are needed and available. Cities can rapidly share information across agency lines to accelerate problem responses and improve project coordination. By providing visibility into KPIs and trends, the solution can also help fine-tune current resource usage and support forward-looking planning activities. City and government leaders and private enterprises around the world are using the IBM Intelligent Operations Center to address a broad range of management and operational needs. These needs include airport management, city operations, emergency management, energy and emissions monitoring, parks and recreation maintenance, port security, stadium operations and security, transportation awareness and prediction, and water utilities monitoring and preventive maintenance.

1.8.2.2 Oracle Smart City Platform   Oracle offers a modular, incremental solution set for local governments that provides a roadmap for transformation [4]. The solution set includes technologies and applications that consolidate already-complex IT infrastructures, rationalize service delivery processes, and support current and future operational systems, as well as supplying an intelligence layer to monitor performance and improve service delivery, program planning, and budgeting.

The following are the key benefits of Oracle's City Platform Solution:

1. 24/7 access to government services without the "city hall shuffle"
2. Single non–emergency number (SNEN) services to support mobile users and those on the other side of the digital divide
3. Face-to-face focused on up-front personal connection (when needed) and to deal with very complex issues
4. Changes the behavior and expectations of constituents
5. Closed feedback loop on political policy to desired outcomes through KPIs posted to constituents
6. Constituents don't have to understand government organizations to obtain services

1.8.2.3 The Thales Hypervisor Supervision System   This is a key technology [5] supporting the smart city concept through its ability to coordinate separate urban information systems, now or in the future. Its open, service-oriented architecture enables interconnected systems and subsystems to share the data needed to optimize individual applications as needs evolve. From an operational standpoint, the intuitive, Web-based interface gives users a citywide picture in real time, providing unmatched decision support for coordination of operations and emergency responses. Finally, data from the city's transport, security, and other systems are archived in the smart city platform and can be analyzed to yield greater insight into the changing urban context to manage resources and plan future developments.

Hitachi Japan [6] also has an advanced and aggregated IT solution (Figure 1.4) for readily embarking on smart city development projects.

The systems for supporting public infrastructures are centered on the smart city platform and are configured in such a way that a variety of different devices and applications are connected in a hub and spokes structure. This makes it possible for devices and applications to mutually coordinate in each individual system, with independent connections, changes, and updates all possible. The management supporting

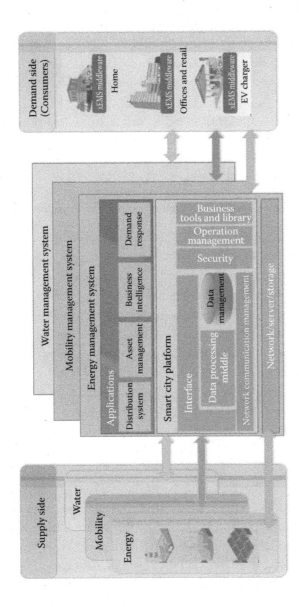

Figure 1.4   The reference architecture for the Hitachi smart city platform solution.

each public infrastructure is of the autonomous and decentralized type, or in other words, is composed of separate and independent clusters, each of which is connected to the other clusters. This allows for the coordination of electric power and transportation management systems, or between the electric power management systems of different regions. For instance, advanced management is possible based on monitoring the balance between power supply and demand to direct electric automobiles to charge stations with available power, and it is also possible to make accommodations for electric power between regions.

Having understood the emerging needs, several corporations have one or more generic as well as specific IT products for freshly starting intelligent city tasks and for enhancing existing cities to be smart.

1.9 The Context-Aware Framework for Smart City Applications

There are sensing, perception, vision, knowledge extrapolation, and actuation technologies flourishing to create and sustain context-aware environments within a city. People are about getting all kinds of information, commercial transactions, knowledge and physical services based on their situation (location, time, etc.) and their various needs (mental, physical, social, etc.). Cyber applications, cloud-based services, user devices, communication gateways and device middleware, digitalized and interconnected objects, and so on are collectively contributing to the swift implementation and delivery of cognitive context-aware services to users. The framework (Figure 1.5) for context-aware computing possesses five main modules.

1.9.1 Data Collection and Cleansing

This is a prime component for carefully collecting data from distributed and difference sources. With the continued growth of data generators and extractors (sensors and actuators, smartphones, social sites, enterprise as well as cloud data centers, devices and instruments from research labs, machines from manufacturing plants and floors, etc.), multiformatted and faceted data are being gathered these days. Further, data gleaned need to be subjected to a series of tasks such as transforming and polishing to make them compatible with the target data storage environment. With the emergence of new kinds of

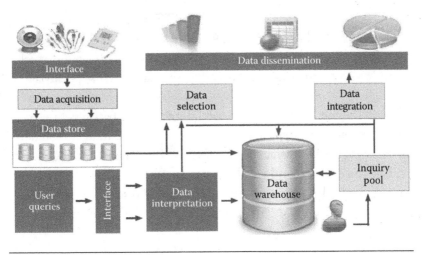

Figure 1.5 The reference architecture for the context-aware framework.

database management systems (Structured Query Language [SQL], NewSQL, and NoSQL), the choice of data management is very critical for the framework. Data connectors, drivers, adapters, and integrators have been made available by product vendors to simplify this arduous task. Data virtualization is a new term in the industry that is gaining momentum for data collection and synchronization in highly distributed and disparate environments.

1.9.2 Data Storage

Once data are refined they are duly stored in an easy-to-access and use storage infrastructure such as a database, data cube and mart, or data warehouse. This enables users to query the data warehouse to retrieve the correct and relevant information to plan ahead and proceed with clarity and confidence. It is a kind of batch processing and pull mechanism. Slicing, dicing, report generation, and other kinds of macro- as well as microlevel operations can be accomplished on data stored to squeeze out usable information.

1.9.3 Data Interpretation

On the other hand, as data pour into different places, context-sensitive information needs to be retrieved and dispatched to the people concerned through a variety of devices, displays, and so on; centralized monitoring; measurement and control systems; any appropriate actuation systems, and so on. That is, a competent real-time data interpretation mechanism has to be in place for extracting situation details quickly to act on them. Knowledge discovery is a crucial cog in context-aware computing. There is a need to have special knowledge bases, policies/rules repository, and other viable solutions to facilitate accurate interpretation of incoming data to extract timely insights. Thus knowledge engineering and enhancement are achieved through multiple tasks such as data integration, aggregation, classification, clustering, composition, processing, analyzing, mining, and so on done individually and collectively.

1.9.4 Cloud-Based

The context-aware framework has a module to enable cloud connectivity. These days, sensors and devices in our everyday environments are connected not only with one another in the vicinity but also with remotely hosted applications, services, and data in cloud environments. With a device integration standard such as Open Service Gateway initiative (OSGi), devices in our physical places are being empowered by dynamically downloading all kinds of enabling services and installing and configuring them to be highly relevant for the widely discoursed and discussed digital living. Thus cloud integration is indispensable for future context-aware solutions. These days, different sorts of data are being generated outside our living environments and they are of high value for people if leveraged smartly. For example, there are unprecedented advancements in the forms of social networking sites, knowledge communities, smarter cars with in-vehicle infotainment systems, financial industries pumping trillions of bytes every day, and so on. The projected data growth is simply phenomenal.

1.9.5 Data Dissemination

Knowledge engineered needs to be packaged and shared among users in a preferred and presentable format. Reports, maps, charts, and graphs are the main mechanisms for sharing knowledge. Data visualization is a popular topic bombarded with a bevy of techniques, tools, and tips facilitating the dissemination of knowledge to people in time.

Context-awareness is an important criterion for city services. With the proliferation of sensors in city environments, data capture, interpretation, and knowledge dissemination aspects are essential for crafting people-friendly services.

1.10 Conclusion

The goals of smart cities are the ubiquitous availability and simplified access of various urban resources, infrastructures, facilities, and services. Further, cities ought to be self-sustaining ecological environments and prime service providers for residents, enterprising endeavors and adventures, institutions, and visitors. Cities need to be deeply connected, functionally integrated, technologically automated, and equipped to use their precious resources and infrastructures optimally to visualize and deliver hitherto unforeseen services. Finally, smart cities will be thriving, scintillating, and increasingly attractive hubs with at the same time substantially reduced living costs and minimization of the climate footprint. Smart city initiatives are clearly mission driven and aptly enabled by mashups of many proven and promising technologies. The key use cases for intelligent cities include

- Smart traffic for reducing congestion on city roads
- Smart healthcare for enabling appropriate access to healthcare data for early disease detection and prevention, informed diagnosis and medication prescription, compassionate care, and so on
- Smart safety and security to improve public and property safety by reducing crime incidents and providing faster responses for both man-made and natural disasters
- Smart service delivery by streamlining, tailoring, and personalizing scores of social, physical, and information services for residents
- Smart energy for environmental sustainability
- Smart banking for synchronized and simplified cash transactions
- Smart businesses to be sufficiently anticipative of consumers' needs and come out with people-centric offerings

The list is actually growing with the fluent arrival and acceptance of pioneering technologies; multipurpose yet handy devices; indispensable, disposable, disappearing, and diminutive sensors and actuators; sustainable and resilient infrastructures; city-specific and converged IT platforms; outside-in thinking in product design; and co-creation of city services, data analytics and knowledge engineering systems, and so on.

References

1. TCS Innovation Labs (2013). Intelligent Cities: A City Process Management Approach (white paper).
2. Alcatel-Lucent (2012). Getting Smart about Smart Cities: Understanding the Market Opportunity in the Cities of Tomorrow.
3. IBM (2012). IBM Intelligent Operations Center for Smarter Cities Administration Guide (Redbook).
4. Oracle (2013). How Smart Are Your City's Services? Oracle's City Platform Solution (white paper).
5. Thales Smart City Platform, https://www.thalesgroup.com/en.
6. Hitachi Smart City Platform, http://www.hitachi.com/.
7. Information Technology (IT) Portal, http://www.peterindia.net.

2

MOBILE TECHNOLOGIES AND APPLICATIONS FOR INTELLIGENT CITIES

Abstract

The spectacular growth of mobile devices and mobile device–related technologies has had a profound impact on the lives of people across the world. Mobile device–related technologies and applications is one of the fastest growing technological spaces. Mobile devices and the plethora of technologies that are a part of it have found an application and made an entry into each and every sector of a city. This has made mobile devices and related technologies inevitable components of an intelligent city. This chapter discusses mobile technologies that are mandatory for creating the backbone of an intelligent city. The chapter starts with an overview of the mobile device ecosystem, which comprises the various generations of mobile technologies and the various prominent mobile platforms that exist in the present-day market. In the next part of the chapter, the role of mobile technologies and their application in the various city sectors are examined in detail with the help of appropriate real-life implementations. The role of the mobile device ecosystem in transforming a city into an intelligent city is discussed in detail. The chapter concludes by examining the various cutting edge mobile technologies that are still in their nascent stages of evolution, the impact they could create, and the value proposition they could provide to present-day cities.

Key Terms Used in the Chapter

Android: An open-source operating system that uses the Linux platform. It was developed by an organization called the Open Handset Alliance.

BlackBerry: A brand of smart phones and tablets developed by an organization called BlackBerry Limited.

Code division multiple access (CDMA): A channel access method that allows several wireless transmitters to send data at the same time through the same channel. To differentiate various transmitters, this method uses a special coding scheme in which a unique code is assigned to each transmitter.

Dual-tone multifrequency (DTMF): A tone signaling scheme used for controlling various types of activities via the telephone network, such as remote control of an answering machine.

Frequency division multiple access (FDMA): A channel access method used in multiple-access protocols as a channelization protocol. FDMA gives users an individual allocation of one or several frequency bands, or channels.

Global Positioning System (GPS): A navigation system that uses satellites to provide time and location information of a user. It is a very robust system that operates under all weather conditions anywhere on Earth. It is maintained by the U.S. government. It can be accessed by anyone free of charge with the help of a GPS receiver.

Global System for Mobile Communications (GSMs): A standard developed by the European Telecommunications Standards Institute (ETSI). It is used to describe protocols used for communication by the second generation (2G) wireless networks.

Smart phone: A category of mobile phone with advanced computing and connectivity features. Smart phones generally contain a digital camera, media player, and personal digital assistant. Apart from these basic features, present-day smart phones contain various other advanced features such as GPS. However, the presence of these advanced features is at the discretion of the manufacturer.

Symbian: An operating system designed for smart phones. It is currently being maintained by Accenture.

2.1 Introduction

Mobile technologies are a vibrant and fast growing industry that has revolutionized the everyday lives of people across world boundaries. Every year, on average, the mobile subscriber base is increasing by more than a million worldwide. Roughly a billion new mobile subscribers were added in the last four years, and this number is expected to increase further in the years to come. This has laid out a strong growth trajectory and innovation space using mobile devices and the plethora of other technologies that form a part of mobile devices.

Fueled by the rapid increase in the mobile subscriber base, mobile service providers are constantly on the lookout for new ways and means to use mobile devices to establish connectivity among various domains that a mobile subscriber comes across in his or her day-to-day life and activities. Some of these domains that prominently cut across a subscriber's life are automotives, utility services, health, education, and financial transactions.

Another prominent mobile technology that is at the heart of innovation every day is mobile broadband. Mobile devices coupled with broadband, which provides seamless interconnectivity, have made connected living a reality for millions of mobile subscribers who stay in geographically dispersed regions. The mobile device manufacturers are always in a constant innovation race to make their mobile devices smarter, faster, and lighter. To keep up with this rapid pace of evolution, the entire mobile ecosystem, which includes network infrastructure service providers, is also working at a constant pace of innovation to make better and more high-performance network facilities available at affordable prices. Content providers are also harnessing new ways to make their products and services available for access using mobile devices.

Some of the interesting findings about the growth of mobile devices as per the IDC survey titled IDC Predictions 2013: Competing on the 3rd Platform [1], are summarized as follows:

1. The 3rd platform technologies—mobile devices and apps, cloud services, mobile broadband networks, big data analytics, and social technologies—will drive 40% of industry revenue and 98% of industry growth.
2. Over the next four years, the number of people accessing the Internet through PCs will shrink by 15 million as the number

of mobile users increases by 91 million. In 2015, there will be more U.S. consumers accessing the Internet through mobile devices than through PCs.

3. Sales of smart mobile devices—smart phones and tablets—will grow by 20%, generating 20% of all IT industry sales in 2013 and 57% of all information technology (IT) market growth. Excluding these devices, the IT industry's growth will be just 2.9%.

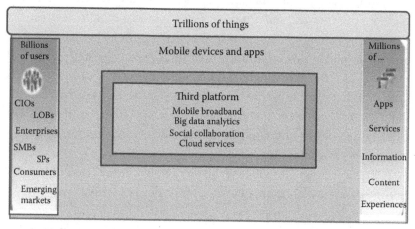

This figure illustrates the stupendous growth of the mobile device market and the intelligent industry trend that is driven by the mobile devices. This trend in turn is the key guiding factor that summarizes the importance of mobile devices, applications, and mobile broadband networks for the evolution and growth of technology-driven intelligent cities across the world.

Another trend that is fueled by mobile devices is the concept of machine-to-machine (M2M) communication. The term M2M describes solutions that focus on remote collection and transfer of data from embedded sensors or chips placed on remote assets that are fixed or mobile. Today smart mobile devices are used extensively to interact and control various machines and hence they are excellent candidates to perform communication with remote devices. One excellent example of M2M communication using mobile devices is Qualcomm's AllJoyn™. This is an open-source software platform that facilitates the concept of Internet of Everything (IoE) by allowing communication among all devices that use AllJoyn. For instance, we could consider a system that allowed remote control of a coffee maker by using a smart phone; when the coffee was ready, the coffee maker would send automatic alerts to the smart phone and television, and could turn the television on as well.

Data analytics is one of the top trends of the industry at this time. Analytics is applied to all types of data to make useful inferences about future trends and patterns. Present-day smart mobile devices provide many features and tools that help to visualize the results of this analytics in the form of various types of dashboards that will be available any time anywhere for officials to make smart decisions. Mobile visualization technologies for analytics have revolutionized the way in which results of analytics are perceived and used.

In short, mobile devices are an inevitable component of building intelligent cities. The various value propositions offered by a mobile device for an intelligent city are summarized in the diagram that follows.

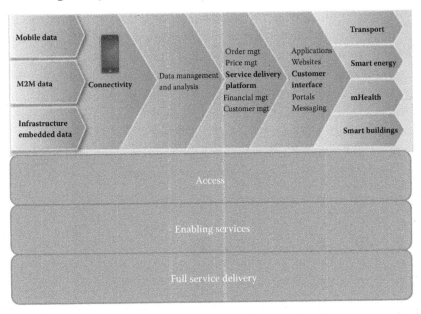

The main components of the diagram are as follows:

1. Data are collected from a wide range of sources and equipment using mobile phones. These data include data from remote sensors and other electronic devices, data that are generated by various infrastructure components such as buildings, water networks, transportation systems, and so on.

2. These data are transferred using the various wired and wireless networking options. They are then collected and stored

in some kind of a database or a data warehouse. Analytics is applied to these data to derive meaningful insights that define the future course of action.

3. These data are used as input for the service delivery platform (SDP), which runs several applications for city services. These services span all domains that are important for a city, such as transportation, healthcare, water networks, and so on. These SDPs will provide open application programming interfaces (APIs) that will help developers to design new value-added services for the residents.

4. The user interface will be accessible to all residents through mobile devices and it will provide a rich set of applications that will improve their quality of life.

These points summarize the value proposition offered by mobile devices to improve the quality of life of residents and visitors in a city, which in turn would contribute to transforming a city into an intelligent city.

In the next few sections, we focus on the various components of the mobile ecosystem. Some of these components are the various mobile generations and standards that are responsible for the various value-added services provided by the mobile devices and the various platforms and frameworks that are used for building smart phones.

The chapter is organized as shown in the figure.

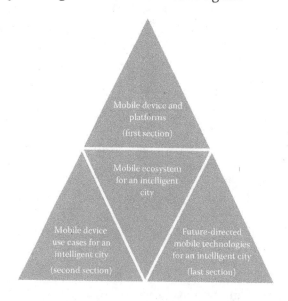

2.2 Evolution of Mobile Wireless Technologies

The evolution of mobile wireless technology has already reached its fourth generation (4G) and is quickly leaping forward toward its next generation (5G). Each generation of mobile wireless technology is clearly characterized by three distinct features:

- Nature and spectrum of services that are offered
- Transmission technology that is not backward compatible
- New frequency bands for transmission of signals

There has been an evolution of a new mobile wireless technology generation once every 10 years starting from the early 1980s. The evolution of first-generation (1G) mobile wireless technologies started in the United States with the release of the advanced mobile phone service (AMPS) system in 1983. In the early 1980s, mobile wireless technologies used an analog mode of transmission. The main drawback of these 1G technologies was the inability to scale to growing needs in a cost-effective manner. This led to the evolution of second-generation (2G) networks that used a digital mode of transmission.

The main differentiating factor between the 1G and the 2G network was that 2G networks used superior digital multiple-access technologies such as frequency division multiple access (FDMA) and code division multiple access (CDMA). These technologies in turn contributed to superior spectrum efficiency, better data services, and advanced roaming facilities which were not offered by 1G networks. The noted wireless technology advancement in the 2G network was the evolution of the global system for mobile communication (GSM) standard. GSM has laid down a framework for mobile communication by defining the functions and interface requirements of a mobile wireless network. However, it does not specify anything about the hardware that needs to be used to build the framework. Some of the major subscription services offered by GSM are dual-tone multifrequency (DTMF), fax services, short message services (SMS), voice mail, and fax mail. Another key mobile wireless technology standard, referred to as part of the 2.5G network, is the general packet radio service (GPRS).

GPRS uses a packet-switching technology for transfer of data across mobile wireless networks. It provides various advanced features such as mobile Internet and multimedia messaging service (MMS). The theoretical speed limit of GPRS is 115 kbps; however, the actual speed in most networks is around 35 kbps.

3G mobile wireless networks support higher data rates when compared to 2G networks. The shift from 2G to 3G gives mobile users the capability to use services such as mobile Internet, e-mail, instant messaging, and video conferencing at a much higher speed. 3G also provides presence and location-based services available to mobile users. Though some of the features of 3G networks were already available with 2.5G networks, the competitive edge of the 3G networks will be the speed at which those services are offered to end-users.

The most recent trend shows that mobile Internet users want instantaneous access to video content with a very superior quality of user experience and the ability to access more convergent mobile services than ever before. This is emphasized by the fact that during the London 2012 Olympic Games, more than 50% of various types of search requests were delivered from mobile devices. Mobile subscribers also want the capability to access any type of content anytime, anywhere. To complicate this situation still further, many content aggregating applications such as App stores and Amazon are making all types of content available on a variety of mobile devices. This has posed a tough challenge for mobile network operators to find new innovative technologies that would enable them to satisfy their customer demand and at the same time ensure that their economies of scale are being met. This changing landscape in the mobile technology arena has led to the evolution of an innovative technology called long-term evolution (LTE), which is often considered a component of the 4G wireless mobile network.

LTE, also referred to as 4G LTE, is a standard for wireless mobile networks and provides high-speed data transfer rates for wireless networks. It will provide 50 times performance improvement for existing wireless networks. LTE broadcast is a single-frequency network (SFN) that operates in a broadcast mode. It is part of the series of standards known as evolved Multimedia Broadcast Multicast Service (eMBMS). Some of the key use cases of LTE from an intelligent city perspective are summarized in Table 2.1.

GM plans to start outfitting cars with 4G LTE, introducing in-vehicle hot spots, streaming entertainment, and applications designed

Table 2.1   Key Use Cases of Long-Term Evolution from an Intelligent City Perspective

LTE SERVICE OFFERING	USAGE FOR INTELLIGENT CITIES
Live event streaming	Live coverage of key events happening in a city such as sports, concerts, award ceremonies, elections, and so on.
Real-time TV streaming	Real-time delivery of important sports events, news channels, and other popular TV shows. This will enable entertainment amidst work which will in turn go a long way in boosting productivity. This could prevent employees taking time off from work to watch a key TV event. (The facility to watch TV shows amidst work should be used judiciously.)
News, stock market reports, weather, and sports updates	Provides news, stock market reports, weather, and sports updates several times during the course of a day with on device caching features.

for its proprietary browser. It's the first mass-market automaker to do so (Audi was the first to introduce 4G LTE, in its A3 model). 4G LTE will be included in most of the Chevrolet, Buick, GMC, and Cadillac vehicles in North America starting in 2014 (via a partnership with AT&T), and GM said it will subsequently expand to brands including Opel and Vauxhall in Europe. GM also demonstrated a prototype vehicle with embedded cameras that enable owners to monitor their car remotely [2].

2.3 Mobile Application Development Platforms

Mobile application development is the process of developing application software for mobile devices. These are mostly installed on phones during manufacturing or can be downloaded by consumers from various mobile software distribution centers. Mobile application software developers have various design considerations such as the screen size of the mobile devices, hardware and software requirement specifications, and so on, as a vast variety of mobile platforms are available. Many mobile application development platforms are available in the market. Each of them has an integrated development environment (IDE) that provides all tools required for a mobile application developer to write, test, and deploy applications into the target platform environment. Some of the key mobile platforms are iOS, Android, Blackberry OS, Windows, etc.

As many mobile platforms are available, the target mobile platforms for which each mobile application should be built have always been a matter of concern for mobile application developers. This has led to the evolution of cross-OS platforms for mobile application development. These platforms offer an excellent alternative to ignoring one mobile OS in favor of another and provide support for developing mobile applications that work across multiple mobile application development platforms. The following are some of the key cross-OS platforms available in the market.

1. RhoMobile provides Rhodes, which is an open source, Ruby-based framework. It helps development of many native mobile applications for a wide range of smart phone devices and operating systems. The operating systems that are supported include iOS, Android, Windows Mobile OS, RIM, and Symbian.

   This framework has capabilities that allow users to develop their source code once and use it to quickly build applications for all major mobile platforms. Native applications that are developed using this framework have the capability to use the mobile device's hardware, including GPS, camera, as well as location data to enhance the application capabilities further. In addition to Rhodes, RhoMobile also provides RhoHub, which is a hosted development environment, and RhoSync, which is a stand-alone server that keeps application data current up to date on end-users' mobile devices.

2. Appcelerator belongs to the free or open-source software (FOSS) framework. The Titanium development platform offered by the company allows the development of native mobile, tablet, *and* desktop applications through typical Web development languages such as JavaScript, HyperText Markup Language (HTML), and so on. Titanium users will also have access to more than 300 social and other APIs and their associated location information. The native applications that are developed using this platform can be stored either in a cloud or in the mobile device. They are designed to take

full advantage of the mobile device hardware, especially the camera and the video camera.

3. WidgetPad is a collaborative, open-source mobile application development environment. It can be used for creating smart phone applications using standard Web technologies such as CSS3, HTML5, and JavaScript. This platform provides features such as project management, source code editing and debugging, collaboration, versioning, and distribution. It can be used to create mobile applications that work on iOS, Android, and Web OS.

4. PhoneGap™ was the winning pitch at Web 2.0 Expo San Francisco's 2009 Launch Pad event. It is a FOSS framework that helps users develop mobile applications for iOS Android, Symbian, and BlackBerry platforms using Web development languages such as JavaScript and HTML.

5. MoSync is another FOSS cross-platform mobile application development software development kit (SDK) that supports common programming standards. The SDK includes tightly integrated compilers, runtimes, libraries, device profiles, tools, and utilities. MoSync provides an Eclipse-based IDE for C/C++ programming. It is expected to provide support for JavaScript, Ruby, PHP, and Python languages soon. This framework supports a large number of operating systems such as Android, Symbian, and Windows Mobile.

6. Cross-OS mobile platform from IBM—IBM® Worklight [3]. IBM Worklight helps you extend your business to mobile devices. It is designed to provide an open, comprehensive platform to build, run, and manage HTML5, hybrid, and native mobile apps. IBM Worklight can help you reduce both app development and maintenance costs, improve time-to-market, and enhance mobile app governance and security.

IBM Worklight consists of five components. IBM Worklight Studio is designed to provide a comprehensive environment for advanced, rich, cross-platform mobile app development. IBM Worklight Server is mobile-optimized middleware that serves as a gateway among applications, back-end systems, and cloud-based services. IBM Worklight Device Runtime Components offer run-time client APIs designed to enhance security, governance, and usability. IBM Worklight Application Center enables you to set up an enterprise app store that manages the distribution of production-ready mobile apps.

IBM Worklight Console is an administrative graphical user inter-face (GUI) for the server, adapters, applications, and push services to help users manage, monitor, and instrument mobile apps.

With IBM Worklight one can

- Support multiple mobile operating environments such as iOS, BlackBerry®, and Windows mobile devices with the simplicity of a single, shared code base
- Connect and synchronize with enterprise data, applications, and cloud services
- Safeguard mobile security at the device, application, and net-work layers
- Govern a mobile app portfolio from a central interface

In the next section, we examine some of the challenges of intelligent cities and the solutions offered for them by the 3G and 4G wireless mobile networks.

2.4 Challenges of Intelligent Cities and Solutions Offered by Mobile Wireless Networks and Devices

Some of the key challenges faced by intelligent cities are

- Inability to effectively monitor and track various types of energy consumption, which in turn leads to situations such as energy theft and energy grid inefficiencies
- Congestion on roads due to the unavailability of information on various transport options, their routes, timings, and so on
- Inefficient supply chain management, which in turn affects the entire retail ecosystem
- Lack of availability of anytime, anywhere healthcare facilities for residents

- Excessive cost due to the maintenance of multichannel ticketing systems
- Inability to extract useful insights from data as data from different agencies within a city are maintained in different silos and there is no possibility to integrate and extract meaningful insights and use them for the benefit of residents

The solutions for these challenges, which can be worked out using mobile devices, are summarized in the diagram that follows. These solutions are the most prominent use cases of mobile devices for intelligent cities.

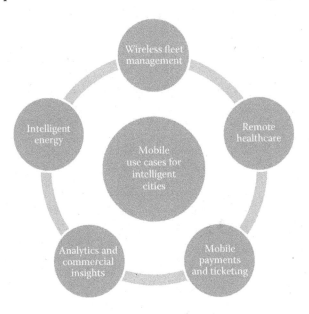

The role of mobile devices in addressing these challenges is summarized in Table 2.2.

2.4.1 Mobile Payments and Ticketing

Mobile devices have an inevitable role in developing an integrated infrastructure and platform for managing ticketing applications and other micropayments in an intelligent city environment. One important use case for mobile ticketing would be public transport services, which are the most important mode of travel to interconnect different parts of a city. They typically involve a high volume of low-value

Table 2.2   Role of Mobile Devices in Addressing Challenges of Intelligent Cities

MOBILE USE CASES FOR AN INTELLIGENT CITY	URBAN CHALLENGE	MOBILE-BASED SOLUTION
Intelligent energy	• Access to electricity for development of cities • High levels of electricity theft • Inefficiencies of traditional grid • High levels of electric vehicle charging • Inability to track energy consumption and usage in real time	A mobile-based energy management service that helps consumers track and manage energy consumption in real time and pay bills using mobile devices; provides features to track energy theft and identify energy leakage.
Wireless fleet management	• Inefficiencies in supply chains	A mobile-based intelligent fleet management solution for mobile tracking of fleet and routing using embedded telematics.
Remote healthcare	• Reliance on costly healthcare models • Aging infrastructure and outdated technology • Limited real-time data about patient's body parameters	Remote patient monitoring and healthcare solutions using mobile devices.
Mobile payments and ticketing	• Cost of maintaining multichannel ticketing systems • Inconvenience for consumers	A mobile ticketing platform that uses near-field communication technology to provide end-to-end ticketing solutions for customers.
Analytics and commercial insights	• Disconnected data sets in silos • Inability to track and derive useful insights about various aspects pertaining to residents in diverse city domains	Mobile business intelligence platforms that provide real-time insight for city government.

transactions that take place throughout the course of the day. If there is a possibility to devise a cashless transaction mechanism using mobile devices, it would immensely benefit both the public and the transport authorities. The benefits would be twofold if there was a possibility for the ticket itself to be distributed back to the mobile device. Many cities today have disparate independent ticketing systems for different modes of transport and other city services such as stadium access, museum entry, and so on. The result is a lack of good user experience for end-users, higher rates of theft or loss, and a loss of opportunity to generate a consolidated view of urban traffic patterns. To best understand the concept of mobile ticketing, it is very important to know more about near-field communication (NFC) technology.

NFC is a combination of radio frequency identification (RFID) and networking technologies. It is a unique wireless technology that enables easy and convenient short-range communication between electronic devices. It connects all types of consumer devices and facilitates easy communication among them. It acts as a secure gateway and allows consumers to use NFC-enabled mobile devices to store and access all kinds of data. If two NFC-enabled devices are brought closer to one another, they can automatically initiate network communication without the need for any preconfiguration or setup.

2.4.1.1 Role of NFC in Mobile eTicketing An eTicket is a token or pass that is used by consumers for various purposes such as travel on public transportation and gaining entry to various entertainment/sports venues. With the help of NFC, the eTicket process takes just a matter of seconds for completion. It also provides much convenience for consumers. After completion of payment information, the purchased eTicket will be transferred to the consumer's mobile device. The different steps involved in eTicketing using NFC are described in the diagram that follows.

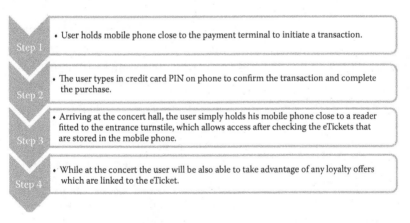

Step 1
- User holds mobile phone close to the payment terminal to initiate a transaction.

Step 2
- The user types in credit card PIN on phone to confirm the transaction and complete the purchase.

Step 3
- Arriving at the concert hall, the user simply holds his mobile phone close to a reader fitted to the entrance turnstile, which allows access after checking the eTickets that are stored in the mobile phone.

Step 4
- While at the concert the user will be also able to take advantage of any loyalty offers which are linked to the eTicket.

NFC technology will enable consumers to use their mobile devices as contactless payment and ticketing devices. One successful trial of NFC is the O2 NFC initiative in London for mobile eTicketing services. The success of this trial opens the door for the wealth of opportunities that are available for various contactless mobile payment options in cities. To facilitate mobile payment options, in many intelligent cities, the necessary infrastructure for contactless mobile eTicketing and payment options is already available. So setting up the necessary infrastructure to facilitate contactless mobile payment options is the need of the day for any city to move forward and climb up the ladder to become an intelligent city.

Launch of mobile ticketing options could open the door for many other innovative contactless mobile cities that form the foundation of an intelligent city. For example, the use NFC enable mobile devices for eTicketing and payment options will in turn trigger other sectors of industry to invest and explore contactless mobile ticketing options and the infrastructure required to support such options. Some examples of new innovative services in other industry sectors could be

- Universal mobile payment options for retail outlets, vending machines, parking areas, and so on
- Data transfer options to allow real-time display of schedules, advertisement options, and so on
- Point of sale coupons, redeemable vouchers, and other loyalty scheme cards
- Access solutions for vehicle, building, office, and home access
- Tracking of public and personal assets, patient tracking, and tracking of field staff

The move to mobile eTicketing and payments would deliver immense value for the public as it provides easier access to public services and also spurs the growth of numerous industries. The main candidate industry that would benefit the most is the retail industry. Retailers will hesitate to explore and invest in mobile payment and eTicketing options until and unless they see a strong interest in such options from the public. Mass adoption of mobile eTicketing and payment as the key public transport ticketing system would convince retailers that consumers are ready to shift to a cashless society and that NFC-enabled handsets are readily available. This in turn would stimulate further investment in mobile payment infrastructure in the retail sector.

Government support of mobile eTicketing and payment options for its transport infrastructure is a critical and strategic move to stimulate the rest of the market. Consumers benefit from mobile ticketing and payment option by having the facility to use a single device across all transport platforms [4]. This in turn provides a consistent user experience, speed, convenience, security, and near universal availability (e.g., non–credit card holders, tourists). The benefits for the city transport provider(s) include reduced costs as a result of having a scalable, integrated ticketing platform across all modes of transportation, dematerialization (i.e., reload platforms), and reduced fraud. Enabling payments to be made from a mobile device would make it possible for tickets to be acquired from outside congested stations, reducing crowding and the need for multiple ticketing staff and ticketing machines [4].

MOBILE PAYMENT AND eTICKETING IN PRACTICE

The Cityzi Project is a large-scale pre-commercial roll out of mobile contactless services. French mobile operators will market the first NFC handsets for use by several thousand customers. Customers will be able to discover, for the first time in France, a multiservice offer of mobile contactless services, delivered through the support of mobile operators. The first commercial mobile NFC handsets were marketed to 500,000 residents in the Nice metropolitan area along with a set of mobile NFC applications. In the summer of 2010 Orange sold the phone in its nine stores in Nice and nearby Manton and Beau Soleil, with approximately 30 retailers selling the NFC-enabled phones. The scope of the initiative covers the entire urban community of Nice, including the city as well as the 24 neighboring communities. The first services on offer within the framework of "Mobile Contactless Nice" will include

- Public transport—ticketing, passenger information
- Promotion of local heritage and education—e-campus project
- Trade and retail—local bank transactions, mobile loyalty and couponing programs
- Cultural/tourist information—museums

The Nice transport company Lignes D'Azur, which operates buses and the trams in the city, has an NFC option similar to Oyster in London and Octopus in Hong Kong. Cityzi customers can load up the Bpass Java application resident on the phone with a credit card to make journeys through an over-the-air transaction. Tickets can be bought at €1 each, or for €2 with parking, or in packs of €10. Each tram journey costs €1 and users can have credit of up to €19 on a phone at any one time. The price of the tickets is charged to the subscriber's phone bill and the mobile operator runs a revenue share with Lignes D'Azur. The phone can be used to take the tram or bus for journeys even if the phone's battery is flat, although one needs a connection to add a ticket to the phone. Perhaps the most powerful part of the technology is the use of NFC tags with a link to the phone's Web browser. Waving the phone over a tag takes the browser directly to a preprogrammed page, providing access to real-time tram and bus times, TV listings, news, weather, restaurant booking, and directory enquiries. The scheme has been a huge success, with other locations anxious to replicate the program.

2.4.2 Intelligent Energy Conservation Using Mobile Devices

The following are some of the main challenges that exist in the energy and utilities sector.

2.4.2.1 Excessive Growth in Customer Demands   By 2050, the demand for energy will almost double compared to existing consumption. Finding new avenues for energy generation and satisfying the demands of the ever-increasing customer base is a real challenge.

2.4.2.2 Increase in Infrastructure Cost   To meet the growing needs for energy, it is necessary to invest in the creation of new infrastructure and at the same time spend to maintain the existing infrastructure. With limited budgets, it becomes very difficult to accomplish these tasks, which become all the more challenging because most existing energy infrastructures and power generation systems have become worn out and obsolete due to aging.

2.4.2.3 Regulations Imposed by Government Rules   Governments across the globe continuously bring out new laws with the aim of reducing the carbon footprint and greenhouse gases. This in turn imposes many restrictions on the agencies that are involved in the energy and utilities sector.

The majority of these problems faced by the energy and utilities sector can be eliminated by the use of M2M technologies. It is estimated that by 2020 there will be around 1.5 billion M2M communications in the utility sector, the majority being in smart meters.

Smart meters are a new type of energy meter. They have the capability to track power consumption and periodically send the readings to the energy supplier. The intervals at which the readings are sent back to the energy supplier are configurable. These smart meters help consumers to keep track of their power consumption and help energy companies to create custom usage plans according to the consumption patterns. This will also provide a great deal of customer satisfaction, as customers can track their usage on a regular basis. This in turn will help reduce calls to the customer care centers.

Mobile devices and mobile network operators have a vital role to play in this ecosystem, which can be summarized as follows:

1. They can provide connectivity among the various devices and the utility operators by leveraging their existing wireless network infrastructure.
2. They can deliver energy consumption alerts to mobile devices and in this way can provide a series of value-added services for the consumers.
3. They can leverage the existing capability to transfer data and bill end-users to exchange huge amounts of real-time data and discrete transactions.

In addition, NFC technology can be leveraged to make bill payment possible using mobile devices.

Mobile devices can be used as part of the smart energy grid as well. The smart energy grid helps to monitor consumption versus demand on a larger scale. Sensors and other components that are part of the smart grid monitor energy usage patterns of homes and industrial buildings and come with patterns that depict power usage. These patterns help predict the times of peak usage, which in turn would help in the creation of real-time adaptive pricing plans that can be communicated to the various stakeholders as alerts to their mobiles. These options to track and analyze usage patterns help to balance the load at peak times by using distributed energy storage and also help to prevent energy wastage during non-peak hours.

The smart grid also allows consumers to give the excess power that they have self-generated back to the grid, without any technical or regulatory barriers. By analyzing and understanding energy demands, a consumer can conserve more energy and is better placed in terms of the decision to utilize alternative power sources.

An architecture for intelligent energy conservation using M2M and mobile devices is given by

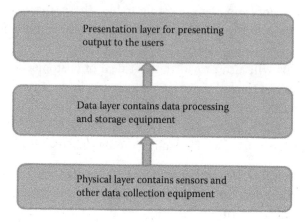

The lowest layer pertains to the actual physical devices and contains sensors and other smart meters that are used to obtain data about energy conservation and usage.

The data from this layer are collected and sent to the next layer, which processes them. The following are the main types of such processing.

- Store the data in various meter data management systems.
- Route the data to various asset tracking and management systems if applicable. This in turn will be used to perform further analysis such as the power consumption of various assets in a building, predict maintenance schedules for various assets, and so on.
- Analyze the usage patterns and the various usage scenarios.
- Use intelligence embedded in the platform to determine energy optimization techniques by finding out peak and non-peak hours and the difference in the usage levels.
- Send message alerts to consumers about their energy consumption levels and customized energy tariffs or plans that may be beneficial for them.
- Route the excess power if available to the various devices or other infrastructural components that may need them.

The last layer is the presentation layer through which the processed data can be viewed by the consumers. Some of the commonly used options are mobile devices, tablets, customer portals where customers can log in to view their usage, dashboards for energy suppliers to get a consolidated view of usage of their customer base, and reporting tools for generating various types of reports. The various options available in this layer could vary from one service provider to another.

In short, mobile devices can form an important part of the energy and utilities ecosystem. This in turn will deliver many value-added services to consumers and will help to transform a city into an intelligent city by enabling intelligent collection, analyses, and usage of data.

INTELLIGENT ENERGY IN PRACTICE

Ampla is an electric energy distributor owned by Endesa Brazil that provides electricity to 73% of the state of Rio de Janeiro and services more than 2 million customers. The rate of urbanization, the nature of the accommodation (slums), and the high crime rate led to an unsustainable level of energy theft and bad credit risk. A large number of customers did not have access to personal banking services and were limited in their ability to budget and manage their finances. Meters at residential and commercial sites were prone to tampering and bribes to employees encouraged fraud.

Ampla was averaging 23.6% energy losses on its network—reaching up to 52% in some areas. The result was a negative impact on the utility's profitability and a higher cost of energy passed through to its consumers. In 2003, Ampla began to roll out a pilot for a new mode of smart metering—located at the pole top—entitled Rede DAT. With Rede DAT the consumption per household is recorded at the transformer and energy consumption data are communicated by the utility over a mobile network. Energy customers receive consumption data through their mobile phones. The pilot proved a great success, with losses from theft reduced by more than 50%, the number of supply interruptions reduced by more than 40%, and operating costs lowered. A wider rollout provided hundreds of thousands of Ampla's residential and business customers with access to the Rede Ampla service.

2.4.3 Analysis and Commercial Insights

Cities across the world face the universal problem of the inability to integrate different types of data that are present in disparate systems and making them available to derive meaningful insights and patterns that would help city officials to devise value-added services that would be beneficial for their inhabitants. This would be the key characteristic of an intelligent city. To make this possible using mobile devices, mobile visualization technologies or mobile business intelligence (BI) plays a major role.

2.4.4 Drivers for Mobile BI Adoption

- Mobile BI facilitates quick decisions. In a typical usage scenario, some amount of waiting time is involved in making an application process data and then use the data to enable decision making. With the help of mobile BI, it is possible to make instantaneous decisions by making the entire data processing and visualization happen in the mobile device.
- Mobile BI allows location-independent decision making. There is no dependency on any office/location to fetch and process data. The widespread penetration of the mobile wireless networks across geographies has made data available anytime, anywhere.
- All data are available for analysis in mobile devices. This, combined with the availability of 3G and 4G networks and the rapid proliferation of mobile devices, has enabled all types of end-users to learn data analysis quickly using mobile devices. There is no more waiting for a decision because critical data can't be accessed.

2.4.5 Key Trends in Mobile BI

- *High levels of importance*—According to a survey conducted by Dresner Advisory Services in September 2011, 68% of organizations feel that mobile business intelligence is very important for their growth and sustenance in the market.
- *Functionality drive*—Mobile devices will be the key focus area for BI in the coming year, according to 2012 predictions from

Gartner. Use of mobile devices will become mainstream to the extent that more than one-third of BI functionality will be taken over by mobile devices within the next couple of years.

- *Large-scale implementation*—33% of enterprises will implement some level of mobile BI by the end of 2012, which is in addition to the 25% of enterprises that already have a mobile BI application in place, according to the independent telecom industry research organization Heavy Reading. More enterprises are finding operational efficiency, real-time analytics, and customer responsiveness from mobile BI and this in turn will drive the large-scale adoption of mobile BI tools and technologies.

- *Collaboration using mobile BI*—Increased use of mobile devices is contributing to the overall growth in collaboration over BI, according to a survey from business intelligence tool and strategy advisory BI Scorecard. The enterprises that will succeed in sharing business data in the next year and going forward are the ones that will continually be the forerunners in the field of innovation in the mobile BI space as per the studies by business intelligence tool and strategy advisory BI Scorecard group.

2.4.6 *Steps to Get Started with Mobile BI*

The following are the key common steps to be followed to integrate and view data using various mobile visualization technologies.

Step 1: Setting up or creating a data source. In this step, a data source is created. Data source refers to the source from which data need to be pulled out by the analytical applications to make predictions. The data source can vary from a huge database to a small set of files. As part of this step, it needs to be ensured that the format in which data are fetched from the data source are compatible with the data type supported by the analytical application. This step is very important to get accurate prediction results because if there is any error in the input data, it will adversely affect the prediction results. Typically the user interface to create a data source will have options to upload the data directly or fetch it from a remote source using some kind of a protocol at fixed time intervals. Data input provided at this stage can be structured or unstructured and it can also be in multiple formats.

When data source inputs are specified for analytical applications, it is very important to evaluate whether it is required to capture real-time data for analytical purposes. If this is the case, it is very important to consider aspects such as network bandwidth available to capture real-time data.

Step 2: Dataset creation. In this step, data from the data sources are pulled out and normalized to a common format to be used to create a prediction model. In some cases, it is required that only specific data fields from the data source be used for analytical purposes. This step provides the option to define those fields. If no specific fields are chosen, data from all the fields in the data source defined are used for building the prediction models. This step converts all different types of data from different sources to one specific format with specific defined fields and data types for data present in each field.

Step 3: Prediction model creation. In this step, the data from the data sets will be used to generate a prediction model based on some underlying statistical concepts such as regression or correlation.

The output of this step typically will be in a visual diagrammatic format. This output will be a predictive model that will show the most relevant patterns present in the data set. The most commonly used visual representation format is the tree structure. Apart from this, there are several other formats such as spirals, bar graphs, pie charts, and so on.

Step 4: Prediction result generation and mobile visualization. In this step, the models generated in the previous step are pulled out to be viewed in mobile devices. Several mobile BI products are available in the market. Some mobile BI products support only specific mobile platforms. Some of the major players in this domain are Cognos, Roambi, and Tabloo.

2.4.7 Mobile Healthcare

Mobile healthcare (mHealth) refers to the use of mobile devices for healthcare and communication services. There has been an increasing interest in this field in countries across the world. The proliferation of mobile devices, availability of high-speed wireless networks, and their impact on the day-to-day lives of large segments of the population have been the key factors driving the adoption of mobile devices in the healthcare sector. In addition, in many parts of the world, there is still an acute shortage of healthcare workers and this has been a matter of concern for city officials. Studies in the healthcare sector have also revealed that healthcare services offered through mobile devices have better reachability and impact even in very remote and resource-poor environments.

mHealth has emerged as an aftermath of eHealth, which refers to the use of information and communication technology for healthcare-related services. Both mHealth and eHealth are interlinked and they work hand in hand. For example, eHealth may involve digitization of patient records, thereby creating an electronic infrastructure for storing patient data, and mHealth could be used to gather and enter patient-related data into city health information systems and also answer various health-related queries for healthcare workers on their mobile devices.

The following are key applications of mHealth.

Education and awareness: SMS using mobile devices has evolved as a simple and effective technique for addressing a wide range of health issues. SMS messages can be sent to mobile devices on various aspects of healthcare such as disease management, disease symptoms, and the availability of various healthcare services at various locations in a city. SMS campaigns for healthcare services can be configured as one-way alerts or as two-way communication. In case of two-way communication, an individual may be asked to take a healthcare survey that may be input to the healthcare information system of the city. These SMS campaigns have proved to have a powerful impact when compared to other modes of communication such as radio and television.

Remote data collection: It is very important for healthcare departments in cities to collect information about the various healthcare policies and their impact on the residents so that they can create better policies that are more aligned to the requirements of the residents. The data collection process is very efficient if done with the help of a mobile device, as it helps in automated entry of data directly into the healthcare information systems rather than paper-based surveys that require manual entry into the information systems. Lastly, manual entry may also introduce errors at the time of data entry.

Remote monitoring: Remote monitoring using mobile devices ensures one-way or two-way communication to monitor various health parameters, provide doctor appointments, and also send reminders about medication regime or upcoming doctor visits. In some cases, remote sensors can be used to monitor various heath parameters and take immediate corrective action if the situation demands it.

Communication and training for healthcare workers: Training new healthcare workers and empowering existing healthcare workers is the key requirement existing in the healthcare sector. Mobile devices can be used to empower healthcare workers by providing them access to the city's healthcare databases. Another current need is to provide effective communication among various healthcare centers so that they can all work together efficiently and effectively to cater to the city's healthcare requirements. This can also be achieved with the help of mobile devices.

Disease and epidemic outbreak tracking: Diseases often start in small pockets and later develop into widespread epidemics. Mobile devices play a very important role in making people aware of the disease symptoms as well as the preventive measures. This will help in the containment of diseases at a very early stage.

Diagnostics and treatment support: mHealth applications are capable of providing expert advice and tips to healthcare workers by providing them access to medical databases with the help of their mobile devices. With the advancement of mHealth, people are able to receive timely treatment at remote places without the need for hospital visits, which might otherwise have proved to be a difficult or impossible task for them.

The mobile devices of healthcare workers are typically equipped with built-in software. Through this software, healthcare workers can enter the various symptoms of the disease in a step-by-step manner and use those steps to get expert advice from senior doctors or from the knowledge bases present in the hospital/city.

2.4.7.1 Value Chain for Mobile Heathcare The value chain for a mHealth system is shown in the diagram that follows. The various stake-holders are

- *Ministry of health/government health agencies*—Need to take the initiative to devise and implement mHealth-related initiatives in the city
- *Funders*—Provide the funds that are necessary for the development and implementation of various mHealth applications
- *Content providers*—Design and create various types of content to be used as a basis for various mHealth initiatives
- *Application developer/platform developer*—Develops various platforms/applications for mHealth initiatives
- *Mobile service providers*—Provide the infrastructure and wireless networks that are used for implementing mHealth initiatives

It is very important that all these stakeholders work in very close collaboration for the success of each mHealth initiative.

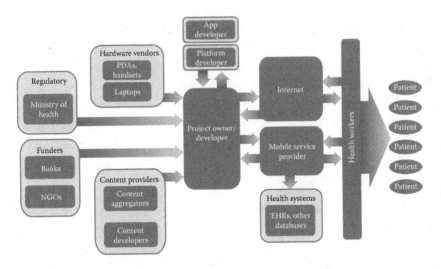

2.4.8 Wireless Fleet Management

Seamless and flawless fleet management is key to the success of any fleet management organization. The main aspects of an efficient fleet management system are the following:

1. *Scheduled maintenance*: Regularly scheduled maintenance is a vital factor to minimize vehicle downtime. All types of maintenance activities such as regular oil changes are essential to improve the life of a vehicle. To chart out preventative maintenance schedules, it is very important to know some key details about the vehicle, such as the type of vehicle, the average usage of the vehicle, and the typical road and environmental conditions in which the vehicle is most likely to be used, warranty details, and regulatory requirements as applicable. In addition, it is always better to know the various types of diagnostic problems that are most likely to occur with different vehicle types.

2. *Vehicle performance*: Details about individual vehicle performance parameters on the road are a key aspect to reduce their maintenance costs. For example, when trucks are running on bad roads with high heat and steep grades, it is very important to monitor various engine parameters such as the engine, the air intake temperature, and oil pressure. This can help fleet managers to monitor engine performance. Collection of these data will also facilitate vehicle analytics at later stages to determine if a vehicle is performing optimally.

3. *Fuel economy*: It is vital to improve vehicle performance through preventative maintenance, which in turn can improve fuel economy. Monitoring unauthorized vehicle usage and excessive speeding of the vehicle can help to reduce fuel usage. Studies have shown that repairing a vehicle that is out of tune can increase its mileage by an average of 4 percent. In addition, fixing a serious maintenance problem can improve a vehicle's mileage by about 40%.

Wireless fleet management solutions have revolutionized the fleet management sector by slicing and dicing the various pain points that are experienced in the fleet management sector. The proliferation of mobile devices and high-performance wireless networks has created a profound impact in the fleet management sector. The various capabilities offered by the different wireless fleet management solutions are the following:

- *Wireless tracking of routes*: With the help of integrated GPS systems, it is possible for fleet management systems to track and provide the exact location of a vehicle and the route that is used for the vehicle's travel. This will help to ensure that vehicles follow only stipulated routes with no possibility for bifurcation. This in turn will help to track fuel expenses and reduce fraudulent activities such as unaccounted fuel usage and unaccounted route traversal for activities that would be of personal interest for the drivers of the vehicles. Fleet managers can monitor the location and other details of the vehicle with the help of their smart phones, which can connect and communicate with the fleet management systems.

- *Scheduled maintenance SMS alerts*: Fleet management systems typically have some software components added to the vehicle's engine. These components continuously monitor various vehicle parameters such as speed, fuel consumption, and odometer readings. With the help of these monitored parameters, fleet management systems have the capability to calculate the maintenance schedule for the vehicles and also send SMS alerts to the fleet managers informing them about the maintenance schedule and the various vehicle parameters or components of the vehicle that may need replacement or repair during the maintenance.

These wireless fleet management systems also have the capability to use wireless networks to store data about the various parameters of a vehicle in a remote database that can be used later for vehicle analytics to derive various meaningful patterns about the vehicle's usage.

2.5 Enabling Mobile Technologies for an Intelligent City

In this section, we discuss some other mobile technologies that will help in the evolution of intelligent cities.

2.5.1 Mobile Augmented Reality

The increasing proliferation of smart mobile devices has led to the emergence of new mobile, wearable, and pervasive computing applications. These applications make anytime, anywhere availability of online resources a reality. The aftermath of this is the penetration of augmented reality (AR) applications into the mobile device sector. This has led to the evolution of a new set of augmented reality applications called mobile augmented reality systems (MARSs). This technology provides techniques to blend virtual imaging technologies into the video stream of a mobile device's camera in real time.

AR applications in general provide a powerful user interface that will facilitate infusion of the context-aware computing environments. AR applications blend context-based virtual information into a person's physical environment. Using this technique, users of AR applications tend to perceive that the information actually exists in their surroundings. MARS extend this feature to mobile devices without considering the mobile device user's whereabouts or location. MARS work everywhere by adding a palpable layer of information to the mobile device user's environment as and when it is desired or required by the user. This technology revolutionizes the manner in which information is made available to people by integrating all Web-related and other types of information available to a mobile device user. This technology also allows users to interact directly with the information that is displayed, pose queries, and collaborate with the people around to exchange thoughts or seek opinion on aspects of interest.

The main components of any AR system are summarized in the following diagram:

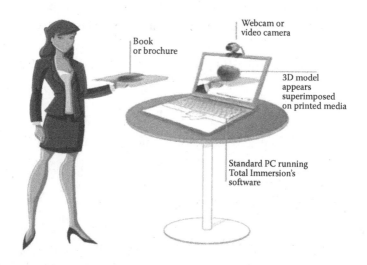

To extend this concept to mobile devices, there should be the possibility to provide position and orientation of the mobile device user as well. In short the components of a MARS are the following:

1. *Camera*—The camera is used for image acquisition and rendering.
2. *MARS applications*—Many MARS applications are available in the market. These applications are used to add the palpable layer of information that is required by the user. Some of these applications are discussed in the next section.
3. *Global positioning system (GPS) and accelerometer*—These components are required to identify location details and track the movement of the user.
4. *Magnetometer*—This component determines the direction that a mobile device user is facing.
5. *Gyroscope*—This component is used to determine the mobile device's orientation in space.

2.5.1.1 MARS in Practice   In this section, some of the popular mobile AR applications (apps) and the various features provided by them are discussed.

2.5.1.1.1 Layar   The Layar mobile application is the world's most downloaded mobile AR application, and, on an average, it continues to grow at an average rate of almost 1 million downloads per month [5]. Layar works on an iOS platform. Layar uses the mobile device's camera and GPS capabilities to gather location information. Layar then provides information about restaurants or other buildings in the surrounding area by overlaying this information on the mobile device's screen. If pointed at a particular building, Layar has the capability to give details about the companies in the building and also details about the companies that are hiring. Apart from this, the mobile application will be able to provide photos of the building that are available in Wikipedia or any other public domain and provide more details about the building such as the history, year of construction, and so on. This application can provide a wide range of use cases for an intelligent city such as intelligent workforce management, intelligent tourism development, and intelligent travel.

2.5.1.1.2 Blippar   This mobile application works on Android and iOS platforms. Blippar has the capability to add an interactive experience to any object that exists around us. The objects could include anything like a movie poster, product label, or any magazine label or advertisement. If a mobile device loaded with a Blippar application is pointed at any such object, all the digital content related to that object such as interactive advertisement and promotional videos will be displayed in the mobile device. This application can provide an intelligent and technology-enabled shopping experience in a city.

2.5.1.1.3 Google Googles   This mobile applications works on an Android platform. It is a visual search application that takes advantage of a smart phone's camera to look up famous landmarks, scan bar codes and QR codes for additional information about a product, translate foreign language text, and so on. This application has the capability to quickly pull out historical facts or encyclopedia entries, publishing details, related products, reviews, and so on about any item to which it is pointed. This application can provide intelligent shopping and intelligent toursim development capabilities for a city.

2.5.1.1.4 iOnRoad   This is an augmented driving mobile application that works on Android and iOS platforms. It helps drivers on the road by providing warnings about possible accidents/collisions, alerts about alternate routes with less traffic congestion, and other kinds of data that will be of use for drivers on the road. This mobile application has a "visual radar" that uses the mobile device's sensors and camera to track the speed of a driver's vehicle and distance of the vehicle from the other vehicles that are in close proximity. This mobile application then calculates and provides various audio and visual collision warnings and speeding alerts. The application also has a provision for recording the speed at which a vehicle is driven and for taking geotagged snapshots. These data can be used later to provide useful insights about driving with the help of driving analytics. This application will be extremely useful to enforce intelligent traffic management, which in turn is a key component of intelligent public safety, which is a vital aspect of an intelligent city.

2.5.1.1.5 Theodolite   This is an intelligent digital viewfinder mobile application that provides users with an excellent data overlay that is comparable to a military heads-up display. The application combines several navigational tools along with the mobile device's internal sensors and GPS, such as a compass, inclinometer, rangefinder, and mapping features. This application also offers the capability to take geo-tagged photos and videos. It will be very useful for intelligent travel planning, especially if the travel involves traversing hills, mountains, and other natural features. This application can also be used by military forces to plan their navigation and movement in high-risk situations such as wars or when they are involved in rescue operations posed by natural calamities such as floods, storms, and landslides. This in turn is a very important aspect of intelligent public safety for cities.

2.5.1.1.6 Motion Coprocessor Apple's iPhone 5s is equipped with a new "M7" chip that is otherwise known as a "motion coprocessor." The M7 motion coprocessor continuously measures the user's motion data, even when the mobile device is not working. It is designed to work by capturing motion data from the mobile device's compass, accelerometer, and gyroscope. The concept of motion coprocessor was designed to facilitate creation of a new generation of health and fitness applications [6].

2.5.1.1.7 Geofencing in Mobile Devices Geofencing is another important mobile application that adds immense value to a city. It is supported by most of the leading mobile platforms in the market such as Android and iOS. A geofence is a virtual boundary of interest that can be set up to send SMS notifications when it is entered or exited. A geofence combines a mobile device user's location awareness to the location awareness of other nearby features that are in closer proximity to the mobile device user's defined virtual boundary of interest. A virtual boundary of interest can be defined by specifying its latitude and longitude values. To adjust the proximity of the location, a value for the radius can also be added. In short, the latitude, longitude, and radius values are used to define a geofence. It is also possible to have multiple active geofences at the same point in time.

Location services present in mobile devices treat a geofence as an area rather than as a point. This allows it to detect when a particular user or device enters or exits a geofence. For each geofence, it is possible to configure location services to send an SMS alert whenever a user or device enters or exits a geofence. It is also possible to limit the duration of a geofence by specifying an expiration duration in milliseconds. After the geofence expires, location services automatically remove it.

Geofencing has many interesting applications such as tracking the location and action of an employee in the context of a mobile workforce, which will facilitate intelligent workforce management; intelligent fleet management by tracking the movement of trucks and other vehicles such as when they enter or leave specific defined boundaries or locations; intelligent device tracking by tracking a mobile device that is supposed to be used only within the hospital premises and by disabling it if it moves outside of them. Another interesting application is to monitor transactions and detect theft or fraud. For example, in case of a fuel purchase, this can be done by matching the location data with fuel purchases. This in turn will help to monitor the distance traveled versus the fuel filled, which would easily help in the detection of fuel theft. An example of a geofence created using a Google map and the kind of mobile notification that is received is given in the figure that follows.

2.5.1.1.8 Beacons Beacons are small low-cost pieces of hardware that can be easily attached to walls or roof tops of buildings. They are capable of using battery-friendly blue tooth connections to send

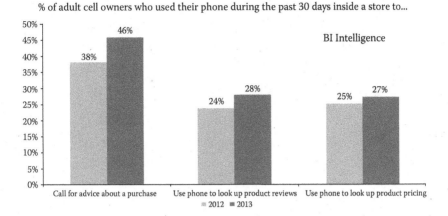

% of adult cell owners who used their phone during the past 30 days inside a store to...

Figure 2.1   In-store mobile shopping experiences. (From Pew, January 2013.)

messages and alerts to a smart phone. They are used mainly for indoor communications, as indoor spaces often block signals, making use of GPS difficult or almost impossible.

They have revolutionized and transformed the way retailers, event organizers, and enterprises communicate with people indoors. They have already found their way into home automation systems as well. As per a recent study, most Americans already use mobile devices in stores for various aspects, as shown in the Figure 2.1 that follows.

Lastly, beacons can also find widespread applications in airports, railway stations, and other transit hubs so that alerts on various aspects of travel such as arrival and departure timings, delays, gate, and other platform-related information can be delivered directly to the mobile devices of the passengers.

2.5.1.1.9 Mobile Backend as a Service   Mobile backend as a service (MBaaS) refers to a cloud computing service delivery model comprising companies that offer services for mobile application developers to set up, use, and operate a cloud backend for developing their mobile applications. MBaaS, also referred to as backend as a service (BaaS), can typically offer two categories of services: consumer BaaS and enterprise BaaS. Consumer BaaS focuses mainly on the development of lighter weight mobile applications and games, whereas the latter concentrates on the development of applications that focus on mobilizing business critical data from enterprise systems. In short,

MBaaS as a whole is disrupting the concept of on-premise "mobile enterprise application platform," while providing much more turn-key functionality for the mobile application development strategy rather than just providing the traditional API management that is offered by platform as a service vendors.

2.6 Conclusion

In this chapter we presented an overview of the mobile devices and mobile device ecosystem. The various applications of mobile devices in the day-to-day activities of cities were exemplified. The emergence of 4G networks and new high-end smart phones will further fuel the pace at which mobile devices are getting integrated with the various city agency activities. This is very evident from recent trends that denote a soaring rise in the number of mobile applications and platforms that are custom made for city processes.

The various mobile device use cases for an intelligent city were examined in detail with apt real-life implementation examples. Futuristic mobile technologies that hold great promise for intelligent cities were also covered in detail in the latter half of this chapter.

Mobile augmented reality technology holds great promise for the future with the plethora of applications it offers to the various domains of the city such as travel and tourism, retail, and workforce management. Geofencing in mobile devices is yet another concept that holds a powerful promise for the future of intelligent cities.

One of the key trends in mobile devices that is expected in the near future is the evolution of wearable mobile devices. They are expected to replace smart phones by means of their integration with various wearable components that form part of a person's daily activities such as watch, wrist bands, sunglasses, and so on. Once these technologies fully mature, they will provide a more seamless experience for infusing mobile device technologies in a person's daily routine. This in turn will help mobile devices to break through the barriers and the constraints that are imposed by the smart phone screens and will help open up avenues for mobile devices to become more people-centric.

References

1. IDC (2013). IDC Predictions 2013. Competing on the 3rd Platform.
2. J. Walter Thompson Worldwide (2013). Mobile Trends for 2013 and Beyond.
3. IBM. http://www-03.ibm.com/software/products/en/worklight/.
4. Philips. http://www.sacg.com.tw/sacweb/marcom/epaper/images/NFC .pdf.
5. Layar. https://www.layar.com/about/layar-facts/.
6. http://www.mgacrumors.com/2013/09/10/iphone-5s-includes-new -m7-motion-coprocessor-for-health-and-fitness-tracking/.

THE ROLE AND RELEVANCE OF SOFTWARE-DEFINED CLOUD INFRASTRUCTURES

Abstract

It is incredibly true that every common, casual, and even cheap thing in our midst is becoming smart in its operations, outlooks, and offerings through a host of technological advancements. Every kind of physical, mechanical, electrical, and electronic good is being made smarter through deft instrumentation starting with its conceptualization stage and followed by the interconnectivity capability. With the enhanced maturity and stability of smartness-enabling technologies, practices, patterns, platforms, and processes, every tangible thing in our personal as well as professional environments is set to become smart in its actions and reactions. That in turn leads to scores of smart environments including homes, hotels, hospitals, and so on. With the faster realization of implementation technologies, the level of interest is gaining momentum among product vendors, system integrators, service providers, government agencies, and consulting organizations toward setting and sustaining smart, safe, and sustainable cities across the globe. The highly popular cloud technology is an interesting phenomenon destined to contribute immensely to the establishment and sustenance of intelligent cities. In this chapter, we look at the essence behind cloud computing, the latest innovations in the cloud paradigm, and some classic use cases for hosting and delivering city-specific applications, services, and data via clouds (centralized as well as federated).

3.1 Introduction

Technologies are playing an important role in sustainably and smartly transforming any ordinary city into an intelligent city or in developing smart cities from the ground up to meet varied people's expectations. The choice of technologies, platforms, tools, and methodologies is crucial for the intended success of smart city projects in any part of the world. As illustrated in the picture below, a smart city engagement is a very complex one because it is the result of seamless and spontaneous integration and orchestration of multiple independent and unique domains such as smart homes, offices, transports, retail, healthcare, public safety, government, utilities, energy security, education, entertainment, and so on.

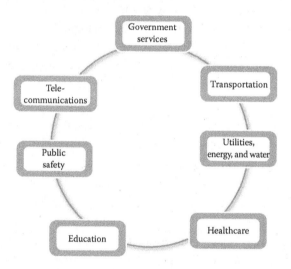

There are several competent yet contrasting technologies in the IT space today and hence the selection of implementation technologies has to be strategically planned and carefully leveraged. Technology usage needs to be rolled out very seriously; otherwise, even if the technologies chosen are sound the project may not see the success initially envisaged. Further, history tells us that many technologies had emerged and disappeared from the scene without contributing anything substantial because of a lack of inherent strengths. Very few technologies could survive and contribute copiously for a long time. The intrinsic complexity in attempting all-round utilization and the lack of respected innovations are the main reasons for their abject failure and so they have vanished into thin air. Thus factors such as the fitment/suitability, competency, capability, sustainability, and extensibility of technologies ought to be taken into consideration while deciding technologies, tools, and other enablers to straighten and smooth the path toward the envisioned targets.

Wireless connectivity, service enablement, digitation, distribution, machine-to-machine (M2M) integration, the Internet of Things (IoT), cloud infrastructures, software platforms, big data analytics (BDA), and so on are the most prominent technologies evolving quickly toward facilitating the charters behind the establishment and sustenance of smarter cities across the globe. Profound information technology (IT) transformation will result in intelligent cities that directly enhance the quality of human living. In this chapter, we discuss the reverberations and repercussions of the cloud paradigm in the context of formation of smart cities.

There are several cloud service providers (CSPs) such as IBM, AWS, Google, Microsoft, HP, and so on laying a strong and scintillating foundation for smarter cities. On the cyber side, aspects such as provisioning, monitoring, and management of cloud resources; hosting an increasing array of cloud-enabled software applications; and keeping cloud-resident data are becoming widespread. At the ground level, a variety of input/output devices are emerging and ceaselessly captivating people. Slim and sleek, trendy and handy smart phones, tablets, wearables, and other personal and professional gadgets are flooding the market these days. Digital assistants come in various sizes, scopes, strengths, and structures to capture the market. Thus IT industrialization, through the powerful position of cloud infrastructures at one end and IT consumerization through a family of handhelds, portables, mobiles, pocketable, and so on at the other, are bringing both evolutions and revolutions to the IT landscape that in turn lead to a bevy of people-centric transitions. Business augmentation, automation, and acceleration are at the forefront with the realization of powerful technologies. It has been proven beyond any kind of doubt that cloud-based services actually have triggered greater business opportunities and possibilities for individuals, innovators, and institutions. The seamless connectivity and integration between physical devices with cloud applications will bring forth a number of benefits in the form of enhanced care, choice, convenience, and comfort.

Cloud infrastructures and platforms are extensively utilized for running numerous software applications for different industry sectors. For instance, home networking, integration, management, and automation software solutions are being taken to a cloud residence so that the creation and sustenance of smarter homes is becoming simplified. Similarly there are specific clouds such as sensor and device clouds, data, information and knowledge clouds, science clouds, and so on for various industry verticals. Generic/horizontal application packages too are being modernized and migrated to cloud environments to reap all the originally envisaged benefits. Intelligent management software solutions are deployed in cloud environments for upkeep of equipment and devices. As illustrated previously, the integration between devices at the ground level with remote applications (device-to-cloud [D2C] integration) is easily brought to fruition through a few pragmatic mechanisms such as open and industry-strength standards for connectivity. In the recent past, the representational state transfer (REST)ful application programming interface (API) was the dominant factor for device integrations. Whether it is installation, maintenance, or updates of device functionalities, the cloud-native as well as enabled systems come in handy. Fresh bundles of functional modules can be dynamically downloaded, installed, and configured into devices to empower them to exhibit exemplary actions and reactions. Remote monitoring, management, repair, enhancement, replacement, substitution, and even decommissioning of several kinds of instruments, machines, ware, appliances, utensils, equipment, and instruments across various environments can be accomplished with just a few clicks. Automation is gearing toward its peak in every aspect of our personal as well as professional lives. Digital living is being guaranteed with the praiseworthy technological advancements.

Signage administrators used to regularly send staff to check digital signage equipment located in public places. But now with the surging popularity of clouds, those remote diagnostic, management, and enhancement applications are being taken to clouds, and with this transition, such equipment can be remotely operated and controlled over any network. Also, public institutions could authorize some of their management tasks such as traffic intersection monitoring to cloud service providers so as to optimize resources and achieve the most efficient operation. In short, cloud-based systems will empower intelligent cities of the future, and industrial clouds are the final piece of the puzzle that will make it happen.

3.2 About Cloud Technology

With the overwhelming acceptance of cloud concepts, there is a big turnaround waiting to happen in IT. Especially on the infrastructure front, there are possibilities for radical optimization. The cloud paradigm has also brought in newer delivery, pricing, and consumption models. Applications are bound to be hosted, managed, and maintained in centralized and converged infrastructures and platforms to be discovered, accessed, and used over the Internet, which is being positioned as the common, affordable, and competent communication infrastructure for universal connectivity. In short, the incoming trends and technologies will require organizations to look seriously at consolidation, standardization, automation, and rationalization. Before plunging into the cloud landscape, there has to be a deeper analysis and greater understanding of its intrinsic capabilities besides any hidden charges and constraints. There are some scenarios in which the cloud is the best bet whereas there are some other areas where the cloud may be a laggard. There are a few well-known shortcomings such as security, lack of controllability and visibility, and so on. Distinct views are being expressed based on different viewpoints around cloud computing. It is much more than that—it is an amalgamation of a number of established technologies. Professors, pundits, and professionals have come out with a variety of enabling tools, best practices, and key guidelines to make cloud adoption simpler and faster. It is a fact that businesses are getting real benefits with the cloud movement, at least in the long run; end-users are being provided with the facility of anytime, anywhere, any network, any device access of cloud resources; software developers are gaining numerous advantages with cloud-based software development platforms; the once widening gaps between development and operational phases are closing with cloud embarkation; and so on. With the heightened simplicity, ubiquity, availability, and consumability of cloud infrastructures, platforms, applications, and data, cloud adoption is climbing.

3.3 Key Motivations for Cloud-Enabled Environments

At one time IT was disparaged as a cost center for any enterprise. Today that sentiment is fast changing as IT is being increasingly recognized and repositioned as the biggest business enabler. However, with the topsy-turvy world economy, the budget allocated for IT operations and for bringing newer IT capabilities and competencies for continuously bolstering businesses to fulfill changing customers' expectations is increasingly flat and even sometimes lower than in previous years. In a nutshell, businesses want more out of IT investments. Thus "more with less" has become a mantra for IT consultants, architects, and professionals to chalk out a viable and venerable IT strategy to bolster business activities without any lethargy and letup. IT luminaries and visionaries ceaselessly ponder on and work out robust and resilient mechanisms (competent technologies, synchronized processes, facilitating frameworks, futuristic and flexible architectures, highly optimized and automated infrastructures and platforms, scores of enabling tools and patterns, best practices, reusable assets, key guidelines and metrics, etc.) to enable businesses in their long and illustrious journey. As part of that IT rejuvenation and renaissance mission, a variety of IT concerns, constrictions, and challenges are being meticulously decoded and articulated widely.

IT departments of medium and big businesses are saturated with expensive IT resources. First, an indisputable fact is that across the globe, the IT utilization is very low, in the range of 10 to 15%; that is, expensive IT resources are sitting idle most of the time. Therefore concerted and calculated efforts have been underway to enhance significantly the purposeful utilization of all kinds of underutilized as well as unutilized IT infrastructures (servers, storage arrays and appliances, and network solutions). This assumes a bigger proposition for businesses, especially in the context of continuously shrinking IT budgets. There are rationalization, simplification, standardization, consolidation and centralization, automation, and orchestration initiatives toward organized and optimized IT. When utilization increases sharply, there can be substantial IT savings that in turn will lead to the addition of more right and relevant capabilities in the IT kitty. Resource sharing is another interesting option for enhancing IT utilization. Thus the aspect of IT optimization to take on business challenges and changes in a more casual and calm manner is the gist of the cloud paradigm.

Second, the need for programmability of IT infrastructures is being insisted on these days, and thereby their administration, configuration, prognosis, performance engineering and enhancement, provisioning and deprovisioning, operations, governance, maintainability and so on can be elegantly simplified and streamlined. All sorts of IT resources enabling businesses are expected to be extremely lean, green, nimble, elastic, versatile, and above all workload aware. That is, resources need to be aware of their workloads and their expected service qualities and ought to be intrinsically adaptive to meet them comfortably without any deviation, deficiency, and disturbance. The much-mandated capabilities such as resource accessibility, extensibility, elasticity, maneuverability, consumability, sustainability, malleability, and so on can be quite easily accomplished through the lavish incorporation of software into various IT resources. That is, the future-directed goal of attaining autonomic IT toward smarter computing can be achieved through software-defined environments (SDEs) that in turn comprise software-defined storage (SDC), software-defined networking (SDN), and so on. That is, IT is becoming totally virtualized totally and the time when everything will be software defined is not too far away.

These are the two top drivers for all the articulated advancements in the cloud landscape these days. All of the traditional data centers are being systematically refurbished with a swarm of proven cloud technologies to be presented as cloud centers. With this technology-driven cloud enablement, IT utilization has gone up 50%. Still not satisfied with that figure, thinkers and pundits are collectively endeavoring to raise the value through the embedding of more intimate and intense software-inspired automation and orchestration capabilities on various types of IT assets to make them grandly supple, smart, and sophisticated. It is predicted that with this solid and sound enhancement, IT utilization is bound to increase remarkably.

3.4 Why Cloud Technology Is Being Aggressively Pursued by Worldwide Governments

Governments across the globe today are confronting severe challenges in their solemn obligations to formulate and deliver a bevy of people-centric services to their constituents and citizens in a responsive, transparent, speedy, and cost-effective manner. Administrators and bureaucrats are faced with the harsh realities of swelling city populations that demand more, aging infrastructures, and declining budgets in the uncertain world economy scenario. As indicated previously, the appropriate usage of technologies is the way forward in this pressing situation. Cloud computing is a radical yet realistic enabler of many things for people and governments. The raging cloud idea, besides bringing down the capital as well as operational costs, is the leading contributor for scores of people-centric innovations. It can bring forth new capabilities and competences to all kinds of stakeholders. Cloud-based applications can be subscribed to and used by any device over a network at any point of time at any place. Thousands of smart city applications and services are being developed, deployed, and delivered via cloud infrastructures and platforms [1]. The picture below shows how different users access and use different software applications that are being hosted and maintained in clouds.

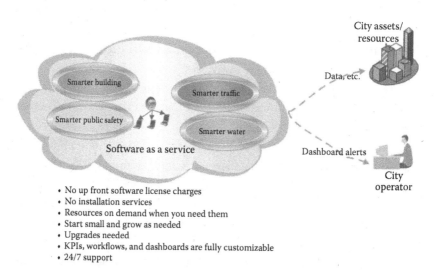

3.5 A Look at Cloud-Inspired Enterprise Transformations

A few noteworthy transitions are expected as cloud technology is embraced. On the one hand, there is a renaissance in the IT discipline; different cloud environments for distinct purposes are bound to erupt and evolve. On the other side, businesses will acquire immense benefits; cloud-inspired IT agility, adaptivity, and affordability result in businesses becoming inspiringly agile, adaptive, and affordable. A third factor is becoming apparent. As energy efficiency is turning out to be crucial for the future, the cloud movement will be a game-changer for environmental sustainability.

3.5.1 The Emergence of Cloud Environments

The key driver for the raging cloudification is that expensive IT resources are lying idle. The first and foremost requirement for cloud building is to do initial assessment of all the resources for the proposed cloud infrastructure. Clouds are being positioned as the consolidated, virtualized, automated, and shared IT infrastructure for efficiently hosting, managing, and delivering scores of service-centric and enterprise-scale IT resources (applications, platforms, and even infrastructural modules) as services to worldwide users via the public Internet, which is being touted and trumpeted as the cheapest communication infrastructure. In other words, as the knowledge-driven service era sets in and stabilizes steadily, the utility and ubiquity of clouds as the path-breaking and promising service deployment and delivery container is set to climb further. From an opening as centralized and converged infrastructures, with the maturity of a series of enabling techniques and standards, clouds are being empowered significantly to solve high-end problems through a seamless federation of multiple geographically distributed clouds.

The main turnarounds and transformations accruing from the pioneering cloud idea is that clouds enable IT agility, affordability, and autonomy, which in turn provides business automation, acceleration, and augmentation. The goals of IT simplicity and sensitivity are being readied and realized with a greater understanding of novelty-packed cloud concepts. IT resource utilization goes up remarkably, and IT resource elasticity, self-service, and application scalability are getting automated using competent software solutions. Cloud infrastructures are extremely lean, green, and programmable. Numerous delightful enhancements such as the amenability, usability, and consumability of IT modules at different layers and levels of the enterprise IT stack are portending good days for cloud computing. The increased IT efficiency is easily translated into overall business efficiency and this has the immense and immeasurable potential to unleash scores of fresh

IT capabilities and business opportunities. On the operational side, there are several solid and sustainable improvements on the aspects of modifiability, performance tuning, scalability, and simplicity. All of these clearly drive business executives and entrepreneurs to refocus on the viability, vitality, and value-additions of the innovation-breeding cloud idea. By delegating the management and governance of infrastructure and software platforms to a team of highly skilled professionals being employed by CSPs, customers could offload their workloads' operational responsibilities and risks to CSPs.

A cloud environment predominantly gives an illusion of infinite processing and storage capabilities and capacities. This radical and radiant empowerment does a great deal of good for some specific enterprise applications. Applications that are designed from the ground up to spread their workloads across multiple servers will be able to benefit immensely from the provision of automated scaling of resources to match varying demands. Users and workloads are bound to change very frequently. This is quite appealing for applications with unpredictable or cyclical usage patterns, because a cloud orchestrator/broker/service bus can monitor usage and can dynamically scale resources up or down on an as-needed basis. This behavior, in sync with the pay-by-usage characteristic of clouds, could lead to significant cost savings.

With the greater and deeper understanding of the business and technical and use cases of clouds, organizations across the world are preparing judicious strategies and roadmaps to plunge into the cloud space, which is steadily expanding through a host of innovations and improvisations. However, the cloud onboarding has to be very carefully and calculatedly articulated and accomplished, as it is associated with several constrictions and challenges. The cloud movement is picking up across industrial sectors. This chapter elucidates all the right and relevant improvements such as SDEs occurring in the cloud space. This transformation puts the cloud idea in a better position in visualizing, implementing, deploying, and delivering a bevy of sophisticated services for smarter cities. Further, cloud-based orchestration engines simplify crafting people-centric, context-sensitive, service-oriented, event-driven, and knowledge-enveloped applications.

It is keenly expected that next-generation cloud environments will play a stellar and sparkling role and will be insightfully tuned to be the core, converged, and cognitive one-stop platform for hosting all kinds of software applications and hardware resources. Clouds are inherently capable of fulfilling the long-drawn vision of utility computing, IT industrialization, consumerization, and so on.

Enterprise transformation becomes a neat and nice reality via a wide array of actions such as process excellence, infrastructure consolidation, and intrinsic assimilation of potential architectural styles and technologies. If there is a glut in IT infrastructure, then infrastructure rationalization, consolidation, and optimization procedures are being widely and wisely recommended. That is, a lean infrastructure is the most desired state of any growing and glowing business and this significantly reduces the tightly aligned infrastructural complexity and cost (capital as well as operational) in due course. With the adoption of autonomic computing concepts, infrastructures are turning out to be the prime target for innately incorporating self-diagnosing, self-healing, self-configuring, self-defending, and self-managing capabilities to sharply decrease human intervention, instruction, and interpretation.

Process innovation is the next thing to be contemplated very seriously for enterprise automation, acceleration, and augmentation. Process reengineering, integration, orchestration, management, and governance techniques need to be leveraged to bring in lean processes that in turn would have a cascading effect on shifting enterprise operations, outputs, and offerings. Third, newer architectural styles are showing much promise and potential in refining enterprise outlooks. The recently erupted enterprise-scale and business-critical service-oriented architecture (SOA), event-driven architecture (EDA), model-driven architecture (MDA), Web-oriented architecture (WOA), resource-oriented architecture (ROA), and so on are becoming very popular in designing, developing, deploying, delivering, and sustaining on-demand, adaptive, real-time, dynamic, flexible, and modular applications.

Finally, disruptive, transformative, and inventive technologies are emerging and evolving rapidly in the IT landscape. Verifying and validating these technologies to be fit for the purpose are vital for success. There are path-breaking technologies that can be generically or specifically utilized for different IT functions. Miniaturization, connectivity, service orientation, virtualization, mobility, cloud, analytics (traditional as well as the most recent phenomenon of big data), and visualization are some of the shining and sustainable trends in the technology space.

3.5.2 Energy Optimization

Energy security and environmental sustainability are the top two global concerns with immense societal impacts [2]. Significant energy assets go toward electricity generation and electricity is a pervasive service whose reliable supply is essential for modern civilization. Not only generation but also transmission and distribution need to be systematically accomplished toward energy conservation. There is a strong view that clouds enable greenness. To assess the environmental impacts of cloud computing, Microsoft engaged with Accenture—a leading technology, consulting, and outsourcing company—and WSP Environment & Energy—a global consultancy dedicated to environmental and sustainability issues—to compare the energy use and carbon footprint of Microsoft cloud offerings for businesses with corresponding Microsoft on-premise deployments. The analysis focused on three of Microsoft's mainstream business applications (Microsoft Exchange, Microsoft SharePoint, and Microsoft Dynamics CRM). Each application is available both as an on-premise version and as a cloud-based equivalent. The team compared the environmental impact of cloud-based versus on-premise IT delivery on a per-user basis and considered three different deployment sizes—small (100 users), medium (1000 users), and large (10,000 users).

The study found that, for large deployments, Microsoft's cloud solutions can reduce energy use and carbon emissions by more than 30% when compared to their corresponding Microsoft business applications installed on-premise. The benefits are even more impressive for small deployments: Energy use and emissions can be reduced by more than 90% with a shared cloud service. Though large organizations can lower energy use and emissions by addressing some of these factors in their own data centers (private cloud), providers of public cloud infrastructure are best positioned to reduce the environmental impact of IT because of their scale. By moving applications to clouds, IT decision makers can take advantage of highly efficient cloud infrastructure, effectively "outsourcing" their IT efficiency investments while helping their company achieve its sustainability goals.

3.5.3 Cloud-Enabled and Hosted Smarter City Applications

Table 3.1 describes where the cloud stands in the realization of smarter cities.

As indicated previously, clouds emerge as the one-stop, all-encompassing, fast-growing, state-of-the-art, malleable, green, and lean IT environment for depositing, deploying, and delivering a host of enterprise, mobile, Web, wearable, social, environment-specific (smart home, office, manufacturing, retail, hospital, etc.), and embedded applications in an affordable, articulative, and adaptive manner. Not only applications, but also all kinds of IT platforms (design, development, execution, integration/middleware, management/governance/security, rule/policy/knowledge engines, orchestration, and so on) are finding these newly crafted, competitive, and elastic cloud infrastructures comfortable, convenient, and caring. In this section, we consider some sample applications (associated with smarter cities) moving to be operated from cloud environments [3]. We have on-premise home automation/networking/integration solutions fully installed in advanced homes. However, with the unprecedented maturity and

Table 3.1   The Cloud Advantages for Smarter Cities

SMARTER CITIES—THE PREREQUISITES	CLOUD ADVANTAGES
Collaborate with others by overcoming the silos (city, leaders, citizens, universities, businesses, etc.)	Affordability ➤ Shifts from capital expenditure to operational expenses ➤ Less total cost of ownership and high return on investment
Make urban requirements transparent	IT and business scability ➤ Elastic resource provisioning ➤ Gives an illusion of infinite resources
Harmonize and standardize processes, data structures, and interfaces	Market adaptability ➤ Faster time to market ➤ Supports innovative ideas
Protect government data privacy and security	Masked complexity ➤ Expand product sophistication ➤ Simpler for customers/users
Handle big data volumes	Context-driven variability ➤ User defined experiences ➤ Increase relevance
Increase efficiency, optimize resources/expenses and manage complexity	Ecosystem connectivity ➤ New value nets ➤ Potential new businesses

stability of cloud environments, most of the common, shareable, and sustainable functionalities are tenderly separated and hosted in remote clouds while home-specific features are with on-premise home gateways. This judicious segregation goes a long way in extolling and employing the middle path.

3.5.4 A Cloud-Enabled Context-Aware Framework for Smarter Environments

Having understood the inherent need for context awareness to develop and sustain a variety of smarter environments, we have described here how we designed and implemented a viable and value-adding context-awareness framework. IT product vendors and academic institutions have been working together and bringing forth a number of nimbler computing paradigms to accomplish widely changing expectations of businesses and users. However, as it turned out, the reality is that computing systems could do only preprogrammed things. That is, on receiving specific inputs software applications are capable of producing predetermined outputs. Inputs are typically fixed beforehand and the outputs are as per the expectations. However, with the penetration of IT into different industry sectors, the roles and responsibilities of IT are bound to grow substantially. All kinds of runtime changes need to be taken care of by software packages to be distinct in their actions and reactions. As context changes naturally or forcefully, the processing software has to accurately absorb the changes in time to turn and tune the outputs. The challenge lies in empowering software services to perform real-time capture of all kinds of changes (social, business, environmental, spatial, temporal, etc.) to come out with more situation-specific and aware results. The next-generation software will thereby be more aligned and applicable directly or indirectly to end-users rather than businesses.

Future compute machines would take several types of internal as well as external input data from distributed and disparate sources to produce smarter results that are more relevant to humans' situational needs. That is, user(s)' context is being flawlessly captured and profusely leveraged by computing clusters to produce right and relevant results for humans. Users' context is being decided based primarily on the implicit capability of establishing seamless and spontaneous connectivity and integration with a dynamic pool of software services and applications (social, enterprise, mobile, embedded, and cloud), multiple data sources, scores of devices, appliances, and sensors in the user(s)' environment. In a nutshell, the fast-emerging paradigm of context-aware computing will produce context-sensitive outputs for human beings to act on with clarity and confidence. The picture below illustrates how different systems, sensors, and actuators are being quickly integrated to do real-time capture of disparate data and distribute and leverage them cognitively to arrive at appropriate and actionable insights.

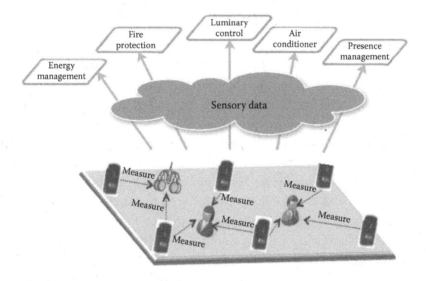

3.5.5 A Sample Use Case

As mentioned previously, several types of smarter environments are emerging and attractive use cases are being proposed. Ambient assisted living (AAL) is a very prominent use case for smarter homes. The goal is to empower bed-ridden, debilitated, and diseased people to lead independent and digitally assisted lives. For example, if a person living alone wants to have a cup of filtered coffee, he or she can instruct the coffee maker in the kitchen through a smart phone command. Once the coffee is ready, a robot can be ordered to fetch the prepared coffee to his or her bedside. Similarly medicine cabinets can have an alert/reminder facility to take tablets on time; the movement of the person can be monitored remotely; household items can be bought through mobile commerce sites; food can be purchased online; and all kinds of consumer electronics, energy managers, kitchen vessels and wares, instruments, microwave ovens, infotainment and edutainment systems, dishwashers, toasters, refrigerators, healthcare monitors, and so on can be instrumented and interconnected to have intelligent behaviors. Everyday activities and requirements thereby can be met with choice and convenience. New services being loaded in cloud-based platforms and infrastructures can be automatically subscribed to by home-bound devices to be relevant for homeowners and occupants.

3.5.6 Cloud–Based Smarter Home Applications

Home automation elements are being manufactured in quantity; linking of distributed and disparate devices is being smoothed out; elaboration of newer and nimbler services is in full swing; enabling frameworks and infrastructures are virtualized and pooled; proven processes are in place; clustered, brokered, federated, and cloud architectures are being worked out; and so on.

The present-day smart home involves bringing servers into the home for integrating diverse household electronics and for their effective control and usage. However, the need to manage, even if done remotely, very complex IT devices in the home has prevented this approach from being widely adopted. A more effective approach is to connect the devices to services in the cloud, which enables the centralization of services. Putting the intelligence into services in the network cloud reduces the complexity of managing software in the home devices and simplifies the interoperability of devices. This is accomplished by bridging the services throughout the network through Web service interfaces, translating the different device protocols to a common platform, and then connecting the devices through the network cloud. This is a far less expensive and more flexible way to aggregate services and compose new services on existing devices than has been possible in past attempts. This takes the complexity out of the connected devices in the home. Consumers move from being the IT managers of their homes to consumers of services through their connected devices. A local services "clone" or services cache in the home can safeguard the availability of services against network problems and guarantee continuous high quality, all with simple control by the consumer. With new cloud services, new possibilities exist for an appliance as simple as a pool pump or refrigerator when it has the ability to sense and respond to changing conditions, to communicate with other systems, and to inform decision making.

In summary, a smarter home is a personal and personalized place specifically designed to add life value, comfort, choice, care, and convenience, energy efficiency, safety and security, and future expansion. Without an iota of doubt, a home is the liveliest and loveliest place for people in their everyday lives. A growing array of smart environment technologies is being retrofitted to be usable and useful for easily and quickly producing and sustaining smarter homes. Abundant home automation elements; industry strength and open standards; trendy electronics; dynamic, virtualized, and converged infrastructures; and proven processes are being given a fresh lease on life and impetus to build digital homes.

Wireless broadband communication; ambient, agile, and adaptive sensors and actuators; smart heating, lighting, ventilation, and air control systems; sophisticated, energy-efficient and connectable edutainment and infotainment electronics; home security appliances; kitchen utensils; and so on will be profusely and prominently utilized in future home environments to sufficiently enhance the quality of life. Digital electronics, technology-enabled and -equipped spaces, the information superhighway, and the Internet of Services and Things and Energy all individually contribute to the goals of smarter homes. Sophistication and smartness are the decisive trends in home information and communication technology (ICT). Powerful cloud technology works in sync with the smart home technologies and methodologies to lead to smarter homes.

3.5.7 Cloud-Enabled Smart Grids

Due to vociferous demands, the modern power grid is transforming into a cyber-physical system (CPS), where the physical infrastructure and cyber infrastructure must coordinate to ensure an efficient and reliable power energy grid [4]. However, there are some practical challenges. Existing grid operations require human decisions. Also, renewables such as wind and solar are inherently unreliable and cause the electricity supply to be susceptible to the vagaries of nature. On the demand side, intelligent appliances, electric vehicle adoption, and rooftop solar panels make the consumer load profile variable. Any demand–supply mismatch causes grid instability unless rapidly rectified. Here the importance of BDA (we have allocated a separate chapter [Chapter 4] for explaining BDA and its growing influence on establishing and sustaining smart cities) plays a critical role toward empowering automated decisions, as human grid operators are actually ill equipped to analyze large amounts of data from millions of distributed smart electric meters and from other data and control points. BDA infrastructures and platforms are able to capture, store, process, analyze, and mine an unprecedented influx of sensing data from multiple sources toward the timely extraction of actionable insights to decisively empower control systems to proceed without any specific human interpretation, instruction, and involvement.

The typical requirements include energy usage events streaming from millions of smart meters, sampled every 15 minutes, and collected and correlated with a consumer's historical profile. Data mining and pattern matching are necessary for online detection of critical situations and their correction with low latency for grid stability. Analytical and computational models can help predict the power supply and demand to make it possible to take preemptive actions to curtail demand by notifying consumers in time. These efforts are incidentally multidisciplinary and require power engineers, data analysts, behavioral psychologists, and microgrid managers to share knowledge for optimal operations with the active participation of consumers. Having understood these specific requirements, the authors have built a cloud-based software platform for data-driven analytics that takes a step toward the smart grid vision.

Their efforts have addressed dynamic demand response (D2R) optimization, a unique challenge application in which supply–demand mismatch must be detected and preemptively corrected by initiating demand-side management from consumers. This software platform supports D2R activities through a semantic information integration pipeline to take in real-time data from sensors and dynamic data sources; a secure repository for researchers and engineers to collaborate and share data and results; scalable machine-learning models that are trained over massive historical datasets to predict demand; and a Web portal and mobile app to visualize current and historical energy-consumption patterns. This software package was deployed in a cloud environment and has been found to be fruitful in many ways.

3.5.8 A Cloud-Based Monitoring Framework for Smart Homes

Lingshan Xu and his team have proposed a cloud-based monitoring framework to implement the remote monitoring services of a smart home [5]. The main technical issues considered include data-cloud storage, local-cache mechanism, media device control, network address translation (NAT) traversal, and so on. The implementation shows three use scenarios: (1) operating and controlling video cameras for remote monitoring through mobile devices or sound sensors; (2) streaming live video from cameras and sending captured image to mobile devices; and (3) recording videos and images on a cloud computing platform for future playback. This system framework could be extended to other applications of a smart home.

Busan Green u-City Technological innovations such as extremely and deeply connected devices; distributed, disposable, and diminutive sensors and actuators; the emergence of the Internet as the open, public, and affordable wide area network (WAN) communication infrastructure; and clouds as the core, centralized, and cognitive one-stop platform for hosting software applications and services, and so on are enabling cities to capture valuable data, develop and deploy new services, and enhance existing services substantially, ushering in the era of smarter cities. These services can bring definite improvement in the effectiveness of city management, generate new growth opportunities for businesses, empower innovations in all aspects, and raise the quality of residents' lives.

An early example of a smart city, South Korea's Busan Green u-City, is using a cloud-based infrastructure delivered by a successful collaboration between the local government and a global technology supplier [6]. The benefits of these new services to citizens are varied and numerous.

- Increase residents' benefits by timely welfare services information distribution
- Improve information accessibility by delivering information through various media channels and devices

- Improve learning experiences by two-way video communication-enabled mentoring
- Increase free education contents and its quality for low-income community residents and students, and thus help to deal with social divide issues
- Reduce overall/regular healthcare cost, especially for low-income residents and elderly people living alone
- Improve access to care services for chronic diseases, reducing the need for patients to visit remote hospitals
- Create new markets for participatory urban regeneration projects applying u-City technologies
- Provide wider revenue creation opportunities by open innovation–based urban regeneration framework

3.5.9 Cloud-Inspired Smarter Healthcare Services

The unprecedented adoption of cloud concepts by various business verticals has impacted the healthcare industry as well [7]. The healthcare industry's technology infrastructure has been highly fragmented, inflexible, closed, and expensive. Because of the widely expressed concerns regarding data security, IT platforms and healthcare applications and data are overwhelmingly maintained in in-house IT infrastructures. Having understood the strategic benefits, the healthcare sector across the world is now keen to leverage systematically the cost and agility benefits of the cloud paradigm without compromising data security. The key question here is whether the cloud scheme is a definite and decisive game changer for every aspect such as operating models, premium service offerings, collaborative capabilities, and end-user services of the healthcare industry. As per the changing scenarios, the healthcare segment too is going through a variety of elegant transformations such as tirelessly appropriating the digitization, connectivity, and collaboration technologies. Healthcare data volume, velocity, and variety are consistently on the climb with the mass availability of high-end and connected machines, instruments, and devices for precisely and perfectly enabling healthcare services and process automation. Therefore the appetite for the latest cloud infrastructures and platforms for hosting healthcare applications and depositing patient data safely and securely is growing. Electronic health record (EHR) services are increasingly cloud-based. Tele-diagnosis and tele-medicine tasks are being activated and accomplished through cloud-based software applications.

Healthcare data posted in cloud environments are easily accessible and shared across the regions by doctors, practitioners, and so on. Governmental rules and regulations stringently mandate storage of data for an extended period of time. Besides the mainstream applications, the data backup, archival, and recovery requirements force hospitals and clinics' IT managers to consider the cloud movement. Medical imaging is a very critical need in healthcare. Extracting reusable patterns and insights from medical images in time goes a long way in empowering physicians, medical experts, and caregivers in prescribing or administering the correct medicine in the perfect dosage. It is therefore clear that cloud technology is going to be critical for visualizing next-generation medical applications and delivering them with all the quality of service (QoS) attributes embedded. Clouds will emerge as the one-stop solution for taking patient care to the next level fluently and elegantly.

3.5.10 Sensor-Cloud Integration for Smarter Cities

Sensors and actuators are the eyes and ears of future IT for the effortless capture of disparate data from an increasing array of distinct sources. Correspondingly there are cloud-based analytical solutions to incredibly capitalize the accumulated data to extract actionable knowledge toward achieving and sustaining the smarter world vision. With clouds emerging as Web-scale, enterprise-class, highly organized and optimized IT infrastructures, there is a persistent and pressing need for sensors on the ground to be seamlessly and spontaneously integrated with online, on-demand, and on/off-premise cloud environments. That is, sensors and actuators could be interfaced with remote clouds for exchanging data and control messages then and there. It is going to be a two-way communication. That is, data are transmitted to the cloud and cloud-based services in turn monitor, measure, manage, and maintain scores of physical sensors and devices. In a nutshell, by adding sensors and actuators into the mix, new opportunities and fresh possibilities for contextualization and geo-awareness arise continuously. In the future, we may read, feel, and even experience "sensing and actuation as a service" (SAaaS). Thus ordinary objects are connected with one another as well as service-enabled to interact with cloud-based applications so that they could exhibit exemplary behavior. Sensors are thereby empowered to be smart to join in the mainstream computing to be a great enabler of people in the days ahead. All small and big environments filled and saturated with a number of different sensors are going to be greater contributors toward smart cities [8].

3.5.11 Social and Sensor Data Fusion in Cloud

Mobile phones are not only enabled with communication capabilities but also possess computing power these days. Further, a variety of minuscule sensors are smartly embedded inside mobile phones to make them multifaceted in their offerings and outputs. That is, with the unprecedented advancements in miniaturization technologies, phones are becoming slim and sleek, trendy and handy, yet are multimedia, multisensor, multiplatform, and multipurpose devices. Phones are also cloud-enabled; thereby all kinds of applications and data being deposited in cloud environments can be discovered, accessed, and used using phones at any time and any place. That is, mobile phones become smart through the internal integration of multiple electronics and the external integration with on-demand and online cloud infrastructures.

Smart phones could capture/record and accumulate large volumes of data related to our daily lives and upload them in social websites and in remote powerful computing machines and storage systems. Smart phones facilitate connected people just as sensors and actuators enable common, casual, and cheap items to become connected entities. That is, people are increasingly connected with one another all the time as well as with the outside world through smart phones. In a nutshell, phones are not only effective input/output devices but also a data aggregation and transmission platform. A wider category of cloud-based people-centric applications are being delivered to humans through smart phones.

Without an iota of doubt, today the two popular types are social and sensor data, collected from different and distributed sources and fused to be right and relevant for people in their daily personal and professional lives. Social-networking services facilitate users to share their ideas, opinions, pictures, videos, news, and other various forms of contents over the Internet, the most pulsating and pioneering communication infrastructure. Sensors are primarily for gathering environmental data toward self, surroundings, and situation-aware information. In short, advanced context-aware applications run in the cloud; social and sensor data are gleaned and fed to cloud-based applications as the cloud provides tremendous processing, memory, and storage capabilities; and the resulting insights can be readily and rewardingly shared with people through smart phones in time. Thus mobile cloud computing is a greater enabler for smarter cities.

Surender Reddy Yerva and his team [9] have built a travel recommendation system that allows blending the heterogeneous social and sensor data for integrated analysis and then extracting information on weather predictions for times and places where users wish to travel. The architecture of the recommendation system comprises several components for accomplishing effective, large-scale social and sensor data fusion. Such sensor and social data fusion features and functionality lead to a sequence of activities toward ultimate knowledge engineering and delivery: gleaning and fusing of data from multiple sources; applications deployed in clouds receiving and leveraging them in real-time to aggregate, process, transform, mine, and analyze to emit actionable insights; smart phones emerging as the all-encompassing device for disseminating the emitted context knowledge to empower those concerned to ponder the next course of action with full confidence and clarity; and so on.

3.5.12 Integrating Sensors with Cloud Using Dynamic Proxies

Sensor networks exceedingly contribute to real-time data capture, processing, and analytics. However, they have a few noteworthy constraints and clouds are capable of overcoming them to the fullest. Therefore the integration of sensors with cloud environments has picked up very recently through a host of viable approaches [10]. The first approach is based on message-oriented communication that uses low-level application-specific APIs to exchange messages between sensors and motes platforms such as TinyOS and Contiki. These are integrated with clouds by using a lightweight IP stack. This approach provides communication infrastructure, but doesn't provide application-level service distribution. The second approach is to use services (simple object access protocol [SOAP] or RESTful) and the application layer functionality of services can be accessed via ports. Sensor data are encapsulated in SOAP packets that lead to high complexity and resource requirements. The RESTful approach is quite simple. An example is TinyREST, which uses a gateway to connect sensor nodes to clouds by mapping messages to HTTP requests. Another example is CoAP, which reduces the HTTP overhead by using a subset of HTTP. This approach adds overhead from processing HTTP requests. A further example is LooCI, which provides an extensible networking framework and an event bus abstraction to bind reusable components. LooCI has a key advantage in that its communication is based on Inter Isolate RPC (IIRPC). Its macro-components can support multiple threads and utility libraries by running each macro component in isolation. LooCI can implement multicast to multiple nodes network-wide. The LooCI middleware has been deployed on a variety of platforms such as the SunSPOT, Contiki, and OSGi. Thus the topic of sensor–cloud integration has been rapidly gaining momentum. There are approaches, middleware solutions, and frameworks for simplifying and streamlining sensor-to-cloud integration to come out with a number of people-centric and city-critical services.

3.5.13 The Next-Generation Hybrid Clouds

For a variety of reasons, private cloud options are being seriously considered by business establishments. Especially for the sake of having deeper visibility of the total IT environment, the end-to-end controllability, the guaranteed performance, and dependability with nil network latency, and above all, impenetrable and foolproof security, private cloud environments are being prescribed as part of enterprise IT strategy. Public clouds are also important as they are Web-scale; cost-effective; manned by trained, experienced, and skilled experts; continuously standardized toward open, interoperable, connected, and federated clouds; and so on. Other noteworthy cases for public clouds include the fact that every kind of customer-facing application is being modernized and migrated to public clouds and there are a number of social networking sites on the Web. That is, everything is service-, Web, and cloud-enabled to be found, bound, and composed toward bigger and better things. Thus public clouds are turning out to be the core and central service-oriented platform for all kinds of applications (social, business, embedded, mobile, analytical, transactional, and IoT) and data. Thus for any growing enterprises, the hybrid cloud, which is the seamless combination of private as well as public clouds, is the way forward.

As we all know, read, and experience, the device ecosystem is on the fast track these days. Every human being is all set to be assisted by tens of devices (wearable, portable, pocketable, implantable, etc.) in his or her daily life. Every home is being filled with scores of hi-fi electronics, appliances, media players, Wi-Fi routers, and so on; every car is being empowered with a large number of electronics such as in-vehicle infotainment system, network gateway, controllers, sensors, chips, and actuators; every manufacturing floor is saturated with a number of connected machines, equipment, instruments, and so on; and every library is filled with hundreds of tagged books; and so on. We have heard, read, and even written about device clouds. All kinds of physical devices in our entire environment are being linked to faraway clouds for data transmission and analytics and are being significantly dynamically empowered with a growing array of cloud-based software services. However, our focus here is not on the extreme connectivity but rather on smartly leveraging the computing, storage, and network capabilities of devices among us to create a kind of personal cloud for accomplishing an emerging array of real-time and personal applications with complete security and judiciousness.

The industrialization and commoditization aspects that considerably elevated the power of cloud computing are now penetrating everyday devices in our midst. Devices are becoming steadily miniaturized yet computationally powerful, fitted with more storage capability, increasingly interconnected and service enabled. It is expected that these new-generation devices will substantially embolden and extend the traditional cloud model to form and firm up an even bigger, less expensive, high-performing, resource-aware, extensible, versatile, and resilient cloud that is more right and relevant for end-users. Now with the abundant arrival and overwhelming acceptance of generic as well as purpose-specific devices, the prevailing concept of the hybrid cloud is bound to change forever. Time- and mission-critical and real-time data processing could happen locally using the computing, networking, and storage capabilities of one or more networked devices. That is, some of the computational resources could reasonably be drawn from the ensemble of personal devices that commonly surround us such as our own smart phones, tablets/phablets, home automation gateways, set-top boxes, connected cars, home and portable storage devices, wearables, and special-purpose computing hardware.

This development suggests a kind of private cloud comprising different yet well-connected devices within an environment is being visualized here. Further, as devices are being integrated with public clouds, ad hoc computation needs are being met locally by on-premise devices whereas data and process-intensive tasks are being performed at powerful and elastic remote public clouds or even in traditional private clouds. (A cloud environment is typically defined as a dynamic pool of compute [virtual and bare metal] and storage appliances being networked and secured inside as well as outside through a host of network solutions such as firewalls, load balancers, application delivery controllers [ADC], network gateways, routers, switches, and so on.)

Everyday devices are thus joining the mainstream computing arena, with most of the high-end data storage, processing, mining, and analytics largely delegated to remote clouds. Coarsely defined, small data analytics is accomplished through a host of devices at the ground level whereas BDA is readied for large-scale cloud infrastructures at the cyber level. In summary, computing tasks will be distributed to nearby devices and the cloud. Storage on a mobile device expands seamlessly by including local and cloud storage under a common namespace. Finally, media distribution occurs over home and public Wi-Fi networks with even media pre-caching on Wi-Fi routers.

Emiliano Miluzzo [11] states that this well-intended and mixed approach would help mitigate some of the perpetual shortcomings of a pure cloud-centric model. Local processing can reduce network latency and ensure QoS attributes such as performance. Edge device participation in personal data storage can increase data privacy, allow faster data storage and retrieval, and reduce the monetary cost for storing data in the cloud by reducing traffic in the backbone network. At the same time, less traffic in the network promotes bandwidth savings and could reduce congestion in a scenario where a growing number of devices and sensors are network enabled. Local device interaction for computing and storage requirements occurs over short-range radio technology such as Wi-Fi and Bluetooth using single-hop connections whereas communication with the cloud is enabled via high-speed wireless data connections (such as long-term evolution [LTE]), wired broadband (WAN), and the open, public, and affordable Internet communication infrastructure.

3.5.14 The Compelling Use Cases for Next-Generation Hybrid Clouds

Our personal gadgets and gizmos such as smart phones, tablets, and laptops are becoming exceedingly powerful and varying in their offerings, operations, and outputs. For example, cell phones are fast transitioning to be smart phones. There are multiple smart phone operating systems and even microvisors (the device version of hypervisors). A variety of powerful sensors and actuators are being squeezed inside smart phones these days. Further, smart phones, besides slim and sleek, are inherently empowered through a seamless and spontaneous integration with remote cloud-based services. The integration of myriad internal and external modules and the much-demanded cloud-connectivity together stand out as factors in the mesmerizing success of today's smart phones.

Owing to the microscopic embedding of several smart sensors that could learn our activities/assignments and monitor our physical health parameters ceaselessly, smart phones are turning out not only to serve as our faithful digital assistants but also to participate decisively in our physical well-being. This trend is bound to continue with the exciting advancements in miniaturization and automation technologies. Heart monitors (electrocardiogram), brain monitors (electroencephalography), blood sugar and blood pressure monitors, hi-fi 3D or stereo cameras, projectors, biometrics, radar/sonar sensors, and so on will be attached with future smart phones to be adequately self, surroundings, and situation aware. Smart phones are also tending toward the universal remote operator for all kinds of devices.

3.5.15 Use Cases—Computation and Actionable Insights

Emiliano Miluzzo further writes that with air quality sensing, municipalities could rely on 24/7 crowd-sourced pollution-level measurements without setup and maintenance of specialized and costly measurement stations across town. Cameras with 3D or stereo capabilities will enable advanced and touch-free gesture recognition on mobile devices. Radar and sonar sensing will make people more aware of their surroundings, for example, of incoming cars when walking and cycling, and can issue preemptive alerts to any incoming perils. People with visual impairments could rely on radar or sonar sensing on their mobile devices to navigate in any environment. Smart glasses, with their on-board cameras and microphones, are expected to become the mainstream mechanism along with other wearables to monitor vital signs ahead on the move. Connected cars are emerging and evolving with the unprecedented success and stability of connectivity technologies. Vehicles could talk to other vehicles on the road, and vehicles will be connected with roadside diverse infrastructures and also to off-premise clouds for acquiring a variety of new capabilities and competencies while on the move.

By applying intelligence and machine learning reasoning to the growing volumes, variety, and velocity of sensor data, we can interpret and infer hidden and prospective patterns to actuate multiple components, realize higher level applications, and offer new forms of interactions such as context-awareness, activity recognition, augmented reality, or voice commands. In a nutshell, the next-generation hybrid cloud will leverage local computation to a major extent to tackle a number of specific use cases. Besides local computation, real-world and real-time intelligence can come from a single device or through a federation of multiple and co-located devices.

Speech recognition engines and image-processing algorithms for, respectively, voice commands and augmented reality applications on smart phones and smart glasses could complete their compute tasks on their own or through interactions with each other. Because of these devices' powerful processing power, less engagement of the cloud might be necessary, resulting in less bandwidth usage and possibly a smoother user experience owing to faster application responsiveness. If sensor data are needed in the cloud to improve a machine-learning algorithm, the local device could send these data to the cloud opportunistically at a later time, for example, during off-peak hours. If the device generating the data is a mobile platform, it can send data when it is in the Wi-Fi range or during battery charging sessions.

3.5.16 Storage Use Cases

Although big data is maturing as an important business paradigm, there is another paradigm steadily attracting the attention of professionals. Researchers refer to this new paradigm as small data, which lets users draw interesting inferences, extract hidden patterns related to a person's own well-being, and enable applications to mine life-logging data. Small data storage requirements, along with users' growing digital footprint including the still and dynamic pictures from mobile devices that account for most personal storage needs, are driving the demand for more capable personal storage solutions.

Not surprisingly, when it comes to cloud services, one of the most popular is cloud storage. For one thing, it frees users from having to maintain and manage personal storage hardware while providing a seamless user experience through transparent and cross-device synchronization. With the average household digital footprint skyrocketing and the high costs of cloud storage services, the new-generation hybrid cloud can be a viable solution to expand cloud storage capabilities and meet users' storage requirements at a lower cost. To achieve this goal, hybrid clouds can intelligently combine traditional cloud storage with available storage from personal edge devices. This free space, on the order of tens of gigabytes today, is likely to increase to terabytes in the near future. This could be well suited to transparently expanding the storage available to users beyond the boundaries of centralized cloud offerings.

The empowered hybrid cloud storage services can provide a flexible and scalable platform for personal data storage, including backup, intelligent file placement and retrieval, and data sharing. By applying smart data-replication techniques across different personal devices, this solution provides not only flexibility but also resiliency to failure. In addition, this new storage model offers enhanced scalability properties: users can add more storage as needed by provisioning a new device to their existing personal storage systems, which transparently reconfigures with no need for manual data migration or painful data synchronization.

3.5.17 Data Dissemination

Smart phones and tablets are fueling the rapid growth of mobile video streaming traffic, surpassing media consumption on PCs. Connected cars will soon accelerate this phenomenon, with thousands of vehicles simultaneously fetching media on the go. Content delivery networks (CDNs) are a solution introduced to meet increasing traffic demand and deliver high-quality customer experience by decentralizing media storage and caching infrastructures. The new cloud model can enable new generations of CDNs by pushing the ability to store and cache content further out to edge nodes to enhance the user experience and reduce the backbone traffic load.

By storing media content on the roadside infrastructure, a data download session from moving cars could complete more quickly because of the high-speed, short-range radio connection. When, in a few years, autonomously driving cars make their appearance, passengers will be busier consuming data than driving. Similarly smart caching on a set-top box based on television users' watching patterns could promote an enhanced user experience by making content readily available and reduce backbone data traffic during peak hours. For example, if Bob watches the first episode of a 20-episode TV show, the next time, he would most likely select the second episode. This prediction can allow intelligent pre-fetching of the episode on Bob's set-top box at a prior time during off-peak hours.

In summary, the new hybrid cloud model looks very promising and potentially fabulous. That is, processing and storage are distributed across all kinds of devices including traditional computers and storage appliances; thereby the network bandwidth usage and costs are bound to come down sharply. By optimally using local computing and storage capabilities, the remote clouds and the network infrastructures are being spared from heavy bombardment.

3.5.18 Software-Defined Infrastructures and Software-Defined Environments

There are many white papers, business case studies, product sheets, research publications, PhD dissertations, book chapters and monographs, conference proceedings, technical articles, briefs, critiques, and write-ups on cloud computing. There are cloud modernization and migration methodologies, best practices, implementation patterns, key guidelines, evaluation metrics, dos and don'ts, knowledge repositories, and so on. The number of confluences, symposiums, workshops, and technical congregations on cloud technology is definitely on the higher side. Because of its tremendous impacts on business operations, offerings, and outputs, there is a huge following for this path-breaking technology. Key distinctions as enunciated and enumerated by many cloud luminaries and leaders are described in the paragraphs that follow.

3.5.18.1 Simplified and Synchronized Operations of Cloud Infrastructures through Standard APIs This is the era of APIs. By front-ending the virtualized infrastructure with a layer of software that provides APIs for accessing, activating, and adapting various IT resources, any users (business as well as technical) can easily invoke one or more APIs and bring forth any resources into existence. A classic example here is using the OpenStack Nova API or AWS EC2 API to provision virtual machines running desired operating systems. From the end-user's perspective, as long as an API is there, it does not matter who the provider is. The easy-to-use API is the game-changer for the IT industry.

3.5.18.2 Instant-On IT HP has coined the concept of "Instant-on Enterprises" and could substantiate the ideals behind it through their noteworthy advancements in realizing highly converged infrastructures. Today everything happens quickly in a cloud environment; hence the capability of cloud-enabled IT agility has a stronger and more sustainable influence on the long-standing goal of business agility. Infrastructures are being consolidated, centralized, converged, virtualized, and shared. The interconnectivity between various modules such as servers, storage, and network solutions is becoming more accurate. Capacity planning is therefore comprehensive and compact. Workload packaging and deployment are being automated; resource provisioning is faster; application configurations and changes are being enabled through highly competent tools; infrastructure management solutions are powerful and path-breaking, the DevOps capability is being fulfilled through a host of technologies and tools; business processes are being provided as a service with the unprecedented maturity and stability of automation, management, and orchestration engines; and so on. Resources are being created on-demand and instantly assimilated with existing resources to achieve the requirements of scalability and availability, and so on.

3.5.18.3 Programmable Infrastructures   The concept of abstraction and virtualization has caught up with IT infrastructures to bring in the much-needed programmability. IT administrators gain programmatic access to infrastructure services. The remote yet centralized monitoring, measurement, management, and maintenance of geographically distributed IT infrastructures are made possible. Real-time diagnosis, troubleshooting, and decommissioning of resources are seeing the light. Several manual tasks are being automated through powerful tools. The result is that we have optimized, extensible, and malleable infrastructures in place to anticipate and accomplish business tasks in a reliable and cost-effective fashion. Cloud service providers therefore can stick to the service-level agreement (SLA) and keep their customers loyal.

3.5.18.4 Deeper Visibility and Higher Controllability   By front-ending the virtualized infrastructure with a cloud software platform, IT administrators could monitor every action and transaction touching the underlying physical and virtual infrastructures. This generates massive amounts of log data and there are machine analytics platforms (open-source as well as commercial grade) to capture, store, process, and analyze in real time to emit actionable insights. This empowerment goes a long way in providing visibility and controllability to administrators in keeping up with workloads and their dependencies. Any kind of slowdown and breakdown can be judiciously avoided.

3.5.18.5 Business Continuity   Building on the intelligence gathered from infrastructure data, IT administrators can now quickly analyze root cause for failures and implement remediation procedures. Using automation, coupled with BDA, IT administrators can further reduce the recovery time sharply by either pre-provisioning additional capacity ahead of the failure event or rapidly deploying spare capacity on-demand to enable quick recovery. Through pre-provisioning, failures can be minimized or eliminated, while rapid deployment helps reduce the time to recover from failures. The recovery time objective (RTO) and recovery point objective (RPO), the major constituents of any business strategy, can be substantially decreased with automation techniques. Disaster and data recovery requirements are being accomplished easily in cloud environments.

3.5.18.6 Enhanced Utilization   Operating the infrastructure resources to the optimum capacity, without risking the SLAs, is every IT owner's goal. Using virtualization and ingrained automation tools, IT administrators could better leverage different hardware components. Perfect capacity planning and resource allocation at a granular level are the key mechanisms for improved utilization of IT infrastructures. By carving out smaller units of resources and putting them together near the application users, an IT administrator can deftly match the capacity needs. Any released sources can be recycled back to the resource pool to be served for other users and uses.

3.5.18.7 Utility Computing   End-users are now able to pay for the exact amount of resource usage. By doing so, they avoid paying for capacity that they did not use and also have the confidence that additional capacity will be available when they need it. Monitoring, billing, and charging are fully automated in cloud environments.

Owing to the increased responsiveness, assertiveness, and pervasiveness of information and communication technologies (ICTs) in realizing the goals of digital living, the indisputable and incredible reason behind the systematic and judicious journey toward the smarter world, there have been a bevy of versatile transformations in the IT field. There is a perceptible change in the form of IT moving from a cost center to a strategic center across all kinds of worldwide enterprises today. A family of business augmentation, acceleration, and automation technologies and tools and tips is being meticulously listed out and leveraged to bring IT closer to business expectations and to readily tackle any business changes and challenges. There have been different kinds of attempts in the form of IT consolidation, convergence, virtualization, rationalization, standardization, simplification, orchestration, and so on to bring in real IT optimization so that the aims of IT agility, adaptability, and affordability could be accomplished to the fullest satisfaction of business executives, end-users, and other stakeholders.

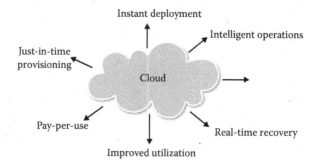

The arrival of cloud concepts has brought tremendous changes in the IT landscape that in turn led to realizing huge transitions in the delivery of business applications and services and in the solid enhancement of business flexibility, productivity, and sustainability. Formally cloud infrastructures are centralized, virtualized, automated, and shared IT infrastructures. The utilization rate of cloud infrastructures has gone up significantly. Still, there are dependencies curtailing the full usage of expensive IT resources. Employing the decoupling technique among various modules to eliminate all kinds of constricting dependencies; more intensive and insightful process automation through orchestration and policy-based configuration, operation, management, delivery, and maintenance; and attaching external knowledge bases are widely prescribed to achieve still more IT utilization to cut costs remarkably. Bringing in the much-discoursed modularity to enable programmable IT infrastructures and extracting and centralizing all the embedded intelligence via robust and resilient software, distributed deployment, centralized management, and federation are being touted as the viable and respected courses of action for attaining the originally envisaged success. That is, creating a dynamic pool of virtualized resources; allocating them on demand for their fullest utilization; charging for their exact usage; putting unutilized resources back into the pool; monitoring, measuring, and managing resource performance; and so on are the hallmarks of next-generation IT infrastructures. Precisely speaking, IT infrastructures are being software defined to bring in much-needed accessibility, consumability, malleability, elasticity, and extensibility.

On-demand IT has been the perpetual goal. All kinds of IT resources need to have the inherent capability of preemptively knowing users' as well as applications' IT resource requirements and accordingly fulfill them without any instruction, interpretation, and involvement of human resources. IT resources need to be scaled up and down based on changing needs so that the cost can be controlled. That is, perfect provisioning of resources is the mandate. Overprovisioning raises the pricing whereas underprovisioning is a cause for performance-degradation worries. The cloud paradigm transparently leverages a number of software solutions and specialized tools to provide scalability of applications through resource elasticity. The expected dynamism in resource provisioning and deprovisioning has to become a core and concrete capability of clouds.

Thus providing right-sized IT resources (compute, storage, and networking) for all kinds of business software solutions is the need of the hour. Users increasingly expect their service providers' infrastructures to deliver these resources elastically in response to their changing needs. There is no cloud services infrastructure available today capable of simultaneously delivering scalability, flexibility, and high operational efficiency. Deeper automation and software-based configuration, controlling, and operation of hardware resources are the main enablers behind the vision of software-defined infrastructure (SDI).

An SDI is an enabler of private, public, and hybrid clouds. That is, software-defined computing, networking, and storage are the principal components in an SDI of the future. With the ultimate flexibility and full-fledged automation capabilities, an SDE is a vital component of the cloud that enables data center administrators to use a single graphical user interface to do everything from deploying virtual machines to assigning storage to configuring networks, hence allowing clouds to become more streamlined, simplified, and adaptively responsive. There are a few connotations such as software-defined data centers (SDDCs), cloud-enabled data centers (CeDCs), and so on for SDEs. Originally it was just data centers for every decent enterprise across the globe. The next milestone is the much-published and pampered server consolidation through virtualization. This server consolidation results in a dynamic pool of virtual as well as bare metal compute systems. That is, data centers have been continuously subjected to a series of noteworthy technology-inspired transformations, optimizations, and so on. The next in line is the availability and adoption of several tools to automate many manual activities. Automated capacity planning, job scheduling, billing and charging, resource provisioning and deprovisioning, resource monitoring, performance measurement, governance, self-service, and so on are being activated through highly efficient configuration and management tools. These enhancements have laid the foundation for the flourishing of cloud centers in prime locations across the world.

Having tasted the expected successes on server machines, the focus has been directed toward storage and network virtualizations. The tried and tested abstraction and decoupling have been the hallmarks for virtualization. Further, all the hardware-bound intelligence is smoothly extricated and developed in centralized and clustered controllers that are extensively filled with software for attaining extensibility, modifiability, and sustainability. Controllers facilitate policy and configuration changes, remote access, policy-based operations, and so on. The Gartner Group [12] breaks down the software-defined data center into four processes.

- *Abstraction*—the decoupling of a resource from the consumer of the resource
- *Instrumentation*—the process of opening up the decoupled infrastructure elements with programmatic interfaces (typically XML-based RESTful APIs)
- *Automation*—the use of APIs to wire the exposed elements using scripts and other automation tools to remove "human middleware"
- *Orchestration*—the automation of provisioning through linkages to policy-driven orchestration systems

These four processes are the keys to the data center of the future—a data center defined and controlled by software. This new paradigm removes existing barriers related to the management of server, storage, and network resources. Changes to infrastructure that used to require days and weeks to implement can now be made in minutes. In this new era for IT, application workloads are not tied to dedicated servers, storage, and network resources. Instead, they move dynamically to balance workloads and optimize infrastructure utilization.

3.6 Building Blocks of Software-Defined Data Centers

The software-defined data center (SDDC) encompasses software-defined compute, storage, and networking components. The substantially matured server virtualization leads to the realization of software-defined compute machines. Highly intelligent hypervisors (alternatively recognized as virtual machine monitors [VMMs]) act as the perfect software solution to take care of the creation, provisioning, deprovisioning, live-in migration, decommissioning of compute machines (virtual machines, baremetal servers, etc.), and so on. In the sections that follow, we focus on software-defined networking and storage.

3.6.1 Software-Defined Networking

The emerging technology trends indicate that networks and network management are bound to change forever. Today's data centers extensively use physical switches and appliances that haven't yet been virtualized and are statically provisioned. Further, the current environment mandates significant and certified expertise in each vendor's equipment and lack of an API ecosystem toward the envisioned programmable networks. It is quite difficult to bring in the expected automations (resource provisioning, scaling, etc.) on the currently running inflexible, monolithic, and closed network modules. The result is the underutilization of expensive network equipment. In addition, the cost for employing highly educated and experienced network administrators is on the higher side. Thus besides bringing in a bevy of pragmatic yet frugal innovations in the networking arena, the mandate for substantially reducing the capital as well as the operational expenses incurred by the traditional network architecture is playing in the minds of technical professionals and business executives.

As virtualization has been contributing immensely to server consolidation and optimization, the idea of network virtualization has picked up in the recent past. The virtualization aspect on the networking side takes a different route compared to the matured server virtualization. The extraction and centralization of network intelligence embedded inside all kinds of network appliances such as routers, switches, and so on brings a number of strategic advantages toward consumable and cognitive networks. The policy-setting, configuration, and maneuvering activities are being activated through software libraries that are modular, service-oriented, and centralized in a controller module and hence the new terminology "software-defined networking" (SDN) has become hugely popular. That is, instead of managing network assets separately using separate interfaces, they are controlled collectively through a comprehensive, easy-to-use, and fine-grained interface. The API approach has the intrinsic capability of putting a stimulating and sustainable foundation for all kinds of IT resources and assets to be easily discoverable, accessible, usable, and composable. Hardware infrastructure programming and thereby their remote manipulations and machinations are gaining momentum.

Therefore standards-compliant SDN controllers provide a widely adopted API ecosystem that can be used to centrally control multiple devices in different layers. Such an abstracted and centralized approach offers many strategically significant improvements over traditional networking approaches. For instance, it becomes possible to completely decouple the network's control plane and its data plane. The control plane runs in a cluster setup and can configure all kinds of data plane switches and routers to support business goals as demanded. That means data flow is regulated at the network level in an efficient manner. Data can be sent where it is needed or blocked if it is deemed a security threat.

A detached and deft software implementation of the configuration and controlling aspects of network elements also means that existing policies can be refurbished whereas newer policies can be created and inserted on demand to enable all the associated network devices to behave in a situation-aware manner. As we all know, policy establishment and enforcement are the proven mechanism to bring in the required versatility in network operations. If a particular application's flow unexpectedly needs more bandwidth, the SDN controller proactively recognizes the brewing requirement in real time and accordingly reroutes the data flow. Precisely speaking, the physical constraints are being eliminated through software-defined networking. If a security appliance needs to be inserted between two tiers, it is easily accomplished without altering anything at the infrastructure level. Another interesting factor is the most recent phenomenon of "bring your own device" (BYOD). All kinds of employees' own devices can be automatically configured, accordingly authorized, and made ready to access the enterprise's network anywhere, anytime.

3.6.2 *The Key Motivations for SDN*

In the IT world, there are several trends mandating the immediate recognition and judicious adoption of SDN. Cloud-enabled data centers (CeDCs) are being established in different cool locations across the globe to provide scores of orchestrated cloud services to worldwide businesses and individuals over the Internet on a subscription basis. Application and database servers besides integration middleware solutions are increasingly distributed whereas the governance and the management of distributed resources are being accomplished in a centralized manner to avail the much-needed single point of view (SPoV). Because of the hugeness of data centers, data traffic, both internally as well as externally, is exploding these days. Flexible traffic management and bandwidth on demand are the emerging requirements.

The consumerization of IT is another gripping trend. Enterprise users and executives are being increasingly assisted by a bevy of gadgets and gizmos such as smart phones, laptops, tablets, wearables, and so on in their daily chores. As noted elsewhere, the BYOD movement requires enterprise networks to inherently support policy-based adjustment, amenability, and amelioration to support users' devices dynamically. BDA has a telling effect on IT networks, especially on data storage and transmission. The proprietary nature of network solutions from worldwide product vendors also plays an unhealthy role in traditional networks and hence there is a clarion call for bringing in necessary advancements in network architecture. Programmable networks are therefore the viable and venerable answer to bring the desired flexibility and optimization to corporate networks. The structural limitations of conventional networks are being overcome with network programming. The growing complexity of traditional networks leads to stasis. That is, adding or releasing devices and incorporating network-related policies are truly difficult in the current setup.

As per the leading market watchers, researchers, and analysts, SDN marks the largest business opportunity in the networking industry since its inception. Recent reports estimate the business impact tied to SDN could be as high as $35 billion by 2018, which represents nearly 40% of the overall networking industry. The future of networking will rely more and more on software, which will accelerate the pace of innovation for networks as it has in the computing and storage domains (explained later). SDN has the capacity to transform today's static and unhealthy networks into calculative and cognitive platforms with the intrinsic intelligence to anticipate and allocate resources dynamically; the scale to support enormous data centers; and the virtualization needed to support workload-optimized, converged, orchestrated, and highly automated cloud environments. With its many advantages and astonishing industry momentum, SDN is on the way to become the new norm for cloud and corporate networks.

3.6.3 Tending toward Network Virtualization

With the cloud era developing quickly, a greater concern is being expressed about the slow pace of innovations on the networking front. Though virtual machines can be provided on demand and the resources such as processing power and storage can be added to them dynamically as needed, there is often no optimized control of network bandwidth. As a result, services can easily become starved for bandwidth, resulting in a sharp decline in their performance. There are automations here and there but the end-to-end automation is the need of the hour toward virtual computing.

Because of server virtualization, there are hundreds of computing nodes that need to be cleverly networked and managed. Networks today are statically provisioned with devices that are managed at a box-level scale and mostly underutilized. SDN enables end-to-end network equipment provisioning, reducing the network provisioning time from days to minutes and distributing data flows more evenly across the fabric, resulting in better utilization. SDN offers the prospect of making network resources as fluid and network management as centralized and automated as the rest of the cloud. Organizations benefit immensely as SDN enables network administrators to control network traffic centrally through programming instead of relying on more manual approaches; eliminates vendor lock-in for network products because of its open and vendor-neutral software; makes it possible to provide new services and applications quickly; reduces operational costs because of its simple and automated approach to deployment; and automates multitier system configuration and optimization including the network appliances used between the tiers.

In short, SDN is an emerging architecture that is agile, adaptive, less expensive, and ideal for network-intensive and dynamic applications. This architecture decouples the network control and forwarding functions (routing), enabling the network control to become directly programmable and the underlying infrastructure to be abstracted for applications and network services, which can treat the network as a logical or virtual entity.

3.6.4 The Need of SDN for the Cloud

Because of a number of enterprise-wide benefits, the adoption and adaption rates of the cloud paradigm have been growing. However, the networking aspect of cloud environments has typically not kept pace with the rest of the architecture. A number of enhancements such as network virtualization (NV), network function virtualization (NFV), and SDN have become available. SDN is definitely the comprehensive paradigm of the future. With the explosion of compute machines (both virtual machines as well as bare metal servers) in any cloud centers, the need for SDN is sharply felt. Networks today are statically provisioned, with devices that are managed at a box-level scale and are underutilized. SDN enables end-to-end based network equipment provisioning, reducing the network provisioning time from days to minutes, and distributing flows more evenly across the fabric, allowing for better utilization.

Google has launched Andromeda, an SDN underlying its cloud. Google has been at the forefront of the SDN revolution. It has gone live with Andromeda, the underlying SDN architecture that will enable Google's services to scale better, more inexpensively, and quickly. It has the added benefit of making the network faster, as well. Google describes Andromeda as its newly integrated networking stack in with the diagram below. Andromeda's goal is to expose the raw performance of the underlying network while simultaneously exposing NFV. They have exposed the same in-network processing that enables our internal services to scale while remaining extensible and isolated to end-users. This functionality includes distributed denial of service (DDoS) protection, transparent service load balancing, access control lists, and firewalls.

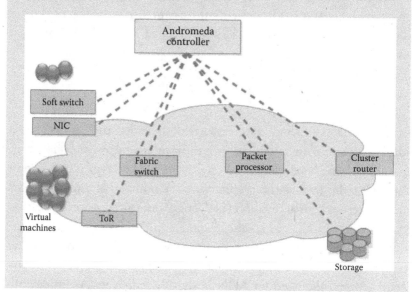

In summary, SDN is the definite game-changer for next-generation IT environments. SDN considerably eliminates network complexity in the midst of multiple and heterogeneous network elements. All kinds of network solutions are centrally configured and controlled to eliminate all kinds of dependencies-induced constrictions and to realize their full potential. Network capabilities are provisioned on demand at the optimal level to suit application requirements. In synchronization with other infrastructural models appropriately, the on-demand, instant-on, autonomic, and smart computing goals are easily delivered.

3.6.5 Software-Defined Storage

We are slowly yet steadily getting into the virtual world with the faster realization of the goals allied with the concept of virtual IT. The ensuing world is leaning toward the vision of anytime, anywhere access of information and services. This projected transformation needs a large number of perceivable and paradigm shifts. Traditional data centers were designed to support specific workloads and users.

This has resulted in siloed and heterogeneous storage solutions that are difficult to manage, provision newer resources to serve dynamic needs, and finally to scale out. The existing setup acts as a barrier for business innovations and value. Untangling this goes a long way in facilitating instant access to information and services.

Undoubtedly storage has been a prominent infrastructural module in data centers. There are different storage types and solutions in the market. In the recent past, the unprecedented growth of data generation, collection, processing, and storage clearly indicates the importance of producing and provisioning of bigger and better storage systems and services. Storage management is another important topic not to be sidestepped. We often read about big, fast, and even extreme data. Because of an array of technology-inspired processes and systems, the data size, scope, structure, and speed are on the climb. For example, digitization is an overwhelming worldwide trend affecting every facet of human life—digital data are everywhere and continue to grow at a stunning pace. Statisticians say that every day, approximately 15 petabytes of new data are being generated worldwide and the total amount of digital data doubles approximately every two years. The indisputable fact is that machine-generated data are larger compared to human-generated data. The expectation is that correspondingly there need to be copious innovations to accommodate and manage big data cost-effectively.

Software-defined storage (SDS) is a relatively new concept and its popularity is surging as a result of the abundant success attained in software-defined computing and networking areas. As explained previously, SDS is part and parcel of the vision behind the establishment and sustenance of software-defined data centers (SDDCs). With the virtualization concept penetrating every tangible resource, the storage industry also gets inundated by that powerful trend. SDS is a kind of enterprise-class storage that uses a variety of commoditized and therefore inexpensive hardware with all the important storage and management functions being extricated and performed using an intelligent software controller. With such a clean separation, SDS delivers automated, policy-driven, and application-aware storage services through an orchestration of the underlining storage infrastructure. That is, we get a dynamic pool of virtual storage resources to be picked up dynamically and orchestrate them accordingly to be presented as an appropriate storage solution. Unutilized storage resources could then be incorporated into the pool for serving other requests. All kinds of constricting dependencies on storage solutions simply vanish with such storage virtualization. All storage modules are commoditized and hence the cost of storage will decline with higher utilization. In a nutshell, storage virtualization enables storage scalability, replaceability, substitutability, and manageability.

An SDS solution remarkably increases flexibility by enabling organizations to use nonproprietary standard hardware and, in many cases, leverage existing storage infrastructure as part of their enterprise storage solution. In addition, organizations can achieve a massive scale with an SDS by adding heterogeneous hardware components as needed to increase capacity and improve performance in the solution. Automated, policy-driven management of SDS solutions helps drive cost and operational efficiencies. As an example, SDS manages important storage functions including information lifecycle management (ILM), disk caching, snapshots, replication, striping, and clustering. In a nutshell, these SDS capabilities enable users to put the right data in the right place, at the right time, with the right performance, and at the right cost—automatically.

Unlike traditional storage systems such as storage area network (SAN) and network-attached storage (NAS), SDS simplifies scale out with relatively inexpensive standard hardware, while continuing to manage storage as a single enterprise-class storage system. SDS typically refers to software that manages the capture, placement, protection, and retrieval of data. SDS is characterized by a separation of the storage hardware from the software that manages it. SDS is a key enabler modernizing traditional, monolithic, inflexible, costly, and closed data centers toward software-defined data centers that are highly extensible, open, and cost-effective. The promise of SDS is that separating the software from the hardware enables enterprises to make storage hardware purchase, deployment, and operation independent from concerns about over- or underutilization or interoperability of storage resources.

The cities of the future are bound to generate a tremendous amount of data to be captured, stocked, and processed in time to squeeze out actionable insights. So it is clear that smart cities insist on modern storage mechanisms. This is a stark reminder for IT professionals to innovate quickly to meet the fast-growing storage requirements.

There are predominantly block-level storage, file storage, and object storage types. NAS, direct attached storage (DAS), and SAN are the leading storage solutions.

3.6.6 Cloud-Based Big Data Storage

Object storage is a recent phenomenon. Object-based storage systems use containers/buckets to store data known as objects in a flat address space instead of the hierarchical, directory-based file systems that are common in block- and file-based storage systems. Nonstructured and semistructured data are encoded as objects and stored in containers. Typical data include emails, pdf files, still and dynamic images, and so on. Containers stores the associated metadata (date of creation, size, camera type, etc.) and the unique Object ID. The Object ID is stored in a database or application and is used to reference objects in one or more containers. The data in an object-based storage system is typically accessed using HTTP via a Web browser or directly through an API-like REST. The flat address space in an object-based storage system enables simplicity and massive scalability. But the data in these systems can't be modified and every refresh is stored as a new object. Object-based storage is predominantly used by cloud services providers (CSPs) to archive and back up their customers' data.

Jeda Networks [13] has applied the SDN approach to the storage domain to have truly virtualized connection between applications and their data. They call this technology Software Defined Storage Networks (SDSN™). SDSNs virtualize the network between applications and their data, referred to as the storage network, by decoupling the complex storage networking control plane (the intelligence that tells the hardware what to do) from the physical network. This results in an abstracted and simplified storage network capable of being "programmable" by software. SDSNs solve the limitations of a fixed and rigid physical storage network—namely scalability, high cost, high complexity, and lack of agility. As organizations of all sizes take advantage of a fully virtualized IT infrastructure, SDSNs free them from the limitations of an all-hardware–based storage networking infrastructure.

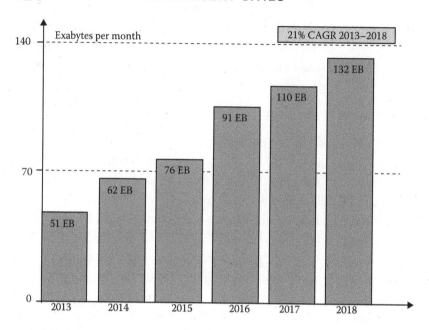

Analysts estimate that more than 2 million terabytes (or 2 exabytes) of data are created every day. The range of applications that IT has to support today spans everything from social computing, big data analytics, mobile, enterprise and embedded applications, and so on. All the data for all those applications needs to be made available to mobile and wearable devices and hence data storage acquires an indispensable status. As per the main findings of Cisco's global IP traffic forecast, in 2016, global IP traffic will reach 1.1 zettabytes per year or 91.3 exabytes (one billion gigabytes) per month, and by 2018, global IP traffic will reach 1.6 zettabytes per year or 131.9 exabytes per month. IDC has predicted that cloud storage capacity will exceed 7 exabytes in 2014, driven by strong demand for agile and capex-friendly deployment models. Furthermore, IDC had estimated that by 2015, big data workloads will be one of the fastest growing contributors to storage in the cloud. In conjunction with these trends, meeting SLAs for the agreed performance is a top IT concern. As a result, enterprises will increasingly turn to flash-based SDS solutions to accelerate performance significantly to meet emerging storage needs.

3.6.7 Key Characteristics of Software-Defined Storage

SDS is characterized by several key architectural elements and capabilities that differentiate it from the traditional infrastructure [14].

3.6.7.1 Commodity Hardware   With the extraction and centralization of all the intelligence embedded in storage and its associated systems in a specially crafted software layer, all kinds of storage solutions are bound to become inexpensive, dumb, off-the-shelf, and hence commoditized hardware elements. Not only the physical storage appliances but also all the interconnecting and intermediate fabric too become commoditized. Such segregation goes a long way in centrally automating, activating, and adapting the full-storage landscape.

3.6.7.2 Scale-Out Architecture   Any SDS setup ought to have the capability of ensuring fluid, flexible, and elastic configuration of storage resources through software. SDS facilitates the realization of storage as a dynamic pool of heterogeneous resources and thereby the much-needed scale-out requirement can be easily met. The traditional architecture hinders the dynamic addition and release of storage resources because of the extreme dependency. For software-defined cloud environments, storage scalability is essential to have a dynamic, highly optimized, and virtual environment.

3.6.7.3 Resource Pooling   The available storage resources are pooled into a unified logical entity that can be managed centrally. The control plane provides fine-grained visibility and control to all available resources in the system.

3.6.7.4 Abstraction   Physical storage resources are increasingly virtualized and presented to the control plane, which can then configure and deliver them as tiered storage services.

3.6.7.5 Automation   The storage layer brings in extensive automation that enables it to deliver one-click and policy-based provisioning of storage resources. Administrators and users request storage resources in terms of application needs (capacity, performance, and reliability) rather than storage configurations such as RAID (redundant array of inexpensive [independent] disks) levels or physical location of drives. The system automatically configures and delivers storage as needed on the fly. It also monitors and reconfigures storage as required to continue to meet SLAs.

3.6.7.6 Programmability In addition to the in-built automation, the storage system offers fine-grained visibility and control of underlying resources via rich APIs that allows administrators and third-party applications to integrate the control plane across storage, network, and computing layers to deliver workflow automation. The real power of SDS lies in the ability to integrate it with other layers of the infrastructure to build end-to-end application-focused automation.

The maturity of SDS will quicken the process of setting up and sustaining software-defined environments for the tactic as well as the strategic benefits of cloud service providers as well as the consumers at large.

3.7 Conclusion

IT optimization is continuously getting enthusiastic attention from technology leaders and luminaries across the globe. A number of generic as well as specific improvisations are being brought in to make IT aware and adaptive. The cloud paradigm is being touted as the game-changer in empowering and elevating IT to the desired heights. There have been notable achievements in making IT the core and cost-effective enabler of both personal as well as professional activities. There are definite improvements in business automation, acceleration, and augmentation, but nonetheless opportunities and possibilities waiting for IT to move up further.

The pioneering virtualization technology is being taken to every kind of infrastructure such as networking and storage to complete the IT ecosystem. The abstraction and decoupling techniques are lavishly utilized here to bring in the necessary malleability, extensibility, and serviceability. That is, all the configuration and operational functionalities hitherto embedded inside hardware components are now neatly identified, extracted, centralized, and implemented as a separate software controller. That is, the embedded intelligence is being developed now as a self-contained entity so that hardware components could be commoditized. Thus the software-defined computing, networking, and storage disciplines have become the hot topic for discussion and dissertation. The journey of data centers to SDEs is being pursued with vigor and rigor. The result is that the pursuit of intelligent cities is being simplified and streamlined with the smart leverage of SDEs.

References

1. IBM Global Services (2011). IBM Smarter City Solutions on Cloud (white paper).
2. Accenture (2010). Cloud Computing and Sustainability: The Environmental Benefits of Moving to the Cloud.
3. Roger Arpagaus and Alexander Auner (2012). A Presentation on Smarter Cities on Cloud. IBM.
4. Yogesh Simmhan et al. (2013). Cloud-Based Software Platform for Big Data Analytics in Smart Grids. University of Southern California, co-published by the IEEE CS and the AIP.
5. Lingshan Xu et al. (2012). Cloud-Based Monitoring Framework for Smart Home. Presented at IEEE 4th International Conference on Cloud Computing Technology and Science.
6. GSMA Connected Living Programme (2012). South Korea: Busan Green u-City Smart City Builds on Cloud Services Delivered by Public-Private-Partnership.
7. Mark Grindle, Jitendra Kavathekar, and Dadong Wan (2013). A New Era for the Healthcare Industry—Cloud Computing Changes the Game (white paper by Accenture).
8. Nathalie Mitton et al. (2012). Combining Cloud and Sensors in a Smart City Environment. *EURASIP Journal on Wireless Communications and Networking* August 2012, 247. http://link.springer.com/article/10.1186%2F1687-1499-2012-247.
9. Surender Reddy Yerva et al. (2012). Cloud Based Social and Sensor Data Fusion. Presented at the International Conference on Information Fusion, Singapore.
10. Wei Wang et al. (2012). Integrating Sensors with the Cloud Using Dynamic Proxies. Presented at IEEE 23rd International Symposium on Personal Indoor and Mobile Radio Communications (PIMRC).
11. Emiliano Miluzzo, AT&T Labs Research (2014). I'm Cloud 2.0, and I'm Not Just a Data Center. IEEE Computer Society, May/June (18, 03), pp. 73–77.
12. HP (2013). Managing Performance in Dynamic IT Environments (technical white paper).
13. A Jeda Networks (2013). Software Defined Storage Networks™: An Introduction (white paper).
14. Coraid (2013). The Fundamentals of Software-Defined Storage—Simplicity at Scale for Cloud Architectures (white paper).

4

BIG DATA ANALYTICS FOR REAL-TIME CITY INSIGHTS

Abstract

As explained in the beginning of this book, the overwhelming leverage of miniaturization, digitization, distribution, consumerization, industrialization, and deeper connectivity technologies has a number of trendsetting and transformational implications for IT as well as for businesses across the globe. The principal one among them is the enormous growth in data size and the greater variability in data scope, structure, and speed. With a growing array of data sources, the data being generated, captured, transmitted, stored, and analyzed are tremendously huge. As data are turning out to be a strategic asset for any organization to be decisive, distinctive, and disciplined in its operations, offerings, and outputs, newer technologies, tips, and tools are being unearthed to smartly stock and subject all incoming data to a variety of deeper investigations to gain actionable insights in time. Extracting and extrapolating knowledge out of data heaps in time especially goes a long way in empowering every kind of enterprise to be exceptionally efficient. The fast-evolving domain of big data analytics (BDAs) is therefore being viewed as a blessing in disguise by worldwide institutions, innovators, and individuals aiming to be competitive and cognitive in their deals, deeds, and decisions. Governments, cities, and citizens are bound to be affected owing to the continuous growth of data (data through business transactions and scientific experiments; social and people data; system, sensor, actuator, and machine data, etc.). Any organization that takes care of all the data being produced within as well as outside is going to be highly right and relevant toward its constituents, customers, clients, and consumers. In this chapter, we illustrate how BDA plays an enormous role in bringing in the expectant big transformations for city infrastructures and ultimately in the quality of city residents' lives.

4.1 Introduction

Leading market watchers, analysts, and researchers have clearly indicated that the data being generated are doubling every two years [1,2]. According to one report, the total amount of data created every two days is equivalent to that created between the dawn of time and 2003. Several noteworthy developments are cited as the principal reason for such a monumental growth of data. Data sources are simply multiplying; edge technologies are empowering every object to be computational, communicative, sensitive, and responsive; all kinds of physical, mechanical, and electrical systems are being functionally enabled through a seamless integration with cyber applications and services to be participative and contributory; every commonly found, cheap, and casual article in our living and working environments are becoming digitized artifacts signaling their valiant and salient entry into the mainstream computing arena; clouds are being positioned as the core and central platform for hosting databases, data warehouses, data marts, and cubes; millions of websites (Web 1.0) and tens of social sites (Web 2.0) are producing volumes of social, enlightening, entertaining, and people data; and so on.

Further, every noticeable event, transaction, interaction, request and reply, and so on are being expectantly captured and saved in storage appliances and arrays for real-time as well as posterior investigations. Ordinary objects are being digitized to be extraordinary in their actions and reactions and these then are capable of being interconnected with one another in the vicinity and with remote ones; thus the foreseeable networks being formed out of these empowered elements are going to be creatively autonomic, people-centric, dependable, extensible, and efficient. In a nutshell, the realization of extremely connected and service-enabled digital objects and machines in our midst is the grand foundation for big data, which is multistructured; massive in volume; and mesmerizing in variety, velocity, and value.

As widely experienced, data are the fountainhead for information and knowledge that can be wisely used for bigger and better things. For the envisioned knowledge era, data are being carefully collected, cleansed, classified, clustered, and conformed as a simplifying and streamlining process toward their final destination. Big data storage solutions are feverishly prevalent these days. The most respectable activity on big data is to do synchronized and systematic analytics to correctly and readily emit big insights. BDA frameworks primarily comprising data processing and storage modules, toolsets, connectors, drivers, and adaptors are made available by open-source as well as commercial-grade solution vendors. Because of the extreme complicity and complexity induced by multiplicity and heterogeneity of big data, enabling BDA products, platforms, patterns, practices, and processes are being derived and released by IT professionals to do big data analysis easily and quickly.

Large and mega cities are beset with scores of problems in housing, infrastructures, safety and security, transport, energy, communication, water, the quality of life, and so on. The receding and recessionary economy puts more stress and strictures on our declining and deteriorating cities. At the same time, cities also open up fresh possibilities and opportunities for thinkers and practitioners to contemplate and activate different things differently. People need to change their structure and behavior significantly to fit cogently with the distinctly identified ideals of the smarter world, a next-generation idea or vision being proclaimed and pursued vigorously and rigorously by leading IT infrastructure and product companies these days. This incredible notion of a smarter world is being presented as the next logical move by worldwide technology creators and service providers to be relevant in their long and arduous journey. There are several key drivers and decisive trends for the surging popularity of this game-changing concept. A series of enabling developments and advancements in realization technologies are being unfolded to simplify and streamline the hitherto unknown path toward the desired and marvelous transformation. The BDA discipline is on a fast track and its contributions are leveraged to design and develop smarter cities. This chapter describes how BDA will contribute immeasurably and flawlessly toward the faster realization and sustenance of next-generation cities.

4.2 Data Analytics and Intelligent Cities

Our cities are becoming more complex these days and hence integrated, insightful, and intelligent IT systems need to be in place to anticipatively monitor and manage the intricacies and intimacies of the world's cities. Today IT is penetrating all kinds of industry verticals. For example, modern airlines are activated and automated through a host of IT systems. Similarly, as the complications and convulsions of today's cities are on the rise, the smart leverage of all the superb advancements of IT has to be elegantly ensured [3].

- Realization of intelligent operations will originate from the boundary-less and ubiquitous access to and flow of data across multiple sources. There are tools to collect, correlate, and corroborate data accurately, analyze it rapidly, and see the resulting information visually anytime, anywhere to enable informed decision making and to make agencies more nimble, transparent, and adaptive.
- All of the polystructured data being gleaned are not value-adding. There are repetitive and redundant data. City-specific data systems must understand the difference between significant and nonsignificant data in their specific contexts and hence data management platforms, practices, processes, and patterns are mandatory to attain the desired success.
- Master data management (MDM), city performance management (CPM), and BDA platforms; data virtualization and visualization tools; and predictive and prescriptive analytics capabilities can layer on top to deliver intelligent operations.

Thus it is clear that IT, especially data analytics, along with a flexible and future-directed strategy, will play a very critical role in shaping up our sliding and sagging cities.

4.2.1 The Prominent Sources of Big Data

As discussed earlier, big data represents huge volumes of data in petabytes, exabytes, and zettabytes for the near future. As we move around the globe, we leave a trail of data behind us. Business-to-consumer (B2C) and consumer-to-consumer (C2C) e-commerce systems and B2B e-business transactions, online ticketing and payments,

Web 1.0 (Simple Web), Web 2.0 (Social Web), Web 3.0 (Semantic Web), Web 4.0 (Smart Web), still and dynamic images, and so on are the prominent and dominant sources of data. Sensors and actuators are deployed abundantly in specific environments for security and for enabling the occupants and owners of the environments to be smart. In short, every kind of integration, interaction, orchestration, collaboration, automation, and operation produces streams of decision-enabling data to be plucked and put into transactional and then into analytical data stores. As the world and every tangible item in it are connected purposefully, the data-generation sources and resources are bound to grow ceaselessly, resulting in heaps and hordes of data.

4.2.2 Describing the Big Data World

We have discussed the fundamental and copious changes happening in the IT and business domains. The growth of service enablement of applications, platforms, infrastructures (servers, storages, and network solutions) and even everyday devices besides the varying yet versatile connectivity methods has laid down strong and simulating foundations for big interactions, transactions, automations, and insights. The tremendous rise in data collection along with all the complications has instinctively captivated both business and IT leaders and luminaries to act accordingly and adeptly to take care of this impending huge and data-driven opportunity for governments, corporations, and organizations. This is the beginning of the much-discussed and discoursed big data computing discipline.

This paradigm is becoming formalized with deeper and decisive collaboration among product vendors, service organizations, independent software vendors, system integrators, and research organizations. Having understood the strategic significance, all the different stakeholders have come together in complete unison to create and sustain simplifying and streamlining techniques, platforms, and infrastructures; integrated processes; best practices; design patterns; and key metrics to make this new discipline pervasive and persuasive. Today the acceptance and activation levels of big data computing are consistently on the climb. However, it is bound to raise a number of critical challenges but at the same time, if taken seriously it will be highly impactful and insightful for business organizations to traverse confidently along the right route. The continuous unearthing of integrated platforms is a good indication of the bright days ahead for the eminent and strategic big data phenomenon.

The implications of big data are vast and varied. The principal activity is to do a variety of tools-based and mathematically sound analyses of big data for instantaneously gaining bigger insights. It is a well-known fact that any organization having the innate ability to swiftly and succinctly leverage the accumulating data assets is bound to be successful in what it is operating, providing, and aspiring to. That is, besides instinctive decisions, informed decisions go a long way in shaping and confidently steering organizations. Thus, just gathering data is no longer useful but IT-enabled extraction of actionable insights in time out of those data assets serves well for the betterment of world businesses. Analytics is the formal discipline in IT for methodically doing data collection, filtering, cleaning, translation, storage, representation, processing, mining, and analysis with the aim of extracting useful and usable intelligence. Big data analytics is the newly coined term for accomplishing various sorts of analytical operations on big data. With this renewed focus, BDA is gaining a higher market and intellectual share across the world. With a string of new capabilities and competencies accruing from this recent and riveting innovation, worldwide corporations are optimistically jumping on the BDA bandwagon. This chapter aims to demystify the hidden niceties and ingenuities of the raging BDA.

4.2.3 Big Data Characteristics

Big data is the general term used to represent massive amounts of data that are not stored in the relational form in traditional enterprise-scale databases. New-generation database systems based on symmetric multiprocessing (SMP) and massive parallel processing (MPP) techniques are being framed to store, aggregate, filter, mine, and analyze big data efficiently. The following are the general characteristics of big data.

- Data storage is defined on the order of petabytes, exabytes, and so on in volume to the current storage limits (gigabytes and terabytes).

- There can be multiple structures (structured, semistructured, and less structured) for big data.
- Multiple types of data sources (sensors, machines, mobiles, social sites, etc.) and resources are available for big data.
- Data are time-sensitive (near real-time as well as real-time). That means big data consists of data collected with relevance to the time zones so that time-sensitive insights can be extracted.

Thus big data has created a number of advantageous repercussions for businesses to give it a prominent place in their evolving IT strategy so as to be competitive in their dealings and decisions.

4.2.4 A Perspective on Big Data Computing

A series of revolutions on the Web and the device ecosystem have resulted in polystructured data being produced in large volumes, gathered, and transmitted over the Internet communication infrastructure from distant and distributed sources. They are then subjected to filtering, cleansing, formatting, refinement, and prioritization through numerous compute and data-intensive processes and stocked in high-end storage appliances and networks. For decades, companies have been making business-critical decisions based on transactional data (structured) stored in relational databases. Today the scene is quite different and the point worth mentioning here is that data are increasingly less structured, exceptionally huge in volume, and complicatedly diverse in data formats. Of course, the data-induced business value is definitely greater. Decision-enabling data are being generated and garnered in multiple ways and they can be classified as human- and machine-generated. Incidentally, machine-data sizes are huge compared to the ones generated by people. Cameras' still images and videos, clickstreams, industry-generic and specific business transactions and operations, knowledge content (email messages, pdf files, word documents, presentations, Excel sheets, e-books, etc.), chats and conversations, data emitted from sensors and actuators, and scientific experiments data are the latest less and medium-structured data types.

Every day, millions of people use a number of Web 2.0 (Social Web) platforms and sites that enable users from every nook and corner of this connected world to read and write their views and reviews on all subjects under the sun; to voluntarily pour their complaints, compliments, concerns, comments, and clarifications on personal as well as professional services and solutions; to share their well-merited knowledge to wider groups of people; to form user communities for generic as well as specific purposes; to advertise and promote newer ideas and products; to communicate and collaborate; to substantially enhance people productivity; and so on. Thus weblogs and musings from people across the globe lead to an explosion of data. These can be appropriately integrated, stocked, streamed, and mined for extracting useful and usable information in the forms of tips, trends, hidden associations, alerts, impending opportunities, reusable and responsible patterns, insights, and other hitherto unexplored facts.

Data have become a torrent flowing into every area of the global economy. Companies churn out a burgeoning volume of transactional data, capturing trillions of bytes of information about their customers, suppliers, and operations; and millions of networked sensors are being embedded in the physical world in devices such as mobile phones, smart energy meters, automobiles, and industrial machines that sense, create, and communicate data in the age of the Internet of Things. Indeed, as companies and organizations go about their business and interact with individuals, they are generating a tremendous amount of digital "exhaust data," that is, data that are created as a by-product of other activities. Social media sites, smart phones, and other consumer devices including PCs and laptops have allowed billions of individuals around the world to contribute to the amount of big data available. And the growing volume of multimedia content has played a major role in the exponential growth in the amount of big data. Each second of high-definition video, for example, generates more than 2000 times as many bytes as required to store a single page of text. In a digitized world, consumers going about their day communicating, browsing, buying, sharing, and searching create their own enormous trails of data.

Source: McKinsey Global Institute Report on Big Data, 2011.

Big data computing involves a bevy of powerful procedures, products, and practices to analyze comprehensively and computationally a multi-structured and massive data heap to create and sustain fresh business value. Sharp reductions in the cost of both storage and computing power have made it feasible to collect, crunch, and capitalize this new-generation data proactively and preemptively with greater enthusiasm. Companies are looking for ways and means to include nontraditional yet potentially valuable data along with their traditional enterprise data for predictive and prescriptive analyses. The McKinsey Global Institute (MGI) estimates that data volume is growing 40% per year. Four important characteristics will define and defend the era of ensuing big data computing.

- *Volume*—As indicated previously, machine-generated data are growing exponentially in size compared to the volume of human-generated data. For instance, digital cameras produce high-volume image and video files to be shipped, succinctly stored, and subjected to a wider variety of tasks for different reasons including video-based security surveillance. Research labs such as CERN generate massive data; avionics and automotive electronics industries also generate a great deal of data; and smart energy meters and heavy industrial equipment such as oil refineries and drilling rigs generate huge data volumes.
- *Velocity*—Today social networking and micro-blogging sites create a large amount of information. Though the size of information created and shared is comparatively small here, the number of users is huge and hence the frequency is on the higher side, resulting in a massive collection of data. Even at 140 characters per tweet, the high velocity of Twitter data ensures large volumes (more than 8 terabytes [TB] per day).
- *Variety*—Newer data formats are arriving, compounding the problem further. As enterprise IT is continuously strengthened with the incorporation of nimbler embedded systems and versatile cloud services to produce and provide premium and people-centric applications to the expanding user community, new data types and formats are evolving.
- *Value*—Data are an asset and have to be purposefully and enthusiastically processed, prioritized, protected, mined, and analyzed utilizing advanced technologies and tools to bring

out the hidden knowledge that enables individuals and institutions to contemplate and carry forward the future course of actions correctly.

There are other characteristics such as data veracity, variability, and viscosity. Big data computing is the IT part of extracting and emitting actionable insights out of big data. This fast-emerging computing model is all about the technological solutions and their contributions in tackling the positive and the negative factors of big data.

4.2.5 Why Big Data Computing?

The main mandate of information technology is to capture, store, and process a large amount of data to output useful information in a preferred and pleasing format. With continued advancements in IT, a stream of competent technologies has arisen to derive usable and reusable knowledge from the expanding information base. The much-wanted transition from data to information and to knowledge has been simplified through the meticulous leverage of those IT solutions. Thus data have been the main source of value creation for the past five decades. Now with the eruption of big data and the enabling platforms, corporations and consumers are eyeing and yearning for better and bigger value derivation. Indeed the deeper research in the big data domain breeds a litany of innovations to realize robust and resilient productivity-enhancing methods and models for sustaining business value. The hidden treasures in big data troves are being technologically exploited to the fullest extent to zoom ahead of competitors. The big data inspired technology clusters facilitate the newer business acceleration and augmentation mechanisms. In a nutshell, the scale and scope of big data will ring in big shifts. The proliferation of social networks and multifaceted devices and the unprecedented advancements in connectivity technologies have laid a strong and stimulating foundation for big data. Several market analysts and research reports are coming out with positive indications that bright days are ahead for big data analytics.

4.2.6 The Application Domains

Big data is increasingly becoming pivotal and paramount for the forthcoming knowledge era. As every concrete thing is slated to be instrumented, interconnected, and intelligent, its interactions are bound to generate a tremendous amount of data. Social sites also join in the data accumulation process. Though most of them are repetitive, redundant, and routine, it is very critical to subject them to a series of filtering and funnelling tasks to subsequently emit value-adding patterns, tips, fruitful associations, and insights that are disruptive, generative, transformative, and corrective if applied properly. The opportunities afforded through big data can be tactically as well as strategically immense.

Every technological innovation in our everyday lives is being recognized and celebrated when it has the inherent wherewithal to accomplish new things or to elevate existing things to newer heights. There is an old saying that necessity is the mother of invention. As the data germination, capture, and storage scene is growing exponentially, knowledge discovery occupies center stage. This has pushed technology consultants, product vendors, and system integrators to ponder a library of robust and resilient technologies, platforms, and procedures that come in handy in quickly extracting practical insights from the data heaps. Today a number of industry segments are coming out of their comfort zone and capitalizing on the noteworthy advancements in big data computing to zoom ahead of their competitors and to seriously plan and provide premium services to retain their current customers as well as to attract new consumers. In the paragraphs that follow, I describe a few verticals that will benefit enormously with the maturity of big data computing.

For governments, the big data journey ensures a bright and blissful opportunity to boost their efficacy in their citizen services' delivery mechanisms. IT spending will come down while IT-based automation in governance is enhanced. There are research results that corroborate the view that the public sector can boost its productivity significantly through the effective use of big data. For corporations, when big data are dissected, detailed, and analyzed in combination with traditional enterprise data, the corporate IT can gain a more comprehensive and insightful understanding of its business, which can lead to enhanced productivity, a stronger competitive position in the marketplace, and an aura of greater innovation. All of these will have a momentous impact on the bottom-line revenue.

For people, there is a growing array of incredible benefits. For example, the use of in-home and in-body monitoring devices such as implantable sensors, wearables, fixed and portable actuators, robots, computing devices, light-emitting diode (LED) displays, smart phones, and their ad hoc networking capabilities to measure vital body parameters accurately and to monitor progress continuously can in the future improve people's health immensely. Sensors are the eyes and ears of new-generation IT and their contribution ranges from environmental monitoring to body-health monitoring. This is an incubator for establishing elegant and exotic services for the entire society. Sellers and shoppers can gain much through communication devices and information appliances. The proliferation of smart phones and other GPS devices offers advertisers an opportunity to target consumers when they are in close proximity to a store, coffee shop, or restaurant. This opens up uncharted and hitherto unforeseen avenues for fresh revenues for service providers and businesses. The market and intellectual share of those pioneering businesses is bound to grow by leaps and bounds. Retailers can make use of social computing sites to understand people's preferences and preoccupations to smartly spread out their reach. The hidden facts and patterns elicited can enable them to explore and execute much more effective micro-customer segmentation and targeted marketing campaigns. Further, they come in handy in eliminating any supply chain disturbances and deficiencies. Thus big data computing will contribute to propping up the productivity of all kinds of enterprises. It has become a compelling reason for people to ponder its tactical as well as strategic significance.

4.3 Describing Big Data Analytics

Without an iota of doubt, the world's iconic cites have outlived empires, human-generated and natural disasters, and enigmatic civilizations successfully and are continuously evolving to absorb all kinds of changes wrought by a bevy of factors such as environmental shifts, population growth, business enterprising and industry clusters, technological advances, infrastructure impacts, people needs, and so on [3]. As a result, cities have become highly congested and complicated systems. Multiple disparate and distributed systems are intertwined together within any growing city environments and hence cities are being aptly touted as systems of systems. As diverse systems including millions of smart sensors and actuators interact with one another, the first and foremost implication is well known. That is, data in different sizes, structures, speeds, and scopes are being emitted in massive volumes. For drawing viable and value-adding insights for designing, developing, and deploying next-generation city systems and services for people, the captured and stocked data have to go through a series of specific processing, mining, and analyzing. Considering the hugeness of data getting gleaned, the traditional information management systems are often found inadequate and obsolete.

The timely arrival and the overwhelming acceptance of the Hadoop frameworks is seen as a boon for deriving actionable insights that can empower transformational leaders by reducing complexity and enable those concerned to make informed decisions. Data are turning out to be an asset for city management. Converting data to information and knowledge has become a challenge. Today every country head, county governor, metro mayor, city manager, and agency director is harnessing existing information to transform city management. For example, in most cities, ambulances are stationed at a single and central location even though data often suggest that ambulances parked at specific city locations based on predicted events and historical needs would be able to respond to emergencies more quickly. To realize their vast economic, social, and cultural potential, cities clearly need to become substantially IT-enabled. BDA in particular, through its prime ability to ingest and crunch big data and to emit pragmatic insights in time, is the need of the hour for cities to zoom ahead toward deftly and decisively fulfilling the evolving aspirations of city dwellers.

This recent entrant of BDA into the continuously expanding technology landscape has generated a great deal of interest among industry professionals as well as academicians. Big data has become an unavoidable trend and it has to be solidly and succinctly handled to derive time-sensitive and actionable insights. A dazzling array of tools, techniques, and tips is evolving to quickly capture data from diverse distributed resources and process, analyze, and mine it to extract actionable business insights to bring in technology-sponsored business transformation and sustenance. In short, analytics is the thriving phenomenon in every sphere and segment today. Especially with the automated capture, persistence, and processing of the tremendous amount of multistructured data being generated by humans as well as machines, the analytical value, scope, and power of data are bound to blossom further in the days ahead.

Precisely speaking, data are a strategic asset for organizations to plan insightfully to sharply enhance their capabilities and competencies and to embark on the appropriate activities that decisively and drastically power up their short- as well as long-term offerings, outputs, and outlooks. Business innovations can happen in abundance and be sustained too when there is a seamless and spontaneous connectivity between data-driven and analytics-enabled business insights and business processes.

In the recent past, real-time analytics has gained much prominence and several product vendors have been flooding the market with a number of elastic and state-of-the-art solutions (software as well as hardware) for facilitating on-demand; ad hoc; real-time; and runtime analysis of batch, online transaction, social, machine, operational, and streaming data. There are a number of advancements in this field as a result of its huge potentials for worldwide companies in considerably reducing operational expenditures while gaining operational insights. Hadoop-based analytical products are capable of processing and analyzing any data type and quantity across hundreds of commodity server clusters. Stream computing drives continuous and cognitive analysis of massive volumes of streaming data with sub-millisecond response times.

There are enterprise data warehouses, analytical platforms, in-memory appliances, and so on. Data warehousing delivers deep operational insights with advanced in-database analytics. The EMC® Greenplum® Data Computing Appliance (DCA) is an integrated analytics platform that accelerates analysis of big data assets within a single integrated appliance. IBM® PureData™ System for Analytics architecturally integrates database, server, and storage into a single, purpose-built, easy-to-manage system. The SAP HANA is an exemplary platform for efficient BDA. Platform vendors are conveniently tied up with infrastructure vendors, especially cloud service providers (CSPs), to take analytics to the cloud so that the goal of analytics as a service (AaaS) sees a neat and nice reality sooner than later. There are multiple startups with innovative product offerings to speed up and simplify the complex part of big data analysis.

4.3.1 The Big Trends of BDA

The future of business definitely belongs to those enterprises that swiftly embrace the BDA movement and use it strategically to their own advantages. It is pointed out that business leaders and other decision makers, who are smart enough to adopt a flexible and future-directed big data strategy, can take their businesses toward greater heights. Successful companies are already extending the value of classic and conventional analytics by integrating cutting-edge big data technologies and outsmarting their competitors. There are several forecasts, exhortations, expositions, and trends on the discipline of BDA. Market research and analyst groups have come out with positive reports and briefings, detailing its key drivers and differentiators, the future of this brewing idea, its market value, the revenue potentials and application domains, the fresh avenues and areas for renewed focus, the needs for its sustainability, and so on. The top trends emanating from this field are discussed in the following section.

4.3.2 BDA Use Cases

Enterprises can understand and gain the value of BDA based on the number of value-added use cases and how some of the hitherto hard-to-solve problems can be tackled easily with the help of BDA technologies and tools. Every enterprise is mandated to grow with the help of analytics. As elucidated previously, with big data, big analytics is the norm for businesses to make informed decisions. Several domains are eagerly enhancing their IT capability to have embedded analytics, and there are several reports extolling the elegance of BDA. The following are some of the prominent use cases.

4.3.2.1 Customer Satisfaction Analysis This is the prime problem for most product enterprises across the globe. There is no foolproof mechanism in place to understand customers' sentiments and obtain feedback about their products. Gauging people's responses correctly and quickly goes a long way toward introducing proper rectifications and recommendations in product design, development, servicing, and support, which has been a vital task for any product manufacturer to be relevant for its customers and product consumers. Thus customers' reviews regarding product quality need to be carefully collected through various internal as well as external sources such as channel partners, distributors, sales and service professionals, retailers, and recently, through social sites, micro-blogs, surveys, and so on. However, the issue is that the data being gleaned are extremely unstructured, repetitive, unfiltered, and unprocessed. Extraction of actionable insights becomes difficult here and hence leveraging BDA for a single view of customers (SVoCs) will help enterprises gain sufficient insights into the much-needed customer mindset and to solve their problems effectively and avoid them in their new product lines.

4.3.2.2 Market Sentiment Analysis   In today's competitive and knowledge-driven market economy, business executives and decision makers need to gauge the market environment deeply to be successful in their goals, decisions, and deeds. Through a deeper analysis conducted legally and ethically they need to address certain questions: What are the shining products in the market; where is the market heading; who are the real competitors, what are their top-selling products, and how are they doing in the market; what are the bright spots and prospects; and what are customers' preferences in the short- as well as long-term perspective? This information is available on a variety of websites, social media sites, and other public domains. BDA on these data can provide an organization with the much needed information about strength, weakness, opportunities, and threats (SWOTs) for their product lines.

4.3.2.3 Epidemic Analysis   Epidemics and seasonal diseases such as flu start and spread with certain noticeable patterns among people and so it is pertinent to extract hidden information to secure a timely arrest in the outbreak of the infection. It involves capturing all types of data originating from different sources, subjecting them to a series of investigations to extract actionable insights quickly, and contemplating the appropriate countermeasures. A news item reports how spying on people data can actually help medical professionals to save lives [4]. Data can be gathered from many different sources, but few are as superior as Twitter; tools such as TwitterHose facilitate this data collection, allowing anyone to download 1% of tweets made during a specified hour at random, giving researchers a nice cross section of the Twitterverse. Researchers at Johns Hopkins University have been taking advantage of this tool, downloading tweets at random and sifting through these data to flag any and all mentions of flu or cold-like symptoms. Because the tweets are geo-tagged, researchers can then determine where the sickness reports are coming from, cross-referencing this with flu data from the U.S. Centers for Disease Control and Prevention to build up a picture of how the virus spreads, and more importantly, predict where it might spread to next.

In a similar line, with the leverage of the innumerable advancements being accomplished and articulated in the multifaceted discipline of BDA, myriad industry segments are jumping on the big data bandwagon to make themselves ready to acquire superior competencies and capabilities especially in anticipation, ideation, implementation, and improvisation of premium and path-breaking services and solutions for the world market. BDA brings forth fresh ways for businesses and governments to analyze a vast amount of unstructured data (streaming as well as stored) to be highly relevant to their customers and constituencies.

4.3.2.4 Using BDA in Healthcare   The healthcare industry has been a late adopter of technology when compared to other industries such as banking, retail, and insurance. As per the trendsetting McKinsey report on big data from June 2011, if U.S. healthcare organizations could use big data creatively and effectively to drive efficiency and quality, the potential savings could be more than $300 billion every year.

- *Patient Monitoring.* Inpatient, out-patient, emergency visits and ICU—everything is becoming digitized. With rapid progress in technology, sensors are embedded in weighing scales, blood glucose devices, wheelchairs, patient beds, X-ray machines, and so on. Digitized devices generate large streams of data in real time that can provide insights into a patient's health and behavior. If these data are captured, they can be put to use to improve the accuracy of information and enable practitioners to better utilize limited provider resources. It will also significantly enhance patient experiences at a healthcare facility by providing proactive risk monitoring, improved quality of care, and personalized attention. Big data can enable complex event processing (CEP) by providing real-time insights to doctors and nurses in the control room.

- *Preventive Care for ACO.* One of the key accountable care organization (ACO) goals is to provide preventive care. Disease identification and risk stratification will be crucial to business function. Managing real-time feeds coming in from health insurance exchanges (HIEs), pharmacists, providers, and payers will deliver key information to apply risk stratification and predictive modeling techniques. In the past, companies were limited to historical claims and health reimbursement account (HRA)/survey data but with HIE, the whole dynamic to data availability for health analytics has changed. Big data tools can significantly enhance the speed of processing and data mining.
- *Epidemiology.* Through HIE, most of the providers, payers, and pharmacists will be connected through networks in the near future. These networks will facilitate the sharing of data to better enable hospitals and health agencies to track disease outbreaks, patterns, and trends in health issues across a geographic region or across the world, allowing determination of source and containment plans.
- *Patient Care Quality and Program Analysis.* With exponential growth of data and the need to gain insight from information comes the challenge to process the voluminous variety of information to produce metrics and key performance indicators (KPIs) that can improve patient care quality and medical aids programs. Big data provides the architecture, tools, and techniques that will allow processing terabytes and petabytes of data to provide deep analytic capabilities to its stakeholders.

4.4 Machine Data Analytics by Splunk®

All of your IT applications, platforms, and infrastructures generate data every millisecond of every day. Machine data is one of the fastest growing and most complex areas of big data. It is also one of the most valuable insights containing a definitive record of users' transactions, customer behavior, sensor activity, machine behavior, security threats, fraudulent activity, and more. Machine data hold critical insights useful across the enterprise.

- Monitor end-to-end transactions for online businesses providing 24/7 operations
- Understand customer experience, behavior, and usage of services in real time
- Fulfill internal SLAs and monitor service provider agreements
- Identify spot trends and sentiment analysis on social platforms
- Map and visualize threat scenario behavior patterns to improve security posture

Making use of machine data is challenging. It is difficult to process and analyze by traditional data management methods or in a timely manner. Machine data are generated by a multitude of disparate sources, and hence correlating meaningful events across these is complex. The data are unstructured and difficult to fit into a predefined schema. Machine data are high-volume and time-series based, requiring new approaches for management and analysis. The most valuable insights from these data are often needed in real time. Traditional business intelligence, data warehouse, or IT analytics solutions are simply not engineered for this class of high-volume, dynamic, and unstructured data.

As indicated in the beginning, machine-generated data are more voluminous than human-generated data. Thus without an iota of doubt, machine data analytics is occupying a more significant portion in BDA. Machine data are being produced 24/7/365 by nearly every kind of software application and electronic device. The applications, servers, network devices, storage and security appliances, sensors, browsers, compute machines, cameras, and various other systems deployed to support business operations are continuously generating information relating to their status and activities. Machine data can be found in a variety of formats such as application log files, call detail records, user profiles, KPIs, and clickstream data associated with user Web interactions, data files, system configuration files, alerts, and tickets. Machine data are generated by both machine-to-machine (M2M) as well as human-to-machine (H2M) interactions.

Outside of the traditional IT infrastructure, every processor-based system including HVAC controllers, smart meters, GPS devices, actuators and robots, manufacturing systems, and radio frequency identification (RFID) tags and consumer-oriented systems such as medical instruments, personal gadgets and gizmos, aircrafts, scientific experiments, and automobiles that contain embedded devices are continuously generating machine data. The list is constantly growing. Machine data can be structured or unstructured. The growth of machine data has accelerated in recent times with the trends in IT consumerization and industrialization. That is, the IT infrastructure complexity has increased remarkably, driven by the adoption of portable devices, virtual machines, bring your own devices, and cloud-based services.

The goal here is to aggregate, parse, and visualize these data to spot trends and act accordingly. By monitoring and analyzing data emitted by a deluge of diverse, distributed, and decentralized data, there are opportunities galore. Someone wrote that sensors are the eyes and ears of future applications. Environmental monitoring sensors in remote and rough places bring forth the right and relevant knowledge about their operating environments in real time. Sensor data fusion leads to develop context and situation-aware applications. With machine data analytics in place, any kind of performance degradation of machines can be identified in real time and corrective actions can be initiated with full knowledge and confidence. Security and surveillance cameras pump in still images and video data that in turn help analysts and security experts to stop any kind of undesirable intrusions preemptively. Firefighting can become smart with the utilization of machine data analytics.

The much-needed end-to-end visibility, analytics, and real-time intelligence across all of their applications, platforms, and IT infrastructures enables business enterprises to achieve required service levels, manage costs, mitigate security risks, demonstrate and maintain compliance, and gain new insights to drive better business decisions and actions. Machine data provide a definitive, time-stamped record of current and historical activity and events within and outside an organization, including application and system performance, user activity, system configuration changes, electronic transaction records, security alerts, error messages, and device locations. Machine data in a typical enterprise are generated in a multitude of formats and structures, as each software application or hardware device records and creates machine data associated with their specific use. Machine data also vary among vendors and even within the same vendor across product types, families, and models.

A number of newer use cases are being formulated with pioneering improvements in smart sensors, their ad hoc and purpose-specific network formation capability, data collection, consolidation, correlation, corroboration and dissemination, knowledge discovery, information visualization, and so on. Splunk is a low-profile big data company specializing in extracting actionable insights out of diverse, distributed, and decentralized data. Some real-world customer examples include

- *e-Commerce*—A typical e-commerce site serving thousands of users a day will generate gigabytes of machine data that can be used to provide significant insights into IT infrastructure and business operations. Expedia uses Splunk to avoid website outages by monitoring server and application health and performance. Today, around 3000 users at Expedia use Splunk to gain real-time visibility on tens of terabytes of unstructured, time-sensitive machine data (not only from their IT infrastructure, but also from online bookings, deal analysis, and coupon use).
- *Salesforce.com*—Salesforce Developer Community (SFDC) uses Splunk to mine the large quantities of data generated from its entire technology stack. It has more than 500 users of Splunk dashboards, from IT users monitoring customer experience to product managers performing analytics on services such as Chatter. With Splunk, SFDC claims to have taken application troubleshooting for 100,000 customers to the next level.
- *Digital publishing*—NPR uses Splunk to gain insights of their digital asset infrastructure, to monitor and troubleshoot their end-to-end asset delivery infrastructure, to measure program popularity and views by device, to reconcile royalty payments for digital rights, and to measure abandonment rates and more.

Figure 4.1 illustrates how Splunk captures data from numerous sources and does the processing, filtering, mining, and analysis to generate actionable insights out of multistructured machine data.

Splunk Enterprise is the leading platform for collecting, analyzing, and visualizing machine data. It provides a unified way to organize and extract real-time insights from massive amounts of machine data from virtually any source. This includes data from websites, business

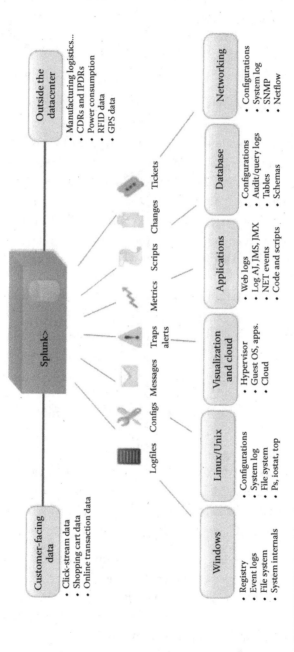

Figure 4.1 The Splunk reference architecture for machine data analytics.

applications, social media platforms, application servers, hypervisors, sensors, and traditional databases. Once your data are in Splunk, you can search, monitor, report, and analyze it, no matter how unstructured, large, or diverse it may be. Splunk software gives you a real-time understanding of what is happening and a deep analysis of what has happened, driving new levels of visibility and insight. This is called operational intelligence.

Most organizations maintain a diverse set of data stores—machine data, relational data, and other unstructured data. Splunk DB Connect delivers real-time connectivity to one or many relational databases and Splunk Hadoop Connect delivers bidirectional connectivity to Hadoop. Both Splunk apps enable you to drive more meaningful insights from all of your data. The Splunk App for HadoopOps provides real-time monitoring and analysis of the health and performance of the end-to-end Hadoop environment, encompassing all layers of the supporting infrastructure.

4.5 Open Data for Next-Generation Cities

Peter Hinssen [5] writes about the power of open data in establishing and sustaining smart cities. Cities are producing a large amount of data. However, the data have to be open to be accessed and subjected to a series of deeper investigations to extract pragmatic knowledge. Today's cities are the true magnets, invigoratingly attracting people from everywhere to consciously explore and enjoy a variety of exciting opportunities. But cities are severely groaning under the weight of their incessant expansions and extensions. City roads and streets are clogging up with congestion and traffic snarls; city inhabitants consume electricity faster than utilities could produce it; crime is increasingly difficult to anticipate and control; people are dissatisfied with civil services because of the faster life patterns; and so on. But the answer is nigh. City users with all their smart phones, cars, social interactions, houses, offices, energy consumption, online transactions, professional assignments and engagements, and so on leave behind a sumptuous amount of data. Not only people, but also all the enabling machines, handhelds and digital assistants, street security and surveillance cameras, RFID readers, in-car devices, smart meters, and so on produce a great deal of data every second. Now any responsible city has to make sense out of this fast-growing data treasure to comprehensively meet the varying expectations. The insights extracted help administrators to chalk out viable and value-adding strategies and associated plans toward the betterment of cities and their inhabitants. The data-driven insights bring much confidence and clarity in effective and future-directed city planning. For example, instead of building more power plants, it is more judicious and analytical to have smart grids and smart meters in place to tackle rising energy requirements of cities. Enterprise resource planning (ERP)–type software solutions for cities (city resource planning [CRP]) can be a better option for future cities.

The author insists that all the aggregated data have to be open to be leveraged by different entities and stakeholders (government officials, nongovernment organizations [NGOs], individuals, etc.). This openness facilitates the realization of right intelligence in time and the derived insights empower different service providers (communication, healthcare, energy, government, e-business, IT, etc.) to be proactive, preemptive, and prompt in all their obligations to their constituents. Smart cities are inherently capable of optimized usage of all kinds of city resources through the smart leverage of highly proven IT tools, platforms, and infrastructures; well connected (wired as well as wireless); purposefully collaborative; transparently sharing; and elegantly sensitive and responsive to city dwellers.

4.6 Edge Data for Cities of the Future

It is a known fact that the unprecedented rise in data sources has led to the emergence of the strategically sound big data discipline and its allied technologies. The big data landscape is relentlessly growing as a result of the convergence of various divergent trends. Besides the enormity of the data being produced by knowledge workers and social animals every single minute, the growing size of machine-generated data will gain prime importance in the impending big data era. Machine data, especially of edge devices, are progressively playing a very pivotal role in shaping the crucial aspect of data-driven intelligence. The story thus far is that first there is a voluminous production and extensive deployment of smart sensors and actuators in a variety of environments (home, industrial, social, entertainment, education, etc.) for different purposes. The much-discussed connectivity, which is constantly becoming deeper and extreme, connects them via different modes: wireless, wireline, and a mix of both. That is, there are millions of devices at the edges of networks and it is projected that the number of devices will be in the range of billions in the years ahead [6].

All of these are being intensively deciphered and deliberated these days because of the unparalleled advancements in the device and connectivity domains. Both resource-rich and constrained devices are systematically networked together in an ad hoc fashion to interchange their data and share their unique capabilities. Further, edge devices are grandly integrated with cyber applications and services hosted at distant cloud environments. These direct as well as indirect integrations and interactions have laid a strong and stimulating foundation for a sharp hike in edge-data generation. Data are being collected by an enormous variety of equipment, such as smart utility meters, surveillance and security cameras, actuators, robots, RFID readers, biometrics, factory-line sensors, mobile phones, fitness machines, defense weapons, launchers and satellites, avionics and automobiles, information appliances, household utensils and wares, electronic gadgets and gizmos, lab-experimentation devices, and medical instruments.

The ubiquitous connectivity and the ceaseless growth of modern sensors and actuators have opened up a whole new powerhouse for valuable information. It is clear that edge data can bring forth significant value to all stakeholders including end-users. The careful and cognitive capture, processing, and analysis of edge data in time can go a long way in empowering organizations to respond to both positive as well as negative events preemptively and solve many problems that were previously out of reach.

The point here is that this untapped resource of edge data has the inherent potential to deliver dependable insights that can transform the operations and strategic initiatives of public and private sector organizations. Incidentally the edge data are becoming larger, speedier, and trickier but the hidden value is greater and hence a distinct research endeavour toward making sense out of edge data is drawing phenomenal attention. On the other hand, there are standards-compliant BDA platforms (open source as well as commercial-grade), data ingestion and crunching toolsets, data virtualization and visualization tools, knowledge engineering techniques, high-performance multi-core processors, gigabit Ethernet solutions, and inexpensive storage options including object storage to extract and extrapolate knowledge.

In summary, as the size of edge data is growing significantly, there is a bigger challenge to information management professionals to evolve a pragmatic strategy for effectively leveraging all sorts of edge data for the well-being of their organizations. With the faster maturity and stability of data analytics platforms, knowledge-enabled everyday systems are bound to flourish.

4.6.1 Edge Data for Smarter Cities

According to Intel, the smart city concept mandates the use of smart-grid infrastructures to improve environmental sustainability, manage energy consumption, better coordinate public resources, and protect the quality of life for urban and metropolitan residents and plan for sustainable growth. The edge data here play a very incredible role. For example, utility companies and governments are using data from the smart grid to understand the complex relationships among generation, transmission, distribution, and consumption with the goal of delivering reliable energy and reducing operating costs. Consumers are also empowered with insights from the smart grid to better manage their personal energy requirements. For example, a "not-home" setting might turn off lights, shut down unused equipment, and adjust home temperature. Utility meter readings and grid data are brought into centralized analytical systems to bring forth timely insights.

Thus edge devices collaboratively contribute immensely to arriving at better decisions than only at a centralized control center. Communication between devices helps determine when, where, and how much energy should be produced and consumers can use home management tools to monitor and adjust energy consumption accordingly.

4.6.2 Edge Data for Smart Retailers

It is well known that supermarkets and hypermarkets across the globe duly collect a great deal of data every day. If the data are properly collected, cleansed, and categorized, retailers can substantially enhance their influence on customers and their buying patterns. This incredible knowledge of customers prepares retail stores to think big and to bring forth scores of premium services in time to retain and delight their loyal customers as well as to attract new customers. The enduring challenges brought on by the hugeness in the data being captured and processed are being tackled through the highly versatile Hadoop framework that can totally change the retail economics by radically lowering the cost of data storage and processing, bringing in new flexibilities to gain new insights, automated replenishment, and more accurately market to individuals rather than a demographic.

Retailers are using a variety of intelligent systems that gather data and provide immediate feedback to help them to engage shoppers fruitfully. Well-known data-generation systems include digital signage, point of sale systems, vending machines, transaction, in-store cameras, dispensing kiosks, and so on. The ability to gain reliable insights from the data shared by these systems makes it possible to provide customer-centric "connected stores." Context awareness is the main theme of these connected machines to understand the customer situation precisely and perfectly. The context information then greatly differentiates in showering customers with a host of unique services. In short, the insights-driven shopping experience is enabling customers to purchase items for the best price. Based on the edge data, retailers can integrate their supply chain activities intelligently. Further, retailers can provide their customers with opportunities to engage with their preferred brands in more meaningful ways to cement customer loyalty.

4.6.3 Edge Data for Smart Automobiles

The number of digital electronics and other automation elements in a vehicle is steadily on the climb for providing different kinds of services to drivers and the occupants. The convenience, care, choice, and comfort brought about through these connected devices are undeniably awesome. Sensors are being attached in every critical component in a car to preemptively get to know the component's status and this reading provides some leeway for drivers to ponder the next course of action. Another interesting and involving module is the in-vehicle infotainment system, which is emerging as the core and central gateway for securing and strengthening the connectivity outside for a range of use cases. All kinds of communication, computing, and entertainment systems inside vehicles will have a seamless connection with the outside world through the well-defined in-vehicle system so that the occupants can enjoy their travels in a fruitful manner. GPS devices and smart meters of cars generate a great deal of data to be captured and analyzed.

Sensors provide information to automated parking systems to lessen the driver's workload substantially. There are sensor-enabled driver assistance systems for automobiles. Location data could be combined with road work and other traffic information to help commuters avoid congestion or take a faster route. Digital signage, cameras, and other infrastructures on the roadsides in synchronization with the in-vehicle infotainment module (V2I) aid drivers to give a pleasant travel experience for all. Vehicles today talk to other vehicles (V2V) on the road and interact with remote cloud services and applications (V2C). Vehicles share their data to the remotely held databases to facilitate the different aspects of vehicle analytics. Maps are the other salivating tool for reaching out the destination in a cool and controlled manner. Detecting real-time traffic flow from each direction and automatically changing traffic signals will improve flow. Edge data further enable automated, intelligent, and real-time decisions to optimize travel across the transportation infrastructure as cars become capable of connecting to the roadway, safety systems, and one another.

4.6.4 Edge Data for Smart Manufacturing

Every tangible machine and tool in manufacturing floors and production facilities is being filled with manifold of smart sensors, communication modules, and so on. As such, today's devices are instrumented to interoperate and be intelligent in their operations and obligations. Machines are networked not only with others in the neighborhood but also with remote cloud environments. Today all the production-related data are being shared to centralized systems in the form of Excel sheets at the end of the day through emails. But new-generation machines are capable of integrating with cloud-enabled software applications and cloud storages instantly and insightfully. That is, machines transfer all the ground-level information to the cyber-level transaction and analytical systems then and there. This technology-inspired real-time connectivity facilitates a number of fresh possibilities and opportunities for corporations in visualizing hitherto unforeseen competencies. In addition, chief executives and other decision makers, who are on the move in a faraway land, can be provided with decision-enabling productivity details through a real-time notification capability to initiate any course-correction if necessary, commit something solid to their customers with full confidence and clarity, ponder new offerings, bring operational efficiencies, explore newer avenues for fresh revenues, and so on.

That is, smart factories connect the boardroom, the factory floor, and the supply chain for higher levels of manufacturing control and efficiency. Sensors and actuators in devices such as cameras, robotic machines, and motion-control equipment generate and use data to provide real-time diagnosis and predictive maintenance, increased process visibility, and improved factory uptime and flexibility. Thus edge data lay a sparkling foundation for smart manufacturing.

4.6.5 Edge Data for Facilities and Asset Management

The big data generated by increasingly instrumented, interconnected, and intelligent facilities and assets is useful only if transactional systems could extract applicable information and act on it as needed. The appropriate and real-time usage of this big data is to help improve decisions or generate corrective actions that can create measurable benefits for an organization. BDA can help generate revenue by providing contextual understanding of information that the business can then employ to its fullest advantage. For example, geographic information systems (GISs) can help location-sensitive organizations such as retailers, telecommunications, and energy companies determine the most advantageous geographies for their business operations. The world's largest wind energy producer has achieved success using a big data modeling solution to harvest insights from an expanded set of location-dependent factors including historical and actual weather to help optimize wind turbine placement and performance. Exactly pinpointing the optimal locations for wind turbines enables energy producers to maximize power generation and reduce energy costs as well as to provide its customers with greater business-case certainty, quicker results, and increased predictability and reliability in wind power generation.

An effective facilities and asset management solution has to leverage BDA to enable organizations to proactively maintain facilities equipment, identify emerging problems to prevent breakdowns, lower maintenance and operations costs, and extend asset life through condition-based maintenance and automated issue notification [7]. To help mitigate risks to facilities and assets, predictive analytics can detect even minor anomalies and failure patterns to determine the assets that are at the greatest risk of failure. Predictive maintenance analytics can access multiple data sources in real time to predict equipment failure which helps organizations avoid costly downtime and reduce maintenance costs. Sensors could capture the operating conditions of critical equipment such as vibrations from ship engines and communicate the captured data in real time to the company's command center for commencing failure analysis and predictive maintenance. Similarly the careful analysis of environmental and weather-pattern data in real time is another way to mitigate any kind of visible or invisible risks. Organizations can receive alerts of potential weather impacts in time to shut down facilities operations or pre-locate emergency response teams to minimize business disruption in case of any advancing storms.

Big data is admirably advantageous when applied to the management of facilities and assets (everything from office buildings to oil-drilling platforms to fleets of ships). This is due to the increased instrumentation of facilities and assets, where the digital and physical worlds have synchronized to generate massive volumes of data. Therefore considering the mammoth volume of data, tools-supported analysis of big data can lead to bountiful benefits such as increased revenue, lowered operating expenses, enhanced service availability, and reduced risk. Sathyan Munirathinam [8] clearly describes how big data predictive analytics ensures proactive semiconductor equipment maintenance. In a nutshell, edge data is a ground-breaking phenomenon for all kinds of industrial sectors to zoom ahead with all the required conviction.

4.7 Integrated BDA Platforms

Integrated platforms are essential to automate several tasks enshrined in the data capture, analysis, and knowledge discovery processes.

A converged platform comes out with a reliable workbench to empower developers to facilitate application development and other related tasks such as data security, virtualization, integration, visualization, and dissemination. Special consoles are being attached with new-generation platforms for performing other important activities such as management, governance, enhancement, and so on. Hadoop is a disruptive technology for data distribution among hundreds of commodity computing machines for parallel data crunching, and any typical big data platform contains a Hadoop software suite.

Further, the big data platform enables entrepreneurs; investors; chief executives; information, operation, knowledge, and technology officers; and marketing and sales people to explore and perform experiments on big data, at scale at a fraction of the time and cost required previously. That is, platforms will endow all kinds of stakeholders and end-users with actionable insights that would in turn lead them to consider and make informed decisions in time. Knowledge workers such as business analysts and data scientists could be the other main beneficiaries through these empowered platforms. Knowledge discovery is an important phase here and the platform has to include real-time and real-world tips, associations, patterns, trends, risks, alerts, and opportunities. In-memory and in-database analytics are gaining momentum for high-performance and real-time analytics. New advancements in the form of predictive and prescriptive analytics are emerging fast with the maturity and stability of big data technologies, platforms, infrastructures, tools, and finally a cornucopia of sophisticated data mining and analysis algorithms. Thus platforms need to be fitted with new features, functionalities, and facilities to provide next-generation insights.

4.7.1 Software-Defined Infrastructures for BDA

There is no doubt that consolidated and compact platforms accomplish a number of essential actions toward simplified big data analysis and knowledge discovery. However, they need to run in optimal, dynamic, and converged infrastructures to be effective in their operations. In the recent past, IT infrastructures went through a host of transformations such as optimization, rationalization, and simplification. The cloud idea has captured the attention of infrastructure specialists these days as the cloud paradigm is being proclaimed as the most pragmatic approach for achieving the ideals of infrastructure optimization. Hence with the surging popularity of cloud computing, every kind of IT infrastructure (servers, storages, and network solutions) is being consciously subjected to a series of modernization tasks to empower it to be policy-based, software-defined, cloud-compliant, service-oriented, networkable, programmable, and so on. That is, BDA will be performed in centralized/federated, virtualized, automated, shared, and optimized cloud infrastructures (private, public, or hybrid). Application-specific IT environments are being readied for the big data era. Application-aware networks are the most sought-after communication infrastructures for big data transmission and processing. Figure 4.2 illustrates all the relevant and resourceful components for simplifying and streamlining BDA.

As with data warehousing, data marts, and online stores, an infra-structure for big data too has some unique requirements. The ultimate goal here is to easily integrate big data with enterprise data to conduct deeper and influential analytics on the combined data set. As per the white paper titled "Oracle: Big Data for the Enterprise" [9], there are three prominent requirements (data acquisition, organization, and analysis) for a typical big data infrastructure. NoSQL (Not only Structured Query Language) intrinsically has all these three. Readers can find more on NoSQL databases in the subsequent sections.

- *Acquire big data*—The infrastructure required to support the acquisition of big data must deliver low and predictable latency in both capturing data and in executing short and simple queries. It should be able to handle very high transaction volumes often in a distributed environment and also support flexible and dynamic data structures. NoSQL databases are the leading infrastructure to acquire and store big data. NoSQL databases are well suited for dynamic data structures and are highly scalable. The data stored in a NoSQL database are typically of a high variety because the systems are intended to simply capture all kinds of data without categorizing and parsing the data. For example, NoSQL databases are often used to collect and store social media data. Although customer-facing applications frequently change, underlying storage structures are kept simple. Instead of designing a schema with relationships

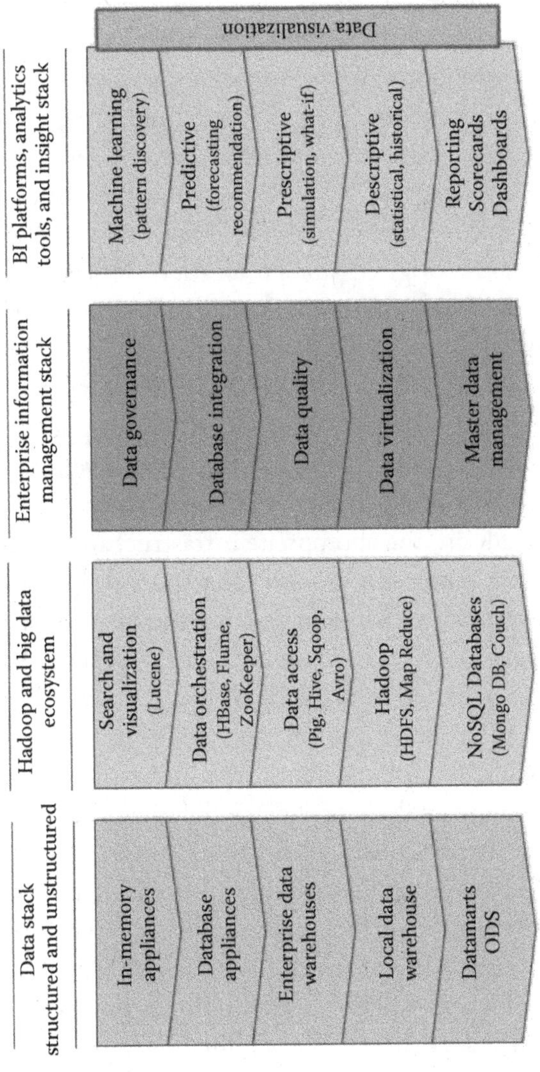

Figure 4.2   Big data analytics platforms, appliances, products, and tools.

between entities, these simple structures often just contain a major key to identify the data point and then a content container holding the relevant data. This extremely simple and nimble structure allows changes to take place without any costly reorganization at the storage layer.

- *Organize big data*—In classical data warehousing terms, organizing data is called data integration. Because there is such a huge volume of data, there is a tendency and trend gathering momentum to organize data at its original storage location. This saves much time and money as there is no data movement. The brewing need is to have a robust infrastructure that is innately able to organize big data and process and manipulate data in the original storage location. It has to support very high throughput (often in batch) to deal with large data processing steps and handle a large variety of data formats (unstructured, less structured, and fully structured).

- *Analyze big data*—The data analysis can also happen in a distributed environment. That is, data stored in diverse locations can be accessed from a data warehouse to accomplish the intended analysis. The appropriate infrastructure required for analyzing big data must be able to support deeper analytics such as statistical analysis and data mining on a wider variety of data types stored in diverse systems, to scale to extreme data volumes, to deliver faster response times driven by changes in behavior, and to automate decisions based on analytical models. Most importantly, the infrastructure must be able to integrate analysis of the combination of big data and traditional enterprise data to produce exemplary insights for fresh opportunities and possibilities. For example, analyzing inventory data from a smart vending machine in combination with the events calendar for the venue in which the vending machine is located will dictate the optimal product mix and replenishment schedule for the vending machine.

4.7.2 Civitas: The Smart City Middleware

The concept of a smart city has been drawing a great deal of attention these days across the globe. Governments, research labs, product vendors, and service organizations are showing exemplary interest in collaborating with one another to make current cities more people-friendly, efficient, and sustainable. As noted elsewhere, several departments or divisions in a city environment need to team up together to bring about the perceptible changes. Therefore the smart city paradigm can be summarized as a greatly complicated and distributed system. As we all experience, standard-compliant middleware solutions are being pressed into service for the seamless integration of diverse software applications and data sources in an IT environment. Here, too, the role and relevance of highly competent middleware is on the climb for attaining the anticipated success in integrated cities.

City-specific applications are being developed, deployed in abundance, and delivered to users. Service middleware (service bus, hub, and fabric) in synchronization with data middleware (a growing collection of data adaptors) are prominent in the middleware space. Service delivery platform (SDP) is another important constituent in the service IT ecosystem in appropriately choosing and composing distributed services from multiple sources and delivering the people-centric, situation-aware, knowledge-filled, and cost-effective composite services dynamically to requesters. Thus service discovery, integration, orchestration, management, and delivery aspects are classified as the IT portion of smart city establishment and sustenance strategy.

However, the traditional IT middleware might be found wanting for smart city projects because of the multiplicity and heterogeneity-induced complexity. The authors [10] have designed a special middleware for integrating smart city services. This middleware provides services that range from environmental sensor deployment to the necessary hardware for high-performance algorithms devoted to extract information from raw data. To cope with the multifaceted nature of the smart city paradigm, Civitas has been enhanced with reasoning capabilities. Leveraging reasoning capabilities enables the middleware to have few hard-coded features that are rather deduced from the available data. In this sense, Civitas is able to adapt to the deployed city, without requiring important modifications or adaption works. The main intention of this work is to promote tightly integrated systems and managed smart cities to simplify the IT environment for service developers. Figure 4.3 illustrates the macro-level architecture of the middleware.

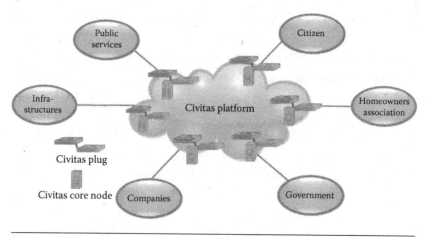

Figure 4.3 The reference architecture of the Civitas platform.

National governments across the globe, urban planners, and metro and city officials are keen on embarking on transitioning their cities into livable, lovable, green, and knowledgeable hubs for facilitating entrepreneurships. All along, IT has been a business enabler and now there is an added twist: IT is being prescribed and presented as the prospective enabler for our city systems also. Because of the inherent and growing heterogeneity, city-specific IT middleware solutions will play a telling and transforming role in the days ahead. In this section, we discussed one such middleware and many more will arrive and flourish considering the fact that there is a big market waiting for smart cities.

4.7.3 Hitachi Smart City Platform [11]

The infrastructural requirements for our cities are constantly on the rise. We have social infrastructures for services such as energy, water, road, and so on. For sustainability goals such as slowing down greenhouse gas emissions into our fragile environment, existing social infrastructures need to be considerably extended and optimized. This involves understanding patterns of usage or consumption and operationalizing appropriate decisions to ensure the different types of social infrastructure are functioning efficiently. It is paramount therefore to collect and process a wider variety of operational and consumption data to extract decision-enabling patterns. Because of the nature of these data, its frequency of collection, and the size of activity records, their quantity is expected to be large enough to justify the term "big data."

The Hitachi smart city platform plays an important role in concise and clear understanding of the changing patterns of use and leveraging them precisely to ensure and enhance the efficiency of different types of social infrastructure. The dominant roles of the smart city platform are (1) data collection, (2) data analysis, and (3) coordination of the systems (applications) that activate, automate, and augment social infrastructures. There are incredible interrelationships between different social infrastructure systems to be captured and used. All of the extracted knowledge needs to be the center of attention for implementing and sustaining next-generation operational applications for smart cities.

4.7.4 Data Collection

The smart city platform includes a database function. Details such as equipment performance and configuration data ought to be given prime importance. Because of the extra capability of M2M integration, the network topology data also play an indispensable role. Further, the city platform also handles the collection and management of large quantities of other useful data such as the consumption and operational records, malfunctions, and so on. For example, data on the supply of electric power are collected from sensors fitted on various instruments and equipment in power plants, transmission and distribution lines, and so on. Similarly, details of consumption are collected from sources such as smart meters installed in buildings, home energy management systems (HEMSs), building and energy management systems (BEMSs), and electric vehicle (EV) charging equipment. As the service area expands and with a greater number of users, the amount of data that will be generated and collected is going to be enormous.

The smart city platform also has a bus function that is used to collect control information. The bus buffers equipment control information is sent from control applications and then forwards it to the destination device. The buffered data are also saved in the database for posterity. The in-memory data storage capability provides a zero-latency guarantee, meaning that the control information reaches the target device within the allocated time.

The smart city platform also collects journal data at intervals of several seconds to several minutes, including data on equipment operation or alarms (notification of malfunction). This provides timely updates on whether equipment is operating normally. If malfunctioning, then the identification of the root cause is facilitated through the journal data.

4.7.5 Data Analysis

The perpetual procedure is that data are systematically collected, cleansed, and catalogued to enable appropriate analysis with the aim of producing actionable insights in time. There are several matured algorithms for data mining, machine learning, data interpolation, prediction, knowledge generation, and dissemination. The data interpolation is all about interpolating the overall situation from collected sampling data. Electric power data, for example, may not be collected from all buildings. Instead, statistical analysis or other viable techniques could be leveraged to estimate the power consumption for the entire district.

Similarly the collected data can be time-stamped and stored in a database. All kinds of changes in historical data can be readily analyzed to identify any usable trends. With more data, prediction accuracy is bound to go up significantly. The prediction capability helps to determine emerging and evolving trends in electric power or water use or for assessing conditions such as traffic congestion. The ultimate derivative of analytics is to extract knowledge to work on with clarity and confidence. There are data visualization tools too in abundance these days to disseminate all the acquired knowledge in preferred formats.

4.7.6 Application Coordination

Data collected from social infrastructure and data obtained from analyses are made available to applications to take account of the tactic as well as the strategic interrelationships between different aspects of the infrastructure including its control and usage pattern. This city-specific platform has the ability to empower application by sharing data among them.

One prominent example is the way in which greater use of EVs increases demand for electric power for charging vehicle batteries. Therefore by collecting all the information on EV use, it is made easier to determine factors such as where charging equipment has to be placed, at what times, if there is a higher demand for power, and so on. Similarly, interrelationships also exist between existing grid power and renewable energy. If power-usage information such as times of peak demand can be obtained, it is possible to determine the times when renewable energy will be used. Also predictions about the deterioration of facilities can be made by coordinating information about the provision and use of electric power or EVs with enterprise asset management (EAM) systems. Thus data capture and crush for information are going hand-in-hand. In the days ahead, there will be several smart city platforms from IT products vendors and software solutions providers for transforming our clogged cities into smart and sustainable ones.

4.8 BDA Frameworks and Infrastructure

There are predominantly two types of big data processing: real-time and batch processing. The data are flowing endlessly from countless sources these days, which are continuing to climb. Innumerable sensors, varying in size, scope, structure, smartness, and so on are pouring data continuously. Stock markets are emitting a large amount of data every second; system logs are being received, stored, processed, analyzed, and acted on ceaselessly. Monitoring agents are working tirelessly to produce a large amount of usable and useful data; business events are captured; knowledge discovery is initiated; information visualization is realized; and so on to empower enterprise operations. Stream computing is the latest paradigm being aptly prescribed as the best course of action for real-time receipt, processing, and analysis of online, live, and continuous data. Real-time data analysis through in-memory and in-database computing models is gaining much ground these days with the sharp reduction in computer memory costs. For the second category of batch processing, Hadoop technology is being recommended with confidence. It is clear that there is a need for competent products, platforms, and methods for efficiently and expectantly working with both real-time as well as batch data. There is a separate chapter for in-memory computing toward real-time data analysis and for producing timely and actionable insights.

The following section provides fuller details about Hadoop technology. As explained previously, big data analysis is not a simple affair and there are Hadoop-based software programming frameworks, platforms, and appliances emerging to tackle the innate complications. The Hadoop programming model has turned out to be the central and core method to propel the field of big data analysis. The Hadoop ecosystem is continuously spreading its wings wider and enabling modules are being freshly incorporated to make Hadoop-based big data analysis simpler, succinct, and quicker.

4.8.1 *Apache Hadoop Software Framework*

Apache Hadoop is an open-source framework that allows for the distributed processing of large data sets across clusters of computers using a simple programming model. Hadoop was originally designed to scale up from a single server to thousands of machines, each offering local computation and storage. Rather than rely on hardware to deliver high-availability, the Hadoop software library itself is designed to detect and handle failures at the application layer. Therefore, it delivers a highly available service on top of a cluster of inexpensive computers, each of which may be prone to failures. Hadoop is based in modular architecture and thereby any of its components can be swapped with competent alternatives if such a replacement brings noteworthy advantages.

Despite all the hubbub and hype around Hadoop, few IT professionals know its key drivers, differentiators, and killer applications. Because of the newness and complexity of Hadoop, there are several areas where confusion reigns and restrains its full-fledged assimilation and adoption. The Apache Hadoop product family includes the Hadoop Distributed File System (HDFS), MapReduce, Hive, HBase, Pig, Zookeeper, Flume, Sqoop, Oozie, Hue, and so on. HDFS and MapReduce together constitute core Hadoop, which is the foundation for all Hadoop-based applications. For applications in business intelligence (BI), data warehousing (DW), and BDA, core Hadoop is usually augmented with Hive and HBase, and sometimes Pig. The Hadoop file system excels with big data that is file based, including files that contain nonstructured data. Hadoop is excellent for storing and searching multistructured big data, but advanced analytics are possible only with certain combinations of Hadoop products, third-party products, or extensions of Hadoop technologies. The Hadoop family has its own query and database technologies and these are similar to standard SQL and relational databases. That means BI/DW professionals can learn them quickly.

The HDFS is a distributed file system designed to run on clusters of commodity hardware. HDFS is highly fault-tolerant because it automatically replicates file blocks across multiple machine nodes and is designed to be deployed on low-cost hardware. HDFS provides high-throughput access to application data and is suitable for applications that have large data sets. As a file system, HDFS manages files that contain data. Because it is file-based, HDFS itself does not offer random access to data and has limited metadata capabilities when compared to a DBMS. Likewise, HDFS is strongly batch-oriented and hence has limited real-time data access functions. To overcome these challenges, one can layer HBase over HDFS to gain some of the mainstream DBMS capabilities. HBase is one of the many products from the Apache Hadoop product family. HBase is modeled after Google's Bigtable and hence HBase, like Bigtable, excels with random and real-time access to very large tables containing billions of rows and millions of columns. Today HBase is limited to straightforward tables and records with little support for more complex data structures. The Hive meta-store gives Hadoop some DBMS-like metadata capabilities.

When HDFS and MapReduce are combined, Hadoop easily parses and indexes the full range of data types. Furthermore, as a distributed system, HDFS scales well and has a certain amount of fault-tolerance based on data replication even when deployed atop commodity hardware. For these reasons, HDFS and MapReduce can complement existing BI/DW systems that focus on structured and relational data. MapReduce is a general-purpose execution engine that works with a variety of storage technologies including HDFS, other file systems, and some DBMSs.

As an execution engine, MapReduce and its underlying data platform handle the complexities of network communication, parallel programming, and fault tolerance. In addition, MapReduce controls hand-coded programs and automatically provides multithreading processes so they can execute in parallel for massive scalability. The controlled parallelization of MapReduce can apply to multiple types of distributed applications, not just analytic ones. In a nutshell, Hadoop MapReduce is a software programming framework for easily writing massively parallel applications that process massive amounts of data in parallel on large clusters (thousands of nodes) of commodity hardware in a reliable and fault-tolerant manner. A MapReduce job usually splits the input dataset into independent chunks that are processed by the map tasks in a completely parallel manner. The framework sorts the outputs of the maps, which are then input to the reduce tasks, which in turn assemble one or more result sets.

Hadoop is not just for new analytic applications; it can revamp old ones too. For example, analytics for risk and fraud that is based on statistical analysis or data mining benefit from the much larger data samples that HDFS and MapReduce can wring from diverse big data. Further on, most 360-degree customer views include hundreds of customer attributes. Hadoop can provide insight and data to bump up to thousands of attributes, which in turn provides greater detail and precision for customer-based segmentation and other customer analytics. Hadoop is a promising and potential technology that allows large data volumes to be organized and processed while keeping the data on the original data storage cluster. For example, weblogs can be turned into browsing behavior (sessions) by running MapReduce programs (Hadoop) on the cluster and generating aggregated results on the same cluster. These aggregated results are then loaded into a relational DBMS system for analytical solutions to take care of.

HBase is the mainstream Apache Hadoop database. It is an opensource, nonrelational (column-oriented), scalable, and distributed database management system that supports structured data storage. Apache HBase, which is modeled after Google Bigtable, is the right approach when one needs random and real-time read/write access to one's big data. This is for hosting of very large tables (billions of rows × millions of columns) on top of clusters of commodity hardware. Just as Google Bigtable leverages the distributed data storage provided by the Google File System, Apache HBase provides Bigtable-like capabilities on top of Hadoop and HDFS. HBase does support writing applications in Avro, REST, and Thrift.

4.8.2 *NoSQL Databases*

Next-generation databases are mandated to be nonrelational, distributed, open-source and horizontally scalable. The original inspiration is the modern Web-scale databases. Additional characteristics such as schema-free, easy replication support, simple API, eventually consistent/Basic Availability, Soft-state, Eventual Consistency (BASE) and not Atomic, Consistent, Isolated, Durable (ACID), and so on are also being demanded. The traditional Relational Database Management Systems (RDBMSs) use Structured Query Language (SQL) for accessing and manipulating data that reside in structured columns of relational tables. However, unstructured data are typically stored in key-value pairs in a data store and therefore cannot be accessed using SQL. Such data are stored in so-called NoSQL data stores and are accessed via get and put commands. There are some big advantages of NoSQL databases compared to the relational databases as illustrated in http://www.couchbase.com/why-nosql/nosql-database.

- *Flexible data model*—Relational and NoSQL data models are very different. The relational model takes data and separates them into many interrelated tables that contain rows and columns. Tables reference each other through foreign keys that are stored in columns as well. For looking up data, the desired information needs to be collected from many tables and combined before it can be provided to the application. Similarly, when writing data, the content needs to be coordinated and performed on many tables.

  NoSQL databases follow a very different model [12]. For example, a document-oriented NoSQL database takes the data you want to store and aggregates it into documents using the JavaScript Object Notation (JSON) format. Each JSON document can be thought of as an object to be used by your application. A JSON document might, for example, take all the data stored in a row that spans 20 tables of a relational database and aggregate it into a single document/object. The resulting data model is flexible and easy to distribute the resulting documents. Another major difference is that relational technologies have rigid schemas whereas NoSQL models are schema-less. Changing the schema once data are inserted is a big deal, extremely disruptive, and frequently avoided. However, the exactly opposite behavior is desired in the big data era. Application developers need to constantly and rapidly incorporate new types of data to enrich their applications.

- *High performance and scalability*—To deal with the increase in concurrent users (big users) and the amount of data (big data), applications and their underlying databases need to scale using one of two choices: scale up or scale out. Scaling up implies a centralized approach that relies on bigger and bigger servers. Scaling out implies a distributed approach that leverages many commodity physical or virtual servers. Prior to NoSQL databases, the default scaling approach at the database tier was to scale up. This was dictated by the fundamentally centralized, shared-everything architecture of relational database technology. To support more concurrent users and/or store more data, you need a bigger server with more central processing units, memory, and disk storage to keep all the tables. Big servers tend to be highly complex, proprietary, and disproportionately expensive.

  NoSQL databases were developed from the ground up to be distributed and scale out databases. They use a cluster of standard, physical, or virtual servers to store data and support database operations. To scale, additional servers are joined to the cluster and the data and database operations are spread across the larger cluster. Because commodity servers are expected to fail from time to time, NoSQL databases are built to tolerate and recover from such failures, making them highly resilient. NoSQL databases provide a much easier and linear approach to database scaling. If 10,000 new users start using your application, simply add another database server to your cluster. To add 10,000 more users, just add another server. There's no need to modify the application as you scale because the application always sees a single (distributed) database. NoSQL databases share some characteristics with respect to scaling and performance.

- *Auto-sharding*—A NoSQL database automatically spreads data across servers without requiring applications to participate. Servers can be added or removed from the data layer without application downtime, with data (and input/output) automatically spread across the servers. Most NoSQL databases also support data replication, storing multiple copies of data across the cluster and even across data centers to ensure high availability and to support disaster recovery. A properly managed NoSQL database system should never need to be taken offline, for any reason, supporting high availability.

- *Distributed query support*—Sharing a relational database can reduce or eliminate in certain cases the ability to perform complex data queries. NoSQL database systems retain their full query expressive power even when distributed across hundreds of servers.
- *Integrated caching*—To reduce latency and increase sustained data throughput, advanced NoSQL database technologies transparently cache data in system memory. This behavior is transparent to the application developer and the operations team, compared to relational technology where a caching tier is usually a separate infrastructure tier that must be developed and deployed on separate servers and explicitly managed by the operations team.

There are some serious flaws on the part of relational databases that get in the way of meeting the unique requirements of modern-day social Web applications, which are gradually moving to reside in cloud infrastructures. Another noteworthy fact is that data analysis for business intelligence is increasingly occurring in clouds. That is, cloud analytics is emerging as a hot topic for diligent and deeper study and investigation. There are groups in academic and industrial circles striving hard to bring the necessary advancements to prop up the traditional databases to cope with the evolving and enigmatic requirements of social networking applications. However, NoSQL and NewSQL databases are the new breeds of versatile, energetic, and respected solutions capturing the imagination and attention of many.

The business need to leverage complex and connected data is driving the adoption of scalable and high-performance NoSQL databases. This new entrant will sharply enhance the data management capabilities of various businesses. Several variants of NoSQL databases have emerged over the past decade to handsomely handle the terabytes, petabytes, and even exabytes of data generated by enterprises and consumers. They are specifically capable of processing multiple data types. That is, NoSQL databases could contain different data types such as text, audio, video, social network feeds, weblogs, and many more that are not being handled by traditional databases. These data are highly complex and deeply interrelated. Therefore the demand is to unravel the truth hidden behind these huge yet diverse data assets besides understanding the insights and acting on them to enable businesses to plan and surge ahead.

Having understood the changing scenario, Web-based businesses have been crafting their own custom NoSQL databases to elegantly manage the increasing data volume and diversity. Amazon's Dynamo and Google's Big Table are shining examples of home-grown databases that can store large amounts of data. These NoSQL databases were designed for handling highly complex and heterogeneous data. The key differentiation here is that they are not built for high-end transactions but for analytic purposes.

4.9 Conclusion

Enterprises squarely and solely depend on a variety of data for their day-to-day functioning. Both historical and operational data have to be meticulously gleaned from different and disparate sources and then cleaned, synchronized, and analyzed in totality to derive actionable insights that in turn empower enterprises to get ahead of their competitors. In the recent past, social computing applications have been delivering a cornucopia of people's data. The brewing need is to seamlessly and spontaneously link enterprise data with social data to enable organizations to be more proactive, preemptive, and people-centric in their decisions, discretions, and dealings. Data stores, bases, warehouses, marts, cubes, and so on are flourishing to congregate and compactly store different data. There are several standardized and simplified tools and platforms for accomplishing data analysis needs. Then there are dashboards, visual report generators, business activity monitoring, and performance management modules to deliver the requested information and knowledge to the authorized persons.

Data integration is an indispensable cog in that long and complex process of transitioning data into information and knowledge.

However, as in the past, data integration is not easy and rosy. There are patterns, products, processes, platforms, and practices galore for smoothening data integration goals. In this chapter, we described the necessity of information architecture for next-generation cloud applications.

References

1. http://www.emc.com/leadership/digital-universe/index.htm.
2. McKinsey Global Institute (June 2011). Big Data: The Next Frontier for Innovation, Competition, and Productivity.
3. Joe Dignan, Nishant Shah, and Fredrik Tunvall (2013). Deriving Insight from Data for Smarter Urban Operations. London: Ovum.
4. http://siliconangle.com/blog/2013/07/09/big-datas-still-on-track-to-save-the-world/.
5. Peter Hinssen. Open Data Power Smart Cities. http://www.datascience series.com.
6. Intel (2012). Intel's Perspective on Data at the Edge (vision paper).
7. IBM Software (2013). Harness the Value of Big Data to Build Smarter Infrastructures (thought leadership white paper).
8. Sathyan Munirathinam and Ramadoss (2014). Big Data Predictive Analtyics for Proactive Semiconductor Equipment Maintenance: A Review. ASE BIG DATA/SOCIALCOM/CYBERSECURITY Conference, Stanford University, May 27–31.
9. Oracle (2011). Big Data for the Enterprise (white paper).
10. Felix J. Villanueva et al. Civitas: The Smart City Middleware, from Sensors to Big Data. Innovative Mobile and Internet Services in Ubiquitous Computing (IMIS-2013), Asia University, Taichung, Taiwan.
11. Kazuaki Iwamura, Hideki Tonooka, Yoshihiro Mizuno, and Yuichi Mashita (2014). Big Data Collection and Utilization for Operational Support of Smarter Social Infrastructure. *Hitachi Review* 63(1): 18–24.
12. Neo Technology (2011). NOSql for the Enterprise (white paper).

5

THE INTERNET OF THINGS FOR CONNECTED AND COGNITIVE CITIES

Abstract

We have been discussing the significant contributions of several proven and promising technologies in ensuring the desired success of smart cities. However, the selection of technologies for establishing intelligent cities has to be made after a careful consideration of multiple factors. Several technologies come and go without contributing anything substantial toward meeting the originally visualized and articulated needs and hence the choice plays a vital role in shaping and strengthening our cities for future challenges and changes. Another noteworthy point is that instead of going for a single technology, it is prudent and pertinent to embrace a cluster of technologies to reach the desired state comfortably. Technology clusters are becoming prominent these days. Especially considering the growing complexity of smart cities (being touted as the system of systems), the need for a collection of technologies is being felt everywhere. Not only the technology-cluster choice but also its appropriate usage is pivotal in achieving the target in a risk-free and relaxed manner. Thus any smart city strategy has to clearly illuminate resilient technologies and methodologies together toward accelerating and attaining the varied goals of smart cities across this vast and vibrant planet. In this chapter, we discuss the immense potential and promise of the newly coined paradigm of the Internet of Things (IoT) in creating next-generation cities that sharply elevate the features, facilities, and functionalities of our crumbling and clogging cities.

5.1 Introduction

The future Internet will comprise not only millions of computing machines, personal/professional electronic devices, and distributed software services but also billions of diminutive sensors, actuators, robots, and so on and finally trillions of sentient or digitized objects. It is overwhelmingly accepted that the fast-emerging and evolving Internet of Things (IoT) idea is definitely a strategic and highly impactful vision to be decisively realized and passionately sustained with the smart adoption and adaptation of state-of-the-art technologies, composite and cognitive processes, optimal and versatile infrastructures, integrated platforms, enabling tools, pioneering patterns, and future-directed architectures. Industry professionals and academicians are constantly looking out for appropriate use, business, and technical cases to confidently and cogently proclaim the transformational value and power of the IoT concept to the larger audience of worldwide executives, end-users, entrepreneurs, enthusiasts, and engineers.

A growing array of open and industry-strength standards are being formulated, framed, and polished by domain experts, industry consortiums, and standard setting bodies to make the IoT concept more visible, viable, and valuable. National governments across the globe are setting up special groups to come out with pragmatic policies and procedures to take forward the solemn ideals of IoT and realize the strategic significance of the envisioned IoT in conceiving and concretizing a bevy of people-centric services to ensure and enhance people's comfort, choice, care, and convenience. Research students, scholars, and scientists are working collaboratively toward identifying the implementation challenges and overcoming them via different ways and means, especially utilizing standard technological solutions.

In this chapter, we aim to give a broader perspective of what exactly is the idea of IoT, as well as trends setting the stimulating stage for IoT realization and demonstration; why it has to be pursued with seriousness and sincerity; what the prickling and prime concerns are; changes and challenges associated with it; where it will be applied extensively and expediently; its near- and long-term future; the key benefits, nightmares, risks; and so on. The dominant theme of this chapter is revealing the usefulness of IoT for shaking up the world's cities to be smart and sustainable.

5.2 Envisioning the IoT Era

As a result of digitization, distribution, and decentralization, there is a renewed focus on realizing a legion of digitized objects, which are termed and touted as sentient materials/smart objects that are being derived from ordinary and everyday objects. Common and casual things are being empowered or modernized to possess certain IT capabilities such as computing, networking, communication, sensing, actuation, and display. Not only computers and electronic devices but also everyday articles and artifacts in our midst are joining in mainstream computing. In short, minimization, integration, federation, consolidation, virtualization, automation, and orchestration technologies are fast maturing toward producing disappearing, disposable, affordable, connected, dependable, people-centric, context-aware devices. These are service-enabled to form high-quality device services. The Web journey as a whole has been very admirable.

The initial Web (Web 1.0) was just for reading (Simple Web), followed by Web 2.0 for not only reading but also writing (Social Web). In addition to its reading and writing functions, Web 3.0 (Semantic Web) links linking multiple Web content, applications, services, and data. The future is definitely Web 4.0 for the envisioned era of knowledge (Smart Web). Thus every important thing in our environments is Web enabled to interact with cloud-based data, applications, services, content, and so on. Further, everything is connected with entities in the vicinity. Cloud infrastructures are being continuously enhanced to be a centralized and core platform for the Smart Web. The future Internet is therefore the IoT.

IoT is all about enabling extreme connectivity among various objects across the industry domains. In this book, we focus on the following themes and titles: the key drivers for the IoT vision, the enabling technologies, infrastructures and platforms, prominent solutions, facilitating frameworks and tools, enabling architectures, business and use cases, concerns and challenges, and so on.

As mentioned previously, a string of promising and positive trends in the IT space have laid a strong and sustainable foundation for the out-of-the-box visualization of the future prospects of the raging IoT idea. In a nutshell, the prevailing trend is all about empowering all kinds of common and casual articles and artifacts in our everyday environments to be IT enabled, networking them in an ad hoc manner using a variety of communication technologies on an as-needed basis to leverage their distinct capabilities individually as well as collectively to decisively and concisely understand the various needs of people in that particular environment, and deciding, disseminating, and delivering the identified services and information unobtrusively to the right people at the right time and at the right place.

5.3 Emerging IoT Trends

5.3.1 Deeper Digitization toward Smart Objects

Every tangible thing is getting digitized with the aim of attaching the much-needed sensing and communication capabilities so that each and every article in our midst is capable of participating in and contributing to mainstream computing. There are multiple ways for empowering ordinary objects to become useful, usable, and extraordinary artifacts. Minuscule tags, stickers, chips, sensors, motes, smart dust, actuators, light-emitting diode (LED) displays, and so on are the most common elements and entities for the speedy, simple, and copious realization of smart objects. As a prime example, we are increasingly and intimately connected to the outside world for outward as well as inward communication through slim, sleek, handy, and trendy smart phones. The ubiquity and utility of multifaceted phones augur positively for the days ahead. In the same way, each and every commonly found item in our environments becomes connected and smart in its operations, outlooks, and outputs. The smartness derived via such internal as well as external enhancements enables them to be elegantly and eminently constructive, cognitive, and contributive.

The maturity and stability of mesh network topology and technologies ensure these empowered and emboldened materials find and bind with other similarly enabled articles (local as well as remote) to leverage their unique functionalities and features to fulfill the varying needs (information, transaction, and physical) of people. Such a longstanding empowerment goes a long way in unearthing a host of nimbler business and IT models and services, fresh possibilities and opportunities for businesses and people, scores of optimization methods for swiftly heading toward the vision of people IT, solid and sharp growth in user experience of diverse business and IT offerings, and so on.

John Hagel and John Seely Brown write that big and marvelous shifts are happening in how things get made from scratch and how hitherto untapped value is being created and aggregated. And digital technologies aren't just impacting production and manufacturing; they're changing the physical world altogether. Our physical world is now technology enabled by the digitization of everything from books to movies to tools such as the flashlights, cameras, calculators, day planners, music players, and bus schedules that now reside on our handhelds and smart phones. The Internet communication infrastructure and digital technologies are the most powerful and path-breaking combination to bring forth big transformations in our physical world.

Owing to a growing litany of praiseworthy improvisations, we have achieved much in the virtual/cyber world. Now is the time to embark on the delayed modernization of the physical world. The principal transition for empowering our physical environments to be smart is to make ordinary things smart. The idea is to meticulously enable dumb things in our daily environments to join in and contribute to mainstream computing.

Already with the maturity of cyber physical system (CPS) technologies, the effective utilization of physical assets and articles is going up steadily. The efficiency of physical machines may be achieved in a number of ways such as improving the "up-time" for a costly machine that has become self-correcting or by renting out excess capacity to external parties to generate new revenue streams.

Digital technology can locate a car and deliver it to us when we need a ride. It matches an individual with a spare bed who is looking for income with an individual in need of a place to stay. It lets us find and modify a design rather than create one and then lets us use a manufacturing-grade tool to execute the design, with limited skill or invested time. The pavement we drive on becomes smarter with sensors that communicate traffic information; heavy earth-moving equipment becomes smarter when sensors monitor tire wear to reduce the risk of down-time. Smart materials can collect and conduct information for the clothing a runner wears or the pipe that water flows through. All of these examples require a degree of human intervention to make them useful and the next step seems to be eliminating the human intervention.

Tech-enabled physical objects are starting to be able to adapt or take action automatically. Think of the anti-skid technology or collision-avoidance features in a car, a set of components communicating with each other and taking action as a result. That type of real-time adjustment and feedback that eliminates or reduces the need for human intervention has begun to extend into larger systems, such as wind turbines and complex machinery interacting within a processing plant. Self-correction and automated load adjustment increase efficiency. There will be far more value unlocked when that information can be fed back to humans for pattern analysis and systematic intervention.

The goal is to pull all of the data back into a human sphere where people can add value. Imagine a beverage company that faces fairly frequent stock-outs that cause customer dissatisfaction and lost sales. A year's worth of data shows that the stock-outs typically occur in conjunction with local and hyper-local events. Now the company has the opportunity not only to track and respond to stock-out situations faster, but also to program the inventory-replenishment system to cross-check with event calendars, weather reports, and Twitter feeds to prepare. Companies' skills in tapping use data will determine the data's value, but the potential is greater than just cost efficiencies.

5.3.2 The Growing Device Ecosystem

The device space is fast evolving (implantable, wearable, mobile, portable, nomadic, fixed, etc.). The rough and tough passage from the mainframe and pervasive PC cultures to trendy and handy portables, handhelds and wearables, disappearing implantable and invisible tags, stickers, labels, chips, and versatile mobiles subtly and succinctly conveys the quiet and ubiquitous transition from the centralization to the decentralization mode. This positive and path-breaking trend, however, brings the difficult and dodging issues of heterogeneity, multiplicity, and incompatibility. That is, all kinds of participating and contributing devices, machines, instruments, and electronics in our personal as well as professional environments need to be individually as well as collectively intelligent enough to discover one another, link, access, and use to be competent and distinctive to accomplish bigger and better things for humans. The end result is that constructing and managing cross-institutional and functional applications in this sort of dynamic, disparate, decentralized, and distributed environments is laced with a few unpredictable possibilities. That is, there are chances for risky interactions among varied services, sensors, and systems, resulting in severe complications and unwanted implications for the safety and security of human society. Also it is envisioned that future spaces will be highly digitized environments with a fabulous collection of digital devices and digitized artifacts, each distinct in its face, features, and functionality.

This compendium of devices will be increasingly interlinked to local networks as well as the global network transparently. With this sophisticated yet complicated scenario brewing silently and strongly, it is logical to think about the ways and means of ably and adaptively utilizing, managing, and extracting their inherent capabilities (specific as well as generic) and capacities for arriving at a horde of people-centric, pioneering, and premium services. As we are keenly waiting for the paradigm of "computing everywhere every time" to cherish and flourish, it is imperative to nourish and nudge any variety of participating devices to be extremely agile and adaptive and to empower them to proactively, preemptively, and purposefully collaborate, correlate, and corroborate to figure out the user(s)' contextual needs by dynamically connecting, complementing, and sharing the dynamic resources with one another accordingly and unobtrusively. At the other end, there are a wider variety of input and output devices such as tablets and smartphones to assist people to finish their personal as well as professional assignments effectively and efficiently. That is, devices are becoming device ensembles and clusters through internal as well as external integration.

To summarize, there are a wider variety of machines, appliances, consumer electronics, instruments, smartphones, tablets, notebook computers, sophisticated specific as well as generic robots, personal yet compact and multipurpose gadgets and gizmos, kitchen utensils, and so on. On the other side, there are resource-constrained, low-cost, low-power, yet multifaceted, smart, and semantic elements and entities such as miniaturized yet multifunctional sensors, actuators, microcontrollers, stickers, tags, and so on. The real beauty here is that all of these are getting connected with other objects in their vicinity as well as with remote cloud platforms and infrastructures.

5.3.2.1 Machine-to-Machine (M2M) Integration   The pervasiveness of ultra-high communication (wired as well as wireless) technologies facilitates the important and long-standing goal of enabling devices to interact with one another seamlessly and spontaneously to share their potentials. The communication field is going through a stream of praiseworthy transformations. There are new paradigms such as autonomic, unified, and ambient communication. A number of highly beneficial communication features and models have emerged with the maturity and stability of adaptive communication platforms and infrastructures. Even business processes are tightly coupled with communication capabilities so that more intimate and intensive processes are bound to erupt and evolve quickly toward the neat and nice fulfillment of peoples' aspirations.

This newly found ad hoc connectivity capability among a large number of devices ranging from invisible and infinitesimal tags, smart dust, stickers, and sparkles in our daily environments to highly sophisticated machines on manufacturing floors and in hospitals has resulted in a series of people-centric and premium applications and services. Several industrial domains are very optimistic and looking forward for this paradigm shift in conceptualizing and concretizing a growing array of creative and cognitive applications for their user community. Telecommunication service providers are the vital partners for the unprecedented and inhibited success of device-to-device (D2D) integration. A bevy of next-generation applications are being conceived and constructed based on this grand transformation brought about by D2D integration, as illustrated in Figure 5.1.

A number of noteworthy use and business cases are increasing the popularity of M2M communication. The prominent ones among them include home integration solutions (proprietary as well as standardized) that are abundant these days to simplify and streamline the rough and

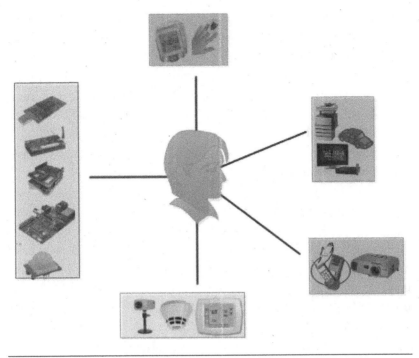

Figure 5.1 Multidevice assistance for humans.

tough tasks associated with home networking and automation. This has led to innumerable smart or intelligent homes, at least in advanced countries. Again, smart metering of all the modules and devices of electricity grids results in scores of smart grids across the globe. Seamless communication among the various components of classic cars has resulted in connected or smart cars. This goes on and on. Fueled by such abundant enthusiasm and optimism among product and platform vendors, telecom companies, IT service providers, system integrators (SIs), government departments, standard bodies, research labs in academic institutions and business organizations, the idea of deeper and extreme connectivity among all kinds of devices of varying sizes, scopes, and structures will produce a multitude of robust and resilient services.

5.3.3 Software-Defined Cloud Infrastructures

5.3.3.1 Cloud-Enabled Embedded Applications As we all know, the much-dissected and discoursed cloud paradigm has laid a stimulating and sound foundation for compactly fulfilling the grand vision of

IT infrastructure optimization through a seamless synchronization of several proven, enterprise-scale and mission-critical technologies such as virtualization, grid, on-demand, utility, autonomic computing models, service orientation, multi-tenancy, and so on. This groundbreaking evolution and elevation in the IT field has brought in innumerable and insightful impacts on business as well as IT domains these days. Clouds are being positioned and proclaimed as the highly consolidated, converged, virtualized, shared, and automated IT environments for hosting and compactly delivering a galaxy of diverse IT solutions and business services. The cloud technology ensures anytime, anywhere, any device information and service access and leverage. The much anticipated ubiquitous service delivery is being fully facilitated with the arrival, articulation, and adoption of the powerful cloud idea. That is, all kinds of services, applications, and data are now being modernized accordingly and adroitly migrated to cloud platforms and infrastructures to reap all the originally envisioned benefits (technical, user, and business cases).

The cloud paradigm has become a versatile IT phenomenon and a fabulous fertile ground that have inspired the development of a number of newer cloud-centric services, products, and platforms that facilitate scores of people-centric, multifaceted, and rich cloud applications to reach a multitude in this connected world. In addition, there have been a variety of generic as well as specific innovations in the form of pragmatic processes, patterns, best practices, key guidelines, metrics, and so on for moderating the rising IT complexity, for enhancing IT agility, autonomy, and affordability and for heightened IT productivity. All the instinctive improvisations happening in the IT landscape with the smart adaptation of the robust and resilient cloud model are directly helping out worldwide business enterprises to achieve the venerable mission of "more with less." Thus cloud as the core, central, inexpensive, and cognitive infrastructure for implicitly taking care of all kinds of business changes, concerns, and challenges portends a brighter and more profitable future for business organizations to surge ahead and keep the edge earned in their offerings, outputs, and outlooks.

With a legion of resource-constrained, embedded, and networked devices joining the IT landscape and with the seamless synchronization with the remote, on-demand, and elastic clouds (generic clouds such as public, private and community or specific clouds such as storage, knowledge, science, data, sensor, device, and mobile), there abound hordes of real-time and sophisticated applications and services.

5.3.3.2 Cloud Infrastructures for Real-Time Big Data Analytics   Today the most visible and valuable trend is nonetheless the unprecedented data explosion in every business domain. As machines and sensors are pervasively deployed and effectively used and managed for a variety of requirements in our everyday environments, machine-generated data are much larger than human-generated data. That is, the data volume is exponentially growing with a number of remarkable advancements in the field of sensors, actuators, robots, connectivity, service enablement, and so on. Embedded systems getting networked locally as well as remotely are the newer attractions. Further, with the data formats ranging from nonstructured to semistructured and to structured style, there are pressures to unearth fresh database modeling and management systems such as Not only Structured Query Language (NoSQL) databases and Hadoop distributed file systems (HDFSs) to swiftly capture, store, and search large-scale and multistructured data and to extract actionable insights without much pain. Besides the volume and the variety, data velocity is another critical factor to be considered very carefully to derive and deduce usable intelligence and to contemplate the next course of action in time with full clarity and confidence. Precisely speaking, big data is all about the three data Vs: volume, variety, and velocity. The traditional data management systems find it difficult to manage terabytes and petabytes of data and hence different NoSQL databases have become very popular to handle voluminous databases with ease.

Besides big data storage and management, big data analytics (BDAs) has become an important phenomenon that cannot be sidestepped at any cost as data across cloud, social, device, mobile, and enterprise spaces need to be comprehensively identified and aggregated, subjected to powerful data mining, processing, and analysis tasks through well-defined policies dynamically and disseminated promptly to be highly beneficial for businesses, governments, financial institutions, and for firms involved in digital marketing, security and retail intelligence, high-performance science and healthcare research, quick customer on-boarding, and so on. The widely used Hadoop implementations, commodity servers, specific data appliances, and so on are the predominant methods being effectively handpicked and handled to accommodate terabytes and even petabytes of incongruent data and to empower executives, entrepreneurs, and engineers to make informed decisions in time and to plan pragmatic action plans with alacrity. With the sustained eruption of inventive technologies, the data architecture for new-generation enterprises will go through a tectonic and meteoric shift. Leading market watchers predict that big data management and intelligence will become common and casual along with the already established data management solutions.

Leading infrastructure solution providers such as IBM, Amazon, HP, Google, and other niche providers (Oracle, SAP, etc.) have developed high-performing and assuring cloud platforms and appliances to accomplish BDA. Thus clouds are filled with numerous integrated platforms for analytics, a growing array of cloud-native software services for multifaceted devices, cloud-enabled enterprise applications, and so on signaling the onset of the IoT era. Clouds will be the marketplace and hosting different repositories of services and data to be easily discovered and used for the ultimate empowerment of devices and people.

5.3.3.3 Cloud Infrastructures for Smart Phone Services   Every application is mobile enabled to allow distributed applications to be accessed and used at vehicular speed. Mobile interfacing is being mandated widely. A number of mobile technologies and tools are facilitating leverage of all kinds of application while on the move. With the explosion of smart phones and tablets, every kind of cloud and enterprise applications is being provided with mobile interfacing. Several operating systems such as Android, iOS, Windows Phones, BlackBerry OS, and so on are available for powering up smart phones and mobile clouds (e.g., iCloud is the mobile cloud for iOS phones, tablets, etc.) are being set up to host and store all kinds of smart phone services, multistructured data, and so on. That is, cloud connectivity is essential for phones to be relevant for users. In short, an integrated network of disparate and distributed resources, assets, and articles is the principal need for the smart world.

5.3.3.4 Device-to-Cloud (D2C) Integration   Different types of devices and digitized objects via multiple types of networks can communicate with a variety of locally as well as remotely deployed applications. The Internet is the global-scale open, public, and affordable communication infrastructure. These applications may have multiple interfaces. A backhaul network, the communication backbone of the Internet infrastructure, is an essential ingredient in enforcing and ensuring devices at the ground level to talk to different applications at cloud-enabled data centers (CeDCs), the new kind of software-defined data centers.

The iDigi Device Cloud (http://www.idigi.com/) is an infrastructure service designed to empower different devices and their networks. The iDigi Device Cloud solves the challenges of massive scalability and service reliability while meeting the requirements for utmost security and privacy. The iDigi Connector is also regarded as the appropriate bridge for integrating client's applications with the iDigi Device Cloud. The cloud paradigm has grown enormously, with an incredible number of applications in several business domains. Specific cloud infrastructures are emerging. That is, we often hear about sensor cloud, device cloud, knowledge cloud, mobile cloud, science cloud, and so on. The pervasiveness and popularity of cloud technology is surging ahead with enhanced awareness about its strategic contributions for the whole of humanity.

5.3.3.5 Cloud-to-Cloud (C2C) Integration Several types of cloud service providers (CSPs) are leveraging diverse technologies delivering different business-centric services. Because of the enhanced complexity and heterogeneity, the goal of cloud interoperability has become a difficult challenge for cloud services and application developers. Cloud brokers, procurers, and auditors are therefore emerging and joining in the already complicated cloud ecosystem. Even cloud consumers are afraid of the vendor lock-in issue as manifold barriers are being erected around cloud infrastructures and platforms. A couple of well-known trends are gripping the cloud landscape. First, geographically distributed and differentiating clouds are being established and sustained.

Second, institutions, individuals, and innovators are eyeing cloud software, platforms, and infrastructures for reaping the originally postulated and pronounced benefits. That is, the same services are being provided by multiple providers with different service-level agreements and operation-level agreements. Incidentally, business processes that span several clouds and services of multiple clouds need to be found, bound, and aggregated to build composite data, services, processes, and applications. All of these clearly attest to the urgent need for competent federation techniques, standards, patterns, platforms, and best practices for a global network of clouds.

Intra- as well as interenterprise integration has to occur via cloud integration services and solutions. Service organizations and system integrators are embarking on a new fruitful journey as cloud broker-ages to smooth the rough edges so that distinct and distributed clouds can be identified and integrated seamlessly and spontaneously to work collaboratively to achieve bigger and better things. Cloud service brokers (CSBs) are a kind of new software solution for cloud data, service, application, and process integration.

5.3.3.6 Sensor-to-Cloud (S2C) Integration   Sensors and actuators are found in many environments these days for different purposes. A sensor network is a group of specialized transducers to monitor and record conditions at diverse locations. Commonly monitored parameters are temperature, humidity, pressure, wind direction and speed, illumination, vibration and sound intensities, power-line voltage, chemical concentrations, pollutant levels, and vital body functions. Every sensor node is equipped with a transducer, microcomputer, transceiver, and power source. The transducer generates electrical signals based on sensed physical effects and phenomena. The microcomputer processes and stores the sensor output. The transceiver, which can be hard-wired or wireless, receives commands from a central computer and transmits data to that computer. The power for each sensor node is derived from the electric utility or from a battery. Potential applications of sensor networks include industrial automation, automated and smart homes, video surveillance, traffic monitoring, medical device monitoring, monitoring of weather conditions, air traffic control, and robot control.

As indicated previously, every empowered entity in our environment is further strengthened by being integrated with local IT and remote cloud IT. As sensors are being prescribed as the eyes and ears of the digital world of the future, sensor networking with nearby sensors as well as with far-off applications needs to be facilitated. There are frameworks and middleware platforms for enabling ad hoc networking of diverse sensors within themselves as well as with distant software components.

In the past few years, wireless sensor networks (WSNs) have been gaining significant traction because of their potential for enabling very intimate and interesting solutions in areas such as smart homes, industrial automation, environmental monitoring, transportation, healthcare, and agriculture. The tremendous progress in WSN design fosters their increasingly widespread usage and leading to growth in both number of nodes per deployment and infrastructure complexity. Today, a city-scale WSN deployment is no longer a novelty. This trendy phenomenon generates lots of data of different types that have to be synchronized, interpreted, adapted for specific needs, interconnected with other data, and/or distinguished in service and application data. If we add a collection of sensor-derived data to various social networks or virtual communities, blogs, musings, and so on, then there will be fabulous transitions in and around us. With the faster adoption of micro- and nanotechnologies, everyday things are destined to become digitally empowered to be distinctive in their actions and reactions. Thus the impending goal is to seamlessly link digitized objects/sentient materials at our environments; other frequently used and handled devices such as consumer electronics, kitchen utensils and containers, household instruments and items; portable, nomadic, and mobile gadgets and gizmos; and so on with remote cloud-based applications via federated messaging middleware. That is, cyber systems are being inundated with streams of data and messages from different and distributed physical elements and entities. Such an extreme and deeper connectivity and collaboration will pump up and sustain cool, classic, and catalytic situation-aware applications.

Clouds have emerged as the centralized, compact, and capable IT infrastructure to deliver people-centric and context-aware services to users with all the desired qualities embedded. This long-term vision demands a comprehensive connectivity between clouds and the billions of minuscule sensing systems.

5.3.4 Big Data Analytics

We discussed this field and its continued impact extensively in Chapter 4. The gist of the matter is how easily and quickly you can transition your data heaps into information and then to knowledge. Any organization that has the innate capacity and capability to extract rightful and right insights is bound to grow and prosper immensely. There are BDA platforms, processes, practices, patterns, and products aplenty to facilitate the hard task of knowledge engineering.

Thus several positive and progressive indications in the hot field of IT are erupting and evolving quickly to spruce up the changing and challenging situations and needs of people. For the knowledge world, the role of BDA is immense and imminent to transform data swiftly into information and into usage knowledge.

5.4 The IoT Reference Architecture

The IoT idea has been making waves these days. Every allied discipline is consciously contributing toward the realization of the IoT vision. It is all about realizing smart objects and enabling them to talk to one another on an as-needed basis to create value for humans in their daily chores. There are exceptional advancements in edge and embedded computing fields. Communication is becoming unified, ambient, and autonomic. Lean communication protocols and stacks and other lightweight network components (switches, routers, modems, application delivery controllers [ADCs], load balancers, network gateways, etc.) are being readied and refined toward digitized objects to find and interact with one another smoothly.

In short, the shining and strategic IoT concept is making the Internet even more immersive and pervasive. By enabling ubiquitous access and interaction with a wider variety of devices such as home appliances, surveillance cameras, monitoring sensors, actuators, displays, terminals, vehicles, and so on, the IoT field is poised to foster the development and deployment of a number of hitherto unseen people-centric applications that implicitly make use of the potentially enormous amount of data. Every sector is bound to go through IoT-inspired disruptive and innovative transformations to facilitate the goals of home and industrial automation, smart healthcare, intelligent energy management, traffic management, smart cars, and so on.

The game-changing IoT domain is innately capable of bringing a number of benefits in the management and optimization of public services such as transport and parking, lighting, surveillance and maintenance of public areas, preservation of cultural heritage, water and energy management, safety of people and public assets, garbage collection, and promoting salubrious hospitals and schools. Further, the ready availability of different types of data emitted by pervasive sensors and actuators and the real-time knowledge extraction capability go hand in hand in bringing about the much-required transparency in public administration, greater responsibility among government officials, and so on. Better and fool-proof service delivery systems can be in place, the co-creation of newer services and outside-in thinking will flourish, there will be a timely awareness of city facilities and events, and so on. Therefore, the IoT paradigm is a huge booster to establish and sustain smart cities.

Building a general architecture for the IoT is hence a very complex task, mainly because of the extremely large variety of devices, link layer technologies, and services that may be involved in such a system as described in Figure 5.2.

The architecture shown in Figure 5.2 primarily comprises the following components.

- *Information capture.* To have context-aware applications, it is prudent and profoundly true that all kinds of situation/ scenario information has to be gleaned. As explained previously, our everyday environments are being filled with scores of digitized entitles, sensors and actuators, instrumented electronics, smart objects, connected devices, information appliances, cyber physical systems, network gateways, communication elements, and so on. These elegantly contribute to information capture about their environments and occurrences therein. Sensors powerful enough to interconnect and interact

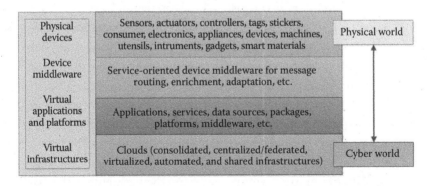

Figure 5.2 Reference architecture for the IoT.

with one another are being used to monitor continuously a person's physiological activities [1] and actions such as health status and motion patterns. Infinitesimal tags, codes, and specks are being overwhelmingly utilized for monitoring and collecting crucial information about various activities in a particular place and sending them to central systems for precise and decisive analysis toward engineering actionable insights.

- *Information delivery.* Today we have a variety of communication technologies and network topologies to carry forward all sorts of collected information. There are sensor networks, body area networks, car area networks, home networks, campus area networks, and so on. There are 3G and 4G communication technologies flourishing across the world. It is anticipated that by 2020, we will have full-fledged 5G technologies and their infrastructures in place to meet rising bandwidth requirements. Bandwidth on demand, video on demand, ambient communication, and ad hoc networks are some of the often heard terms in securely delivering information to different destinations without any compromise.

- *Information processing.* With the emergence of powerful and standards-complying data analytics platforms, frameworks, and tools, the analytics domain is bound to grow substantially. In the case of big data, any Hadoop implementation could filter out routine data to bring forth value-adding information. That is, transitioning multistructured data into structured form so that the stabilized analytical systems such as data warehouses, cubes, and marts can proceed toward fine-grained analytics is the gist of Hadoop technology. There are powerful, optimized, bundled, and purpose-specific appliances for data analytics. Real-time and streaming analytics are also maturing quickly to provide real-time analytics for certain use cases. There are pioneering algorithms toward predictive and prescriptive analytics. Further, information visualization solutions will disseminate any extracted and extrapolated knowledge to the respective users. Thus data crunching, information processing, and knowledge discovery are being simplified with noteworthy advancements in the hot IT field.

- *Smarter applications.* The transition from data to information and knowledge is being facilitated through a plethora of automation and acceleration technologies. There are widespread improvements in effective data integration, virtualization, synchronization, and polishing toward knowledge engineering. Once knowledge is created, it is corroborated, correlated, and then conveyed to appropriate software applications to exhibit the much-wanted smarter behavior.

Thus automated data capture and interpretation resulting in actionable intelligence goes a long way in empowering software applications to be distinct in their operations, offerings, and outputs.

5.4.1 Smart City Communication Architecture

The traditional Internet interconnects various compute machines through a relatively simple network architecture. Today all kinds of professional and personal devices are joining the Internet. For smart cities, all kinds of physical and digital artifacts need to be integrated with the Web and hence an additional layer for sensing is required. This brings many new requirements and challenges as well.

- *Object sensing layer.* Increasingly commonly found, casual and cheap articles are getting the relevant computational, communicating, sensing, perception, decision-making, actuation, and so on from the lavish usage of low-cost, low-power, short-range and low-memory sensors, controllers, and other edge technologies. Robust and resilient network topologies and communication technologies are in place to seamlessly connect these empowered artifacts.
- *Service construction layer.* This layer is for service building purpose. Services are being built afresh from the ground up or can be picked from public and private service repositories to assemble the chosen services to come out with people-centric services. There are generic as well as specific services. There are enterprise, embedded, cloud, mobile, social, and IT services. Based on the data being provided by sensors and actuators, distinctive services can be produced dynamically in runtime

and given to the right set of people. Services are registered and deposited in service repositories.

- *Service delivery layer.* Services being produced need to be delivered as per changing requirements and scenarios. There are service delivery platforms (SDPs) to facilitate service delivery in the right measure to the right person at the right time and location. SDPs pick up services from the local as well as remote service repositories to package them in an appropriate form to be delivered to service requestors. Enterprise service bus (ESB) is the principal service discovery, aggregation, dissemination, intermediation, arbitration, acceleration, security, and optimization solution.

- *Service brokerage layer.* There are several service providers offering the same service with different quality parameters. Service brokerage firms are helping service consumers identify the appropriate service providers and facilitating the establishment of integrating service providers with users. All kinds of specific requirements are being accomplished through the brokers. In a smart city environment, individuals need a variety of city-specific services. There are information portals, government agencies, service integrators, cloud brokers, and so on to enable people with specific services in time in a cost-effective fashion.

Further, there are other layers such as application layer, process layer, application programming, and user interfaces to complete the total stack.

5.4.2 Network Architectures for IoT Applications

By 2050, 70% of the world's population (projected to exceed 6 billion people) is expected to live in cities and outskirts. To survive as the most compact platform enabling economic, social, and environmental well-being, the world's cities and their people-centric services such as administration, education, healthcare, safety, transport, and utilities need to be innately smart. All the city's connectivity, social, physical, and cyber infrastructures need to be hugely sensitive and responsive. In this section, we discuss how the newly arrived and radically benefiting IoT domain will be a solidly contributing partner in establishing and elevating our cities. The IoT, which is a mesmerizing evolution of the current Internet into a dynamic network of digitized objects that have the capability to contribute mainstream computing and communication, is definitely a key differentiator in realizing connected, integrated, and automated cities [2].

It is well known that the IoT networking environment is strongly characterized by multiple network architectures featuring many distinctive applications. Very broadly, network traffic can be categorized into two classes. The first is the high-throughput and delay-tolerant elastic traffic and the second is high-bandwidth and delay-sensitive inelastic (real-time) traffic.

5.4.3 IP-Based Connectivity Models

Typically IoT is an extension of the current Internet and hence the time-tested and proven IP architecture is going to be the prime and prominent connectivity model for the envisaged growth and success of IoT as well. The propensity toward the IP architecture is due to the fact that there is an inherent interoperability among various devices and communication technologies. That is, even resource-constrained embedded devices, implantable, wearables, handhelds, and smart objects are clinically interconnected through this stable, scalable, and manageable IP connectivity model. Figure 5.3 explains the two kinds of access: direct and indirect access.

The authors have defined five types of network architectures for the smart city domain.

- *Autonomous network architecture.* Figure 5.3a illustrates the connectivity model of autonomous networks. Internet access can be made possible via a gateway. While designing autonomous

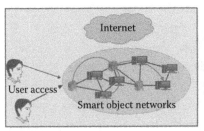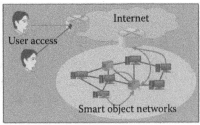

Figure 5.3 Direct access and indirect access.

networks, the IP protocol suite is still commonly adopted because of its scalability and flexibility. With the adoption of the IPv6 stack, a large address space has become available.

A sample application for this kind of network architecture is automatic parking management. We have detailed this use case in the section on IoT application domains.

• *Ubiquitous network architecture.* For ubiquitous networks, Figure 5.3b is the connectivity model, where smart object networks are a part of the Internet. Via the Internet gateway, any authorized users will have access to the information provided by smart object networks, either fetching directly from the device or by means of intermediaries. The network architecture is hierarchical, comprising both wireless multiaccess networks and wireless multihop networks. Wireless multitop networks could be in the form of wireless sensor networks or vehicular ad hoc networks. It is possible to have multiradio applications as there are a number of radio access technologies available to connect to the Internet.

On the application front, there are several applications brewing using this network architecture. A prominent application is the structure-health monitoring fully leveraging the advancements in the field of wireless sensor networking (WSN). Similarly traffic congestion and impact monitoring is another interesting one. We have given sufficient details in the ensuing section.

• *Application-layer overlay network architecture.* The most common operation of any IoT application is to collect a large amount of data from hundreds of thousands of nodes in the physical environments. Because of the data flow from anything to any other thing, traffic congestion is the most problematic point here. Energy consumption is relatively high here because of the multiplicity of participating elements. Therefore a viable alternative is to go for in-network data processing. That is, data aggregation and fusion for squeezing hidden information, policy-based feature extraction, and other data analytics can be accomplished within the network itself instead of transmitting all of the collected data to remote systems for further processing, mining, and analysis. This phenomenon considerably reduces the amount of data getting transmitted over networks. With the unprecedented advancements in the network virtualization technology, a kind of application-layer overlay network of selected nodes can be formed for this task.

The well-known application for this network architecture is the compressive sensing for environmental monitoring. By deploying a variety of environment-specific sensors across a city, a number of decision-enabling city parameters without clogging communication networks can be captured readily to enable officials to plan and execute things meticulously. Owing to the rapid urbanization and the transition toward digital living, several people-centric services can be accomplished. In particular, air quality can be determined, environmental sustainability can be guaranteed, traffic can be regulated, people security and property safety can be ensured, and so forth.

- *Service-oriented network architecture.* The fundamental and foundational point of the IoT concept is that every tangible thing gets interconnected and service enabled. Even fresh devices are instrumented to be inoperable. Therefore for the widespread leverage and usage of the IoT services, besides the elimination of all kinds of dependencies, the multiplicity- and heterogeneity-introduced complexities need to be identified and eliminated through competent technologies. Service-oriented architecture (SOA) has been a guiding factor here to bring in a sense of clarity and complexity mitigation. This generic architecture has pervaded every domain and today there are several architectural patterns such as service-oriented device architecture (SODA), service-oriented network architecture (SONA), and so on. Everything is being expressed and exposed as a service by hiding the underlying infrastructure.

As per the authors, the application of combined noise mapping and video monitoring is in the forefront for the SONA. The well-known implications of this application are enhanced health, well-being, and quality of life as this SONA-based IoT application is capable of providing enough tips to council members for effectively managing noise and its effects. A reliable system for measuring, monitoring, and responding to noise issues is the strong motivation for developing and sustaining an acoustic sensor network. A video sensor network can integrate image processing, computer vision, and networking to do dynamic scene analysis. Surveillance helps track a person, identify suspicious activities, and detect missed luggage and unauthorized access. With the coexistence of acoustic sensor network and video sensor network, there can be more powerful orchestrated applications for users.

- *Participatory sensing.* This is a new concept powerfully emerging in the IoT realm. It is similar to the widespread crowdsourcing idea, which is seeing huge popularity with the runaway success of social sites and digital knowledge societies. Here too, people, rather than deployed sensors, take the responsibility of collecting, analyzing, and sharing sensor data. The unique "human-as-a-sensor" feature of participatory sensing dictates certain network architectures. As human behaviors are highly mobile, erratic, and unpredictable, the most common network architecture is one in which participants connect to a central server directly via reliable wireless technologies such as Wi-Fi, GPRS, or 3G/4G instead of relying on other users as relay nodes. Therefore, unlike ad hoc, mesh, or traditional sensor networks, the interaction between users will have to be intermediated by a central entity. In a certain confined spatial-temporal context (e.g., a conference), where a certain group of people rendezvous for a prescheduled period, a clique (or multiple cliques) could be formed and a cluster-based architecture be applied. Because of the common interest of the participants, most message exchanges would be intracluster only. Thus, a cluster-based structure would be more cost efficient and save substantial bandwidth and energy resources.

The applications of participatory sensing broadly range from environmental monitoring to transportation and from healthcare to lifestyle, among many others. With the vast penetration of smart phones, such emergences will play a significant role in the process of creating a smart city.

To capture the vagaries of IoT-enabled smart city applications, competent and adaptive network architectures are mandatory. The preceding section clearly depicted all the possible network architecture options to be smartly clustered to come out with sophisticated city applications.

5.5 Prominent IoT Technologies

Technologies are coming and going. Many have arrived with much fanfare but could not survive the onslaughts and faded away into thin air silently without making any substantial contributions for human society. Some have withstood time because of their inherent strengths and copious contributions toward business augmentation, acceleration, and automation. In this section, readers can find a number of influential technologies for IoT realization.

- *Computing paradigms*—service, social, cluster, grid, on-demand, utility, mobile, autonomic, trustworthy, green, cloud, and big data computing
- *Communication technologies*—unified, ambient, and autonomic communication models providing standards-compliant 3G, 4G, and 5G communication capabilities
- *Context-aware technologies*—sensing, vision, perception, and actuation technologies
- *Middleware technologies*—integration, intermediation, aggregation, fusion, federation, transformation, arbitration, enrichment, and composition technologies
- *Digitization and edge technologies*—tags, stickers, smart dust, motes, LED, microcontrollers, invisible sensors, and so on
- *Miniaturization technologies*—micro- and nanoscale electronics product design technologies
- *Knowledge engineering technologies*—semantic, event capturing and processing, data mining, processing, analytical, and dissemination technologies
- *Interface technologies*—natural and adaptive, intuitive, and informative interfacing technologies

The good news is that there are several powerful, proven, potential, and promising technologies erupting rapidly to facilitate the right tasks. These days, technologies co-mingle to form technology clusters to fulfill hard-to-crack problems. The much-discussed and dissected cloud technology actually represents a smart collection of several enterprise-scale, mission-critical, and accomplished technologies. That is, the prevailing trend is to leverage potential technologies individually or collectively.

With the commendable advancements in infrastructure optimization, process excellence, state-of-the-art platforms (development, debugging, administration, management, and delivery), and architecture flexibility, the right technologies need to be understood and used rightfully to realize the IoT vision. The IoT concept represents the future Internet, whose capability and complexity are bound to significantly, seamlessly, and spontaneously network heterogeneous and tangible things including physical, mechanical, electrical, and electronics systems across the globe. There are many names such as the Internet of Everything (IoE) (promoted by Cisco), the Industrial Internet (GE), the Internet of Important Things, and so on. All the Internet-centric technologies are bound to converge to emit out spectacular and scintillating applications for mankind. The bountiful and beautiful result is a strategically sound synchronization between the physical and the virtual worlds. Digitization is bound to impact each and every thing in this world.

5.6 The IoT: The Key Results

The resultant applications are a string of intelligent and interactive workspaces and smart environments such as smart or aware homes and offices. For example, Japan Railways (JRs) is planning to set up smart railway stations to enhance the convenience, choice, comfort, and freedom of travelers. A smart environment typically comprises a fluctuating array of infinitesimal electronic gizmos that can perceive the context, act, and react based on the events in it. Further, they achieve seamless mobility, interoperability, and connectivity among the participating devices of the environment. In addition, the stationed and positioned devices can connect and collaborate with any other devices entering the environment by forming small-scale ad hoc networks.

Therefore hitherto unknown and unforeseen applications and services through a judicious mix of shrewd systems and sensors can be created dynamically in real time and granted to any user on demand. The special characteristics of these devices are self-organizing, self-adapting, self-repairing, self-optimizing, self-configuring, and self-recovering. Precisely speaking, they can be able to bounce back to the original state if there is any kind of serious obstructions, disturbances, and disasters, and are capable of forming insightful wireless ad hoc networks with others in the vicinity automatically and seamlessly. Other critical assets and artifacts are various types of high-end server systems and security and storage clusters; other primary components in intelligent zones include smart labels, pads, tags, stickers, dots, motes, dust, and so on. IDC has come out with the following opportunities for businesses in the years ahead.

- *New business models*—The IoT will help companies create new value streams for customers, speed time to market, and respond more rapidly to customer needs.
- *Real-time information on mission-critical systems*—Enterprises can capture more data about processes and products more quickly and radically improve market agility.
- *Diversification of revenue streams*—The IoT can help companies monetize additional services on top of traditional lines of business.
- *Global visibility*—The IoT will make it easier for enterprises to see inside the business, including tracking from one end of the supply chain to the other, which can lower the cost of doing business in far-flung locales.
- *Efficient, intelligent operations*—Access to information from autonomous endpoints will allow organizations to make on-the-fly decisions on pricing, logistics, and sales and support deployment.

Precisely speaking, the extreme connectivity of important things will bring paradigm shift in the way people live, work, interact, think, decide, act, and react. Viable and venerable business models need to be worked out to enable product vendors, IT and telecommunication services providers, cloud integrators, end-users, and national governments to team up together for the knowledge era.

5.7 The Advantages of the IoT Concept for Smart Cities

With the growing stability and maturity of IoT and M2M standards, reference architectures, toolsets, platforms, and infrastructures, inspired innovators, individuals, and institutions could bring forth a number of unique use cases for championing and sustaining the IoT technology campaign [3]. In short, as with the continued emergence and evolution of fresh technologies, newer benefits arise continuously and city dwellers are getting newer enablement and empowerment [4] in their everyday lives with the correct and cognitive usage of technologies. At a macro level, the following advancements are being expected from the revolutionary and raging IoT idea.

1. *Optimized systems.* Optimization has been the primary goal for any system to ensure enhanced efficacy. Powerful technologies enable an optimal sharing of various resources that are becoming scarce. That is, there will be a shared usage of city resources through a plethora of technology empowerments. Cities will see a climb in developing and deploying pioneering IoT applications that will tell us when, where, what, and how to use resources for their preservation and productivity. It is estimated that major cities waste up to 50% of water due to leaky pipes. Similarly there are several other well-known and everyday scenarios. For example, irrigation systems run when it is raining, street lights remain on during daytime, and so on. As explained previously, sensor-attached devices are being increasingly hooked up with cloud services so that they can be locally as well as remotely monitored minutely and activated adeptly. Thus smart sensors enable all kinds of systems to be intelligent, and thereby a variety of automation, simplification, rationalization, and complexity mitigation needs in peoples' lives are easily fulfilled through the incorporation of the IoT's advanced features and functionalities.

2. *Service-enabled and connected systems.* All kinds of devices including resource-constrained ones in our midst will undergo radical transformations with the smart leverage of the proven and potential IoT principles, patterns, and platforms. Every

single object is endowed with a service application programming interface (API) and hence all other artifacts could find, match, and use their unique offerings. Thus connectivity and service enablement are the two prime parameters for all kinds of "dumb" items to be active, articulative, adaptive, participative, and contributive.

For instance, public transportation could work better with the apt usage of IoT-provided features, a growing array of vehicle-centric cloud-based services, and the very recent phenomenon of BDA. Transport operators and control centers can get a 360-degree view of the traffic movement, the whereabouts of vehicles, and other related information in real time. Predictive analytics go a long way in establishing predictive maintenance of transports. Connected systems can supply all sorts of decision-enabling information such as ticket sales, peak hours or seasons, busy junctions, and so on to facilitate the introduction of user-centric and premium service offerings. With the pervasiveness and persuasiveness of smart phones, bus users can save time by having the visuals of the exact location, speed, and occupancy of the buses on their mobile phones. Bus operators can generate newer revenues through location-based advertising and services.

3. *Self-, surroundings-, and situation-aware systems.* Every digitally empowered device is capable of knowing its identity and neighbors explicitly. That is, when a system on its own or in synchronization with others is context aware, then people can easily get context-sensitive services.

4. *People-centric systems: The IoT-inspired capabilities for enhanced care, comfort, choice, and convenience.* We have written about these factors and facets extensively in other chapters. Ambient assisted living (AAL) is one prominent use case. Air conditioners adjust per the users' requirements, washing machines set up the washing level as per the dresses' states and needs, and so on. Residents can monitor the pollution concentration in each street of the city or can get an automatic alarm when the radiation level rises above the threshold in an emergency environment.

5.7.1 The Co-Creation of IoT-Enabled Services for Smarter Cities

Vicini et al. [5] have clearly elucidated the needs and the ways of co-creating technology-stimulated services that are people-aware and -centric. Especially as the IoT idea is transitioning from the conceptual to the realization stage, the quality and quantity of next-generation services will be great. For example, with the surging popularity of smart phones, thousands of fresh and fascinating services are being developed across the globe, deposited, and delivered through a variety of mobile cloud environments. Similarly, it is realistically expected the emergence of specific and generic devices and instruments for smart cities will bring a plethora of city-specific services.

We have already discussed the IoT idea and its huge and untapped potentials for automating, accelerating, and augmenting people's tasks, both trivial and complex. The idea of IoT is to improve the value chain among users, devices, applications, and environments considerably and therefore the synergy is to lay a scintillating and stimulating foundation for innovators for deriving and delivering sophisticated and smart services that have the greatest impact on people's lives. Providing adaptive, innovation-filled, supple, and personalized services based on meaningful data collected via scores of interconnected digital objects, networked electronics, and cloud-based applications enables our cities to be intelligent in their offerings, operations, and outlooks.

5.7.2 Examples of IoT-Inspired Services Co-Created and Tested

The authors have listed a few services in their research paper. The first one is the Interactive Totem Service that is based on a totem equipped with a touch screen monitor and an easy-to-use interface suitable for children. It is placed in the pediatric department of the San Raffaele Scientific Institute (HSR) and allows hospitalized children to interact with a number of games that allow them to learn while playing. A reward system stimulates children to order their own meals and learn about nutrition as well as understand better how to manage their condition during hospitalization.

- *Nutritionally aware vending service.* The vending service developed by HSR offers a service for the promotion of healthy lifestyles, which stimulates users to reflect on the benefits related to healthy living through a new concept of vending machines via an interactive touchscreen. The vending machine not only provides healthy foods, literature, and music, as well as useful information regarding mobility and physical activity, but also personalized information on how to adopt healthy lifestyle choices.

- *Bicycle activity monitoring and tourism service.* The aim of this service is to promote initiatives for healthier and environmentally friendly lifestyles while providing new services for pedestrian-cycle mobility. It involves a digital platform designed for exchanging and sharing information and digital content related to the world of cycling and now includes a wearable monitoring system, which collects biological data from users as they cycle.
- *Infomobility service.* The aim is to improve the mobility of patients, visitors, staff, and students in their travel to and from San Raffaele Hospital by offering a platform through which the latter can access a vast amount of information including the timetable of the shuttle line and information about the condition of the automatic line and the next connections to and from the hospital.
- *Energy management service.* This helps users monitor and improve their energy efficiency. Two pilots are being developed: an office pilot and a hospital pilot (which includes patients' rooms, corridors, and nurses' station). Smart appliances and smart plugs provided by project partners are being positioned in actual work and hospital contexts for those who use these spaces.

Thus the concepts such as co-creation and outside-in thinking are gaining momentum, capturing more intellectual and market shares. As future services and applications are for and by people, the human involvement in conceiving and concretizing trendsetting services is going to grow in the days ahead.

5.7.3 The Role of Advanced Sensing in Smart Cities

As urban areas consume the vast majority of resources that are quickly becoming scarce due to overexploitation by the teeming population, it is vital to make cities optimized and organized to sustain them for future generations. IT is the foremost domain to bring the necessary transformation to our cities. Process orchestration, advanced ambient systems, infrastructure optimization, architecture assimilation, and so on are the major contributions for the envisioned smart cities across the world. From the smart design of buildings, which capture rain water for later use, to intelligent control systems, which can monitor infrastructures autonomously, the possible improvements enabled by sensing, perception, and actuation technologies are enormous. Hancke et al. [6] illustrate several sensing applications in smart cities, sensing platforms, and technical challenges associated with these technologies. Infrastructures are critical for formulating and firming up different services for city dwellers as illustrated in Figure 5.4.

Sensing is a requirement for infrastructures to be smart, as the need for autonomy capability is now mandated for public infrastructures. We have extensively read about, heard about, and even felt self-configuring, diagnosing, healing, defending, governing, and

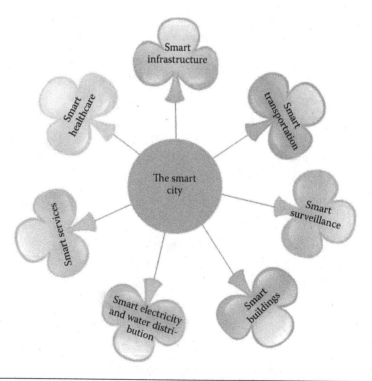

Figure 5.4　The smart city is a system of systems.

organizing computing infrastructures. It is all about having self-managing infrastructural components toward autonomic computing. Here, too, smart physical infrastructures such as bridges, buildings, homes, roads, and so on are the ones that can monitor themselves and act on their own intelligently. Clusters of smart sensors are the main components for deriving smart infrastructures in our daily living.

Using sensors to monitor public infrastructures provides awareness that enables a more efficient use of resources, based on the data collected by these sensors. Real-time monitoring eliminates the need for regularly scheduled inspections, thereby reducing operational costs. Measuring energy consumption in households allows for accurate load forecasting and sensors deployed in roads for traffic monitoring collect data that are necessary for the implementation of intelligent transportation systems (ITSs). For these approaches to be effective, sensors have to be deployed in very large numbers, and they have to be interconnected so that the collected data can be sent to a central information system where intelligent decisions based on this data can be made.

5.7.4 Sensors Everywhere and in Everything

In a nutshell, the emergence of smart sensors is a good omen for self-managing infrastructures. For example, there are sensors for determining gas, electricity, and water consumption. Further, in a smart home, there are light, pressure, gas, temperature, fire, humidity, and presence sensors aplenty. More sophisticated sensors include accelerometers that can be used to measure acceleration and vibration. In the context of structural health monitoring (SHM), for instance, sensors such as corrosion rate sensors work on the principle of an increase in electrical resistivity due to corrosion; acoustic emission sensors are used to detect propagation of sound waves; and magnetostrictive sensors detect the change in magnetic induction in the material caused by strain or stress. With the arrival of miniaturization technologies such as microelectromechanical systems and nanotechnology, sensors are becoming diminutive, disposable, randomly deployable, and indispensable.

The surging popularity of smart phones opens up a totally new sensing scenario. Smart phones are fitted with a variety of sensors such as GPS, gyroscopes, accelerometers, and compasses, enabling a variety of crowd sourcing applications, which will eventually be augmented by the IoT paradigm. In particular, collaborative data collection is a popular crowd sourcing application.

In summary, the usage of heterogeneous sensors and actuators is growing rapidly for monitoring and measurement of different parameters in physical infrastructures and environments, and the resulting knowledge is leveraged for effective control and operation of the infrastructures. Sensors explicitly ensure the functional automation of different elements and entities in our midst.

5.7.5 Sensing as a Service for Cities of the Future

Considering the unique contributions of smart sensors and actuators in facilitating people-centric, situation-aware, and real-time applications, the authors have come out with a new sensor deployment and delivery model to accentuate the sensor technology further. The sensing as a service (SaaS) model consists of four conceptual layers: (1) sensor service providers, (2) sensor service publishers (SSPs), (3) extended service providers (ESPs), and (4) sensor service consumers [7]. This is definitely a stimulating trend toward the vision of everything as a service. Sensor producers and consumers are at the extreme ends. In between, we have sensor service publishers and sensor service integrators. In this model, users view sensors as sensing services. The main responsibility of an SSP is to aggregate all kinds of sensor services and publish them in a cloud-based service registry and repository for public discovery and consumption. Sensor producers and owners have to register their sensors and their services with one or more SSPs so that sensor service consumers can easily find, bind, and leverage those sensor services to compose real-world applications. An ESP is a kind of system integrator and service broker. Sensor service consumers connect with ESPs with all their requirements and ESPs work with them to fulfill their expectations by sensor service connectivity, aggregation, monitoring and measurement, management, arbitration, data dissemination, and so on.

Xively is a public cloud for the IoT that simplifies and accelerates the creation, deployment, and management of sensors in a scalable manner. Further, it allows sharing sensor data. The OpenIoT project focuses on providing an open-source middleware framework enabling the dynamic formulation of self-managed cloud environments for IoT applications. Global Sensor Networks (GSNs) is a middleware that supports sensor deployments and offers a flexible, zero-programming deployment and integration infrastructure for IoT. These developments strengthen the vision toward sensing as a service. The following are some use cases for this new service model.

5.7.5.1 Waste Management　Waste management is one of the toughest challenges that modern cities have to deal with every day. A deeper penetration of ICT solutions, however, may result in significant savings and economical and ecological advantages. For instance, the use of intelligent waste containers that detect the level of load and allow for an optimization of the collector trucks' route can reduce the cost of wastage collection and improve the quality of recycling. To realize such a smart waste management service, the IoT shall connect the end devices, that is, intelligent waste containers, to a control center where an optimization application processes the data and determines the optimal management of the collector truck fleet.

Waste management consists of different processes such as collection, transport, processing, disposal, managing, and monitoring of waste materials. In Figure 5.5, this use case is illustrated how the

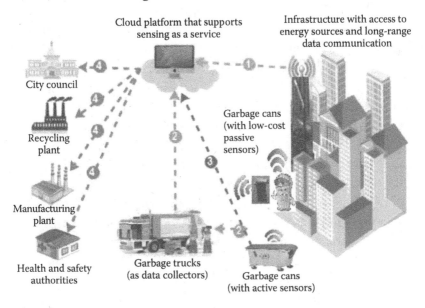

Figure 5.5　Reference architecture for sensing as a service.

sensing as a service model works in the waste management domain. In a modern smart city, there are several parties who are interested in waste management (e.g., city council, recycling companies, manufacturing plants, and authorities related to health and safety). Instead of deploying sensors and collecting information independently, the sensing as a service model allows all the interest groups to share the infrastructure and bear the related costs collectively. The most important aspect of such a collaboration is the cost reduction that individual groups need to spend otherwise. All the interested parties can retrieve and process sensor data in real time to achieve their own objective.

5.7.5.2 Smart Homes   A futuristic scenario explains the interactions in sensing as a service model. The scenario illustrated in Figure 5.6 is based on a smart home domain that also plays a significant role in smart cities.

5.7.5.3 Smart Agriculture   This sensing as a service model can be elegantly extended toward many real-world application scenarios. Currently, the authors are actively involved in designing and developing open platforms for sensor data collection, processing, and sharing in the domain of agriculture. Agriculture is an importation part of smart cities as it contributes to the food supply-chain that facilitates a large number of communities concentrated into cities.

5.7.5.4 Environment Management   Environment monitoring and management is a bigger domain wherein multiple kinds of sensors are being leveraged. Most of the sensors used for environment monitoring are commonly found in other domains such as climate, wild fire detection, and structure-health monitoring. Using the sensing as a service model, interest groups can acquire relevant sensor data without spending for sensors. Further, environment management is a large domain that a single organization cannot deal with (e.g., wild fire) comprehensively. Therefore a model such as sensing as a service comes in handy to stimulate a bevy of innovative solutions that use the same data but produce different results using different processing and analyzing techniques (e.g., prediction, visualization, and simulation).

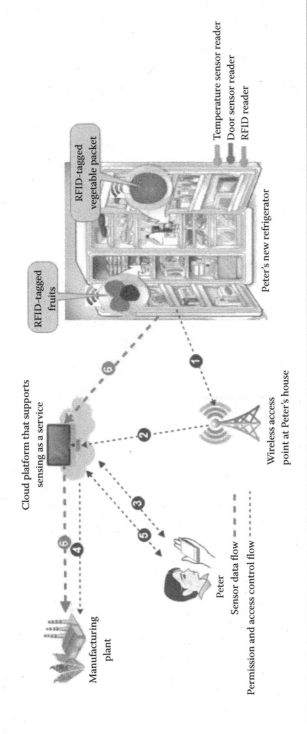

Figure 5.6 Control and data flow in a smart home use case.

5.7.5.5 Near-Field Communication The following are real-world examples of near-field communication (NFC) application [6] within the context of the smart city.

- *Smart energy metering*—NFC-enabled post-pay electricity meters are deployed in various nations. Payment for electricity consumption is automatically done after the encrypted reading has been sent over-the-air to the service's banking back-end.
- *Data acquisition and control*—NFC-enabled smartphones can be used to interface with control systems for remote control and can be used as platforms for advanced measurement and processing.
- *City tourist surfing*—With an NFC-enabled smart phone and smart posters disseminated throughout the city, a user can navigate through points of interest within the city.
- *Smart car parks*—Motorists can use their NFC-enabled smart phone as an electronic ticket to enter the parking lot and when leaving as an electronic wallet to effect payment.

With the addition of NFC to the ubiquitous smart phones, NFC is envisaged as a key enabling technology in smart cities.

5.8 Popular IoT/M2M Applications

As noted elsewhere, the IoT domain is surging as a result of five intriguing trends in the IT field: digitization, distribution, industrialization, commoditization, and consumerization. Therefore the IoT conundrum has a captivating and cognitive impact on every person in this increasingly connected world.

Readers can find a few well-known and widely articulated applications that gain immensely through the aforementioned modernizations. It is a foregone conclusion that fresh technologies would bring fresh perspectives and bring forth provisions for overcoming complexities and foretasting original applications that are really transformative, innovative, and disruptive. In this section and the ones that follow, we discuss a plethora of existing services that are being transitioned to be smart as well as altogether newer and more city-specific applications from the ground up.

5.8.1 A Typical IoT Application

In an extended enterprise scenario, all kinds of functional divisions are interconnected with one another via the cloud-hosted middleware suite. Clearly cloud occupies the prime spot in any integrated environment. All the common services are getting deployed in network-accessible cloud platforms. Only specific functionalities are being maintained at the edges. The cloud service broker (CSB), which is explained in detail in the text that follows, plays a stellar role in streamlining and simplifying the complex integration hurdles and hitches, as shown in Figure 5.7.

There are cloud integration appliances and solutions in abundance to effortlessly integrate date across clouds (private, public, and hybrid clouds). In short, CSBs are very relevant for distributed computing. There are federation approaches for realizing the vision of the intercloud. Standards are being formulated to establish run-time linkage between geographically distributed clouds to attend some specific scenarios. There are cloud orchestration platforms for uniting clouds. Cloud interoperability is demanded as clouds are vital for the success of the IoT concept. Both generic and specific clouds need to be integrated to fulfill the unique demands of any IoT applications and hence cloud integration, orchestration, and automation

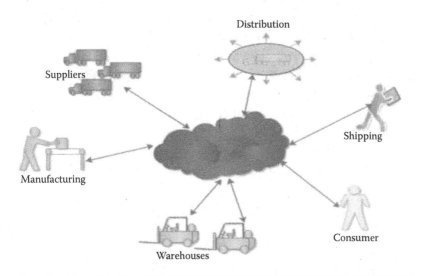

Figure 5.7 The cloud is the central environment for next-generation connected applications.

are essential for the projected success. At different levels and layers, the much-needed linkage is being tackled. There are integration appliances, middleware, service repository, and scores of tools for enabling cloud connectivity and interactions. As in the case of system integrators, we will hear more about cloud integrators/brokers for providing next-generation connected applications to people in the days ahead.

5.8.2 Structural Health of Buildings

The proper maintenance of the historical and cultural buildings of a city requires the continuous monitoring and measurement of the actual health parameters of each building and the identification of the areas that are vulnerable to any easy prey. The urban IoT may set up a distributed database for capturing and storing the sensor readings of buildings. In the recent past, there have been building-specific sensors such as vibration and deformation sensors to monitor the building stress, atmospheric agent sensors in the surrounding areas to monitor pollution levels, and temperature and humidity sensors to provide a complete characterization of environmental conditions.

This database will reduce the need for expensive periodic structural testing by human operators and will allow targeted and proactive maintenance and restoration actions. Finally, it will be possible to combine vibration and seismic readings to better study and understand the impact of light earthquakes on city buildings. This database can be made publicly accessible to make the residents aware of the care taken in preserving the city historical heritage. The practical realization of this service requires the installation and maintenance of specific sensors in the buildings and surrounding areas. These sensors have to collectively collect, corroborate, and correlate to extract the right insights in time in synchronization with a cloud-based cyber application.

5.8.3 Smart Energy

Energy has become a scarce commodity and hence its preservation is very much obligatory. In addition, more energy consumption means more heat dissipation into our fragile environment. With efficient usage of precious power energy, the much-feared environmental degradation and global warming can be significantly minimized to achieve environmental sustainability.

Smart metering solutions (this is an IoT/M2M solution connecting every energy-gobbling device in a network with the centralized smart meter) are very much accepted and used in advanced countries to accurately understand the usage. In other words, smart electricity meters help energy consumers to decode how energy savings can be achieved based on the readings and alerts being rendered by smart meters. The advanced metering infrastructure (AMI) is an active and ongoing research area to generate solutions for energy efficiency.

5.8.4 Smart Healthcare

Healthcare will be a huge industry in the years ahead. There are a number of specific devices for measuring and managing a number of human health parameters. IoT solutions are capable of reminding patients and their families as well as their doctors in case of any emergency arising out of any abnormality in any of the health readings.

5.8.5 Smart Home Security

Sophisticated home networking, integration, automation, security, and control mechanisms are hitting the market very frequently. M2M solutions for home security are merging with energy management to provide remote alarm controls as well as remote HVAC controls for homes and businesses through mobile phones.

5.8.6 Smart Cargo Handling

IoT solutions are being manufactured into a variety of storage/handling containers including cargo containers, money and document bags, and nuclear waste drums. Information on the real-time location of the container, whether it has been opened or closed, and how containers are being handled through motion sensors can be easily obtained to prevent any possible security and theft risks and to increase recovery capability of stolen or lost material.

5.8.7 Smart Traffic Management

M2M solutions are able to provide real-time road traffic information to drivers via automobile GPS devices to enable them to consider better alternatives.

5.8.8 Smart Inventory and Replenishment Management

IoT solutions can be integrated into the sensors measuring the amount of bulk product in a storage bin. This information can be made available to both the supplier and the user so proactive reorders can be initiated when inventories reach a predetermined level. This is very beneficial for manufacturing processes that do not consume a consistent and predictable amount of product or the transport time of the bulk product results in product stock-out.

5.8.9 Smart Cash Payment

M2M/IoT solutions allow mobile credit/debit card readers to provide secure and encrypted data transmissions at the transaction and ticketing counters in hyper malls, hotels, movie theaters, restaurants, and so on. Retailing becomes a smooth process without the need to stand on a queue for cash payment. The seamless connectivity between tags, tag readers, cash cards, merchant banks, retailers, and so on goes a long way toward considerably enhancing the customer experience.

5.8.10 Smart Tracking

IoT/M2M solutions allow parents to track their children very precisely from their workplaces and other locations and empower caregivers to remotely track those with disabilities as well as independently living, disease-stricken, debilitated, and bed-ridden people. Managers can keep track of employees performing their duties in rough and tough places. In particular, those who are, for example, working in oil wells, fighting forest fire, helping out in disaster-struck places, battling in war zones, or hiking in mountains will benefit immensely through such technological innovations.

The items inside vending machines can connect with their suppliers and provide all the relevant information about the number of containers and bottles inside and how many more are needed to fill up the vending machine, which is a sharp improvement over the current practice.

5.8.11 *Smart Displays*

All kinds of machines such as ATMs, vending machines, television sets, security video cameras, sign posts, dash boards, and so on can be intertwined at strategic locations. With such close integration through a competent M2M solution, customized video as well as static images can be dispatched to these machines to flash time-sensitive and preferred details and displays. A hungry person could order his pizza on his mobile phone yet see the pizza details and pictures on the larger screen of any one of these machines or with connected projectors showing the images on a white wall to give a clear vision.

5.8.12 *Smart Asset Management*

Every industry has its own set of specific assets. For example, hospitals have a a variety of devices both large and small, including a number of scanning machines, diagnostic equipment, healthcare monitors, robots, and other instruments. The real challenge lies in their effective location identification in case of any emergency, upkeep, management, monitoring, inventory, security, and so on. There are several unique benefits of an IoT/M2M solution in this complicated scenario. An advanced M2M solution sharply reduces the time consumed by employees to pinpoint the assets' exact location, considerably increments their utilization, and provides the ability to share high-value assets between departments and facilities. With every asset in a hospital environment integrated with each other and with the remote Web/cloud platforms via the M2M product, remote monitoring, repairing, and management are being greatly facilitated. Through the connectivity established with cloud-hosted healthcare applications, every machine could update and upload its data to the centralized and cyber applications; a number of activities are thereby fully automated by avoiding manual intervention, interpretation, and instruction.

5.8.13 *Air Quality*

It is well known that nations across the world have set appropriate mechanisms in place to slow down the threatening climate change. There are attempts through a host of ways to cut down greenhouse gas emissions into our fragile environment, to enforce energy preservation, and subsequently to decrease heat dissipation so that the global objective of sustainability can be realized sooner than later. To such an extent, an urban IoT can provide the means to monitor the quality of the air in all kinds of crowded areas such as open air stadiums, parks and playgrounds, and so on. In addition, communication facilities can be provided to let health applications on joggers' devices capture and transmit data to remotely held applications and data sources. In this way, people can always find the healthiest path for outdoor activities and can be continuously connected to their preferred personal training application or trainer. The realization of such a service requires that air quality and pollution sensors be deployed across the city and the sensor data have to be made publicly available to citizens.

5.8.14 *Noise Monitoring*

Noise can be seen as a form of acoustic pollution as much as carbon monoxide (CO) is for air. An urban IoT can offer a noise-monitoring service to measure the amount of noise produced at any given hour in particular areas. Besides building a space–time map of the noise pollution in the area, this service can also be extended to enforce the safety of people and public properties by means of sound-detection algorithms that can recognize, for instance, the noise of glass crashes or brawls. This service can remarkably improve both the quietness of the nights in the city and the confidence of public establishment owners. However, the installation of sound detectors or environmental microphones is bound to face strong opposition, as these sensors and devices have been portrayed as invasions of privacy.

5.8.15 *Traffic Congestion*

This is an important service for future cities. An urban IoT has the innate capability to closely monitor city traffic and if there is any congestion or complication on the roads, it could be immediately captured and conveyed to those concerned. At this point of time, camera-based traffic monitoring systems are performing a yeomen service. However, minute sensors can do a better job. Next-generation traffic monitoring may be realized by using widely deployed sensors, road infrastructures, and GPS installed on modern vehicles in synchronization with acoustic sensors. This information is of great importance for city authorities to discipline traffic and to send officers where needed and it helps people to plan in advance the route to reach the office or to better schedule a shopping trip to the city center.

5.8.16 Smart Parking

This facility is being given based on road sensors and intelligent displays that direct motorists along the best path for parking in the city. The benefits are many. It helps drivers to find a parking slot quickly; there is a less CO emission from the car and subdued traffic snarl. The smart parking service can be directly integrated in the urban IoT infrastructure to get proper visibility through widespread advertisements. Further, through short-range communication technologies, it is possible to remotely verify whether vehicles are getting parked properly and in the right slots allocated for them. Disabled people can get priority too.

Professionals and experts are exploring, experimenting, and expounding an increasing array of value-added business and use cases for a variety of industry segments to keep the momentum on the IoT/M2M space intact. There is another trend fast picking up these days with the active participation of academicians and industry veterans. Cyber physical systems (CPSs) are the new powerful entities in this complicated landscape. That is, all kinds of physical systems at the ground level are being empowered with scores of generic as well as specific cyber applications, services, and data. That is, not only connectivity but also software-inspired empowerment is being ticked as the next-generation evolution in the machine space. There is no doubt that there will be more IT-automation for all kinds of "dumb" and dormant systems.

5.9 Cyber Physical System for Smart City Needs

Cyber physical systems (CPSs) [8] use wireless communication, sensing, perception and actuation technologies, and distributed decisions overwhelmingly with immensely potential benefits in very diverse areas of human activity such as the personal as well as professional environments; homeland security; transport systems; emergency management; discovery of bombs, mines, and unexploded ordnances; leisure; and tourism. There are fresh possibilities and opportunities in waiting to be eloquently fulfilled with the smart leverage of the distinct concepts and capabilities of the fast-flourishing CPS domain.

5.9.1 CPS for Emergency Response

Numerous review articles have detailed the research activities on sensor-aided CPSs that enable intelligent and fast response to emergencies such as fires, earthquakes, or terrorist attacks. Real-time monitoring and quick response are the two inherent requirements for emergency response.

During a fire, different types of sensors can cooperate and interact with the evacuees and the environment to lower the intensity of fire and material losses. Temperature and gas sensors can help monitor the spread of hazards. Rotatable cameras track the spread of the fire and the movement of civilians. Ultrasonic sensors can range the distance to obstacles in the environment and monitor dynamic changes of maps due to sudden changes in some built structures through destruction and debris. Smart evacuation schemes can help evacuees using the cooperation between first-aid decision nodes, sensors, and civilians with mobile devices. Evacuees with mobiles and wearables can follow personalized navigation paths with distributed decisions that mitigate congestion. Those without smart phones may follow audio or visible LED directions. Integrated applications in clouds can gather sensing information and dynamically predict the movement of evacuees and hazards to make the best decisions regarding resource allocation and response. A search may also be conducted with the help of robotic devices despite their limited autonomy. For emergency response, there are a few challenges as described here.

- *Communication issues.* Many-to-many information flow and opportunistic connections are inevitable in emergency situations. In a fire emergency, to find safe paths, sensing information needs to be aggregated from many live sensors and conveyed to many evacuees on the move in real time. Communication channels are liable to failure and hence it is a serious issue. In addition, query-and-reply communications may also proceed among different groups of people, for example, first responders, evacuees, members of the press, and robots. In these cases, the typical communication protocols, such as broadcast, unicast, and multicast, may be not able to deal with these diverse communication requirements.

- *Information acquirement and dissemination.* Cross-domain sensing and heterogeneous information flow are inherent features in an emergency response system. To guarantee the safety of people, information in different domains must be acquired. Moreover, sensors are not the only information contributors; they include all the interactions among sensors, actuators, people, smart objects, and events. All of the captured information has to be subjected to a series of real-time investigations to extract insights that need to be taken to those concerned.

- *Knowledge discovery.* Data are everywhere in abundance, in different formats, speed, scope, and so on. However, generating pragmatic knowledge is the most crucial aspect in any emergent situations to tide over the crisis effectively. Partial information and dynamic changes are inherent in an emergency. Recently, whatever the volume of data being generated, the data analytics platforms have become capable of squeezing intelligent data to rely and work on.

- *Resource allocation and management.* Limited resources make timely response more difficult. Unlike other sensor-aided applications, the needs of intelligent actuation, scheduling, and efficient resource allocation will increase in emergency response systems. Intelligent scheduling is needed to select the best course of action, while scarce resources must be allocated efficiently to perform actions.

- *Heterogeneous system integration and asynchronous control.* Multifaceted technologies will be accurately chosen and used to enhance the capability and diversity of emergency responses. Further, functionally separated tasks such as sensing, storage, computation, and decision making, need to be accomplished by independent functional units so as to facilitate the integrated asynchronous control of multiple technologies.

As reported previously, with the maturity and stability of CPS technologies, newer application domains will emerge in the smart city space.

5.10 Smart City Platforms and Frameworks

There are smart city solutions in the forms of integrated platforms and enabling frameworks by product vendors. IBM, Oracle, Hitachi, and others are the leading IT solutions providers to facilitate the faster and simpler realization of smart cities across the globe. Many software infrastructure solutions are being developed and deployed along with supporting toolkits and tips to provide end-to-end smart city functionalities. Considering the growing market for smart city solutions, IT product vendors are on a fast track to bring forth highly competent solutions to keep the edge earned. In this section, we discuss a smart city communication platform and a framework for sensor–cloud integration, which is a major aspect in building and enhancing intelligent cities.

5.10.1 A Communication Platform for Smart Cities

M2M communication platforms [9] will take the role of insightful control of the communication between all connected machines to ensure the intended tasks. All kinds of devices are nowadays instrumented to have the innate communication capability. The communication infrastructures (cellular as well as radio) too are becoming pervasive. Thus enabling devices to connect with one another in the vicinity as well as to the remote cyber systems usher in a variety of hitherto unforeseen applications for individuals and institutions. The software development community is at the forefront in designing, developing, debugging, and deploying a variety of device-centric services. All kinds of existing and emerging devices are being shown to be service-providing, requesting, and brokering systems. This means the Internet of Services (IoSs) paradigm will power on the world on many ways. The IoS leads to streams of highly sophisticated cloud, enterprise, embedded, social, and analytical applications being constructed very quickly through integrated platforms, powerful tools and pioneering techniques such as service integration, orchestration, and choreography. The seamless and spontaneous connectivity results in intelligent devices to exhibit distinct behaviors as per the varying scenarios and needs. The point is that M2M communication will lead to a growing array of original smart city applications.

Smart city IT has to have the following four main points: (1) smart infrastructures to connect physical objects and sensors through heterogeneous communication networks realizing the interconnection between human and machines (H2M) and between machines (M2M); (2) smart operations for improving the quality of life for people by offering innovative services in every sector by integrating systems and information and the core elements for supporting urban operation and management; (3) a smart ecosystem, where the analysis of the interconnected information should yield new insights for driving decisions and actions that lead to process innovations and other noteworthy outcomes of pioneering systems, organizations, and industry value chains; and (4) smart governance—the interconnection of urban components with integrated application systems needs to be governed through policy establishment and enforcements. Thus any smart city platform has to have the functionality, features, and facility to provision these four requirements. The authors of this platform also have listed the research challenges as follows:

- *Scalability*. Considering the rapid increase in the number of smart devices coupled with the unfavorable heterogeneity in sensor networks, scalability is a main technical challenge for enabling ubiquitous information and service access. How naming and addressing of all the participants and constituents, networking and communication, data management, service provisioning, and delivery are to be accomplished are some of the research challenges.
- *Governance*. Smart city services involve many different stakeholders such as service developers, integrators and brokers, communication and cloud service providers, device manufacturers, administrators, policymakers, end-users, and so on. To be able to manage the overall system consistently, flexible

and generic solutions are needed for optimized sharing and governance.

- *Lack of test beds.* To perform reliable large-scale experimentations for the verification and validation of research results, the need for a city-scale test bed is being demanded.

5.10.2 A Smart City M2M Platform

Having understood the limitations of the existing platforms, the authors have built a flexible and future-directed platform for smart cities. The main functionalities of the platform are detailed in their research paper. The platform could overcome the aforementioned limitations to a major extent. With the accumulation of connected machines, the direct fallout is the huge growth and heaps of data. Thus communication networks and infrastructures need to have the inherent capability of comfortably carrying data to target systems to initiate the process of knowledge extraction, engineering, and exposition. Representational state transfer (REST)ful services APIs are pervasive and distinctively popular in the cloud, analytics, mobile, and IoT era owing to to its extreme simplicity. That is, data traffic is regulated, tracked, and tackled with the standard interfaces. Devices send out data as well as event messages to be unambiguously understood and acted on by devices on the other side. Data compression, de-duplication, analysis, and processing algorithms are very critical for the success of this platform and hence validated and refined data processing techniques and methods are embedded in this platform. There are other capabilities such as impenetrable security and privacy, ease of participatory development, and simplified use and operation of the platform.

5.10.3 A Framework of Sensor-Cloud Integration

In this section, a robust and resilient framework to enable this exploration by integrating sensor networks to clouds is explained. There are many challenges to realize this framework. The authors of this framework [10] have proposed a pub-sub–based model, which simplifies the integration of sensor networks with cloud-based and community-centric applications. Also there is a need for Internet working cloud providers in case of any violations of service level agreements (SLAs) with users.

Use Cases A virtual community consisting of a team of researchers has come together to solve a complex problem and they need huge data storage, computing capability, security, etc. For example, this team is working on the outbreak of a new virus strain sweeping through a population. They have deployed biosensors on a patient's body to monitor his/her condition continuously and to use these data for large and multidimensional simulations to track the origin and spread of infection as well as the virus mutation and possible cures. This might require large computational resources and a versatile platform for sharing data and results that are not immediately available in the representation of the problem. So the sensor data obtained need to be aggregated, processed, and disseminated based on the subscriptions. However, as sensor data they require a huge team.

Here, researchers need to register their interest to get various patients' status (blood pressure, temperature, pulse rate, etc.) from the biosensors for large-scale parallel analysis and to share this information with each other to find actionable computational power and storage. One cloud provider may not handle this requirement, which demands a dynamic collaboration with other cloud providers. Thus the formation of a virtual organization with cloud integration methods is gaining importance.

In the healthcare domain, doctors need real-time and historical data to thoroughly diagnose and analyze the health of patients and to prescribe the correct course of medication with the right dosage. There are specialized sensors to continuously monitor, measure, and dispatch a variety of healthcare parameters to centralized control centers and caregivers. Further, owing to the unprecedented improvisations in ad hoc networking, there are body area networks (BANs) and smart sensor networks (SSNs) to clinically capture and cognitively collaborate with cloud-based applications to corroborate and correlate the accuracy and recency of the data obtained. Then competent data analytics platforms emit actionable insights that in turn are visualized and disseminated to doctors, specialists, surgeons, and caregivers as well as other actuation systems.

Roads have sensors that can communicate with the vehicles passing over them to determine useful traffic patterns, find more sustainable ways to route cars, and perhaps even generate data to be sold to insurance companies or other businesses seeking to tap transportation and logistics information.

The traditional high-performance computing (HPC) approach such as the sensor-grid model can be used in this particular case, but setting up the appropriate infrastructure to deploy and scale it quickly is not easy in this environment. However, the cloud paradigm is an admirable and awesome move. Current cloud providers unfortunately did not address this issue of integrating sensor networks with cloud applications. To integrate sensor networks to the cloud, the authors have proposed a content-based pub-sub model [10]. A pub-sub system encapsulates and transitions sensor data into events and provides the services of event publication and subscription for asynchronous data exchange among system entities. MQTT-S is an open, topic-based and pub-sub protocol that hides the topology of sensor network and allows data to be delivered based on interest rather than on the individual device addresses. It allows a transparent data exchange between WSNs and traditional networks and even between different WSNs.

In this framework, like MQTT-S, all of the system's complexities reside on the broker's side but it differs from MQTT-S in one aspect— it uses a content-based pub-sub broker rather than the topic-based method. When an event is published, it is transmitted from a publisher to one or more subscribers without the publisher having to do anything to take up the message to any specific subscriber. Matching is done by the pub-sub broker outside of the WSN environment. In a content-based pub-sub system, sensor data have to be augmented with meta-data to identify different data fields. For example, a metadata of a sensor value (also event) can be body temperature, blood pressure, and so on.

To deliver published sensor data (events) to subscribers, an efficient and scalable event matching algorithm is required by the pub-sub broker. This event matching algorithm targets a range of predicate cases suitable to application scenarios and has to be highly efficient and scalable when the number of predicates increases sharply. In this framework, sensor data are coming through gateways to a pub-sub broker that is required to deliver information to the consumers of SaaS applications, as the entire network is very dynamic. On the WSN side, sensor or actuator (SA) devices may change their network addresses at any time. Wireless links are quite likely to fail. Further, SA nodes could also fail at any time and instead of being repaired, it is expected that they will be replaced by new ones. Besides, different SaaS applications can be hosted and run on any machines anywhere on the cloud. In such situations, the conventional approach of using network addresses as the means of communication between the SA devices and the applications may be very problematic because of their dynamic and temporal nature.

Several SaaS applications may have an interest in the same sensor data but for different purposes. In this case, the SA nodes would need to manage and maintain communication means with multiple applications in parallel. This might exceed the limited capabilities of the simple and low-cost SA devices. So, a pub-sub broker is needed and is located on the cloud side because of its higher performance in terms of bandwidth and capabilities (Figure 5.8).

In conclusion, to deliver published sensor data or events to appropriate users of cloud applications, an efficient and scalable event-matching algorithm called Statistical Group Index Matching (SGIM) is leveraged. The authors have also evaluated the algorithm's performance and compared it with the existing algorithms in a cloud-based ubiquitous healthcare application scenario [10]. The authors have clearly described that this algorithm in sync with the foundational and fruitful framework enables sensor-cloud connectivity to utilize the ever-expanding sensor data for various community-centric sensing and responsive applications on the cloud. It can be seen that the computational tools needed to launch this exploration is more appropriately built from the data center "cloud" computing model than the traditional HPC approaches or grid approaches. Based on this creative work, new-generation cloud-sensor platforms and applications should be visualized. Finally, a very important ingredient in the smarter planet is the pervasiveness of adaptive middleware solutions

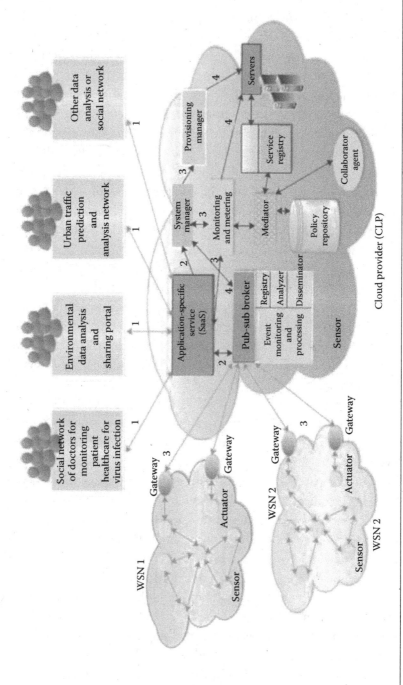

Figure 5.8 Framework architecture of sensor-cloud integration.

for seamlessly and spontaneously integrating devices in the physical world with the business and IT applications and packages in the virtual/cyber world over all kinds of networks.

The final outcome of these interesting and desirable trends and technologies is the Internet of Devices and Services that in turn lead to smarter and sophisticated applications for humans. That is, with self-, surroundings-, and situation-aware devices along with cloud infrastructures and the Internet as the communication infrastructure, people-centric services and applications can be precisely and perfectly decided, developed, and delivered to in real time.

5.11 Homeland Security and the Sensor Cloud

The sensor cloud takes the cloud concepts and applies it to sensor networks. Intelligent wired or wireless sensors store their data in the cloud, subscribers are allowed to view and analyze the data, and administrators carry out remote management of the sensors. The concept of the sensor cloud has caught on because of the ubiquity of sensors consequent on support for a variety of sensors on a standard smartphone platform (accelerometer, cameras, microphone, GPS, compass, proximity, ambient light, etc.). Specialized sensors are embedded in most electronic and electrical equipment.

Companies are now building clouds to store the data captured by such sensors. There are several surveillance sensor networks in place throughout the world. Each national government is responsible for setting up and running its surveillance sensor network and different agencies run their own networks (city surveillance, traffic management, VIP security, critical infrastructure, coastal surveillance, border control, etc.). In addition, other Homeland Security–impacting agencies have their own networks: railways, airports, critical infrastructure, and so on. Each network of sensors (video surveillance cameras in most cases) has its own infrastructure for video/content management (DVRs/NVRs/VMS servers) and storage [11].

The problem with the current decentralized architecture is that many of the agencies do not have the required resources for managing the infrastructure. Older sensor data are not properly archived or are misplaced. Further, silos of surveillance sensor networks prevent the emergence of a common operational picture (COP) at a global level. One solution that would address these issues would be to build a Homeland Security sensor cloud that services all Web-connected surveillance sensor networks: video, audio, radar, trace detectors, access control, motion detectors, and so on. The sensor cloud would store the sensor data and allow authorized users to view and analyze the same. Agency-specific applications can be developed based on the needs of the user agencies. To get such an initiative off the ground, countries and their respective homeland security agencies have to be agreeable to having their data stored in clouds. Some sensor networks will need to be upgraded to meet a minimum quality-of-data level (e.g., optical resolution in the case of video surveillance cameras). Such a move will also allow homogenization of sensor specifications with the objective of ensuring that the most optimum sensors are selected for a particular use case. The sensor networks will need to conform to a common standard (either by upgrading the hardware or by plugging in a gateway) to ensure that they connect to the cloud and that the data streams for each type of sensor can be stored in a common database. The owners of the data will have to be agreeable to share their data (in combination with data from other owners) for analysis, data mining, and other information-extraction techniques.

5.12 Conclusion

In the last decade, the IoT paradigm has slowly but steadily conquered the minds of researchers and engineers to become one of the most exciting, innovative, transformative, and disruptive domains. In this chapter, we have explained the radical contributions of the celebrated IoT concept in setting up and sustaining next-generation cities, the incredible IoT technologies, the noteworthy transformations that are bound to flourish in the days ahead, the network architectures that are to shape the forthcoming applications for simplifying and streamlining city processes, and so on. We have described the industry-strength IoT frameworks emerging to build city-specific applications and services. There are data analytics platforms to create reliable and usable insights and feed them to respective applications to be exceptionally resilient, versatile, and adroit.

References

1. Min Chen (2013). Towards Smart City: M2M Communications with Software Agent Intelligence. *Multimedia Tools Applications*, 67:167–178.
2. Jiong Jin, Jayavardhana Gubbi, Tie Luo, and Marimuthu Palaniswami (2012). Network Architecture and QoS Issues in the Internet of Things for a Smart City. Presented at the International Symposium on Communications and Information Technologies (ISCIT) Incheon, Korea.
3. Satish Phakade Pawar (2013). Smart City with Internet of Things (Sensor Networks) and Big Data. Chichwad, Pune: Institute of Business Management & Research (IBMR).
4. Andrea Zanella and Lorenzo Vangelista (2014). Internet of Things for Smart Cities. *IEEE Internet of Things Journal*, 1(1):22–32.
5. Sauro Vicini, Sara Bellini, and Alberto Sanna (2012). How to Co-Create Internet of Things-Enabled Services for Smarter Cities. In SMART 2012: The First International Conference on Smart Systems, Devices and Technologies. Stuttgart, Germany.
6. Gerhard P. Hancke, Bruno de Carvalho e Silva, and Gerhard P. Hancke Jr. (2013). The Role of Advanced Sensing in Smart Cities. *Sensors*, 13(1):393–425.
7. Charith Perera, Arkady Zaslavsky, Peter Christen, and Dimitrios Georgakopoulos (2014). Sensing as a Service Model for Smart Cities Supported by Internet of Things. *Transactions on Emerging Telecommunications Technologies*, 1–12.
8. Erol Gelenbe and Fang-JingWu (2013). Future Research on Cyber-Physical Emergency Management Systems. *Future Internet*, 5:336–354.
9. Asma Elmangoush, Hakan Coskun, Sebastian Wahle, and Thomas Magedanz (2013). Design Aspects for a Reference M2M Communication Platform for Smart Cities. In 9th International Conference on Innovations in Information Technology. Abu Dhabi.
10. Mohammad Mehedi Hassan, Biao Song, and Eui-Nam Huh (2009). A Framework of Sensor-Cloud Integration Opportunities and Challenges. ICUIMC '09 Proceedings of the 3rd International Conference on Ubiquitous Information Management and Communication, 618–626.
11. The Sensor Cloud the Homeland Security (2011). http://www.mistral solutions.com/sensor-cloud-homeland-security.

Suggested Readings

http://www.peterindia.net. An Information Technology (IT) Portal.
Pethuru Raj (2012). *Cloud Enterprise Architecture*. Boca Raton, FL: CRC Press.

6

Social Media Analytics for People Empowerment

Abstract

The amount of social media data is increasing exponentially year after year. As of the first quarter of 2014, Facebook had roughly 1.28 billion active monthly users. This goes to show the impact of social media networks in the day-to-day lives of people across the world. As a result of the immense proliferation of social media networks in day-to-day activities, many organizations are using social media networks to promote their brand, increase lead generation, promote marketing communications, and so on. This has led to the evolution of a new branch of analytics called social media analytics that deals with the study of social media networks in various facets of an organization. With the increase in the popularity of social media networks, this branch of analytics is gaining momentum. For an intelligent city, it is necessary to have intelligent organizations. Organizations can evolve into intelligent organizations if they are equipped with the necessary information technology infrastructure to utilize cutting-edge technologies such as social media analytics. The first section of this chapter deals with the use of social media analytics for the evolution of intelligent organizations, and the second section deals with the use of social media analytics for the evolution and creation of intelligent cities. It is necessary to have some metrics to measure the impact created by social media networks. The four different types of metrics that are available to measure the impact of social media networks in organizations are discussed in this chapter. In the first section of this chapter, we also examine several use cases of social media analytics for organizations, as well as the various types of social media analytics tools. Social media analytics has found its way into day-to-day activities of city organizations as well. A variant of social media analytics called sentiment analytics is used extensively by city officials to track the sentiments of citizens on various decisions of the city government. An architecture for integration of social media analytics with the intelligent cities of the future is also proposed in the second section of the chapter. The chapter concludes with a short case study of a pilot implementation of social media analytics in an intelligent city. Several real-life examples are provided throughout the chapter to elucidate the importance of social media analytics in present-day organizations and intelligent cities of future.

Key Terms Used in the Chapter

Best-in-class organization: Organizations that are experts in using social media marketing.

Internet of Things (IoT): Refers to billions of computing devices that communicate with one another using the existing Internet infrastructure.

Natural language processing (NLP): A field of computer science that deals with interactions between computers and language of human beings.

Rich site summary (RSS) feed: Uses Web feeds to publish frequently updated information.

Social media platforms: Social media networks such as Facebook, Twitter, LinkedIn, YouTube, and so on.

Social profile: The aggregated interests, comments, and overall behaviors of a fan follower or an RSS feed subscriber to a defined social media network platform of an organization such as an organization's Facebook page or Twitter profile.

Social reach: Aggregate of social profiles of an organization that are present over all types of social media platforms.

6.1 Introduction

Intelligent cities are cities of the future that have the capability and infrastructure to leverage information technology and analytical tools to improve the quality of life of their residents. The analytical tools will help city officials to enhance the productivity of their residents by using the insights that are derived from these analytical tools.

An intelligent city will focus on the following key areas to improve the quality of life of its residents.

- Facilitating rapid economic development by growing the existing businesses and by creating avenues for new ones
- Providing a sustainable environment for their residents by reducing energy wastage and greenhouse gas emissions
- Communicating actively with their residents, businesses, and other community groups and engage them actively in city operations and decision making
- Developing a common ecosystem by coordinating with all city agencies, components, and organizations to find new avenues for products and services that would be beneficial for the overall ecosystem

The value architecture of an intelligent city is summarized in the diagram below. This architecture uses CAMS (Cloud, Analytics, Mobile, and Social) technology as a foundation to develop and deliver value-added services to its residents. In this architecture, the combination of big data analytics and social media networks has led to the evolution of a new stream of analytics referred to as social media analytics.

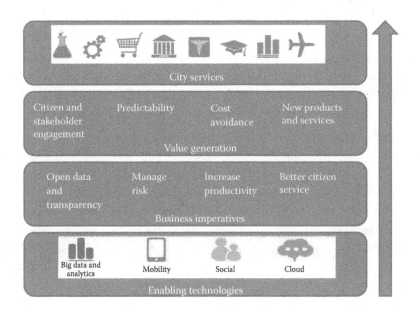

The amount of social data generated is increasing exponentially. As per the most recent statistics, Twitter users collectively produce 100,000 tweets per minute. All other social media websites generate similar amounts of data. With these huge amounts of social data generated in real time, it becomes necessary for businesses to capture the pulse and emotions of their product users and devise strategies to boost brand advocacy, which in turn will increase the sales of their products. This is where social analytics plays an inevitable role. Social analytics equips an organization to analyze and measure the impact of social media data on its brand value by examining data from various internal and external forums, which are listed in the following diagram:

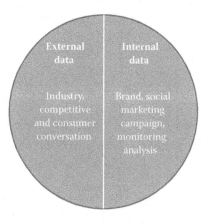

Social media analytics plays a critical role in the building and sustenance of intelligent cities. Of late, there has been a great deal of impetus on how social media analytics can be used to improve the efficiency of city government. A variant of social media analytics that is a very useful aid for city officials is sentiment analysis, which helps city officials to gather actionable insights about citizens by capturing their sentiments from social media conversations. Sentiment analysis is a very nascent area and does not have many use cases in present-day cities. However, in the intelligent cities of the future, sentiment analysis will be a core component as it efficiently tracks the emotions of citizens, which in turn will go a long way in building sustainable and intelligent cities for future. This will also provide a mechanism for the city officials to involve citizens actively in city operations and decision making. Social media analytics for intelligent cities will use equitable proportions of big data analytics and social media collaboration concepts to devise strategies for intelligent city governance.

For cities to be intelligent, apart from the city agencies, the various organizations or businesses that form a part of the city ecosystem should also transform to intelligent organizations by utilizing the power of social media analytic technologies for the benefit and growth of their ecosystem.

The first section of this chapter deals with the use of social media analytics for the transformation and growth of businesses in cities and the second section deals with the use of social media analytics for the evolution and creation of intelligent cities, including sentiment analysis.

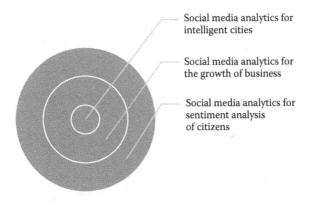

Social media analytics for intelligent cities

Social media analytics for the growth of business

Social media analytics for sentiment analysis of citizens

6.2 Building a Framework for the Use of Social Media Analytics for Business

The benefits offered by social media analytics to an organization are immense. However, it is not possible for all organizations to derive benefits from social media analytics. Adoption of social media analytics by organizations should imply realization of immediate business benefits for an organization. The following framework describes the steps that need to be followed by an organization to realize immediate business benefits.

Strategy	Metrics	Organization	Technology
• Define business objectives • Identify required insights	• Define success • Recommend actions	• Identify required resources • Identify barriers	• Identify tools based on strategy, metrics, and organization

Step 1: Strategy: This is the key step in which the organization's expectations of using social media analytics should be clearly laid out. If any changes are required in the existing processes to attain the organization's expectations, a feasibility study should be done to assess the impact of the change on the organization's existing business.

Step 2: Metrics: The metrics to measure the impact of social media on an organization should be clearly specified. The goals—whether to drive brand awareness, increase awareness about competitors, improve sales, generate business leads, or any other aspect of that kind—should be defined in this step. If any specific actions are required to measure the metrics, those actions should also be clearly mentioned in this step.

Step 3: Organization: An organization's readiness to adopt and use social media analytics should be appraised correctly. This is done by performing an assessment of the following parameters:

- Resource availability
- Skill availability in social media analytics tools
- Availability of tools/processes for social media analytics

Step 4: Technology: Once all of the previous steps are completed, there will be a clear direction in terms of strategy, metrics, and skill availability. In this last step, the tools that are required for performing analytics on social media data are selected. In this selection, it is important to assess various parameters such as cost, success rate of the product, training curve, and license maintenance process for renewal/upgrades.

6.2.1 *Social Media Content Metrics*

The key aspect with regard to the use of social media by organizations is the type of content that is posted in the social media. Development of content for social media needs to be done carefully and should be governed by a set of metrics so that effective content development strategies can be devised for various types of social media networks. This in turn allows companies to leverage social media marketing to achieve an optimal return on investment. The following are the four different types of metrics available for measuring the effectiveness of content:

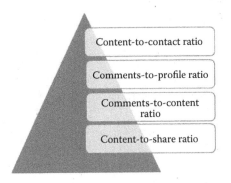

6.2.1.1 *Content-to-Contact Ratio* This measures the ability of an organization to publish engaging content, which in turn helps it to generate new social profiles in social media networks. It has been observed that for average organization, the content-to-contact ratio has been roughly about 8:1. (This means that for every eight pieces of content that are published, a new social profile is created.) For the best companies, the content-to-contact ratio could be as high as 1:1. In this context, usage of the terms average and best refers to the experience of the company in the social media marketing domain. So initially for all organizations, the response using social media marketing could be dull, which in turn will pick up over time as organizations gain more experience in the field of social media marketing.

6.2.1.2 *Comments-to-Content Ratio* This measures the impact of an organization's content campaign. The comments-to-content ratio can be measured with the help of various social media parameters such as likes and comments. The comments-to-content ratio also measures

the capability of an organization's campaign to create successful social profile engagements. A higher number of comments and likes denotes a higher degree of engagement. Organizations that are veterans in social media marketing have a comments-to-content ratio that is much higher than that of the organizations that are new entries into the field of social media marketing.

6.2.1.3 Comments-to-Profile Ratio   This measures an organization's capability to connect with its existing social profiles with the passage of time. This ratio is measured based on the assumption that the higher the number of comments for existing profiles, the higher the possibility that the brand will stay fresh in the minds of customers at the time of purchase. It has been observed that comments-to-profile ratio for best-in-class business-to-consumer (B2C) companies is significantly higher when compared business-to-business (B2B) companies.

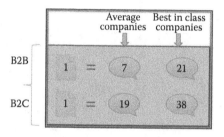

6.2.1.4 Content-to-Share Ratio   This measures the content's capability to extend beyond the reach of social media boundaries into other networks, forums, or communities of people. The higher the ratio, the higher is the success rate of the content. This assumption is based on the fact that only if people like some content, they will go that extra mile to register for the content and share it with others who are outside the network. High values for the content-to-share ratio also denote new social media prospects for an organization's brand and products.

6.2.2 Different Dimensions of Social Media Analytics for Organizations

Organizations can use social media analytics for diverse purposes. Each dimension qualifies as a use case of social media analytics. These different use cases are summarized in the following diagram:

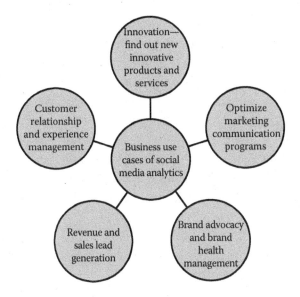

6.2.2.1 Brand Advocacy and Brand Health Management Present-day organizations focus a great deal on brand value and the steps to advocate and maintain brand value. Social media is widely used to propagate brand value by various organizations. Data gathered from social media networks are also used by organizations to understand the sentiments of people toward their brand. Brand health is monitored with the help of a combination of brand-related keywords and words that denote positive and negative sentiments of people. The following are some of the specific applications of this use case in business.

- Track the region or location of maximum brand penetration.
- Assess the strength of your brand versus the brand of competitors.
- Track the highest performing products in the brand.
- Track brand influencers (measured in terms of the discussions of people who get maximum likes or followers in social media).
- Assess sentiment toward the brand (measured by means of the number of likes or positive comments).

6.2.2.2 Social Media Analytics to Calculate Net Promoter Score The Net Promoter Score is a parameter that is used to determine the brand loyalty of customers. It is based on the idea that every brand's customer can be categorized into three groups: Promoters, Passives, and Detractors. Promoters are those who have a score of 9 to 10 on a 10-point scale. Promoters are very loyal to the brand and are expected to fuel the growth of the brand. Passives have a score of 7 to 8; they are satisfied customers, but are susceptible to competitor brand offerings. Detractors have a score of 0 to 6; they are unsatisfied customers who are likely to act as negative propagators of your brand. Social media is widely used today by many organizations to calculate Net Promoter Score by hosting surveys, by tracking the brand sentiments of customers, by calculating the number of brand likes and so on.

6.2.2.3 Optimize Marketing Communication Programs   Marketing promotion campaigns and other activities that are organized for sales promotion involve a great deal of expenditure. These sales promotional programs are often conducted on massive scales in many regions across the world. Today social media are used to judge the responses of people toward such promotional programs by using some kind of measurement strategy that is used later on as a means to improve and enhance the campaigns.

6.2.2.4 American Express Uses Social Media to Measure the Effectiveness of Their Campaigns   American Express recently partnered with YouTube and VEVO to live-stream a Duran Duran concert as part of their "Unstaged" series. They incorporated a Google chat widget to understand better how many people talked about the concert and, if so, whether they referenced American Express in their comments. The goal was to determine whether and how the live-stream experience influenced purchase intent and brand perception to better understand how to tune future initiatives [1].

Another important dimension of social media for marketing communication programs is to use the different types of social media platforms for marketing communication programs. This is referred to as social marketing. In such scenarios, the concept of engagement analysis becomes very prominent. Engagement analysis helps to measure the impact of marketing campaigns on different social media platforms. A framework for engagement analysis is given below.

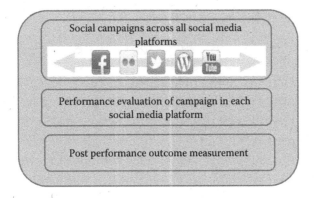

Using the framework given above, the following are the key steps in engagement analysis.

1. Analyze the campaign across all social media platforms where it was used.
2. Analyze the effectiveness of the campaign through each social media platform. This can be done by measuring the maximum number of likes, followers, or click-throughs through each platform.
3. Perform a deeper analysis of the social media platform that created the maximum impact. This can be done by observing the various words in the social media posts that resulted in maximum number of clicks to the assets. This analysis will help to word the campaigns effectively in the future.

The following are some of the specific applications of this use case in business.

- Track people who liked the content used in the campaign and the sentiments of people toward the campaign and the product that was marketed in the campaign.
- Track the effectiveness of the campaign.
- Understand the correct time of the year/month/day to host promotional campaigns of products.
- Analyze the most effective type of campaign. (There are many types of promotional campaigns such as advertisements, campaigns using social media sites, campaigns using brochures or flyers, campaigns organizing live concerts/programs at various locations.)

6.2.3 Revenue and Sales Lead Generation

Social media cannot be directly used for revenue generation. However, they can be used as a means for lead generation and conversion. To achieve complete success in this process, it is important to understand the importance of social media in the buying process of customers and then tune it to influence the customers toward a specific brand.

It is often a difficult task to quantify the impact of social media on the lead generation process and to track the number of leads that are generated using social media. The following is one high-level formula that could be used by executives to track the impact of social media on lead generation.

Lead generation effectiveness of social media = Number of leads generated using social media/total number of leads

Another metric that is very useful in measuring lead generation effectiveness is the content-to-contact ratio.

HOW PETCO USES SOCIAL MEDIA MARKETING FOR LEAD GENERATION

PETCO is an example of a company that takes a holistic approach to social media. "From a revenue perspective," says John Lazarchic, vice president of e-Commerce for PETCO, "Facebook is a low revenue source for us. We don't look at Facebook and Twitter and see that they're driving huge revenue." "For us," he continues, "social is more about engaging the customer, which means conversations about their pets. Our Facebook pages have a little information about products or promotions, but we do it rarely. We try to use Facebook more as an interactive brand tool. When we look at the data on likes and comments, we see almost universally they are comments or conversation about pets. People just love to talk about their pets." But that is only half the story. According to Lazarchic, the social tools on the PETCO site drive significant interaction. The company has seen that ratings and reviews drive conversion and sales and reduce return rates. Further, they've found that people who engage with their "Ask and Answer" tool have higher engagement and higher sales.

When consumers are on Facebook, "they're not in a shopping mode," Lazarchic says. "They may follow a retailer because they have an affinity for a brand, but they're not there because they're looking for dog food." Furthermore, consumers' social graphs don't necessarily mirror their interests. "Let's say I'm into aquariums. Maybe a few of my friends share my interest," he continues. "But if I go to the PETCO community, I'll find a whole group of people who love aquariums. The forums are about technical questions and expertise, whereas Facebook is more about engaging with friends."

But, Lazarchic cautions, what's true for PETCO may not necessarily be true for all brands, such as fashion. "I am in a consumable-driven business. I encourage retailers to look at their consumers, consider their demographics, and figure out their reason for being on social platforms," he stated. "Do you consider your friends to be dog nutrition experts? Probably not, but you might trust them to give you advice on whether something looks good on you." Lazarchic advises brands to take the long view and understand that social media is still new and evolving. "What's true today may change tomorrow, so this is just a snapshot in time of how we engage with our customers," he says [1].

Some specific applications of this use case are the following:

- Track leads by each social media channel and lead conversions using each channel.
- Track the impact of social media marketing on search results and search engine optimization.
- Assess the impact of social media marketing on customer loyalty.

6.2.4 Customer Relationship and Customer Experience Management

Customer experience management, which forms the foundation of customer relationship management, has a heavy dependency on social media. Social media has the capability to create a positive impact on customer experience management, which in turn can imply many other benefits for the organization such as brand value enhancement and cost savings.

6.2.4.1 Dell's Social Media Listening Command Center   Dell operates under the philosophy that "Everyone is listening," and created a Social Media Listening Command Center in December 2010. While Dell is organized in the holistic model for social media, it uses a hybrid holistic/coordinated model for listening. The goal is to embrace social media as an organization and as an integral part of the workday, while supporting all employees with social media "air cover." Though the Social Media Listening Command Center includes a ground control team, it is not the only location in which employees listen. A significant number of the more than 100,000 Dell employees—beyond the command center and social media team—listen to social channels as part of their daily responsibilities.

"We have a dual strategy when it comes to listening," Richard Binhammer says. "The first part is that we push listening deep into the organization. The closer people are connected to customers, the better." To support that philosophy, the company makes training and tools a priority for staff, enabling them to incorporate social media as a tool in their day-to-day operations. The second part of the strategy, Binhammer says, is embodied in the Command Center; the ground control team maintains a macro perspective on issues so that groups within Dell don't duplicate efforts and are instead able to focus on addressing customer concerns. The next evolution of listening, says Maribel Sierra, director of Global Social Media and Communities at Dell, is the notion of a "social radio," which Dell is currently building. The social radio will enable employees at the company to "tune into" conversations relevant to their group or line of business. "This is the next level of how we can bring listening to everyone at Dell" [1].

The level of expectations of the customers using different types of social media channels are different. In some types of social media channels such as communities, the expectations of the customers are not very high and they are happy to sort out their issues with the help of the experience or inputs of other members of the community.

Some specific applications of this use case are the following:

- Track the intensity of a specific product issue.
- Assess the customer relationship weak points of the organization.
- Track the time taken by the organization to respond to specific issues that are raised online.

6.2.5 Innovation

Many organizations use custom-built platforms and websites to gather crowd-sourced innovative thoughts and product ideas. A classic example is the website that is maintained by Starbucks (http://mystarbucksidea.force.com). But not all organizations have the resources and the capability to maintain such dedicated websites. This has made organizations explore alternate avenues to gather innovative inputs of people. One such trend that has become very popular these days is the use of social media networks to gather inputs that could act as feeders of innovation for various organizations. One key component is to make social media listening a constant part of an organization's function. This will help organizations to keep track of the various emerging ideas and also the feedback and responses to various ideas.

AMERICAN EXPRESS USES SOCIAL MEDIA TO GET INNOVATIVE PRODUCT IDEAS

"In an ideal world," says Pepper Evans of American Express, "we would use social analytics to listen and respond to product feedback, ultimately leading to product innovation. We would love to evolve based on what we hear in the industry."

6.2.6 Social Media Tools

Social media tools can be classified into two broad categories.

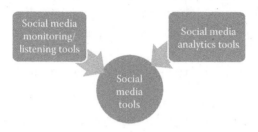

6.2.6.1 Social Media Monitoring/Listening Tools   These refer to a set of tools that listen to the usage of specific terms/phrases across all social media platforms and specific websites that are configured by the service provider. These words/phrases may pertain to specific brand names, sentiments about the brand, new product ideas for the brand, comparison of one brand with another, and so on. These tools will just provide monitoring capabilities and they do have to any in-depth analytical capabilities required by large enterprises. Some of the leading social media listening tools are the following:

- *Hootsuite.* This is a very popular social media listening tool and monitors multiple social media networks such as Twitter, Facebook, LinkedIn, WordPress, Foursquare, and Google+. It also provides limited analytical capabilities by generating weekly analytical reports.
- *TweetReach.* This tool helps an organization to assess the impact and implications of tweets by measuring how far the tweets travel. It helps to track the most influential followers of a brand. These influential followers can be used as brand ambassadors later on to promote and propagate the brand.
- *Klout.* This tool measures the impact or influence created in social media by a specific brand or person and then assigns a score called Klout Score based on the amount of influence created. Influence in this context refers to the response of people toward the content that is posted in social media networks and other online forums.

- *Socialmention.* This is a free social media listening tool and monitors more than 100 social media sites. This tool has the capability to analyze data in four different dimensions: Strength, Sentiment, Passion, and Reach.

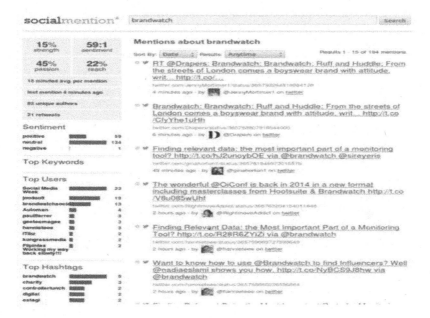

- *HowSociable.* This tool measures a brand's and a competitor brand's social media presence. With a free account it is possible to track 12 social media sites. If an organization is interested, it is possible to use this tool to track 24 more websites with the help of a paid account. This tool assigns scores for a brand on different social media platforms. This will provide insights on which social media platform is the best for a brand.

6.2.6.2 Social Media Analytics Tools   Social media analytics tools have the capability to measure the baseline social media parameters and provide deep analytical insights and patterns. Patterns are predicted for present and future scenarios. These predictions sometimes are made available as reports. In short, the main differentiating factor of the social media analytics tool is the ability to apply analytics to social media data for deep insights.

COGNOS CONSUMER INSIGHT—A POWERFUL SOCIAL MEDIA ANALYTICS SOLUTION FROM IBM

Cognos Consumer Insight allows organizations to track and analyze brand-related conversations in social media networks such as Twitter; Facebook; and any other websites, blogs, and communities as per the organization's requirement. To perform analysis, as a first step the solution collects and processes data from the required sources. The text analytics feature is utilized to read huge amounts of data to identify brand-related conversations, sentiments, and other general trends. The output of this can then be analyzed in a Cognos environment. The output provided by Cognos Consumer Insight is very powerful. It has huge potential as it helps to identify discussions about the brand quality and other issues pertaining to the brand. It also helps to track the product attributes that are of interest for customers and the performance of the brand content on various social media platforms.

6.3 Social Media Analytics Architecture for Intelligent Cities

An intelligent city is one where all the domains such as transportation, water, grids, and so on are interconnected and data coming from sensors of each of these domains are integrated and visualized through a common dashboard so as to facilitate collaborative decision making in real time.

Many times it becomes necessary to integrate data from sensor networks with the data of social media networks. Some examples of scenarios are situations where residents want to understand the reviews about restaurants in specific areas of city by combining data from social media networks such as the number of likes and the number of positive comments, situations where residents want to combine the GPS feature with social media networks to locate social media friends in real time, and so on.

The different layers of the architecture are as follows:

Physical layer. This layer contains sensors, CCTV cameras, video surveillance systems, transportation management systems, water management systems, intelligent grid systems, intelligent home automation systems, and so on that form a part of the intelligent city ecosystem. This layer represents the systems that fetch actual physical data and bring it into the IT Infrastructure of intelligent cities.

Services layer. The diverse types of data from the physical layer are processed appropriately using different techniques. For example, video feeds are processed using some image processing algorithms such as face recognition algorithm for facial recognition, shape recognition for different types of shapes, and so on. Similarly audio feeds could be processed using some speech recognition algorithm and so on. The whole objective of processing data is to create rich metadata that could be streamed in real time to serve as inputs for search operations. The services layer has the capability to combine data from sensors and social media networks to identify specific objects or events of interest. This is possible because of the capabilities offered by the highly sophisticated Internet of Things (IoT) platforms that have the capability to fuse, combine, or filter multiple types and streams of data. The services layer has an intelligent rules engine with the capability to combine multiple complex types of metadata in response to queries from the search engine. This makes it possible for the service layer to extract insights based on the combination of data from sensor networks and social media networks. The services layer stores all types of metadata in a XML/JSON format. This layer can also use representational state transfer (REST) application programming interface (API) to deliver services to the engine layer.

Search engine layer. Search operations are performed using the search engine that is present in the search engine layer. The search engine collects data from the various nodes and indexes them by creating an extremely efficient index structure. The search engine also has the capability to perform ranking of events that are obtained from social media networks and services layer as per their relevance to user queries.

Presentation layer. The results of search operation are presented to the end-users through various types of presentation devices such as mobile phones, laptops, and visualization dashboards.

Xively—A classic example of IoT platform. Xively is the first public cloud purpose-built for the IoT platform. Xively's platform as a service (PaaS) helps organizations to create interconnected devices whose count can scale up to billions of devices. Xively provides an exhaustive list of APIs for many programming languages and platforms. This allows organizations to build embedded software products that can readily connect to the Xively service. Xively has a Web service that provides the capability to provision and manage devices. This in turn provides capability to each device to send and receive data using the Xively platform. Xively also provides visualization of results in the form of interactive graphs and dashboards.

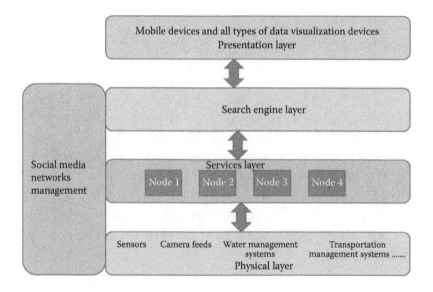

6.3.1 Social Media Analytics for City Government

The key components of an intelligent city are depicted in the following diagram:

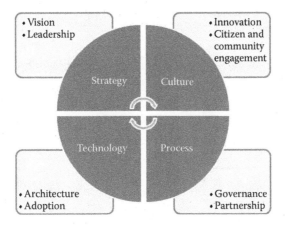

The role of social media analytics is vital for building the culture of an intelligent city. This is because a healthy city culture will evolve only in an environment in which residents actively communicate, collaborate, and participate in the decision-making processes of the city. Social media will be a key channel for the citizens to collaborate, express their views, and voice their concerns over various matters which are handled by the city government. For the city government to know, extract, and use this information effectively, social media analytics becomes an inevitable component. The main component of social media analytics that is very useful for the city government is sentiment analysis, also known as opinion mining. Now let us look at what this sentiment analysis is all about and its importance for city government.

6.3.2 Design of an Architecture for Sentiment Analysis in Intelligent Cities

The Internet is loaded with different types of opinions or reviews by people on different events, products, and personalities. Social media sites such as Facebook and Twitter generate immense amounts of public opinions that can serve as useful inputs for the decision making process. Many of these types of opinion data take various forms, such as reviews, surveys, ratings, and so on and many of them are on local city government services. Each of these opinion data could be treated as an unstructured data input. Sentiment analysis is a discipline that tries to interpret and understand these broad ranges of informal opinions. An example of the outcome of sentiment analysis is given below.

Platform	Objective	Metric	Goal	Alternate metric
Facebook	Customer engagement	Avg number of comments/post	10	Avg number of shares/week
Twitter	General awareness	Avg number of followers/post	10	Avg number of RTs/post
LinkedIn	Thought leadership	Number of best answers	23	Number of recommendations
YouTube	Sales/lead generation	Number of leads/sales	1%	Likes/views
Blog	General awareness	Number of unique visitors/month	500	Comments/post
Slide share	Sales/lead generation	Number of leads/sales	3%	Number of downloads

Sentiment analysis is a branch of computational linguistics that tries to extract emotions from text. An architecture that could be used as a reference for performing sentiment analysis in intelligent cities is given below. Ways to gauge customer sentiment include

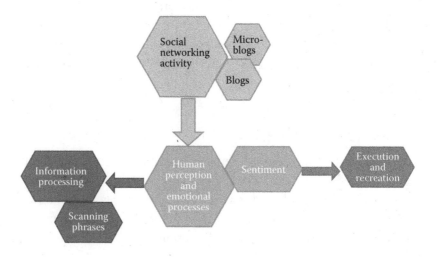

- Blogs
- Microblogs
- Review sites
- Social media networks
- Online communities

The different levels at which sentiment analysis is performed are described in the following paragraphs.

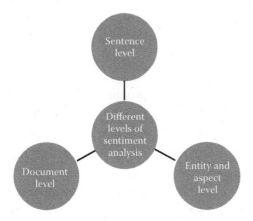

Document level. The main task here is to examine a document in its entirety to assess if it denotes a positive or a negative sentiment. This type of sentiment analysis is commonly used to examine product review documents and other documents of that kind to check whether the sentiment expressed by the entire document is positive, negative, or neutral. This method of analysis is also called document level sentiment classification. However, this analysis has a constraint in that it can be applied only to documents that represent a single entity.

Sentence level. The main task here is to examine a sentence and classify if it expresses a positive, negative, or neutral opinion. Neutral means no opinion.

Entity and aspect level. This level of sentiment analysis performs a high level of fine-grained analysis when compared to document-level and sentence-level analysis. In many situations, some documents will contain a mix of positive and negative sentiments. In such situations, this level of sentiment analysis becomes a very useful option. Entity and aspect–level analysis does not focus on language constructs such as sentence and paragraph. Instead it focuses only on opinion analysis.

The fundamental idea behind this analysis is that any opinion will have basically two parts:

- A sentiment (positive or negative)
- A target (of opinion)

This method works on the assumption that an opinion without its target has only limited use. The concept of opinion target is also very helpful to understand the context of the sentiment analysis problem. For example, although the sentence "Although the service is not that great, I still love this restaurant" clearly has a positive tone, we cannot say that it is entirely positive. In fact, the sentence is positive about the restaurant (emphasized), but negative about its service (not emphasized). In many applications, opinion targets are described by entities and/or their different aspects. Thus, the goal of this level of analysis is to discover sentiments on entities and/or their aspects [2].

The fundamental concept underlying sentiment analysis is natural language processing (NLP). NLP extracts specific emotion-related keywords from data that appear in the data sources from where it has been linked or configured to receive data. One common task that needs to be performed after keyword selection is polarity classification. Polarity classification extracts a particular word or phrase and classifies it into one of three categories:

- Positive
- Negative
- Neutral

This will be used as a basis to decide the review rating of the city service or decision where opinion is sought from the residents. Different types of sentiment analysis software are available in the market. These software extract opinion from textual data. Review aggregators present in the software determine whether the reviews could be categorized as positive, negative, or neutral. Some software even have the capability to assign a score based on the number of positive, negative, and neutral words present in specific data sources. Some city services where sentiment analysis could be used are the following:

- Track sentiments of citizens on specific government decisions pertaining to public welfare.

- Track citizen emotion toward the quality of government services.
- Track sentiments of the citizens on cost-cutting measures introduced by the government.
- Track the well-being and emotions of citizens.
- Assess factors in a city that demand immediate attention based on the feedback and emotions of citizens.

At present, the use of sentiment analytics by city officials to hear the concerns of citizens is limited. However, in the intelligent cities of the future, this will become part of the government's day-to-day activities because of the extensive use of social media in all facets of life.

6.3.3 Use of IBM's Social Sentiment Index to Identify the Factors Impacting People in Five Canadian Cities

IBM analyzed the tweets from thousands of people from five Canadian cities to identify their challenges resulting from traffic congestion in these cities [3]. In the big data age, with its continuous information explosion from data generated by blogs, online communities, and social media networks, social media listening helps to analyze and understand the data to get valuable insights on people's attitudes. This critical capability offered by social media data helps city officials to understand and react to public opinion on key city services such as transportation, which is a city service considered in the current example.

As per IBM's analyses, it was evident that citizens of Toronto were the most vocal, as they had posted about 10,000 tweets about traffic congestion in 11 months. Of these 11,000 tweets, more than 40% were found to be negative. The number of negative sentiments related to vehicle parking issues was the major point of concern for most of the citizens of Toronto. It was observed that after going around the parking area, the citizens tweeted out of their frustration that they were not able to find a parking slot for their vehicles. Citizens of other Canadian cities also had similar negative sentiments about vehicle parking. This fact is a major eye opener for the city officials to devise and deploy IT systems that have the capability to send parking slot availability information on major parking areas in the cities.

Another Canadian city, Halifax, had fewer than 1000 traffic-related tweets, about only 20% of which were negative. But this city had the highest number of traffic tweets in relation to the proportion of the city's population. The status in Vancouver was similar. Montreal had the lowest number of traffic-related tweets, showing that its citizens were not really concerned about traffic-related issues.

Sentiment analysis provides valuable information to city officials to prioritize the matters that require immediate attention and make judicious use of available resources and funds to tackle such concerns. The example that follows sheds light on the importance of sentiment analysis for city officials.

6.3.4 Spain Uses Sentiment Analysis to Track and Improve Standards of City Services

The city of Madrid has added a new feedback mechanism to its social media networks. This mechanism provides options to citizens to give their feedback and comments on various public services in the city such as lighting, irrigation, waste management, and so on. City officials are planning to use this feedback to improve their services and prioritize aspects that demand immediate attention.

6.3.5 Sentiment Analysis to Track the Mood of City Residents

Sentiment analysis can be used to track food habits, which in turn can be used to track the mood of residents with regard to their food.

6.3.6 FoodMood.in Uses Sentiment Analysis to Track Food Mood of Citizens

FoodMood.in is a website that has the capability to combine tweets with geographic locations to predict the present state of mind of citizens with regard to food. Foodmood uses a sentiment classification tool of Stanford University that is a "trained" classifier that can accept millions of tweets as inputs at a time. This website also provides features to classify top 10 favorite foods of a specific city or region. In addition, it has options to compare countries based on their gross domestic product (GDP) and food score.

Bristol University in the United Kingdom gathers the emotions that are expressed in tweets to generate reports about the mood of the country. This report has proved to be very accurate in its calculation, as it has been found that many times when there were riots and natural calamities in the United Kingdom, fear and sorrow were the emotions that emerged as the general mood of the country.

6.3.7 Smart Policing Using Sensors and Domain Awareness System

The New York Police Department (NYPD) implements smart policing by combining sensor data with social media data. This solution was developed by Microsoft and is called the Domain Awareness Solution. It aggregates data from multiple sources such as video feeds, license plate information, witness reports, and social media networks. This solution provides investigators in the NYPD a real-time view of the criminal activity in the city. This solution also provides insights on potential threats.

6.3.8 Case Study of Sentiment Analysis Implementation in an Intelligent City

The city of Santander in Spain is in the process of creating a large intelligent city. Several pilot projects are being implemented in this city [4]. Smart Santander proposes a unique city-scale experimental research facility in support of typical applications and services for an intelligent city. This facility will be sufficiently large, open, and flexible to enable horizontal and vertical federation with other experimental facilities and stimulates development of new applications by users of various types including experimental advanced research on IoT technologies and realistic assessment of users' acceptability tests. The project envisions the deployment of 20,000 sensors in Belgrade, Guildford, Lübeck, and Santander (12,000), exploiting a large variety of technologies. A mobile application was developed for the residents of the city. This mobile application has a tool to display the different types of emotions at the Santander area. The six primary emotions that are included in this mobile application are the following:

- Anger
- Disgust
- Fear
- Joy
- Sadness
- Surprise

• Anger

• Surprise

• Fear

• Disgust

• Sadness

• Joy

When the citizens of this city post messages to social media networks with the help of this mobile application, they can add appropriate emotion-related color to their post at an appropriate location in Santander. This helps to track sentiments of the citizens at various locations in Santander.

6.4 Conclusion

Social media analytics is a niche and fast growing variant of analytics that focuses on the application of analytics on the data that are gathered from the social media networks. The patterns that are gathered as an outcome of social media analytics have diverse applications in various fields. The metrics to assess the impact of social media networks were examined in this chapter. The key use cases of social media analytics were discussed: customer relationship and customer experience management, innovation, marketing communication programs, sales and lead generation, and brand advocacy. The different types of social media tools and some market leading vendors for social media analytics tools were also discussed.

In the next section of the chapter, the key focus was on the use of social media analytics for the various services of city government.

A social media architecture for intelligent cities together with a value chain that specifies the value of social media analytics for intelligent cities was discussed. A variant of social media analytics called sentiment analysis is very useful for city government to track and understand the sentiments of citizens toward various decisions of the city government. Various real-life examples that depict the use sentiment analysis for various aspects of the city were also discussed. The chapter concluded with a short case study of sentiment analysis implementation in an intelligent city.

References

1. Altimeter Group (2011). A Framework for Social Analytics (white paper).
2. Bing Liu (2012). *Sentiment Analysis and Opinion Mining*. Morgan & Claypool.
3. http://www.ibm.com/news/ca/en/2013/04/02/r881108u46877w41.html.
4. http://www.smartsantander.eu/.

7

INTELLIGENT CITIES

Strategy-Making and Governance

Abstract

Cities across the world are in the midst of a conglomeration of challenges such as the rapid increase in population, drastic decline in city budgets, and inability to strike a balance between the supply and demand of resources that are required to sustain them. Present-day cities need to take some drastic steps to meet these ever-increasing demands of their citizens and also improve the quality of services that are being provided to them. Information technology (IT) can act as a catalyst of this change by fueling the automation of various city systems and processes, which would in turn equip cities to deliver more with limited resources and budgets. There are various phases in the transformation of a city based on the levels of technology integration that has been embraced by it. The two main types of cities that we consider in this chapter are digital cities and ubiquitous or intelligent cities. Digital cities devise and implement IT-based strategies and IT-based social initiatives to drive radical changes in the way they function. These in turn will help cities to improve the quality of life of their citizens. Ubiquitous or intelligent cities are cities that have attained very high levels of technology integration in almost all aspects of their infrastructure and processes to an extent that the various infrastructural components can communicate seamlessly with one another. This communication is done with the help of various components such as sensors, actuators, and control systems using diverse types of ubiquitous networks. The value propositions offered by U-cities to its residents are the following: (1) Efficient and effective delivery of services. (2) Efficient use of city infrastructure components. (3) Effective and unprecedented strategic information on the use of the city and its services. These two types of cities, together with the various types of technology integration supported by each of them, and the strategic governance framework required for the digitization of cities are the key topics of this chapter.

7.1 Introduction

Cities across the world are facing numerous challenges that are drawing increasing focus and fueling significant investments. Some of the key issues faced by cities are the following:

- *Increased population levels.* As per the United Nations report, the world's population in urban areas or cities constituted 50% of the entire world's population and is expected to increase further in the years to come. Between 2009 and 2050, the city population is expected to increase by 2.3 billion, the whole of which is expected to move from rural areas to cities, creating a net increase in the urban population by 84% in the next four decades. This soaring rise in the urban population exerts significant pressure on the various city sectors and infrastructure components such as transportation, healthcare, education, and other city services, that in turn will incur a great deal of capital expenditure for the city's rejuvenation.
- *Polarized economic growth.* The 2012 McKinsey report states that the world's top 600 cities will contribute 65% of global gross domestic product (GDP) from 2010 to 2025 [1].
- *Increased environmental concerns.* Owing to the enormous population in cities, greenhouse gas emissions from cities have reached an alarming level. This in turn imposes pressure on cities to devise and implement sustainable and eco-friendly strategies in various sectors such as energy and utilities, transportation, and manufacturing.
- *Declined city budgets.* Cities are under tremendous economic pressure and this in turn forces them to reduce the budgets that are available for city and resident development activities.

To address these concerns, it is necessary to identify and eliminate the concerns that prevail at the grass root levels of the city ecosystem. To that end, it is necessary to identify the key elements that comprise a city ecosystem, as follows:

- Information pertaining to various aspects of a city
- Citizens
- City leaders
- City infrastructure and resources

Information is a strategic asset of a city. Amalgamating information about the city resources and making it available to city leaders is a vital factor that will equip city leaders for proactive decision making about the various aspects of the city such as intelligent resource utilization and communicate it back to other components of the city ecosystem. It is essential to make the residents aware of the vital information about the city's resources so that it can induce a behavioral change in them that in turn would benefit the city significantly. A city's operation and planning should be based on ongoing real-time monitoring of various city parameters, insightful visualizations, and constant feedback loops or mechanisms that create more efficient city systems. They also instill better informed decision-making capabilities for city leaders and citizens. Cities should be treated like real-time systems, and there should be a continuous opportunity to make effective use of city resources swiftly and at the same time feed those decisions back to the various components of the city ecosystem. These aspects of the city ecosystem are summarized in the following diagram:

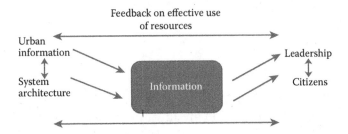

The main constraints faced by cities will require devising intelligent strategies and governance mechanisms to accommodate the increasing population masses with limited resources and constrained budgets. In short, cities need to evolve into intelligent cities to deliver more with fewer resources. Information and communication technology (ICT) will be the key enabling component for the design, implementation, and operation of intelligent cities. Apart from ICT, radio frequency identification tags (RFIDs), sensor networks, geographic information systems (GISs), wireless broadband, location-based services, and smartcard systems have also found their way into the various initiatives devised by the government for the welfare of its citizens. But the key to effective implementation of resident-based services using these components is the efficacious use of these technologies to devise systems that are interoperable and intercommunicable.

City leaders will have a major role in the transformation of cities into intelligent cities as the core task of decision making, strategy formulation, and implementation needs to start from them and then penetrate deeper into all other city hierarchies. The governance framework for the design and implementation of intelligent cities should be designed using the approach shown in the following diagram:

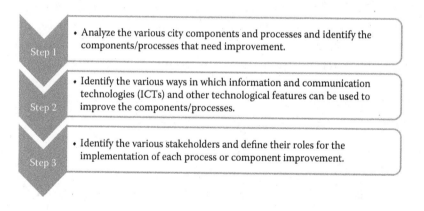

Step 1
- Analyze the various city components and processes and identify the components/processes that need improvement.

Step 2
- Identify the various ways in which information and communication technologies (ICTs) and other technological features can be used to improve the components/processes.

Step 3
- Identify the various stakeholders and define their roles for the implementation of each process or component improvement.

Information technology (IT) is central for the transformation of cities. Cities across the world are in various stages of maturity with respect to their use of IT and all other allied technologies. This has led to the classification of cities in terms of the maturity of their resident-based digital services. Several classifications exist for cities such as digital city, smart city, ubiquitous city, and so on. However, the exact definition of each type of city and the demarcation among the different types of cities is not clearly laid out. The various types of governments based on the level of technology integration can be classified as shown in the following figure (E-government refers to electronic government and U-government refers to ubiquitous government):

Parameters	E-government	U-government
IT strategy	Process reenginerring using IT	Seamless integration and linkage
Service availability	24 hours a day, 7 days a week	365 days nonstop
Service space	Customer's home and office using Internet	Customer's location and physical change

The focus of this chapter is on the various aspects of the city governance framework and how the framework can be used efficiently to build various pillars of a city, which in turn will play a major role in the transformation of cities into intelligent cities. The two types of governments—E-government and U-government—and their frameworks and strategies are also dealt with in detail in this chapter. Throughout this chapter, the terms ICT and IT are used interchangeably.

7.2 IT Initiatives for Intelligent City Governance

The IT initiatives for intelligent governance of cities can take two dimensions: IT-enabled city strategies and IT-enabled social initiatives.

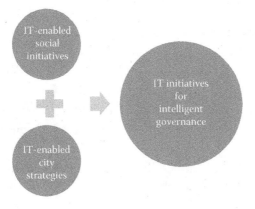

IT-enabled city strategies involve the use of latest IT tools to improve and optimize the existing city infrastructure components. Examples of IT-enabled city strategies are shown in the following diagram:

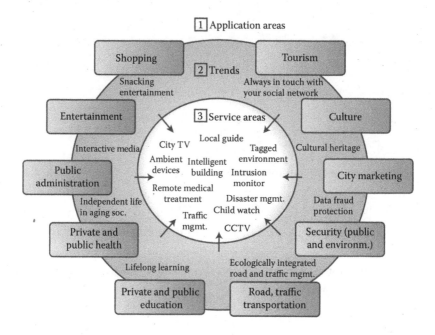

IT-enabled social initiatives stimulate self-help, community endeavors using social media and other IT tools, community-based business initiatives, and other activities that could efficiently use IT tools for the benefit of society. These initiatives cannot replace IT-enabled city strategies; instead they can complement them and make them work more effectively for the benefit of the residents.

IT-enabled city strategies can take several dimensions such as e-governance and digitization of processes involved in various city sectors such as healthcare, education, and transportation, to name a few. Some cities in the world have surpassed these levels of digitization and have attained new heights in the technology-enabled city concept by embracing the concept of ubiquitous computing. Ubiquitous computing deals with embedding computing devices in our surroundings and making them work in an interconnected, interoperable, and seamless manner with the main objective of making computing power available for an average person to smooth everyday activities. For our discussions throughout this chapter, we will use the following evolutionary framework to categorize cities in terms of maturity of their technological infrastructure:

From this diagram, it is clear that there are two stages of evolution for a city:

1. *Digital city.* A digital city is one that uses the Internet and other Web-related technologies for the creation of processes and systems that would benefit its residents. It more tightly aligns itself to the e-governance concept, which at present has its roots in most cities across the world.
2. *Intelligent/ubiquitous city.* An intelligent or ubiquitous city is one that uses a combination of IT and ubiquitous technologies such as RFID, location-based tracking, GIS, and other sensors embedded in the surroundings to automate the daily activities of residents. This requires a matured IT infrastructure backbone that should have the scalability and adaptability to absorb and accommodate many cutting edge technologies.

For a city to evolve into an intelligent city, it is necessary to ensure that it first transforms into a digital city. The concept of a digital city encompasses both a digital city, which involves the use of IT-enabled city strategies, and a digital society, which involves the use of IT-enabled social initiatives. In the next few sections of the chapter, we delve further into these two types of cities, focusing more on the technological aspects, examples of city processes with which the technologies can be integrated, and the benefits the citizens can gain using each of them.

7.2.1 IT-Enabled City Strategies

IT-enabled city strategies provide new ways for governments, municipal authorities, and private sector companies to design and build more efficient infrastructure and services for cities. In the next section some examples of IT-enabled city strategies are discussed, with an in-depth look at e-government, which is the core component of a digital city.

7.2.2 E-Government

An e-government is a government that uses IT for its transformation by making its systems and processes more accessible, effective, and accountable for its citizens. E-government can be described as a social technical system with a social subsystem (government) and technical subsystem (IT). The social technical framework for e-government is shown in the following figure:

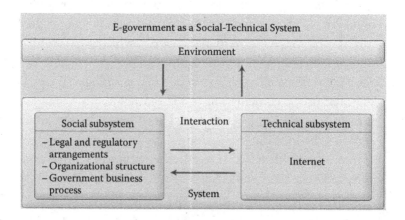

E-government includes

- Facilities that provide good access to government information
- Options that promote citizen engagement by offering more facilities for the public to interact with government officials
- Provisions that make the government more accountable for its operations by allowing more transparency, which in turn alleviates opportunities for corruption
- Options that provide more development opportunities for its residents, especially for the benefit of rural and traditionally underserved communities

The key feature of e-government is the use of IT to connect government very closely to its citizens. E-government cannot be set up overnight simply by a government deciding to buy some computers and set up a website. Instead, it requires careful planning, execution, and the full support of city leaders and other government officials for its complete success. Setting up of an e-government is a three-phase process. The success of each phase determines the success rate of the next phase. The three phases for setting up an e-government are as follows.

Phase 1: Make the government information available and accessible to citizens through IT tools (publish). Government agencies generate huge volumes of information that are mostly useful for their citizens. But most of the time, the citizens are not aware of the availability of such information and hence fail to make use of it judiciously. This can be avoided to a great extent by posting such information online and making it accessible to all citizens. Examples of such useful information could be changes in government policies/rules, forms, and so on. These government websites go a long way in making government information available to large masses of the population.

Phase 1 of E-government in action. The Government of Colombia portal is a true example of a one-stop portal that provides access to all types of government information using a single view. This was set up as a result of a directive from the president of Colombia to all government agencies to create websites that represent their services correctly to the citizens of Colombia. All of these websites were later linked through a single portal. Each government agency paid a great deal of attention to set up high-quality websites that made the citizens aware of its services in the best possible manner. As a result of this effort, this portal is now quoted as a well-established example of an e-government one-stop portal.

Phase 2: Increase citizen participation in government activities (interact). After publishing the government-related policy information on websites, it is the responsibility of the government to make people aware of the information and also provide them appropriate trainings on how to use it. After this is done, the government should motivate its citizens and involve them in the policymaking process. This can be done by advertising various aspects of the proposed government policy online before finalizing them. The citizens should be also encouraged to openly share their views and thoughts in open blogging communities/groups set up by the government for that purpose. The government should also reciprocate by informing citizens that their views are highly appreciated and making them aware of the steps/actions that were taken by the government to address their viewpoints or suggestions. With the increased proliferation of Web 3.0 technologies, interactive websites are no longer a dream or a myth. Government agencies across the world are using interactive communities and forums to understand the views of citizens on various activities that are in the government's pipeline for execution.

Phase 2 of E-government in action. The Government of Namibia has a website that provides opportunities to its citizens to participate in national government discussions. The government using this website wants to involve its citizens in its political discussions, thereby setting an example of a true democratic government. This website provides an opportunity for citizens to be up to date with the latest legislative developments of the Namibian parliament. One specific aspect that needs to be mentioned is that bills that are under consideration are posted on this website and the citizens are provided an opportunity to voice their concerns directly to the parliamentary representatives.

One recent trend that has become increasingly popular in this direction is the use of social media such as Facebook and Twitter for gathering the views of citizens on specific activities that are planned by the government. The various types of interactions (likes, comments, dislikes, etc.) of large masses of population are tracked and reported using various mechanisms and they are used to finalize the appropriate course of action. An entire new stream of analytics has evolved in this direction to track the views of the citizens on various events or policies that are planned by the government. This is called sentiment analytics. More details about this are covered in Chapter 6.

Phase 3: Make services of government accessible to citizens online. Governments can take a step further by creating e-commerce type applications and add them to their websites. This will help citizens to process their government transactions online. This would provide tremendous time savings for citizens by avoiding lengthy queues and waiting times in front of government offices. Some of the key applications that would benefit highly are tax payments, land registrations, fine collection for vehicles, and so on.

Perhaps the biggest benefit for governments utilizing and providing online websites for various government services would be to streamline the currently labor-intensive tasks, which in turn can save a great deal of money for the government in the years to come. Further, by automating and refurbishing the manual procedures and processes, government agencies can curtail corruption to a great extent and also increase their revenue enormously as a result of automation of revenue-generating areas such as tax and fine collection.

Phase 3 of E-government in action: E-procurement system, Chile. The government procurement system in Chile had numerous challenges because of the existence of several systems and processes that were fragmented and followed multiple heterogeneous regulatory frameworks. In 1998, the government of Chile set up the Communications and Information Technology Unit (UTIC). The main objective of this organization was to come out with a set of e-government efforts to reduce costs and make the government systems and processes more transparent. The first step taken by UTIC was revamping the existing procurement systems by centralizing all the purchasing activities with the help of a website.

This website had the capability to automatically send out e-mail notifications to companies that had registered with the government for information such as when contracts come up for bid. This in turn was followed by an online bidding procedure. This new system thoroughly corrected all the flaws that existed in the procurement system and it was also able to create new methods of accountability by providing diverse types of statistics that are very helpful for the successful completion of the procurement process.

Based on the three phases of e-government, there are four prominent types of e-governance models in the present-day scenario.

1. *Government-to-government (G2G)*. In this case, IT is used mainly to restructure the governmental processes among the various government agencies. The issue that requires paramount attention in the government sector is the existence of disparate government agencies with no well-defined processes to ensure communication and coordination between them. This model provides interaction among different government agencies as well as between different functional areas within an organization. This model also provides vertical interactions among the various national, provincial, and local government agencies as well as between different various levels that exist within an organization.

2. *Government-to-citizens (G2Cs)*. In this model, a website, blog, or community is created that acts as an interface between the government and citizens. This will enable the citizens to benefit by direct interactions with the government agencies. Another use case of this model is the provision to make online payments to various government agencies. In short, this model improves the availability, accessibility, and quality of government services to citizens.

3. *Government-to-business (G2B)*. In this model, government websites are used to help the business community interact directly with the government. The objective of this model is to cut red tape, reduce time, reduce operational costs, and create a transparent business environment by handling transactions directly with the government without a third party. The G2B model can be used for transactions such as licensing, permits, procurement, and revenue collection. It can also be used for trade- and tourism-related business.

4. *Government-to-employees (G2Es)*. In most countries, the government is the biggest employer. It becomes necessary therefore for the government to interact with its employees on a regular basis. This is a two-way process between the government agency and the employee. Use of IT tools helps to make these interactions fast and efficient.

7.2.3 Key Challenges for E-Government

7.2.3.1 Infrastructure Development Many cities across the world do not have the basic infrastructure that is required for the implementation of e-government tools and technologies. It is vital to examine the existing infrastructure, find the loopholes, and work with stakeholders to rectify the issues and eliminate the gaps.

7.2.3.1.1 Infrastructure Development in Practice: E-Literacy Model in Gyandoot, India Gyandoot is a community-based literacy program that is a true example of e-government–based service in India. The most important aspect of this program is its success even in remote villages of India where the literacy rate is very low and numerous infrastructure limitations exist, such as limited bandwidth for Internet connectivity. The highlight of this program is the fact that readily available and cost-effective technologies can make even the poorest and most remote populations use e-government services effectively.

The core aspect of this project was the use of kiosks as commercial organizations. To provide additional level of flexibility, the Gyandoot project uses laptops with Internet access that was provided using wireless modems. This project spreads the value of government services even to the most remote villages of Madhya Pradesh. The kiosks offer a host of government services including, for example, information on the price of seeds, fertilizers, and crops through useful government links that make it possible for the people in villages to access the necessary information without the need to undertake long-distance travel to government offices.

7.2.3.2 Public Policy and Law The use of IT for provision of government services may require amendments to existing laws. Appropriate amendments to the laws should be made to ensure that electronic documents and transactions are recognized and approved and that existing policies support and not impede the growth of e-government services.

7.2.3.3 Privacy E-government services collect a great deal of data about citizens and store them in different types of databases. In this scenario, it becomes very important for the government to preserve the privacy of the information that is collected from citizens. Privacy measures must be incorporated during the planning and design of e-government systems. It is very difficult or almost impossible to integrate effective privacy protection mechanisms after a system is built.

7.2.3.3.1 Privacy Impact Assessment, Ontario, Canada: An Online Guide to Fair Information Practices   Ontario Province in Canada has created a Privacy Impact Assessment toolkit. The main purpose of this toolkit is to provide guidelines to educate governments that are interested in evaluating their information policies against the widely accepted privacy criteria.

7.2.3.4 Security   Security is costly, but adequate measures must be taken to ensure appropriate security of e-government systems during their design phase. Breach of security is a serious factor that could drain the trust and faith of the citizens in the e-government system.

7.2.3.5 Interoperability   Interoperability is a vital factor in the design of e-government systems. Instead of designing and implementing separate systems for each department, e-government systems should be designed in such a way that they are interoperable and can be used across various departments of the government. Design of efficient and reliable e-government systems requires a comprehensive overhaul of existing legacy systems.

7.2.3.6 Public/Private Collaboration   Various parties from both public and private sectors should be involved for the effective and successful implementation of e-government services. Techniques to set up public and private collaboration and competition are already a matter of grave concern in the e-government domain. New rules and regulations may have to be framed to define the relationship of the public and private sectors in the e-government ventures. The question in the demarcation of controls between the public and the private sector in e-government efforts is always a matter of concern and debate. The best way to ensure coordination and cooperation in various e-government projects must be considered carefully, with public and private sectors working together as partners with no intention of political or economic gain. Unplanned partnerships and alliances can have brutal consequences, so it is important to review new partner relationships frequently to ensure that both parties involved are pleased with the terms and conditions laid down in the partnership agreement. In short, for the effective implementation of e-government services, the various aspects as summarized in the following figure should be implemented.

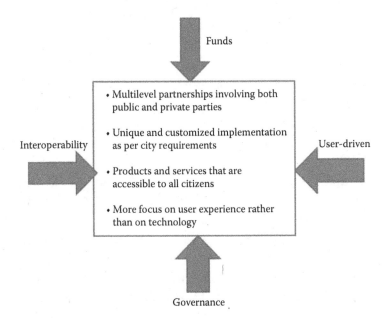

Apart from e-government, some other examples of IT-enabled city strategies are the following:

- *Creation of excellent network infrastructure.* The availability of ubiquitous broadband infrastructure for both wired and wireless networks creates an excellent backbone for fixed and mobile telecommunication services, which in turn goes a long way in contributing to integrate systems that are present in all spheres of a city. This is often considered as a key infrastructure component for a digital city.
- *IT-enabled healthcare.* The digitization of healthcare records and the use of integrated health information systems and networking technology to leverage expert medical care by using facilities such as telemedicine and remote healthcare monitoring go a long way in transforming a city into a digital city.
- *IT-enabled education.* IT has a large role to play in education. The concept of L3—Life Long Learning—and A3—Anybody,

Anytime, Anywhere—is possible through IT. One of the key components that enables L3 and A3 is the concept of e-learning. E-learning refers to a Web-based educational delivery mechanism through which students can access the trainings anytime, anywhere through the use of the Internet. The emergence of e-learning has revolutionized the field of education and is a very crucial component for the development of digital cities.

- *IT-enabled construction.* Use of IT to reengineer the construction industry is a key element of a digital city. This is mainly because IT-enabled building-automation systems help in the design and construction of energy-efficient buildings. These buildings in turn help to reduce energy consumption and facilitate judicious use of space within buildings. Energy-efficient and eco-friendly buildings form the core infrastructural component of digital cities.

- *IT-enabled grids and utilities.* The use of IT to design and develop real-time metering and control systems for electricity networks and gas and water utilities is a vital aspect for the emergence of a digital city. These real-time metering systems reduce fraud and theft by allowing real-time usage monitoring and reporting. These metering systems also help to devise specific tariffs or plans for different types of consumers based on their consumption patterns. It also helps to devise a better alignment of supply and demand to optimize and reduce overall resource consumption.

- *IT-led economic development.* Creation of technology-intensive business units or research and development initiatives and special economic zones to attract fresh investments that catalyze the growth of hardware- and software-intensive industries is a must-have factor for the development of digital cities. Early examples include Japan's Shinanogawa Technopolis, Malaysia's Cyberjaya, Bangalore's software and tech parks, and the Wuxi New District in China. More recent technopolis developments include India's Kochi Electronic Park and Chengdu's Tianfu Software Park, the largest software park in China.

7.3 IT-Enabled Social Initiatives

As discussed previously, IT-enabled social initiatives complement IT-enabled city strategies by using IT to deliver some features as shown in the following figure:

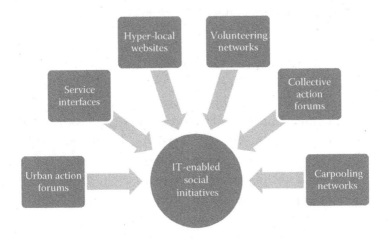

Apart from the previously listed topics, IT-enabled social initiatives also involve the use of social media networks such as Facebook to form communities and mobilize local action.

7.3.1 Urban Action Forums

IT-enabled urban action forums are communities that use information technology for a common cause directed toward the benefit of the citizens. The evolution of Web 2.0 technologies has played a major role in the evolution of such urban action forums that use interactive websites to direct the thoughts of the citizens in an area toward a common goal.

One excellent example of an urban action forum is Your Library, the Web portal that was launched in the city of Edinburgh by the Library and Information Services department of the city. In Edinburgh, libraries were extensively used by people not only as access points for gaining a wealth of information about various aspects, but also as a socializing venue for formal and informal interactions with other citizens.

After the launch of Web 2.0 services, it was decided to integrate IT with various aspects of library processes and also to integrate social media with the library IT infrastructure so that even after digitization, libraries could continue to provide a platform for people to socialize with one another. All of these aspects led to the design of Your Library, the Web portal with the following features:

- The "Virtual Library" Web portal contained links to two main applications: YourEdinburgh and Library2Go.
- Integration of social media sites such as Twitter, Flicker, and YouTube under a common identity, "Tales of One City." The overall aim of integrating the social networks to the library portal was to promote local libraries across the city and to provide a platform for residents to share their views about the library. This also provided a platform for the library staff to receive complaints and take appropriate corrective actions.

7.3.1.1 The Virtual Library Web Portal   The Virtual Library Web portal is a unique portal that united all the digital resources of the library such as catalogues, databases, and other websites under a single portal. The portal also provided various options to renew library membership, reserve books, and download and use the various digital resources of the library.

7.3.1.2 YourEdinburgh   The YourEdinburgh element of the Virtual Library is an important technique that was devised to promote involvement among neighborhoods and community groups. It also aimed to ensure that library users could feel a sense of ownership.

7.3.1.3 Library2Go   This supports downloading of audio books and other e-books to mobile devices. This innovative library system devised by the city of Edinburgh proved to be a huge success and was adopted by many neighboring cities to promote their own libraries.

7.3.1.4 Service Interfaces   Service interfaces are IT resources that act as interfaces between the citizens and the government. One excellent example of a service interface is the website http://www.fixmystreet.com.

At such websites, citizens typically are asked to follow a three-step process to raise a concern or lodge a complaint, as shown in the following diagram:

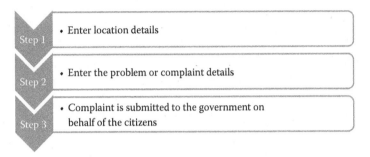

Step 1
• Enter location details

Step 2
• Enter the problem or complaint details

Step 3
• Complaint is submitted to the government on behalf of the citizens

Such useful websites go a long way in incorporating intelligent governance system in cities.

7.3.1.5 Hyper-Local Websites Hyper-local websites are typically used for conveying all kinds of information pertaining to a specific city or sometimes the neighboring cities as well. One classic example of a hyper-local website is EveryBlock (http://www.everyblock.com), which is the leading website for neighborhood discussions and engagement, including the latest local media stories, crime reports, real estate listings, and business reviews. EveryBlock is currently available in Chicago [2].

7.3.1.6 Support Networks Support networks are typically websites that offer customized support services for citizens. Several kinds of support activities are required for the smooth functioning of our everyday lives. Some of them could be support for elderly parents when other family members are at work, property monitoring (especially if the property is in a location that is far away from the current habitation), search for rental houses in a specific locality, and so on.

7.3.1.6.1 Host of Real Estate Property Services from HomeShikari.com (http://www.homeshikari.com/property-services) This website offers a host of real estate property related services to the citizens of Bangalore City, India. Some of the services they offer are property monitoring, sale and purchase of property, and so on.

7.3.1.7 Volunteering Networks   Volunteering is generally considered an activity that is not done for any financial benefit or gain, but rather as a service to mankind. It can be done for socialization and enjoyment as well. There are many types of volunteering such as skill-based volunteering, virtual volunteering, corporate volunteering, and so on. Volunteering activities go a long way toward improving the quality of life of citizens in a city. Many websites are available to support volunteering activities to ensure that their benefits are fully realized by the residents.

7.3.1.7.1 Volunteering Network: International Volunteer HQ   International Volunteer HQ (IVHQ; http://www.volunteerhq.org/) is an organization that provides safe, responsible, and affordable volunteer abroad programs in countries around the world. Each year, IVHQ sends thousands of volunteers on these programs and offers a wide range of volunteer travel opportunities to many countries throughout the world. Established in 2007, this organization has now become one of the world's popular volunteer travel companies. It offers a wide range of projects for volunteer travelers in various domains such as teaching, childcare, community development programs, medical and nursing programs, construction, renovation, and wildlife conservation.

7.3.1.8 Collective Action Forums   Collective action forums help to organize and support initiatives that for various reasons may require the support of a larger audience. For example, someone may decide to host a website for a specific cause only if a certain number of people agree to support or follow the website. In such a scenario, it becomes necessary for a third party to coordinate with others to get their approval and support. Collective action forums refer to websites of organizations that perform the role of a third party in the preceding example.

7.3.1.9 Collective Action Forum—Pledgebank   PledgeBank (http://www.pledgebank.com) allows users to set up pledges and then encourages other people to sign up for them. A pledge is a statement of the form "I will do something if a certain number of people will help me do it." The creator of the pledge then publicizes his or her pledge and encourages people to sign up. Two outcomes are possible—either the pledge fails to get enough subscribers before it expires (in which case, we contact everyone and tell them "better luck next time"), or, the better possibility, the pledge attracts enough people that they are all sent a message saying "Well done—now get going!" [3].

7.3.1.10 Carpooling Networks

Carpooling networks or websites promote the "Go green" concept by decreasing carbon emissions from vehicles by reducing the number of vehicles on the road. This is done by connecting people who use the same route so they could travel in a single vehicle instead of in separate vehicles. Websites that help to advertise routes and other timing information to facilitate carpooling are called carpooling networks. Today with the conglomeration of social media technologies, many carpooling websites provide the option to review the social media profiles and then choose travel partners so that likeminded people can carpool.

7.3.1.10.1 Carpooling Network—Zimride

Zimride (http://www.zimride.com) is a website that offers carpooling services. Those who are interested in joining the existing carpools or who want to advertise the availability of their vehicles for carpooling can use this website to provide all relevant details such as route, timing information, and so on. This website is also linked to social media networks such as Facebook and Twitter. Using this option, any prospective carpooler can view the social media profiles of others who are part of the carpool and choose carpools of people with similar interests, hobbies, professions, and so on.

7.3.1.11 Use of Social Network Forums

Today there is widespread use of social media networks such as Facebook, YouTube, and Twitter as platforms for community collaboration. Many times, specific accounts or forums are set up to mobilize action on specific local issues and in natural disaster situations such as earthquakes, storms, and floods.

In short, both IT-enabled city strategies and IT-enabled social initiatives are required for the emergence and sustenance of digital cities. Both should exist in synergy to keep up the pace and momentum of digital cities.

In the next section, we examine the various building blocks of the ubiquitous city (U-city) or intelligent city. It should be noted that the digital city is the first step in the evolutionary framework of cities and it is not possible for a city without digitization to go to the next phase of a city, termed an intelligent city.

7.4 Ubiquitous or Intelligent City

U-cities are cities that have embraced higher levels of digitization when compared to digital cities by using cutting-edge technology blocks that go much beyond the Internet and Web 3.0 technologies that form the basis of digital cities.

Ubiquitous cities are used to describe a unique urban environment in which the city's physical infrastructures are embedded with computing devices across the entire city, making them present in the everyday lives of citizens in such a way as to be both omnipresent and invisible. These technological devices are fully integrated through interoperability and connected through wireless networks where everyone, anywhere in the city, will have access to computing power, the Internet, and various applications at any time of the day. Residential, medical, government, and business computers will all be connected through a series of all-encompassing wireless networks, broadband systems, and ubiquitous sensory networks [3]. The basic building blocks of a U-city are summarized in the following diagram:

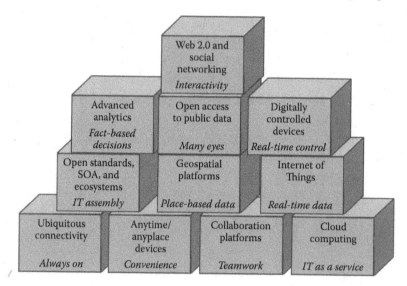

7.4.1 Ubiquitous Connectivity

Ubiquitous connectivity is the essential infrastructure requirement of the 21st century. Access to the high-bandwidth, low-cost Internet is the need of the day to meet the ever increasing demand of connectivity.

The network infrastructure to support wireless networks is the vital component for the effective use of mobile broadband and all other city services that are made available to the residents via mobile devices. According to the most recent statistics, the number of mobile broadband users as of 2014 is about 2.3 billion. The mobile network and mobile device ecosystem with the fully equipped infrastructure in place is the ideal platform to support the sophisticated network of information sharing and communication required to operate a U-city as almost half of the world's population now uses mobile devices as their main mode of communication.

7.4.1.1 Network Broadband Infrastructure Development A key national investment in broadband is epitomized by the Australian government's A\$40 billion network investment in a project called National Broadband Network (NBN). This project has a fiber-to-the-home open-access network that will provide 93% of Australia's homes with 1 Gbps of connectivity. The rest of the homes will have a network with 12 Mbps of connectivity that is provided with the help of satellite and other wireless technologies. The project started in 2010 and is expected to take eight years for completion.

7.4.2 Omnipresent Devices

Present-day smart phones can be termed anytime, anyplace devices (omnipresent) because of the large-scale penetration of mobile broadband networks. Smart phones help us to access any type of content from anywhere. Smart phones have also radically changed the way we interact with the Internet. Facebook recently reported that they have about 680 million active mobile users in addition to a billion active monthly users. The various smart phone platforms, the supported applications, and play stores have virtually changed the way people perceive various applications and their availability.

7.4.3 Collaboration Platforms

Present-day unified communications and collaboration platforms have the capability to bring together many technologies such as voice, short message service (SMS), calendars, online meetings, video conferencing, and other office automation tools that were previously available as standalone tools. These integrated communication and collaboration platforms can create borderless organizations, boost the productivity of the teams, and facilitate mobile or remote working concepts. The latest generation of online meetings and high-resolution video conference systems, such as Cisco's WebEx and IBM® Sametime® meetings, serve as genuine alternatives to face-to-face team meetings.

7.4.4 Cloud Computing

Cloud computing refers to a model of computing in which IT-based services are made available to end-users on a pay-to-use basis over the Internet. The IT services include software applications, platforms for building applications, and huge amounts of storage space and other infrastructural components that are needed by the various organizations. Cloud computing provides a cost-effective and viable alternative for deploying IT-based city strategies and IT-based social initiatives, as the usage of cloud models for deploying these services does not involve any capital expenditure. Cloud-based technologies are already creating a wave of IT innovation across cities because of the cost-effectiveness and a simplicity of use that is offered by this model.

7.4.4.1 Cloud Computing for Intelligent Cities   The European Platform for Intelligent Cities (EPICs) is a pioneer project in the new "Smart Cities" and "Living Labs" initiatives and it is funded by the European Commission. This project experienced many technical stumbling blocks because of which the implementation could not be fully completed. But with the support of IBM's cloud infrastructure, they were able to provision a Web-service delivery platform successfully for the EPIC project.

7.4.5 Open Standards and Service-Oriented Architecture

One of the most important trends in the IT industry is the evolution and development of open standards and published interfaces for development of applications in various domains. This had paved the way for various vendors to produce diverse types of hardware and software systems using the concept of service-oriented architecture (SOA).

This approach facilitates a more dynamic approach where applications can be created or assembled by using the existing components and Web services rather than having them built as monolithic projects. This is an intelligent approach through which various solutions that are required for the various aspects of city automation can be built and deployed rapidly, avoiding huge amounts of waiting time that would have been the case otherwise.

7.4.6 Geospatial Platforms

The availability of free or low-cost geographic information systems such as Google Maps makes visualization of city-based information very easy. These maps, when combined with GPS and other location-based services available in smart phones, have made it very easy to manipulate and visualize various aspects of a city under different scenarios. For example, if there is an accident at a specific location in a city, maps and other location-based services available in a smart phone can be used to locate the nearest hospital and the type of facilities available in the hospital, such as the number of emergency units, ambulances, and so on. These maps provide a powerful mechanism to visualize and locate various assets, resources, and services that are available in a city. These provide highly effective ways for engaging citizens in planning dialogues.

7.4.7 Neogeography in U-Cities

There has been an increasing trend these days to create and distribute various types of geographic information publicly—not by government or organizations but by individuals. This stupendous development in the field of maps could be attributed to two factors—the availability of low-cost geographic information systems and widespread use of the Internet. These maps developed by individuals are often personalized for their own use and provide useful information that can be used by other organizations to create their own set of maps. For example, Wikimapia and Open Street Maps are creating a huge footprint of geographic information that can be used by other individuals or organizations. Google Earth is encouraging individuals to develop their own geospatial applications using their own set of geospatial data. These trends could be taken as indicators of the democratization of the mapping and have paved the way for the emergence of another stream called citizen science. Citizen science refers to an activity in which a group of citizens become engaged in some kind of scientific activity, for example, bird surveys, and then accurately denote them on the maps using time and space coordinates. This field of geography where the maps are freely generated or used by individuals for generation of different kinds of data is referred to as neogeography. These neogeographic data provide a large amount of value proposition for the U-city government and city agencies, as they provide much additional data that would help city officials in urban planning and mapping.

7.4.8 Internet of Things

The Internet of Things (IoT) is the future of Internet technologies, in which every object around us will be connected via some kind of network to every other object and will also have the capability to send and receive data from them. Our living, relaxing, and working environments are envisioned to be filled with a variety of electronic devices including environment monitoring sensors, actuators, monitors, controllers, processors, tags, labels, stickers, dots, motes, stickers, projectors, displays, cameras, computers, communicators, appliances, gateways, high-definition IP TVs, and so on. Apart from these, all physical and concrete items, articles, furniture, and packages will become empowered with computation- and communication-enabled components by attachment of specially made electronics onto them. Whenever we walk into such kinds of augmented environments illuminated with a legion of digitized objects, the devices we carry and even our e-clothes will enter into calm yet logical collaboration mode and form wireless ad hoc networks with the inhabitants of that environment. For example, if someone wants to print a document on his or her smart phone or tablet, and if he or she enters a room where a printer is situated, then the smart phone will begin a conversation with the printer automatically and send the document to be printed. Thus, in that era, our everyday spots will be made informative, interactive, intuitive, and inspiring by embedding intelligence and autonomy into their constituents (audio/video systems; cameras; information and Web appliances; consumer and household electronics; and other electronic gadgets besides digitally augmented walls, floors, windows, doors, ceilings, and any other physical objects and artifacts; etc.). The unobtrusive computers, communicators, sensors, and robots will be instructing, instigating, alerting, and facilitating decision making in a smart way, apart from accomplishing all kinds of everyday needs proactively for humans. Humanized robots will be extensively used to fulfill our daily physical chores. That is, computers in different sizes, looks, capabilities, interfaces, and prices will be fitted, glued, implanted, and inserted everywhere to be coordinative, calculative, and coherent yet invisible for discerning human minds. In short, the IoT world will make our environment much more intelligent. This in turn will be the main technological pillar of ubiquitous or intelligent cities.

7.4.9 Advanced Analytics

The amount of data is increasing exponentially every year, and according to the most recent IDC digital universe study, by 2020, about 33% of the data generated will contain information that will provide valuable insights if they are analyzed using appropriate analytical tools. These valuable insights could be derived from the data patterns that appear in social media usage, correlations in scientific studies that occur in diverse fields, trends in security footage, and so on. These insights can in turn fuel the fact-based decision-making process that will help to monitor and control various events based on real-time statistics. The rise of cutting-edge analytical systems will be fueled by the fusion of the IoT concept (which generates more data) and cloud computing platforms (which provide scalable processing power and massive storage capacity).

7.4.10 Open Access to Public Data

Today, most government agencies are moving toward making their data publicly available for their citizens. This is because they have realized the importance of and the need for "many eyes to view data." This has fueled the creation of many applications that help citizens to derive valuable insights from these government-generated data sets, which in turn will equip citizens to make diligent decisions.

7.4.11 Digitally Controlled Devices

With the IoT concept becoming increasingly prominent, there is also an increasing tendency to develop equipment that is capable of controlling all appliances and devices digitally using some kind of a centralized system. There is also an increased focus on integrating these centralized monitoring and controlling system capabilities to laptops and smart phones. This will help in the easy realization of concepts such as computerized homes, buildings, vehicles, and other infrastructure systems. For example, it would be very easy to control all aspects of home automation such as lighting, cooling, electrical appliances, and so on centrally and remotely with the help of a smart phone. These digitally controlled systems are the key building blocks for the conceptualization of intelligent construction systems, intelligent building systems, and intelligent transport systems. A key concept to be kept in mind during the design of these systems is that the different components of automation such as sensors, actuators, and so on need to be finalized during the design phase itself so that they can be integrated with the systems at the time of development. After development, it is very difficult to retrofit these components into the system.

7.4.12 Social Media Networking

The proliferation of Web 2.0 technologies have offered numerous capabilities for people to communicate and collaborate with one another. Web 2.0 technologies have also fueled the growth and development of communities for diverse aspects such as knowledge sharing, communication on topics of common interest, and so on. The soaring response of the people to social media sites such as Facebook and Twitter have led to an offshoot of social media analytics called sentiment analytics, which is used extensively by government agencies to understand the sentiments of citizens on various decisions and policies of the government. These social media networking platforms are an inevitable component for building social networks in cities.

7.5 Strategic Governance Framework for the Implementation of U-Cities

The strategic governance framework for the implementation of ubiquitous or intelligent cities is shown in the following diagram:

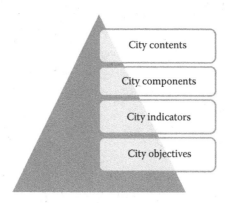

The four layers indicated in the diagram provide a logical framework that can be used by the various city leaders to evaluate the various implementation options available in hand. For example, the first layer is about city objectives. If the prime objective of city leaders is to conserve water based on some metrics that denoted poor water conservation (layer 2), then they have to examine the possibility of building an interconnected water network in the city that has all the features to track real-time water consumption patterns of the citizens (layer 3). After making decisions about the design and the features required in the water conservation system, city leaders will have to examine similar water conservation measures and systems implemented in other cities and derive the best practices so that they can be incorporated in the system under consideration. Each layer in the above framework is detailed in the following paragraphs to provide a better understanding.

7.5.1 City Objectives

City objectives are an important catalyst in the decision-making process. To arrive at the city objectives, the various domains that exist in the city such as finance, energy and utilities, education, public safety, healthcare, and so on should be examined in detail to identify the sectors that need improvement. It is a vital aspect to include the citizen's views in the decision-making process to ensure that the entire cycle of evaluation and decision making is seamless. After analyzing the various domains, it is important to prioritize the sectors that need improvement and the amount of improvement that is required. This is a vital component that will finalize the city objectives and link them to the various projects, policies, and investments that are planned for the city. While planning the city objectives, it is also very important for city leaders to analyze the existing technological infrastructure and the present maturity level of a city, that is, whether it is a digital city, U-city, and so on.

7.5.2 City Indicators

Most of the time, city objectives are qualitative or empirical in nature. Hence it is necessary to quantify them to arrive at various metrics. For this purpose, it is essential to link them to various existing and published city indicator indices. These indices benchmark the cities using well-defined and proved methodologies. Some of the standard city indicators that are available are Global City Indicators Facility (GCIF), Green City Index, and so on. Each of these indicators uses a different set of parameters for the evaluation of cities. Different cities may require different indicators based on their priorities and objectives. For example, if a city's objective is to improve the financial sector, then the Green City Index might be appropriate.

7.5.3 City Components

At some point or the other, city objectives are linked to physical components, assets, resources, or locations. For example, if the city objective is to improve water conservation, then the following assets or resources are components of the process.

- Water network components such as pipes, valves, and so on (asset)
- Water operators (resources)
- IT infrastructure (asset)
- Logistics for water operators (resources)

For the success of the laid out city objectives, it is essential to perform a detailed evaluation of the various components that are part of the system under consideration and design a system to optimize the utilization of each system component.

7.5.4 City Content

Once all the other aspects of the city system under consideration are evaluated carefully, it becomes necessary to look at the diverse implementations that have been done in other cities across the world. It is necessary to do a careful examination of the various implementations to derive the pros and cons of the various implementations. It is very important to generate a framework comprising best practices from the various city implementations, which in turn could form the foundational component for the implementation of city objectives for the city under consideration.

7.5.4.1 First Ubiquitous City in the World [4]   Songdo New City in South Korea is expected to be the first U-city in the world. Its construction began in 2008 and the expected completion date is in 2014. It is an outcome of the partnership alliance between the South Korean government and a private sector organization, Cisco. This city is planned to have a unique urban environment where various computing devices such as sensors and actuators are planned to be embedded across the entire city. This way it is planned to make these devices a part of residents' everyday lives in an omnipresent and omnipotent manner. These technological components are integrated appropriately using wired and wireless networks to ensure that citizens anywhere in any part of the city will have access to them irrespective of infrastructure limitations. The computers used in different sectors will be interconnected through a series of networks that include wired and wireless broadband systems and sensor networks that are ubiquitous in nature. This new way of engaging with the citizens is expected to encourage new forms of participation among citizens that would subsequently ensure increased transparency and democratization of services in the city.

7.6 Conclusion

In this chapter, we analyzed the diverse challenges faced by present-day cities and the need to revamp the systems and processes in the existing cities. IT integration with the various sectors of the city will provide an effective solution for most of the problems faced by present-day cities. Based on the various levels of IT integration with the various facets of the city, cities can be broadly classified into two types: digital cities and ubiquitous or intelligent cities. Transformation of a city into a ubiquitous city is a journey and cannot happen overnight. The first phase of transformation is the transition to a digital city. A digital city uses IT for serving two main purposes: IT-enabled strategies and IT-enabled social initiatives. The various forms of IT-enabled strategies and IT-enabled social initiatives were discussed in detail with appropriate examples. The various changes that are required in the vital components of the city for the success of digitization and transformation were also discussed in the chapter.

The next stage in the transformation of cities is ubiquitous or intelligent cities. This refers to cities that have embraced higher levels of digitization and technology integration in the diverse city domains. The various technological components of U-cities were also discussed in detail. Examples were used appropriately to elucidate the concepts that were explained.

In the last section of the chapter, a strategic governance framework that needs to be embraced by the cities for their transformation to intelligent cities was discussed. Lastly, the cities across the world are in the various stages of their evolution. The need of the day is that these cities need to understand and appreciate the value provided by technology integration to their citizens, which in turn will help them to accelerate the transformation process.

References

1. Cisco (2012). Smart City Framework: A Systematic Process for Enabling Smart + Connected Communities (white paper).
2. EveryBlock. http://www.everyblock.com.
3. PledgeBank. http://www.pledgebank.com.
4. Location-Awareness and Ubiquitous Cities: A Report to the U-City Research Institute, Yonsei University, S. Korea.

8

SMART HOMES AND BUILDINGS

Abstract

Our homes and corporate buildings are becoming increasingly digital environments with the constant accumulation of a growing array of specific as well as generic devices and displays. Consumer and office electronics such as tablets, smart phones, TVs, laptops, printers and scanners, coffee-making machines, toasters, ovens, robots, audio and video systems, and games consoles are ensuring news ways and means through which consumers and knowledge workers compute and communicate, entertain, educate and enable themselves, and so on. Devices are consistently empowered through a host of pioneering technologies, tools, and tips to devise new situation-aware and people-centric services to be intimately and intensively relevant for users. The individual as well as collective operation of all kinds of machines, instruments, wares, equipment, electronics, appliances, and so on is another option gaining popularity these days. The remote access of these gizmos and gadgets anytime from anywhere is growing day by day for a variety of purposes. Not only distant connectivity but also empowering devices to sync with one another in the vicinity on an as-needed basis to implement and incorporate path-breaking capabilities and competencies is gaining momentum. Devices are being empowered internally as well as externally to find, bind, and talk with one another with continued success in formulating and firming up versatile technologies for device integration and orchestration. Establishing and embodying policies onto device middleware is another overwhelming proposition to enhance the device power substantially. Cloud connectivity is being mandated, as most of the device-specific services being developed by inspired developers are deposited in cloud platforms to be readily subscribed to by worldwide users. In addition, cloud infrastructures are being optimized ceaselessly to be deployed in a distributed manner, extremely elastic, managed centrally, accessed publicly, consumed as a service, streamlined through automation solutions, and simplified smartly to position them as the next-generation IT infrastructure for all kinds of IT platforms, professional and personal data, applications, and services. In this chapter, we discuss the various technologies and their implications in setting up advanced homes and buildings that in turn contribute to the realization of smarter cities.

8.1 Introduction

On multiple fronts, there are inescapable trends pointing toward the urgent need for establishing and sustaining technology-inspired, process-centric, service-oriented, cloud-enabled, event-driven, and policy-based smart cities. The highly visible trend is that the urban population is burgeoning for different reasons. It is estimated that more than 6.3 billion people (that is, 60% of the total world population) will be living in cities by 2050 [1]. An aging population especially in developed countries, overcrowded cities, traffic congestions, human crimes, air contamination, administration lacunae, crumbling public infrastructures, the continued dwindling of energy supply, natural and man-made disasters, and so on are the main pain points of worldwide cities. These unwanted developments have put severe stress and led to a series of significant ramifications on cities across the world. City infrastructures (physical, social, cyber, etc.) predominantly are bound to totter and tumble by bursting at their seams.

Governments, city planners and officials, IT product vendors, system integrators, and cloud service providers (CSPs) need to precisely focus on timely understanding and correcting all kinds of infrastructural limitations. However, as cities are becoming extremely complicated systems, the formulation of an appropriate strategy is the main task to start with. Unfortunately cities are turning out to be a very complex system of systems in a number of areas:

- *Food*—world hunger, safety, traceability, distribution, pilferage, and wastage
- *Cloths*—fashion, protection, supply chain management, retails, and online-to-offline commerce (O2O)
- *Living*—cover/protection, comfort, safe, security, costs, and maintenance
- *Traffic*—safety, convenience, congestions, costs, economy, and pollution
- *Education*—quality, equality, continual education, efficiency, effectiveness, learning models, and so on
- *Entertainment*—information and communication technology (ICT)-enabled games, digital convergence, music, distributions and cultural events
- *Healthcare and wellness*

The unprecedented growth of urban populations, catastrophic global warming, and resource limitations are putting immense pressure on all stakeholders to focus more intently on both sides: supply as well as demand. That is, on one hand, efforts are underway collaboratively on how to increase resource generation whereas on the other hand, professionals are exploring workable ways and means to conserve resource usage. Resource efficiency is a serious topic on which there are deliberations and discourses aplenty these days. Optimized usage of scarce resources is therefore being insisted on everywhere for future generations to be able to live on the dwindling amount of various life-critical resources. Water is one such critical entity; in addition, fuels need to be preserved, food production has to be substantially enhanced through revolutionary scientific solutions, transportation facilities need to be in place to take care of increasing demands, various connectivity and cyber infrastructures need to be remarkably enhanced considering population growth, and so on.

Precisely speaking, cities ought to be IT-enabled to meet the afore-mentioned requirements. IT already has proven to be a strategic contributor to worldwide businesses. Now IT is more attuned to bringing in relevant enablement and efficiency in all the spheres that are directly or indirectly linked with the general population. That is, every facet of human living is being empowered by the stream of wonderful advancements in the IT industry. For cities to be smart in their operations, offerings, and outputs, IT is being greatly recommended for achieving the desired results. There are several product vendors consciously working out in bringing forth competent IT products, platforms, and tools toward the quicker and risk-free facilitation of smarter cities. That is, the critical involvement of miniaturization, connectivity, service enablement, sensing, perception, vision, knowledge engineering, visualization, and actuation technologies in shaping the desired goals for the faster realization of smarter cities is growing.

Smart buildings and homes form a substantial part of smart cities. In this chapter, we emphasize the powerful technologies, tools, and tips for building smarter homes and offices from the ground up. There are approaches and solutions enabling transformation of traditional homes into smart environments. The cloud idea also gets special attention in this chapter, as in the future, cloud-based applications and data will be orchestrated in an automated manner to understand perfectly people's situational requirements and fulfill them.

8.2 Elucidating Technological Advancements

Trendsetting computing, communication, and context-awareness (via ubiquitous and real-time sensing, vision, perception, knowledge engineering, decision making, and actuation techniques) technologies are forthcoming. There is a series of noteworthy innovations, consolidations, optimizations, and simplifications in the field of information technology (IT) to continuously and reliably cope with the ever-changing needs of businesses and society. That is, through a variety of converged, virtualized, federated, shared, and automated IT infrastructures (computing nodes, network components, storage arrays, and appliances), there is a solid and substantial renaissance in IT these days. These envisioned and delightful transformations bring paradigm shifts on multiple fronts for all kinds of shareholders and ultimately for end-users.

The way software systems are being developed, deployed, delivered, and decommissioned is all set to enter a new captivating and capitalizing era of online, off-premise, and on-demand paradigm. Further, massive volumes of multistructured data from all kinds of disparate, distributed, and digitalized entities and elements are being systematically captured, cleansed, and stocked in local or/and remote software-defined storages. Increasingly powerful applications and services are being written to process the resulting data tsunami to extract actionable insights in real time. Next-gen software solutions and services are being taken to the greatly optimized IT infrastructures (clouds) to reap the originally envisaged benefits of cloud computing. The Internet has turned out to be the public, worldwide, open, and affordable communication infrastructure. That is, anytime anywhere, any device, any network access and leverage of personal as well as professional applications, services, and data are seeing a neat and attractive reality with the unprecedented adoption of proven and promising technologies.

Processes too are going through a number of striking transformations so that we can have integrated yet lean processes for business and IT applications. The lingering concept of service orientation has taken the whole IT industry through a storm and the result in the enterprise computing arena is truly momentous and mesmerizing. Another conspicuous trend is the emergence of newer and nimbler disruptive, transformative, and imaginative automation elements in the form of elegant and endearing devices, slim and sleek sensors, multifaceted actuators, versatile robots, intuitive displays, and so on. The device ecosystem is fast enlarging as miniaturization and instrumentation technologies are fast maturing and stabilizing. With the availability of extreme and deeper connectivity technologies, everyday devices are becoming interconnected to be intelligent in their actions and reactions. Generic and purpose-specific devices are being produced in massive volumes to be made available widely and affordably.

Further, the onset of service-enablement and edge technologies has resulted in a tremendous amount of digitalized, smart, and sentient objects. That is, every common, casual, and even cheap thing in our everyday environments is being meticulously digitalized to participate seamlessly and smartly in mainstream computing. All sorts of mechanical, electrical, and electronics are instrumented and interconnected to be smart in their operations, offerings, and outputs. There is a positive buzz on purposeful, real-time, and ad hoc interactions of disparate and geographically distributed gadgets and gizmos to craft smarter environments for different industry segments. Several types of semantic and sensitive networks are unfolding as enumerated in the following list based on the distinct ranges of network coverage.

Mesh networking is another inspiring development catapulting IT to greater heights.

1. Body area network (BAN)
2. Personal area network (PAN)
3. Local area network (LAN)
4. Metro area network (MAN)
5. Wide area network (WAN)

Establishing adroit and active environments is streamlined and simplified with the arrival and acceptance of highly competent technologies in several spaces as illustrated in the following:

- *The technology space*—There is a cornucopia of technologies (computing, connectivity, miniaturization, middleware, sensing, actuation, perception, analyses, knowledge engineering, etc.).
- *The process space*—With new kinds of services, applications, data, infrastructures, and devices joining mainstream IT, fresh process consolidation, and orchestration, governance and management mechanisms are emerging. That is, process excellence is the ultimate aim.
- *Infrastructure space*—Infrastructure consolidation, convergence, centralization, federation, automation, and sharing methods clearly indicate the infrastructure trends in the computing and communication disciplines. Physical infrastructures turn out to be virtual infrastructures. Two major infrastructural types are
    - System infrastructure (computing, storage, and network)
    - Application infrastructure—integration backbones, platforms (design, development, deployment, delivery, management, etc.), messaging middleware, databases (Structured Query Language [SQL] and Not only SQL [NoSQL]), and so on.
- *Architecture space*—Service-oriented architecture (SOA), event-driven architecture (EDA), model-driven architecture (MDA), resource-oriented architecture (ROA), and so on are the leading architectural patterns.
- *The device space* is fast evolving (slim and sleek, handy and trendy, mobile, wearable, implantable, portable, etc.). Everyday

machines are connected with one another as well as to the remote Web/cloud.
- *Data space*—Data are being produced in an automated and massive manner.

In a nutshell, it is all about quickly and easily creating assistive, agile, and adaptive environments for intelligently bringing in much-wanted care, convenience, choice, comforts, and controls for humans in their personal as well as professional places. Smart buildings and homes are the most popular and exciting phenomenon in the class of smart environments. Researchers have reported a number of people-centric and pioneering use cases for encouraging businesses, services providers, and people to embrace smarter buildings and homes with clarity and confidence.

8.3 Key Drivers for Smarter Homes and Buildings

The first and foremost application of notable developments in ambient intelligence (AmI), Internet of Things (IoT), cyber physical systems (CPS), cloud computing, ubiquitous sensing, intuitive and natural interfaces, sentient materials, and autonomic communication disciplines is to insightfully establish and sustain smart homes. Besides handy and trendy devices, eye-catching multifaceted yet miniaturized devices are hitting the market these days. In addition, device integration and collaboration standards are being schemed and specified for original equipment manufacturers (OEMs) and devices' components makers for enabling devices to coexist and cooperate purposefully. Machine interfaces are budding and boosting machine-to-machine (M2M) communications toward formulating and firming up innumerable facilities and functionalities that in turn make machines faithful and innovation-filled assistants for people in their daily chores. People-centric applications are being consistently unearthed with the maturity and stability of technologies. Self, surroundings, and situation awareness are being realized with empowered devices and smart objects in capturing and conveying decision-enabling information. There are push-and-pull–based approaches for information capture. Information visualization tools and techniques are other important factors in building smarter environments.

Context awareness is an important ingredient for conceptualizing and concretizing people-centric services. Smart sensor networks, sensor fusion algorithms, device-to-device (D2D) interactions [2], device-to-cloud (D2C) communication, devices subscribing cloud-based smart home services at runtime, the seamless collaborations between smart phones and smart home instruments, the increased usage of data analytics for usable knowledge, the spontaneous integration between physical things at homes with remotely hosted cyber applications through device middleware, and so on are some of the highly discussed and documented aspects for accelerating the realization of smarter homes.

There are standards-complying device integration appliances, gateways, proxies, and brokers toward smart homes. Smart phones are bound to play a vital role in shaping the idea behind smart homes of the future. Embedded and embodied intelligence goes a long way in designing connected and cognitive devices for people empowerment. Internal as well as external connectivity are being insisted on as devices and devices services are different places. Especially with cloud emerging as the core and central place, scores of personal and professional applications are being hosted in multiple clouds (public, private, and hybrid) to be provided as services for worldwide users. Clouds are being positioned as the next-generation IT environment for deploying, subscribing, delivering, and enhancing several sorts of software platforms and applications as services. In a nutshell, the widespread acceptance of highly competent technologies and devices has laid a stimulating foundation for smarter environments.

8.4 Prominent Use Cases of Smarter Homes and Buildings

The following prominent use cases are eliciting greater attention. More and more compound applications can be realized by intelligently combining discrete use cases.

1. Elderly care/ambient assisted living (AAL)
2. Home security (security and safety of people and property)
3. Remote monitoring, diagnostics, repair, management, maintenance, replacement, and even retirement of a growing array of home-bound devices and smart objects
4. Energy-efficient green homes through micro-grids
5. Entertainment, infotainment, and edutainment
6. Enhanced comfort, convenience, choice, and control applications

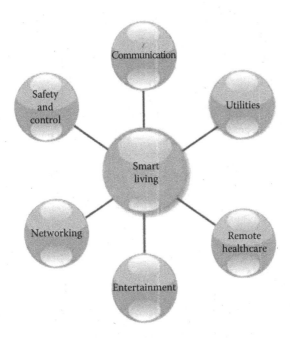

8.5 Smarter Homes and Building Elements

A growing variety of smart sensors, software solutions, connected devices, cloud services, and so on are set to enable us in multiple forms and formats in our living and working environments. That is, apartment and office buildings, manufacturing floors, and other action-centric, lively, and lovely places will be extremely technology-empowered and splurged. Ordinary and everyday objects are being digitalized, connected with one another locally, and cloud-enabled. That is, everything in our places is systematically empowered with relevant and right intelligence through the addition of functional modules internally as well as through integration with remotely hosted software applications. Even communication networks are being filled with appropriate competencies and capabilities to simplify and streamline the task of making every common, casual, and cheap thing smart; every kind of electronics smarter; and ultimately people the smartest.

All kinds of deficiencies and dependencies are being eliminated through a host of measures such as standardization, adaptors, bridges, middleware, common application programming interface (APIs), and so on. Plug-and-play capabilities are being guaranteed. Devices are manufactured accordingly and modernized to connect and collaborate with one another in realizing people-centric tasks. Information capture, aggregation, share, and leverage for actionable insights, information dissemination, and visualization concepts are continuously strengthened toward the vision of smarter environments. Devices are being produced using the highly regarded factory model/industrialization. All high-end IT servers, storages, and networking solutions are being commoditized. This is being achieved by identifying and abstracting all kinds of common functionalities, features, and facilities. Finally all are implemented through software. Important aspects such as modifiability, replacement, substitution, accessibility, consumability, and so on are easily incorporated in software. Policies and knowledge bases in synchronization with a knowledge manager are emerging as the new-generation mechanism for establishing autonomic infrastructures. The software route is being recommended for policy establishment and enforcement. The growing list of prominent home networking and automation solutions includes

- *Security and surveillance elements.* Security sensors for windows, doors, motion, glass break, and smoke can provide critical security information about our homes while at home or in the office. Internet Protocol (IP)-enabled security and surveillance cameras are very important for ensuring tight, unbreakable, and impenetrable security. Intrusion detection and prevention systems are other prominent security modules.

- *Heating, air conditioning, ventilation, lighting, and shade control systems.* Comfort is emerging as the decisive factor in next-generation homes. Novel machines are being instrumented to take care of different environmental conditions. Connectivity among various home-bound devices including light switches, wall-mounted touch panels, and so on is being ensured. Robots come in different varieties for doing physical work for people. Cloud-enabled robots will be a critical and crucial cog in human activities in the days ahead.

- *Computing and communications devices.* A wider variety of computing machines ranging from personal computers (PCs), notebooks/laptops/tablets, Wi-Fi routers and gateways, wearables, and smart phones are being extensively used in home environments these days. With seamless convergence, computer and communicator are often interchanged.

- *Entertainment, edutainment, and infotainment media systems.* There are several notable innovations in media technologies and products. Today we boast about fixed, portable, mobile, and handheld devices for ubiquitous learning. IP-enabled television sets are being produced in mass quantities, increasing our choice, convenience, and comfort considerably. Web, information, and consumer appliances are plentiful and pioneering. Technologies for social sites (Web 2.0) are on the climb, facilitating higher productivity for humans and for forming digital communities for real-time knowledge sharing. Home theaters, music systems, DVD devices, game consoles, and so on are for entertainment.

- *Home networking.* All passive, numb, and dumb items are being transformed into digitalized objects. These are being wirelessly and wisely networked with all sorts of household electronics to connect and communicate (directly [peer-to-peer] or indirectly [through a middleware]) to derive competent people-centric, networked, and embedded e-services. Home networking infrastructures, connectivity solutions, bridging elements, and other brokering solutions are being found in greater numbers these days. Home networks also can connect with the outside world via the pervasive Internet. This enables remote monitoring, management, and maintenance of home devices. Car multimedia, navigation and infotainment systems, parking management systems, and so on are getting connected to household systems directly or via box-based middleware for real-time connectivity and interaction.

- *Home access control.* E-locks are emerging as a crucial security measure for home access control.

- *Kitchen appliances, wares, and utensils.* A modular kitchen comprising all kinds of electronics emerges as a key factor for smarter homes. Coffee makers, bread toasters, electronic ovens, refrigerators, dishwashers, food processors, and so on are being enhanced to be smarter in home environments.

- *Relaxing and mood-creating objects.* Household items such as electric lamps, cots, chairs, beds, wardrobes, windowpanes,

couches, treadmills, tables, and sofas as well as objects in specific places such as gyms, spas, bathrooms, car garages, parking slots, and so on are being linked together in an ad hoc
manner to greatly enhance the experience of users.

- *Healthcare materials.* Medicine cabinets, pill and tablet containers, humanoid robots, and so on are occupying prime slots
in guaranteeing good health for home occupants.

Statistical estimates and forecasts predict that there will be hundreds of microcontrollers in any advanced home/office environment
in the days ahead. The much-touted edge technologies such as cards,
chips, labels, tags, pads, stickers, smart dust and motes, specks, and
so on are enabling the onset of powerful environments. That is, our
everyday places are going to be saturated with a growing array of
event-producing and -consuming entities; environmental monitoring
and measurement solutions; controlling, actuation, and notification
systems; integration fabrics, hubs, and buses; visualization displays
and dashboards; networking and automation elements; and scores of
handhelds, wearables, portables, implantables; and so on to make our
lives and locations pleasant and liveable.

8.6 Envisioning Smarter Homes and Buildings: The Role of the Cloud Theme

Broadband communication, mesh networking, streams of home automation systems, and resilient home integration middleware enable
the realization of smart homes. However, the current trend is the
centralized approach through a home server or gateway. That is, the
box-based central approach dominates current smart homes across
the globe. The complexity is being pushed to the home integration
box and with the addition of newer and nimbler devices will in time
add greater and more uncomfortable complexity. Hence the logical
move is to divide and conquer the threatening complications arising
from the centralized approach, which is also responsible for the single point of failure. Off course, there are dependable approaches for
overcoming the persisting difficulties. The point here is to abstract all
the generic functionalities and put them in the cloud, which is the
core, central, and cognitive IT infrastructure for enterprise, device

(smartphone, wearables, etc.), and Web users. Many consumers could utilize cloud-based applications at the same time through the famous multi-tenancy feature. Only specific features are made available in home/office-bound devices. Further, the connectivity capability is embedded into devices to search and use capabilities of nearby devices as well as remote applications. This way, additional functionalities can be readily added at cloud applications, and ground-level physical devices at any point in time can access and leverage newly added services dynamically to be more powerful and purposeful.

Another unique trend is emanating with the pervasiveness of cloud centers across the world. For smart phones, thousands of creative services are being developed and deposited in cloud-based application stores and service repositories. Mobile users can subscribe to and use them according to their preferences, passions, and purposes. Similarly, new devices are emerging for a variety of needs, situations, spaces, interests, and so on in our personal, social, and professional lives. For example, home integration devices are very popular these days and thousands of imaginative services are being conceived, concretized, and stored in cloud-based stores to facilitate worldwide families to discover, decode, and use them with all confidence.

The cloud paradigm breeds innovations relentlessly and leads to innumerable fresh opportunities and possibilities for all. The telling impacts of the cloud theme are many and momentous for business establishments, service providers, creative thinkers, software engineers, research professionals, and so on. The extraordinary momentum created is still being sustained as a result of the inherent potential of cloud technology. Undoubtedly cloud computing has turned out to be a game-changing factor for business houses these days. Clouds are irrevocably and irresistibly the next-generation IT infrastructure for affordable, optimized, elastic, and instant-on IT.

Techniques have been developed for reliably transforming data to information and to knowledge. The data-driven insights are being smartly leveraged by product vendors and service providers to be proactively and preemptively inventive to provide premium and state-of-the-art services to end-users. With cloud technology, consumers do not need to have knowledge of, expertise in, or mastery and control over the technology infrastructure in the cloud. Chapter 3 in this book provides details on cloud computing.

8.7 Smarter Environments Are Instrumented, Interconnected, and Intelligent

As part of the smarter planet vision, IBM has come out with three distinguished characteristics:

- *Instrumented.* This is the ability to sense and capture changing conditions. Instrumented devices provide detailed information and control about their own functioning and also provide information about the environment in which they operate. For instance, a washing machine can report information about the state of its components to support preventive maintenance for avoiding unforeseen outages. At the same time, it can sense its wash load to optimize its operations; it can send usage information to the manufacturer for data-driven product innovation; and it can be remotely operated when the energy cost is lowest.
- *Interconnected.* This is the ability to communicate and interact with people, systems, and other objects. Interconnection enables devices to make remote access to information about another device and control of it. Thus the Internet of Services (IoSs) will thrive and the complexity is therefore distributed. Consumers get to know the status of their devices from anywhere, any network, any device. Service aggregation will become compact and casual.
- *Intelligent.* This is about the ability to make appropriate decisions based on accurate and recent data. Intelligent devices support the optimization of their use, both for the individual consumer and for the service provider. For instance, a utility can send signals to consumers' homes to manage discretionary energy use to reduce peak loads.

The adoption of smarter home/office devices requires that they also be intuitive. Consumers will adopt new services only if they are easy to use and fit smoothly into their lifestyles. The learning curve for newer services has to be very minimal and the benefits of adopting them must be immediately apparent. The following illustration shows the various advantages for smart homes.

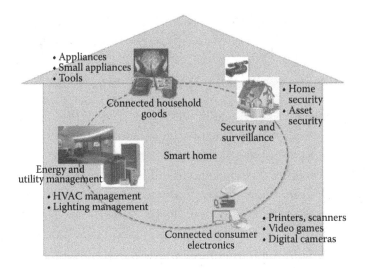

8.8 Smarter Home/Building Capabilities

The outcomes of smarter homes are many, including making consumers' lives more productive, healthier, and happier. The four service areas are

- *Entertainment and convenience.* There is an increased convergence these days. Increasingly Web content is being made available via television, and, conversely, TV programs are being viewed through Web browsers. There are digital, smart, and Internet-enabled TVs aplenty. Product vendors, content creators, IT service providers, communication service providers, and end-users are working harder in taking the entertainment industry to its next level. There are public displays, security and surveillance cameras, and flat panel TVs in public places as the threat quotient is on the rise. The convergence momentum is highly beneficial for people as well as building managers.

- *Energy management.* Future demands on the electrical grid will encourage minute-by-minute home appliance management to prioritize energy services while delivering automatic savings to owners. Automatically synchronizing lighting, home appliances, climate and environmental sensors, and all household smart objects sharply minimizes energy consumption based on changing environment conditions and usage patterns in homes and buildings. Building automation systems (BASs) is a prominent module in streamlining occupants' needs. With the integration of smart grids, the role of BAS in conserving scant energy increases significantly.

- *Safety and security.* Many insurers now offer discounts for existing centralized alarm services using sensors and IP surveillance cameras. The ability to deploy home/building sensors that can instantly notify the homeowner, selected neighbors, or the police and fire departments can enhance home security. These services can also empower family members to remotely check on the safety of children and the well-being of elderly people.

- *Health and wellness.* Healthcare providers could continuously monitor their patients with implanted devices or other at-home medical devices without hospitalization. Smarter home sensors monitor fitness, well-being, and advanced parameters consistently. These health electronic devices can collect evaluative information about current health conditions for disease management and prevention and guarantee overall wellness.

The following figure illuminates how a centralized home device middleware performs a variety of tasks such as device connectivity and message passing for interactions, notifications, control, monitoring, commands, diagnosing, repair, and so on in a secure fashion.

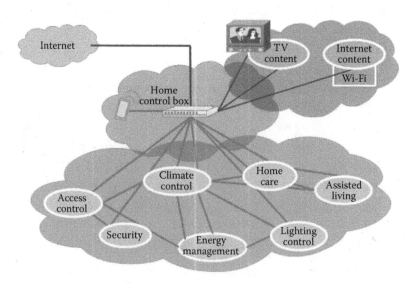

As multifaceted devices are being continuously and consciously added in our living, social, and working places, the quality and quantity of IT-enabled services are on the climb, empowering people in their routine activities. Not only information, commercial transactions, and analytical work but also IT is bound to excel in delivering knowledge-centric, decision-making, context-aware, and physical tasks for people in the days ahead. The cloud as the scalable and optimized IT infrastructure will serve bountifully in providing knowledge services to the right people at the right place and at the right time. As physical systems at the ground level are integrated with cloud-based cyber applications and services, policies, knowledge bases, and information stores, smart environments such as homes and offices are destined to act smarter.

8.9 Smarter Home/Building Services in Clouds

A bevy of enhancements occur in the home/building front. Home automation elements are being manufactured aplenty; the seamless linking of disparate and distributed devices is being smoothened out; all the data emitted by and extracted from those connected embedded devices are being carefully captured, cleansed, and loaded in high-performance analytical systems; platforms (local as well as cloud-based) are made available for conceptualizing and developing smart homes services and applications that are in turn deployed in different execution containers (onsite, offsite, and/or hybrid, virtual or bare metal servers, etc.); IT infrastructures are virtualized, pooled, and software defined to be easily configured and customized as per evolving requirements; and so on. Besides local interactions, the much-touted external integration, especially with remote cloud applications, services, and data, is being insisted on as a long-term growth strategy.

The problem with the current setup is as follows. Present-day smart homes and buildings involve specialized home servers for integrating diverse household electronics and for their effective control and usage. That is, local connectivity is ensured and this approach varies for different homes and buildings; hence reusability of resources is restricted. However, as more features are being incorporated into home devices and appliances, the operational complexity is set to grow. One pragmatic complexity-mitigation pattern is to abstract all the common capabilities to cloud-based software applications so that home appliances, kitchen utensils, medicine instruments, office machines, and so on at the ground level tend to have only specific functionalities. Now with the surging popularity of clouds, remote connectivity is also being given importance. This means home-bound devices are not only being managed remotely but are also empowered through a variety of cloud-based services and applications at runtime. Such kinds of dynamically enabled and insights-driven devices are more powerful and precise in their delivery capabilities.

Thus it has become routine for device manufacturers to empower them with cloud connectivity capability so that all sorts of home-bound devices can connect and leverage a cornucopia of software services, knowledge bases/policies/recipes, decision-enabling data, and so on from clouds. This ultimately leads to the centralization of services and any asset, resource, and article anywhere anytime can subscribe to and get the appropriate capability to be distinct and dexterous. Putting intelligence into services in remote clouds substantially reduces the complexity of managing devices. With the abstraction of functionalities, physical devices are becoming commodities that are less expensive and endowed with very basic capabilities. Devices are deployed in a distributed manner but managed in a centralized manner. Device replacement, substitution, repair, controllability, visibility, and security are heavily simplified. Clouds are furnished with different interfaces, especially representational state transfer (REST)ful interfaces and similarly devices too are provided RESTful interfaces, thereby establishing the initial connectivity to facilitate subsequent exchange of data, functional commands, and even documents. Such thoughtful transitions lead to device-to-device (D2D) and device-to-cloud (D2C) interactions; thereby capabilities are shared and devices are endowed with additional power to join and contribute to mainstream computing, storage, and analytics.

Further, geographically distributed service-enabled devices are easily found, bound, and composed to craft process-oriented, people-centric, event-driven, and context-aware composite services. This is a far less expensive and more flexible way to aggregate atomic and discrete services and compose new pioneering services from existing device services than all the past endeavors together. This takes the complexity out of the connected devices. Clouds are being positioned as the core, common, and affordable platform for realizing connected and cognitive devices. Therefore the eruption of the cloud idea is having a massive and mesmerizing impact on physical systems. The Internet is the communication platform and all these collaboratively set a stunning software-defined platform for the ensuing knowledge era. The result is truly momentous. Consumers move from being the IT managers of their homes to consumers of services through their connected devices. The quality of service (QoS) attributes such as discoverability, accessibility, consumability, modifiability, and sustainability are being radically improved.

With new cloud and device services individually and collectively, newer possibilities emerge for appliances, machines, instruments, wares, and gadgets to grasp the ability to sense and respond (S & R) to changing conditions, to communicate with other systems on an as-needed basis, and to contribute to appropriate decision-making. Important and frequently used services can be cached locally so that there can't be any slowdown or breakdown if there is a network problem or an outage at the cloud. The continuous guarantee of high-end services is being made available to consumers with just a click.

8.9.1 Benefits of Cloud-Enabled Smarter Homes

The coming together of cloud and smart homes opens up a slew of incredible possibilities for end-users. Specific benefits for consumers, cloud service providers (CSPs), home/building service providers, and device manufacturers are listed here.

- *Consumer benefits.* Consumers will find these new electronics and services far easier to handle as the uncomfortable device complexity and device management aspects are being moved onto the cloud. Devices are therefore easy to use and repair. Connecting disparate devices together as well as with the remote cloud is simply a matter of software adaptors at the service provider's place. Mobile devices could operate most of the devices inside and outside homes. Devices will become handy in realizing informational, commercial, knowledge, and physical services for consumers. Sensing and actuation devices can form ad hoc networks to understand citizens' needs in time and provide them instantly in an unobtrusive manner. Path-breaking networked robots and consumer electronics will dot our environments to support and sustain people in times of need. Devices can automatically connect, download the appropriate and relevant software modules from cloud-based applications, and configure them accordingly to be a perfect companion for users in all circumstances. In short, all kinds of mechanical, electrical, and electronics devices are bound to become cloud enabled to be advantageous for humans in their daily chores.

- *Device manufacturers' benefits.* There are standard organizations, consortiums, and agencies across the globe for specifying competency standards for devices and services so that the goal of long-pending interoperability can be achieved. All kinds of constricting dependencies are being eliminated and a smooth flow of information among distributed devices is being ensured through the proven standards-based approach. The open and industry-strength standards lead to massive adoption of devices, and service providers could think of device-centric services and workable models through the smart leverage of standards-compliant devices. The market size is bulging and the business risk for device manufacturers is declining. The previous "walled gardens" tends toward an open ecosystem. The emergence of the cloud is doing much good in hosting and managing a growing array of device-centric services. The bulk of the intelligence is being taken out of devices to be implemented in software. Such digitalization and distribution of functionalities will enhance the forthcoming digital world.

- *Service provider benefits.* Cloud service providers (CSPs) are the main service providers, and there are others for the deployment and management of devices and their bridges (software and hardware). As the types of devices increase, many more newer services can be developed and deployed in clouds to be accessed and used by the devices. Clouds emerge as the centralized platform as service repositories and application stores. Many of the benefits accruing to device manufacturers also apply to service providers. The shared and dynamic cloud infrastructures reduce the capital expenditure for bringing business and IT solutions to the competitive and knowledge-filled market. More devices mean more data, which in turn leads to more realistic and rewarded insights. That is, service providers too benefit along with device producers. These timely insights can yield substantial improvements in services or open up possibilities and opportunities for conceiving premium services. With clouds in place, service providers can focus on their own core strengths by delegating all of their IT obligations to cloud providers.

While clouds take care of the infrastructural and platform needs for devices applications, the power of analytics will energize embedded applications to be more aligned toward people. Analytics are becoming real-time and high-performing with the unprecedented maturity of analytical solutions. Several advancements are occurring in parallel to accelerate the onset of the envisioned smarter planet. Everyday devices are connected to be intelligent, device-specific services are being developed and deployed in device as well as generic clouds, the analytics landscape is continuously on the right track to contribute substantially to devices becoming insightful, and so on.

8.9.2 *Envisioning Service Delivery Platforms*

A typical service delivery platform (SDP) based on industry standards supports cooperative interconnection and creation of novelty-packed services. Application development in cloud-based platforms and the subsequent deployment in cloud execution containers bring a series of definite advantages such as quicker and easier development of services at lower cost with shorter time-to-market, facilitating rapid experimentation for improvisation. Besides service implementation from the ground up, there are other important service-centric obligations such as service assemblage, brokering, deployment, provisioning, monitoring, substitution, profiling, decommissioning, and so on. That is, automation is being demanded in every phase of engineering, configuration, administration, management, delivery, and enhancement. Further, with the availability of highly matured orchestration tools, service orchestration is another important factor gaining momentum these days.

Typically an SDP enables the integration, composition, and management of large and complex sets of distributed services. The SDP concept was initiated in the telecommunications systems domain and is penetrating other domains at a fast and furious pace. Because of the diversity, distribution, and decentralization of services, such types of common and centralized managing entities are gaining popularity. The SDP provides an SOA-based framework to link modular services, including third-party services, to manage different types of service exposure and to leverage common back-end components. In addition, any SDP provides service lifecycle management from the creation of new services, to bringing them online in a controlled way for selected customer sets, to actual operations, bundling with other services, and finally termination of services to make way for competent alternatives. The key benefits of SDP are

- SOA can manage the increasing complexity of multiple yet concurrent service deployments to cut costs on service deployments and operations and to enable people to focus on their specific value-additions and core strengths without having to acquire the skills or expend hard-earned capital to build and oversee a fully functioning service infrastructure.
- Using SOA and Web 2.0 technologies, any SDP enables collaboration for more agile service creation.
- Common storefront technology enables service providers to integrate their business processes and storefronts for monetizing their services efficiently.

The following diagram gives the macro-level architecture for cloud-based SDP for smarter homes.

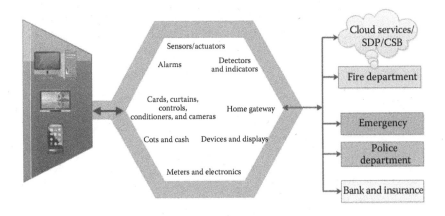

With clouds emerging as the most competent and compact platform, increasingly SDP solutions are being migrated to and operated in clouds. Thus a number of business, technical, and user benefits will inevitably abound. Implementing an SDP in the cloud can very well revolutionize the raging smart home discipline too. Generally speaking, an SDP is a synchronized platform to easily integrate and orchestrate different services, whether they are implemented in cloud or as conventional services and deliver as composite services to end-users dynamically in runtime. Policies are being formulated to ensure complete automation.

An SDP in a cloud environment has the inherent capability to support the expansion of a service's scope by enabling newer services in existing markets and by expanding existing services into newer markets with minimum risks and cost. Exposing service interfaces formulated in standardized formats enables third parties to integrate their services quickly to build novel services in synchronization with the capabilities of the SDP. This paves the way for nimbler business models with unbeatable business opportunities. A smarter home SDP is a specific-purpose SDP for the establishment, governance, and sustenance of smarter homes.

A smarter home is a personal and personalized place specifically designed to add life value, comfort, choice, care, and convenience, energy efficiency, safety, and security. The connected nature ensures further expansion. Without an iota of doubt, the home is the liveliest and loveliest place for people in their everyday lives. A growing array of smarter environment technologies is being retrofitted to be usable and useful for easily and quickly producing and sustaining smarter homes. Abundant home networking, integration, and automation elements; scores of industry-strength and open standards; miniaturized electronics, dynamic, virtualized, and converged infrastructures; and lean processes will ensure building up connected homes for digital living. The following illustration depicts cloud-enabled smarter homes.

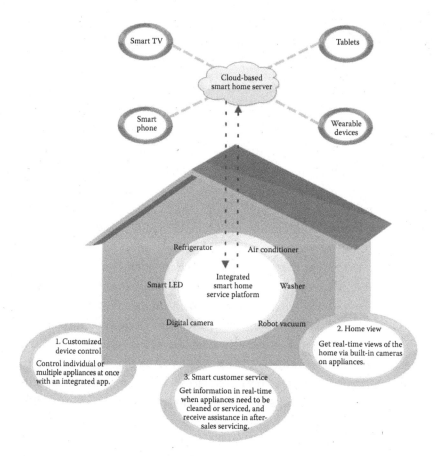

8.9.3 Building Automation System

Apart from independent homes and luxurious houses, deluxe apartments in high-rise buildings; condominiums; gated communities; spas; gardens; resorts; and buildings of different sizes, scopes, and structures occupy more space in any typical city. There are corporate and government offices, manufacturing floors, star hotels, hospitals, auditoriums, food plazas, shopping complexes, and so on. Different sets of stakeholders of these physical entities are providing a wide gamut of newer and nimbler functionalities and facilities. Managing such a complex web of buildings is not a simple affair. IT solution and service providers are increasingly focusing on bringing in impactful automation through scores of IT-enabled products. Energy optimization especially is a vital parameter for energy-gulping and guzzling buildings. There are building management as well as energy management systems to take care of different automation needs of next-generation buildings.

These IT solutions are helpful for building owners, keepers, users, and so on in linking together different building resources, assets, operational as well as controlling elements, people, and so on in visualizing and composing premium services and pragmatic applications. All kinds of noteworthy events are being captured instantaneously and leveraged through analytical platforms. The seamless and spontaneous connectivity among various automation modules within and outside goes a long way to unambiguously orchestrate through formally declared and described policies and preferences to produce sophisticated functionalities for building' users. A building automation system (BAS) has the inherent wherewithal to measure, manage, and maintain all the managed systems. Similarly all the electrical components and systems are optimized for lessening their energy consumption. Energy conservation is increasingly an important consideration. In short, buildings are becoming automated and intelligent. Building control and management systems in synchronization with various digitized objects, sensors, and actuators ensure enhanced user comfort, choice, and care.

The appropriate design and installation of a BAS is the prime factor for achieving the expected success. All sorts of devices inside and applications outside have to be seamlessly integrated through a centralized/clustered or distributed BAS middleware to ensure maximum impact on building users. Devices emit multistructured data and hence the middleware has a big role in data translation. Another constraint is that there are manifold device protocols and they need to be transformed to ultimately have an integrated system. The proprietary nature of the traditional BAS is fast disappearing and a kind of freshness and openness is flourishing, as there is a growing appetite for capturing batches and streams of data being emanated by hundreds of sensors and actuators in buildings and to pass them on to a common platform for further investigations. The BAS space is being widely adopted these days. That is, any BAS product is embedded with the unique capabilities of service orientation, cloud enablement, IPs, constrained application protocol (CoAP), and so on to be relevant for newer buildings. Emerging standards are enabling data sharing between building automation systems and other business applications to improve efficiency and enable real-time control over building systems. BAS plays a vital role in eliminating all kinds of differences and deficiencies so that all kinds of simple as well as sophisticated building systems dynamically cooperate to accomplish bigger and better things for building owners, facility managers, users, guests, and visitors.

8.10 IP-Based Convergence of Building Systems

These days with the adoption of smart technologies, our home, social, and business environments are extremely sensitive, responsive, personalized, and so on. As discussed earlier, there are building-specific software systems that need to be converged to create an optimized outlook. The cost benefits and the operational efficiency of converged systems are increasing steadily. An incremental application support on a converged network provides significant cost savings when maintenance, upgrade, changeover, remote monitoring, dynamic real-time response, and other operational management aspects are taken into consideration. IT systems' increased reliability and real-time performance further heighten the advantages of bringing in true convergence among building IT systems. In the increasingly connected world, building systems across geographical locations need to proactively and preemptively alert, interact, respond, decide, and act. An IP-based system provides an affordable and feasible solution [3].

New IP protocols and technologies are being developed specifically for IP smart objects such as sensors and actuators used in buildings, factories, cities, and so on. These technologies allow for efficient use of the network and enable devices to expose resources and capabilities that historically have been inaccessible to other network participants. Efficient compression methods are in place to address the lingering issue of limited bandwidth of low-speed media often used at the edges and sophisticated routing is being employed to take into account the unique characteristics of these device-level networks (e.g., integrity of links, intermittent connectivity, large number of nodes, and constrained devices [processing, power, and memory]). IP can reach down to the device level while addressing the unique issues associated with the edge devices.

The notion of network convergence using IP is fundamental and relies on the use of a common multiservice IP network supporting a wide range of applications and services. This not only means that such networks are ideal to foster innovation but also leads to dramatically reduced overall cost and complexity, in contrast with a myriad of incompatible, specialized networks interconnected by hard-to-manage gateways. Thanks to its layered architecture, the IP suite has been enriched with a number of new advanced features and capabilities over the past three decades:

- *Multicast* is the technology allowing for sending data traffic to a set of hosts while minimizing traffic replication in the network so as to save network resource usage. For example, you can think of this as a one-to-many communication method.
- *Virtual private networks (VPNs)* can be built on top of a common IP infrastructure, offering a complete isolation between the VPN with technologies such as virtual local area networks (VLANs) and multiprotocol label switching (MPLS) VPNs. You are likely to have used this technology when you logged onto your company's computer network remotely from home or hotels.
- *Quality of service (QoS)* is the ability to provide different priority to different applications, users, or data flows or to guarantee a certain level of performance to a data flow. For example, an application itself can indicate the required priority of the messages as they are routed over the IP network. A number of IP-based technologies have been developed to truly support a

wide variety of qualities of service: IP packets are "colored" when entering the network or by the application itself to indicate the required level of QoS and then they are routed in the network and handled so as to meet the service level agreement (SLA) thanks to scheduling and congestion avoidance techniques. Current QoS technologies allow for the support of real-time application with tight SLA constraints. For example, in a converged building management system and IT network in a building, a fire alarm message would take precedence over email traffic.

- *Reliability.* A number of techniques have been developed to provide an extremely high level of reliability thanks to built-in redundancy, the ability to quickly (in a few dozens of millisecond) re-compute a route should a network element fail, and so on. In other words, the network can intelligently and autonomously reconfigure an alternative route if the first one should fail.
- *Security.* IP networks can be highly secure. A number of technologies have been developed over the years to ensure authentication, support encryption, avoid Denial of Service (DoS5) attack, etc.

Devices (billions of them) are interconnected using IP technologies and more widely deployed in buildings or retrofitted in currently existing infrastructures. These transitions lead to newer and premium services being built and delivered for building users dynamically. The buildings will be thickly populated with IP-enabled devices at all levels and enable an ecosystem of services that will allow interaction among its different components, the environment, and the users. Further, buildings will no longer be limited to standalone entities but will participate as elements of bigger infrastructures (e.g., multi-building groups) enabling streamlined management and participation in services such as load management and demand response to achieve goals set at an enterprise level.

The buildings and their management will be extended to integrate and interact with the majority of those devices in buildings. For example, the users working or even temporarily being in a building can carry devices such as mobile phones that enable them to bidirectionally and collaboratively interact with various devices in the building. All generated information will be captured and exchanged in a service-based manner, which will enable third-party providers to develop innovative applications and services for different stakeholders. When designing and executing new business processes, architects need to be aware that enterprise applications will be able to get near real-time data from the infrastructure itself. Dynamic decision support based on key performance indicators (KPIs) will be realized and coupled with timely monitoring and control capabilities. Such decisions will be enforced across systems in the building(s). New-generation building applications such as facility management, user-centric applications, and so on will depend on runtime mashups of services.

In short, thanks to the development of these IP-based technologies, it became possible to share a common IP network in support of a myriad of applications having a variety of constraints in terms of quality of service, security, VPNs, reliability, and so on. As devices and infrastructures generate a large amount of data and data analytics are being embedded into building systems, sophisticated systems can be visualized and built and deployed. IP technologies in synchronization with smart objects, software-defined infrastructures, building systems, converged networks, and so on foretell better days ahead in realizing smarter buildings.

8.11 Smarter Homes: Architectural Styles, Patterns, and Approaches

Home networking, integration, and automation are some of the buzzwords in the smart home ecosystem. Open and industry-strength standards are being vigorously prescribed as the future-directed solution for dismantling and eliminating all kinds of incompatibilities and barriers among various home-bound devices, artifacts, and assets. The lingering requirement is to have one single common device that takes care of device integration, orchestration, security, enablement, management, maintenance, and so on. The centralized product has to seamlessly connect all differently enabled gadgets while maintaining the flexibility to link future devices a consumer may purchase. Home integration devices (HIDs) are the new entrants to simplify and accelerate the making of smart homes. HID is a middleware device emerging as a viable option for seamless and spontaneous linkage and leveraging of the expanding device ecosystem. Middleware is an affordable, low-power, multipurpose, multichannel, and multidevice platform with plug-and-play installation that connects home digital devices wirelessly and provides easy local as well as distant access. It is a critically bundled solution (highly integrated SoCs, advanced protocols, power management module, switches, etc.), making it simpler for OEMs to design a system quickly, resulting in faster time to market and reduced development cost. A strong software ecosystem is being recommended toward a growing array of applications and services that can use the middleware solutions cognitively to explore smarter home solutions. The home middleware is destined to support always-on connectivity, thereby enabling on-premise devices to become connected and empowered through a host of multitenant and scalable cloud applications such as smart energy management, health monitoring, and personalized entertainment. In this and the ensuing sections, we shed some light on the various decisive parameters for the implementation of smart homes in a risk-free and rewarding fashion.

For the envisioned success, the choice of architectural pattern is very important. Generally any architecture is projected as the pragmatic blueprint that gives the structure, behavior, and direction for the system under implementation. As the development process is becoming difficult and distributed, architecture is bound to play an important role in system building. That is, architecture is the unifying and smoothing factor for the distributed development team. Smart home applications and services are becoming the rage and hence architectural patterns, decisions, drivers, and approaches are acquiring significant traction. In Table 8.1, we list the dominant architectural styles and solutions for the booming home integration field. As widely known, service-oriented architecture (SOA) is the architectural pattern for designing, developing, deploying, and delivering robust and resilient business applications. SOA is mainly for modernization of legacy applications, integration of application and data silos, and composition of novel applications and services.

Table 8.1 Dominant Architectural Styles for Home Integration

ARCHITECTURAL STYLE	DESCRIPTION
Service-oriented device architecture (SODA)	SODA is an adaptation of the SOA principles, which integrate business systems through a set of services that can be reused and combined to address changing business priorities. Services are software components with well-defined interfaces, and they are independent of the programming language and the computing platforms on which they run.
SOA-based field bus integration architecture (SOAFBIA)	The current trends in service consolidation over the Internet Protocol (IP) also stimulate the integration of the industrial automation system with the information technology (IT) infrastructure for more efficient information access and more cost-effective production and management. Field buses have been the de facto communication standard in industrial automation, but mostly based on manufacture-specific protocols. Thus, the interoperability between the manufacturer-specific field bus systems and the external operating environment is the critical factor in enabling the networked industrial automation systems. However, most of the existing field bus integration solutions lack either flexibility or scalability. SOAFBIA is an architecture in which each field bus system is encapsulated with operational interface, manageability interface, and semantic descriptions in a standard format to facilitate interoperability. Moreover, a resource agent is proposed as an enhanced service broker, which implements not only the standard service registry functionality in SOA, but also the resource management functions including admission control, service scheduling, and load balancing.
Service component architecture (SCA)	SCA is a standard with service programming and composition models. Services can be publicly discovered, created, and configured out of legacy application modules; orchestrated and choreographed through linkage and leveraged; and so on.
Event-driven architecture (EDA)	EDA is a strategic architectural style. As a result of multiplicity, decentralization, and diversity, thousands of events will be generated from different places and the event processing engine has to have the required capability to receive all of them in real time and process them quickly to produce and provide real-time notification and actuation. Real-time insights and intelligence will be the norm and SOA in sync with EDA will be an asset.
Cloud architecture	Increasingly personal as well as professional services will be posted in clouds to be offered via subscription for a fee or free to worldwide consumers and customers. There is a need for device-specific cloud architectures.
Model-driven architecture (MDA)	Models soon will become the leading abstraction units in the software engineering field. Formal models in digitalized format can be stored, exported, and imported to transition them into deployable and executable service codes via code generation toolkits, cartridges, and so on.

8.11.1 Smarter Homes—Middleware Platforms

With the surging popularity of smart home applications, there are widespread initiatives and endeavors to creatively, convincingly, and comprehensively support the case for smarter homes. As a result, international projects have been initiated; middleware solutions are being pumped out; development, execution, and change management platforms are being readied; enabling toolkits are being announced and articulated; and so on. Currently available middleware platforms for smarter homes are described in Table 8.2.

8.11.2 Smarter Home Frameworks

Frameworks are the proven enablers in the IT domain. As the developmental complexity of IT applications and services is on the climb, frameworks are being perceived to be simpler and more streamlined. Creating and sustaining smarter home systems and networks are not an easy task and hence frameworks are finding their relevance and roots in this dynamic space. Table 8.3 lists the prominent frameworks that go a long way in smoothing and strengthening the integration task of heterogeneous home IT products, devices, and infrastructures.

8.12 Home Integration Standards: Industry Strength and Proprietary

It is a well-known and recognized fact that standards are essential for any product to thrive in the market. Standards compliance is becoming mandatory for devices and products vendors to enable them to talk to each other seamlessly. Spontaneity is the keyword for devices to dynamically discover, associate, leverage, and compose toward advanced applications. Table 8.4 lists the industry-strength as well as industry-specific standards for the blooming domain of home integration.

Table 8.2 Middleware Platforms for Smarter Homes

NAME	PLATFORM NAME	DESCRIPTION
http://www.pervasa.com/atlas.php	Atlas Middleware	By seamlessly connecting devices to the network, Atlas delivers embedded hardware as a software service to the developer. These services can then be combined to create a vast array of applications and solutions. Atlas follows a modular design offering maximum flexibility, adaptability, and return on investment. An Atlas node consists of several (typically three) layers connected using two board-to-board connectors. Wi-Fi, ZigBee, USB, and Ethernet communication layers are currently available. The processing layer is a low-power Atmel Atmega128L microcontroller supported by a 32K extended external memory. Several device connector layers offer physical connectivity to a large variety of sensors, actuators, and devices. Atlas is not only hardware; it is a middleware residing on the Atlas nodes and in the network. Based on the OSGi standard, Atlas offers the magic of plug-and-play to the widest array of sensors and devices. It does so by automating the sensor-to-service (hardware-to-software) conversion.
http://ws4d.org/	Web Services for Devices (WS4D)	WS4D is an initiative bringing SOA and Web services technology to the application domains of industrial automation, home entertainment, and automotive and telecommunication systems. WS4D is all about using Internet technologies such as XML, HTTP, and Web services to connect resource-constrained devices in ad hoc networks and still conserve interoperability with Web services as specified by the W3C. This enables the usage of high-level concepts for Web services also in low-level distributed embedded systems. So WS4D provides technologies for easy setup and management of network-connected devices in distributed embedded systems. The WS4D toolkits comply with DPWS standards.
https://forge.soa4d.org/	SODA tools, Wikis, and browsers	The SOA4D Forge is the support site for both developers and users of the SOA4D (service-oriented architecture for devices) technologies. SOA4D is an open-source initiative aiming at fostering an ecosystem for the development of service-oriented software components (SOAP messaging, WS-* protocols, service orchestration, and so on) adapted to the specific constraints of embedded devices.

(Continued)

Table 8.2 (Continued)   Middleware Platforms for Smarter Homes

NAME	PLATFORM NAME	DESCRIPTION
http://www.linksmart.eu	The LinkSmart middleware for networked devices	LinkSmart middleware allows developers to incorporate heterogeneous physical devices into their applications by offering easy-to-use Web service interfaces for controlling any type of physical device irrespective of its network technology such as Bluetooth, RF, ZigBee, RFID, WiFi, and so on. LinkSmart incorporates means for device and service discovery, semantic model-driven architecture, P2P communication, and diagnostics. LinkSmart-enabled devices and services can be secure and trustworthy through distributed security and social trust components of the middleware.
http://www.echelon.com/	LonWorks	LonWorks is a networking platform specifically created to address the needs of control applications. The platform is built on a protocol created by Echelon Corporation for networking devices over media such as twisted pair, power lines, fiber optics, and radio frequency. It is used for the automation of various functions within buildings such as lighting and HVAC.
http://felix.apache.org/	Apache Felix	Apache Felix is a community effort to implement the OSGi (Open Service Gateway initiative) service platform and other interesting OSGi-related technologies under the Apache license.
http://www.eclipse.org/equinox/	Eclipse Equinox	Equinox is an implementation of the OSGi core framework specification, a set of bundles that implement various optional OSGi services and other infrastructure for running OSGi-based systems.
http://www.knopflerfish.org/	Knopflerfish	Knopflerfish is the leading universal open-source OSGi service platform. Led and maintained by Makewave, Knopflerfish delivers significant value as the key container technology for many Java-based projects and products.

Table 8.3 Frameworks for Smarter Homes

VENDOR	NAME	DESCRIPTION
Galixsys Networks http://www.galixsys networks.com	Andromeda Embedded Services Framework	Andromeda can enable automated communication for devices in a variety of applications, including sensors, monitors, or controllers with automatic storage and retrieval of captured or generated data. Robotic or device artificial intelligence (AI) enhancement via server or cloud computing Digital still cameras or video players with automatic upload or streaming of pictures and video Remote monitors that need greater functionality or automation over Web page serving
http://www.netmf.com/	.NET Micro Framework	.NET Micro Framework helps easily develop powerful, interactive, and complex applications. Securely connects devices over wired or wireless protocols. Develops reliable solutions faster at lower cost. Develops full solutions using .NET including devices, servers, and the cloud.
http://restlet.org/	RESTful Web framework	The trend is that the Web is becoming ubiquitous and that representational state transfer (REST), as the architecture style of the Web, helps to leverage all HTTP features. Restlet, the open-source REST framework, is already available on regular computers based on Java SE/EE in Web browsers. For the ubiquitous Web, mobile devices have to be empowered further. With the faster commoditization of smart phones, more and more mobile users will have usable access to the Web from their phone. So far, developers have been stuck with proprietary platforms and were lacking the productivity and portability common in the Java world. Thus the Restlet framework is being ported to smart phones.

(Continued)

Table 8.3 (Continued)   Frameworks for Smarter Homes

VENDOR	NAME	DESCRIPTION
http://www.greenpeak.com/	The Open Smart Home Framework	The Open Smart Home Framework (OSF) is an architecture that is composed of the components of the ZigBee (IEEE 802.15.4) standard family that are relevant for the home and the consumer. It combines these components into an architecture that allows for an easy-to-install, maintenance-free, reliable, secure, and cost-effective sense and control network implementation, without any visibility for the user of the different ZigBee network layers or other underlying components that are used.
http://wosh.sourceforge.net/	WOSH Framework	WOSH (Wide Open Smart Home) is an open-source, multiplatform framework (message-oriented middleware) written in ANSI C++, designed to enable (smart) home automation. WOSH is a service-oriented framework (SOA) providing an open-source (network)-independent infrastructure for developing component-based software (services, aka bundles). WOSH Framework and installed services enable rapid development (RAD) and features composition.\nWOSH ships with many implemented services and some end-user applications (such as woshsrv, WorkShop).
http://eclipse.org/smarthome/	Eclipse Smart Home Framework	Smart home adoption will gain momentum only if the different devices can be connected to overarching use cases, but currently the market for smart home systems and IoT gadgets is heavily fragmented. The only way out of this is to establish common interfaces and application programming interface (API).

Table 8.4 Standards for Home Integration

STANDARD	MEDIA	DESCRIPTION
6LoWPAN	Radio frequency	6LoWPAN is an acronym of IPv6 over low-power wireless personal area networks. The 6LoWPAN group aimed to define header compression mechanisms that allow IPv6 packets to be sent to and received from over IEEE 802.15-based networks.
		The targets for IP networking for low-power radio communication are the applications that need wireless Internet connectivity at lower data rates for devices with very limited form factor. Examples include automation and entertainment applications in home, office, and factory environments.
Bluetooth	Radio frequency	Bluetooth is the codename for a technology specification for small form factor, low-cost, short-range radio links among mobile PCs, mobile phones, and other portable devices. The Bluetooth Special Interest Group is an industry group consisting of leaders in the telecommunications and computing industries who are driving development of the technology and bringing it to market.
CEBus	All	The CEBus Standard (EIA-600) is a protocol specification developed by the Electronic Industries Association (EIA) to support the interconnection and interoperation of consumer products in a home.
DLNA http://www.dlna.org	Digital Living Network Alliance	DLNA is a cross-industry organization of leading consumer electronics, computing industry, and mobile device companies. This is a vision of a wired and wireless network of interoperable consumer electronics (CEs), personal computers (PCs), and mobile devices in the home and on the road, enabling a seamless environment for sharing and growing new digital media and content services. In the DLNA digital home, it will be common for consumers to • Easily acquire, store, and access digital music from almost anywhere in the home • Effortlessly manage, view, print, and share digital photos • Carry favorite content anywhere to enjoy while on the road • Enjoy distributed, multiuser content recording, and playback
DPWS (Device Profiles for Web Services)	All	DPWS defines a minimal set of standards and specifications to provide Web service–based communication for embedded devices. It identifies a core set of Web service specifications comprising the following areas: secure message transmission, dynamic discovery, description, subscription, and event notification.

(Continued)

Table 8.4 (Continued) Standards for Home Integration

STANDARD	MEDIA	DESCRIPTION
HAVI (Home Audio Visual Interoperability)	IEEE	HAVi is a CEs industry standard that will ensure interoperability between digital audio and video devices from different vendors and brands that are connected via a network in the consumer's home.
HBS (Home Bus System)	Coax Twisted Pair	A consortium of Japanese companies, supported by government agencies and trade associations, has specified communications standards and equipment for home automation. This encompasses links among appliances, telephones, and audio-video equipment using twisted-pair wires and coaxial cables.
HomePlugAlliance (https://www.homeplug.org/)	Power Line	Created to set a technology specification for home power line networking and to promote its wide acceptance in the marketplace. The alliance's objective is to enable and promote rapid availability and adoption of cost-effective, interoperable, and specification-based home power line networks and products enabling the connected home.
KNX http://www.knx.org/	All	The worldwide standard for all applications in home and building control, ranging from lighting and shutter control to various security systems, heating, ventilation, air conditioning, monitoring, alarming, water control, energy management, metering as well as household appliances, audio, and much more. The technology can be used in new as well as in existing home and buildings.
HomePNA and HomeGrid http://www.homepna.org/home/	Phone Line	The HomeGrid Forum develops extensions to the HomePNA specifications for distributing entertainment and triple play data over existing coax cables and phone wires. It also certifies and promotes member products for residential deployments. The Alliance provides member-only access to a community of HomePNA developers and users including leading equipment OEMs, service providers, and technology developers to help you design, deploy, and support new products and services such as HD IPTV.
OSGi (Open Service Gateway initiative) http://www.osgi.org/	All	The OSGi specification will create an open standard for a service gateway that is inserted between the external network and the internal network.

(Continued)

Table 8.4 (Continued) Standards for Home Integration

STANDARD	MEDIA	DESCRIPTION
UPnP (Universal Plug and Play) http://www.upnp.org/	All	The UPnP architecture offers pervasive peer-to-peer network connectivity of PCs of all form factors, intelligent appliances, and wireless devices. The UPnP architecture is a distributed, open networking architecture that leverages TCP/IP and the Web to enable seamless proximity networking in addition to control and data transfer among networked devices in the home, office, and everywhere in between. UPnP technology targets home networks, proximity networks, and networks in small businesses and commercial buildings. It enables data communication between any two devices under the command of any control device on the network. UPnP technology is independent of any particular operating system, programming language, or network technology.
VESA (Video Electronics Standards Assoc.) http://www .vesa.org/	Various	The VESA Home Network consists of a backbone network, one or more component networks, a number of access devices that connect the home network to external access networks, a number of network devices that connect component networks to the home backbone network, and end devices that provide various functional services to the home user.
ZigBee https://www.zigbee.org/	Wireless	ZigBee standards prove you can rely on the widest variety of smart and easy-to-use products for just about anywhere you work, live, or play. Our innovative standards are designed to let product manufacturers help their customers create their own IoT and M2M wireless sensor networks to gain greater control of, and even improve, everyday activities. ZigBee lets you easily and cost-effectively add intelligent new features that improve the efficiency, safety, security, reliability, and convenience of your products. You can help your customers save both energy and money, or give them the tools they need to gain control of their homes. It's even possible to help people maintain their independence and allow them to closely monitor their health and fitness.

8.13 Conclusion

As we all know, buildings and homes occupy a major portion of any city across the globe. In this chapter, we discussed the technological advancements in realizing smart homes and buildings. We listed the various architectures ranging from centralized and peer-to-peer (P2P) to distributed architectures for producing smart places. Multiple standards are being specified for device makers and the data formats for home-bound devices are diversifying. And frameworks for quickly developing smart environment services are being produced toward the faster realization of smarter environment applications. Thus the penetration and pervasiveness of smarter buildings is highly visible. With the continuing decline in hardware prices including the costs of chips and controllers, there will be a sharp increment in buying, installing, configuring, and leveraging manifold devices in our everyday environments. The role and responsibility of device manufacturers, IT system integrators, independent software vendors, cloud brokerages, telecommunication carriers, cloud service providers, and standards bodies are therefore bound to rise significantly. Market researchers and analysts are also optimistic about the success and scope of smarter environments in the long run. There are standards-compliant connectivity, bridging, and other middleware solutions aplenty in the market place; as a result, the days of smarter homes, offices, buildings, manufacturing floors and plants, educational campuses, hospitals, hotels, stadiums, and so on are not far away.

Appendix

Smart Home Solutions

Having realized the market trend for smart home solutions, companies and vendors across the world have come out with generic as well as specific (standard, technology, platform, application domain, etc.) products. We here list the major products, their application domains, and providers.

PROVIDER NAME	PRODUCT NAME	PRODUCT DETAILS
Xanboo http://www.xanboo.com/	Xanboo	Xanboo provides an end-to-end technology platform that enables access and control of devices locally via a TV or PC, and remotely over the Internet via a mobile phone or PC. Xanboo's technology is market agnostic and provides a platform for a wide range of partners wishing to deliver services based on video monitoring, device control, notification, or data transmission to any location with Internet access. Using the Xanboo Software Development Kit (the SDK), partners can provide a wide range of previously unavailable revenue-generating services to their customers under their own brand. These services, customized to each partner's particular requirements, are being used in markets ranging from security and energy management to home healthcare.
iControl http://www.icontrol.com/	iControl ConnectedLife	iControl ConnectedLife represents a unique opportunity for leading broadband, telecommunications, and home security providers to deliver next-generation broadband home management services to their customers, including interactive home security, remote home monitoring, home management and control, energy management, and home healthcare.

(*Continued*)

PROVIDER NAME	PRODUCT NAME	PRODUCT DETAILS
OpenRemote http://www.openremote.org	Building Operating System Standard (BOSS)	OpenRemote Boss is where all the critical processing such as integration of protocols, routing of messages, and so on occurs. It is mostly software written in Java and is therefore portable across operating systems. OpenRemote Orb is Linux OS based. It runs OpenRemote Boss and the hardware gateway via USB, infrared, and serial interfaces. It is designed to support development. It is Wi-Fi enabled. OpenRemote Controller is an open platform that acts as an integrator for existing protocols. It creates a central point of integration and programming. Various media standards (X10, IR, RS, KNX, UPnP, proprietary) and messaging formats are supported. Today it provides a gateway for the iPhone and a browser to control the devices plugged into the home. OpenRemote for iPhone is the client of the OpenRemote Controller. This client is a native iPhone/iPod Touch application, Android application, or a Web application, supporting any browser. Protocols Supported—The point of the OR Boss is to be open and modular with respect to protocols. In theory, any protocol can be ported and distributed as part of a Boss instance. Currently this supports X10, IR, RS, KNX, and UPnP.
http://www.control4.com/	Home control	Control4 offers the ultimate home automation solution by making the products and systems you already have and use every day work together. By integrating everything from lighting control, music, home theater, climate control, security—even iPads, iPhones, and Android smartphones and tablets—a smart house by Control4 creates personalized experiences that enhance your life and provide added comfort, savings, convenience, and peace of mind.

(*Continued*)

PROVIDER NAME	PRODUCT NAME	PRODUCT DETAILS
http://www.life-ware.com/	Lifeware	Lifelware is an industry leader in digital entertainment and automation. Flexible and scalable, Lifelware is the perfect solution for homes, meeting rooms, buildings, hospitals, hotels, and multidwelling units. The state-of-the-art, standards-based software and hardware is easy to configure and install—no programming required.
http://www.smarthome.com/	KeypadLinc–INSTEON Lamp and Wall Dimmer Control Kit	Remotely controlled lights and lamps with convenient, elegant lighting scenes using an INSTEON Home Automation Network

References

1. UN World Urbanization Perspective (2014). New York: United Nations.
2. Andreas Kamilaris and Andreas Pitsillides (2012). A Restful Architecture for Web-Based Smart Homes using Request Queues. NETworks Research Laboratory, Department of Computer Science, University of Cyprus.
3. IPSO Alliance Smart Building Workgroup (2013). Introduction to IP in Commercial Buildings. http://www.ipso-alliance.org/.

9

SMART ENERGY, UTILITY, AND TRANSPORT

Abstract

The growing concept of intelligent cities is rapidly captivating and capturing the minds and hearts of people who are charged with effective city administration. The general public as well is exerting much pressure on city managers and elected representatives to bring in a stream of reformations in city governance besides a cornucopia of versatile technologies to automate various manual and mundane city tasks. It is no secret that an effective use of mission-critical technologies also ensures the much-needed transparency in city functioning and third-party auditability for nipping any mischievous acts in the bud. Technologies promote insightful thinking and decision making for city officials and bureaucrats; a guarantee of prompt response and timely service delivery by public servants; and a greater responsibility/accountability toward citizens and city projects' execution by authorities with utmost care, clarity, and confidence; and so on. Leveraging multifaceted technologies intelligently lays a stimulating foundation for proactively conceptualizing newer services and facilities for city dwellers, immigrants, and job seekers who are highly qualified, skillful, well trained, and who demonstrate an entrepreneurial spirit, professional experience, and technological expertise. Across the world, many smarter cities are being collaboratively and cognitively built that are aptly touted as the system of systems. In short, smart cities are complex to visualize and accomplish, as they are much more than the sum of many of their complicated subsystems. The predominant subsystems include smart energy, smart buildings, smart transport and logistics, smart water and utilities, and so on. In this chapter, we consider the contributing and participating components in constructing and caring for competent and people-centric smart cities.

9.1 Introduction

In the fields of software and hardware engineering, while traversing from the problem space to its solution architects would simply follow two primary techniques that are catered to and prescribed everywhere: decomposition and composition. For precise and perfect understanding of the problem in hand, the problem is decomposed into many simpler and smaller modules, the appropriate solution for each of them is constructed, and finally they are composed to attain the envisaged solution. This has been the age-old practice. In a nutshell, any sophisticated system can be built successfully through the process of componentization. Today complex systems are pervasive either by choice or sometimes thrust upon us for various reasons. Smart cities too, being so vast, are viewed as a collection of different yet interrelated entities.

There are two foremost approaches for implementing a complex system, whether through software, hardware, or any physical or cyber physical system (CPS): the bottom-up and top-down approaches. Smart city development is also not averse to these avenues. The u-up approach is to start from the local requirements, influences, resources, cultures, and policies and move up toward the top through a seamless and spontaneous accumulation through intuitive and imaginative interfacing. Undoubtedly, smart citizens and communities are the basic building blocks of smart cities. A variety of local systems coexist and lead to a complex, smart, and sustainable city. The growing urban challenges can be met fully through the potential collective intelligence and the proven bottom-up approach. To fulfill local aspirations and to make real and rapid progress, there is an insistence on building doable mechanisms for scanning, evaluating, and cross-fertilizing good ideas. Reusability of existing assets and capabilities can be a boon with this approach while safeguarding inclusive growth.

On the reverse side, the top-down approach is vision-centric, strategically and soundly planned and executed, centrally coordinated, monitored and managed, with a time-bound execution of deals, and so on. Everything starts fresh; there is less possibility for the reuse of existing resources; there is less scope for accommodating people's voice; the concept of outside-in thinking cannot be fully exploited; and so on. This is a time-bound program and can leverage the fully matured technologies; the city landscape will be very modern at the end of the program initiated; the city architecture can be developed for incorporating all kinds of future-directed changes (technology, requirement, social, etc.), and so on. In short, this is being imposed from the top and hence there could be a possibility of not taking care of the ground realities. The local needs could often be suppressed and instead the inside-out thinking would get priority.

There are both advantages as well as disadvantages with the approaches and sometimes a kind of hybrid approach is being recommended so that the vision as well as the ground realities can be cogently combined to implement cities of the future that intrinsically enable the creation of smart citizens and communities. Cities will be innovation hubs, that is, they will ensure digital living and comprise energy-efficient buildings and homes, structured layouts, smart utilities (gas, electricity, and water), unified and connected transports, and so on. The basic and intended goal is to do more with less. That is, as cities are crowded, and various city resources are scarce, expensive, and on the decline, usage can be optimized and simplified through a bevy of means such as rationalization, sharing, streamlining, and need-based supply. There has to be a harmony among people, properties, and places. The other factor being insisted on at local as well as national levels is to emit much less carbon to the fragile environment while enhancing all kinds of amenities for people. In this chapter, we describe the various constituents of smart cities.

9.2 Smart Energy

Multiple tricky challenges such as population growth, climate change due to global warming, demographic changes due to extensive urbanization, and fast depletion of resources are destabilizing our cities. These have forced city planners and architects to exhort all stakeholders to be sensitive and adaptive to survive and thrive in increasingly complicated city environments. Smart cities are therefore being prescribed everywhere as the ultimate solution for all kinds of urban deficiencies and disturbances. Reducing carbon gas emission and increasing living standards substantially are the twin objectives. It is estimated that information technologies are capable of contributing to a 15% reduction in carbon emissions by 2020. Thus it is absolutely clear that technologies, if applied appropriately, are beneficial for city upgrade and community betterment and hence cities are mandated to consciously harness technologies to uplift and sustain human society.

As we all know, electricity is an important ingredient (energy) for powering various systems across the length and breadth of the city. Electricity grids are ubiquitous these days and beset with the problem of leakages in their handling. Further, optimal utilization is sorely missing, as the monitoring mechanism is not fully automated and consumption patterns are not analyzed sufficiently to conceive practical options. As is well known, electrical energy is becoming scarce and its production, transmission, and distribution are becoming complicated and costly. Another point here is that more power consumption leads to more heat generation. The continuous environmental degradation due to excessive heat dissipation of multiple systems can be offset to a major extent through a number of optimizations in electricity networks. Smart electricity grids consequently are being portrayed as the way forward for cities to substantially reduce electricity consumption and to provide a means of energy preservation. It is all about transforming power-hungry urban locations into low-carbon places through the smart leverage of precocious technologies, thereby conserving precious power energy for future generations.

Thus smart energy metering, measurement, and management are accepted as the appropriate ways to handle this perpetual predicament in the energy domain. Generally energy meters are mandatory for social utilities such as gas, electricity, and water across cities and communities. This helps energy producers and suppliers produce invoices from every household to gain a good understanding of the energy consumption pattern at the user level. The usage details are then taken to analytical software systems at the central level to identify workable ways and means of moderating energy usage. Real-time analytics in energy utilization goes a long way in locating bottlenecks and eliminating energy wastage through various energy conservation methods. When usage declines, the cost of energy does as well for users and this has a cascading effect on the value chain. The smart grid is being touted as a holistic and harmonious approach for the various stakeholders in the energy domain. Lately, energy meters have been connected to remote control systems directly, thereby facilitating a kind of automation in extracting energy expenditure.

The analytics system then empowers both energy suppliers and users with real-time intelligence to consider the correct course of action collectively. There are Not only Structured Query Language (NoSQL) databases for capturing, storing, processing, mining, and analyzing such a huge amount of data, as there could be millions of energy meters for every single energy service provider. In short, power usage has to be highly optimal to sustain the environment as well as to keep the cost of energy production down. Every user is going to be assisted by a growing pool of generic as well as purpose-specific devices and hence the energy need is bound to grow in the days ahead. Thus the importance of introducing smartness in energy consumption is a good omen for smart cities. There are other benefits of smart grids such as their capability of preemptively identifying any malfunction and arresting any untoward incident for the utmost safety and security of people and properties.

9.2.1 Smart Grids

Smart grids involve the application of advanced electrical engineering processes in association with a few resilient technologies in the expanding information technology (IT) domain to embed the much-needed smartness in electrical grids. As indicated in Chapter 1, physical systems in our daily environments are methodically empowered to be smart through a light integration with a host of cyber systems. There are other significant advances in sensing and actuation technologies such as the formation of ad hoc sensor networks, the emergence of sophisticated interfacing systems to ensure thorough interoperability, real-time data capture, transmission, processing, knowledge extraction, and so on. Thus through instrumentation and interconnectivity real-time systems provide high-quality services to city residents. Among the projected and perceived benefits are improved operational reliability, reduced resource usage and costs, improved environmental quality with less carbon in the atmosphere, improved governance, and new enterprise and job creation opportunities.

The smart grid is an advanced electricity transmission and distribution network (grid) that uses robust two-way communications, smart sensors, and centralized software applications to improve the efficiency, reliability, and safety of power delivery. Smart grids comprise a range of emerging and evolving technologies that can be applied along the end-to-end electricity supply chain from power generation plants through transmission and distribution to end users (homes, apartments, hospitals, hotels, commercial buildings, etc.). With energy meters in every power-consuming building, the supply chain still expands. Sensor-attached electrical appliances and consumer electronics, smart meters, two-way communication, and distributed computing and centralized analytical system all collaboratively team up to see the light of variable and renewable energy generation, dynamic demand and response (on-demand power supply), variable pricing, and so on. Ultimately energy efficiency, reliability, and safety are being guaranteed. Electricity is the fastest growing element of total global energy demand and smart grids are the best way forward to meet this demand in a cost-effective, secure, and sustainable way. The annual market for smart grid technology infrastructure (including smart meters, sensor networks, fiber optic and wireless networks, and data analytics) will grow to nearly US$16 billion by 2020. The market for energy storage technologies is also growing rapidly.

Smart grids are being named as the mandatory requirement for establishing and sustaining smart cities and contribute immensely to the grand success of smart city initiatives for any nation. As cities go through a series of optimizations, the energy domain too would get its due share. There are several commonalities between smart grids and smart cities. The most visible ones are service enablement, distributed computing, ultrahigh broadband communication, network connectivity, system integration, and actionable and timely insights. The use of technologies such as sentient materials, ubiquitous sensing, vision, perception and actuation, knowledge discovery and dissemination, cloud, big data analytics, mobility, and social computing will ensure the quick and easy realization and management of smart grids and cities. Energy, especially electricity, is essential for our everyday living. As city populations, energy-guzzling electronics, and electric vehicles are on the climb, the need for electricity will grow. There are two major options: the first is that the power generation capacity has to be adequately increased. Unfortunately electricity generation is not coping with impending needs and there is a growing gap between supply and demand for several reasons. The second option is to stringently follow energy conservation mechanisms that include the optimized and on-demand usage by cutting down power leakage, pilferage, and wastage.

9.2.2 Energy Harvesting

Wireless sensor networks are characterized by severe resource constraints, one of which is the reliance on battery life. With the deployment of sensor nodes in very large numbers in smart cities, it is infeasible to replace or recharge batteries in these devices. Creating energy-efficient solutions from protocol design to sophisticated power management schemes are efficient and necessary methods, but not sufficient. A popular way of supplementing power includes solar panels, but sunlight is not always available and it is not the most cost-effective solution. The harvesting of energy from alternative sources in the environment is being actively researched and developed [1]. Examples of these energy sources include thermal, light (solar), wind, mechanical (vibration), and many others. However, efficient ways of capturing this energy are vital, as the energy from these sources is usually available in extremely small quantities. Hence, ways to scavenge energy from the environment to prolong the nodes' lifetimes and improve market adoption are essential. Sources are typically from light, heat, and sources of kinetic energy such as vibrations, and so on. Of course, this technology can also be applied to drive any other low-energy device. Methods of energy harvesting in the context of smart cities include

- *Wind energy.* Small-scale turbine rotation is converted to electrical energy. Such turbines can be located in open places where wind is easily accessible. Nodes used for structural health monitoring, deployed in bridges and similar structures, can use this kind of energy harvesting. Other methods involve the use of piezoelectric materials or vibrating membranes.
- *Radiofrequency (RF) energy.* An antenna receives RF signals and an RF–DC converter module converts the RF signals to

DC voltages. With multiple antennae emitting signals, this type of harvesting is worth exploring.

- *Electric field.* Electric and magnetic fields around power lines, for instance, can be exploited for energy scavenging. Sensors deployed in the near proximity of these overhead lines can exploit these electric or magnetic fields.
- *Light and thermal sources.* These are common both indoors and outdoors. In houses, for instance, these can be ambient artificial light or heat from appliances.
- *Piezoelectric harvesters in bridges and highways.* To meet the demands in power requirements for sensor nodes for structural health monitoring, the structure's vibration, in case of bridges or highways, is a good energy scavenging source.

A great deal of research and development is ongoing in this domain, and these techniques are still not completely mature for powering of low-power devices; even when they are used, it should be for ultralow duty cycles only to preserve as much energy as possible. Among these scavenging techniques, harnessing energy from vibration is probably the most efficient approach.

9.2.3 *The Need for Big Data Analytics for Smarter Grids*

Chapter 4 in this book is devoted to big data analytics. As smart cities are destined to produce a massive volume of data to be collected, preprocessed, stored, and analyzed, the most recent buzz of big data analytics is becoming mandatory for empowering city officials as well as users to be smart in their decision making and actions. The following is an example that clearly demonstrates the need for big data analytics platforms, processes, and infrastructures.

Consider a fictional company called X Utilities that serves 10 million households. Once each quarter, it gathers 10 million readings to produce utility bills. With government regulation and the price of oil skyrocketing, X started deploying smart meters to get hourly readings of electricity usage. They now collect 21.6 billion sensor readings per quarter from the smart meters. Analysis of the meter data over months and years can be correlated with energy saving campaigns, weather patterns, and local events, providing savings possibilities both for the consumers and X Utilities. When consumers are offered a billing plan that has cheaper electricity from 8 p.m. to 5 a.m., they demand 5-minute intervals in their smart meter reports so they can identify high-use activity in their homes. At 5-minute intervals, the smart meters are collecting more than 100 billion meter readings every 90 days, and X Utilities now has a big data problem. Its data volume exceeds its ability to process them with existing software and hardware. So X Utilities turns to Hadoop to handle the incoming meter readings. Figure 9.1 gives the macro-level architecture of data analytics using traditional platforms and infrastructures.

Figure 9.2 illustrates the high-level architecture of big data analytics for facilitating smarter grids by giving real-time and actionable insights with ease. The Hadoop platform plays a very important role in gathering metering and measurement data directly and preprocessing the data accumulated to prepare them to be quickly subjected to data analytics. There are plenty of connectors to spontaneously integrate data between Hadoop and traditional data analytical systems. Traditional business intelligence (BI) suites are better equipped to simplify not only knowledge discovery but also dissemination. Hadoop, on the other hand, is better positioned for intake, validation,

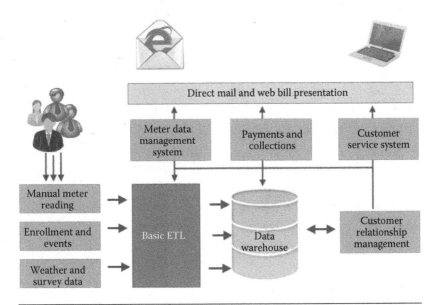

Figure 9.1 Data analytics before the big data era.

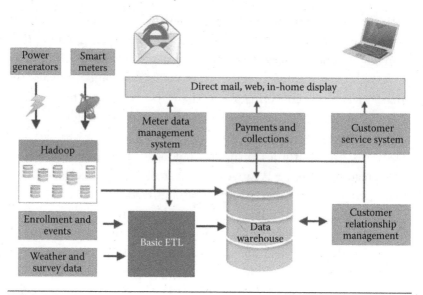

Figure 9.2 The big data-centric architecture.

and verification of data from distributed and diverse sources in large quantities and for preprocessing them quickly through parallelization/ horizontal scalability so that stabilized and successful knowledge extraction systems could breathe easy in bringing forth data-driven insights.

In conclusion, because energy requirements are on the rise, the identification of viable means for solidly conserving energy usage acquires special significance. IT-driven mechanisms are being deeply explored and expedited to realize the mandated and the longstanding goal of energy preservation. The new subject of big data computing is penetrating every industrial domain to ring in the desired insights-driven optimizations and the energy sector is realistic with regard to extracting and employing data-driven insights in time to fulfill the strategic objective of energy efficiency. We all know that IT infrastructures (servers, storage, and networking components) in widely deployed data centers and server farms are drawing a large amount of power energy, thereby leading to more greenhouse gas emissions. Thus concerted efforts toward lean, clean, and green computing are being accelerated. IT solutions and services are being leveraged toward environmental sustainability by moderating catastrophic global warming and climate change.

In summary, historically energy supply has been a one-way process with the utility provider supplying energy to the grid without the ability to receive any feedback or insight about the supply and its quality. The smart grid is all about empowering the utility provider with all the decision-enabling details about the grid and electricity transmission, distribution, leakage, and usage. Thus all the measured values at different levels and junctions are routed back to the utility services provider to contemplate viable and acceptable ways of achieving more energy efficiency. Smart sensors in the grid, buildings, and homes can predict when the energy demand goes up so that the energy supply is accordingly maneuvered by providers. Consumers may pay more for powering energy-draining devices such as electric water heaters, electric vehicle chargers, air conditioners, pool pumps, and so on during peak hours. Smart grids are adept at better usage of multiple power supplies such as solar, coal, wind, and water individually as well as collectively; drive energy conservation; and also provide the much-needed differentiation to suppliers. Smart grids allow customers to self-generate and sell excess power back to the grid, establishing a positive and cooperative relationship between providers and users. The well-known results of smart grids include fewer and reduced outages, reductions in network energy losses, more efficient energy markets, and improved conditions for producers and energy generators.

The smart grid will rely on the use of RF to provide wireless connectivity to the various components of the new electric distribution system. Wireless communications technology has become ubiquitous in our lives, enabling mobile connectivity with cell phones, wireless Internet services, and home area networking with Wi-Fi technology, even cooking our food with microwave ovens.

9.2.4 Envisioned Energy Grid Services for Smart Cities

We have allocated a separate chapter (Chapter 5) for the Internet of Things (IoT) because of its power for realizing next-generation systems across the industry. With the cloud emerging as the core and central platform and infrastructure, there is another nomenclature called the Cloud of Things (CoT) for IoT. The arrival of such powerful technologies has brought a series of delightful developments for people. Several basic services are being built and delivered in every field of merit. For example, as we saw earlier, there are smart meters for all kinds of utilities so that the supply and the demand could be accurately analyzed to identify and rectify any lacunae. These are the days of smart grids powered by the Internet of Energy (IoE) [2]. Power energy conservation is increasing due to the impending paucity of fuels for lighting up our environments. Every electricity-consuming and -guzzling device is being subjected to a variety of tests to formulate pragmatic mechanisms to reduce electricity consumption. The author of this publication has visualized which IoT/CoT technology-inspired energy services are going to be persuasive and pervasive for future generations.

- *Timely energy monitoring* is expected to be a reality, especially when considering the vast investments in smart metering projects. Information acquired at several layers of the smart grid infrastructure can be validated and securely communicated among the different systems and cloud-based services in real time.

- *Fine-grained control/management* capabilities are expected to complement existing scenarios of adaptive management of the infrastructure. This implies a potential understanding of the underlying processes to a certain extent and flexibility of energy consumption/production that can be negotiated; hence it goes beyond simple ON/OFF signals and considers the whole lifecycle of affected devices and systems as well as their operational context, involved processes, and goals locally and at system level.

- *Energy brokering* may be seen as a value-added service with the help of financial management applied to the smart grid infrastructure. Although this is still at early stage, the implications for applications built around it could have a significant impact on the dynamic operation of the grid, as well as on the offering of new innovative services and applications for all stakeholders.

- *Real-time analytics* are expected to operate on the big data provided by the plethora of smart grid city stakeholders. Effective assessment of data will provide new insights on the existing operational aspects and unveil optimization opportunities.

In addition, informed decision making considering real-time data on an unprecedented scale will be possible, which may lead to better decisions and future planning for smart cities.

- *Community management* services will provide customized information adjusted to the goals of the specific community; for example, a neighborhood within a smart city and hence actively enable a critical mass of consumers in the smart city. The communityware smart grid must support the creation of dynamic communities where the (mobile) user may connect and participate with its assets (e.g., electric vehicle, white-label appliances, etc.). These communities may be motivated by several aspects, for example, environmental, economic, social, and so on. Support for intra- but also intercommunity collaboration is desired to increase network effects.
- *Energy application stores* will be required to manage the large number of energy-related services and applications available for the CoT-enabled devices. There users/devices may automatically find, install, and maintain a variety of energy-related applications and services that may enhance their operational context.

Figure 9.3 illustrates future energy services being conceived and concretized for smart cities of this connected world.

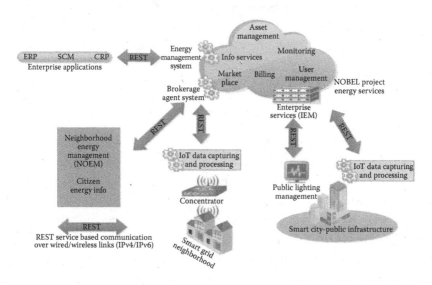

Figure 9.3 The energy management architecture.

9.3 Smart Lighting

Lighting is one aspect not to be taken lightly in the context of cities' energy needs. As we all know, buildings account for one-third of global greenhouse gas emissions and account for up to 40% of total energy consumption. Lights easily consume up to one-fifth of a building's total energy usage. Similarly streets lights, energy-guzzling billboards, and advertisements at important junctions; electric signals at street crossings; lighting for festivities and family gatherings; and ornamental lighting at art galleries also consume a large amount of power, at least at night. Therefore technologies that make lights more energy efficient, customizable, and programmable for achieving more sustainable and vibrant cities are being given extra attention. Emerging lighting technologies are the next frontier in helping growing cities to reduce their energy consumption remarkably and create more enjoyable landscapes for their residents. Undoubtedly lighting is perceived as a low-hanging fruit toward substantial energy savings in buildings and urban infrastructures.

Lighting solution providers are brimming with confidence and bringing in a stream of innovation-packed and technology-driven smarter lighting solutions. Sensors and actuators especially are extravagantly and intrinsically attached; next-generation lights thereby will be sensor-intensive, interconnected, software-defined, and remotely monitored and operated. Corporations are addressing the important theme that minimizing the ecological footprint through a host of energy-efficient systems is a priority.

9.3.1 Smart Lighting Approaches

As indicated previously, at different levels and layers, energy preservation is being set in motion and accomplished. First of all, it is prudent to replace existing lights with energy-efficient lighting sources such as light-emitting diode (LED). Automated management of lighting sources is another sellable and workable option, especially turning off lights when they are not needed and adjusting light levels to suit people's needs. Having automated control over lighting through proven technologies is the best way to go forward. Automation has been rapidly penetrating every tangible domain these days, and the lighting field is not an exception to this overwhelming initiative across the globe. Thus along with lights, lighting control solutions are incrementally gaining market and intellectual shares. New-generation lights are becoming software defined with the accumulation of a wider variety of smart yet minuscule sensors and actuators. With the maturity and stability of wireless technologies, lighting is all set to be smart.

Lighting control systems could deliver the required amount of light according to the location and time requirements. Lights can automatically turn on, off, or dim as per changing needs. Control systems are the best option for bringing the correct and relevant changes to ensure optimal lighting everywhere at all times. Typically lighting control systems have the following features:

- ON/OFF and dimming controls
- Occupancy sensors to detect whether rooms are occupied
- Photosensors to detect the current illumination levels provided by natural and/or artificial light
- Scheduling that turns on, off, and dims luminaires at preset times
- A centralized control system interface (such as a wall panel or computer software) to manage all of the above
- A method of communication between the lighting equipment and control system
- A method of measuring, displaying, and responding to lighting energy usage
- Scheduling and timers

Nimbler sensors are coming up quickly to empower control systems with enough firepower to accelerate smart lighting.

- *Occupancy sensors.* Occupancy sensors are useful not only to address flexible working hours, but also to control lights in areas with irregular usage patterns. When the sensors detect that someone has entered an area, the lights corresponding to the location in which the person is detected can be brightened to provide sufficient illumination. Occupancy sensors can also be used to create "corridors of light" to follow people such as security guards and housekeeping staff as they move through a building.

- *Photoelectric and daylight sensors.* One of the greatest areas of potential savings is to reduce lighting when illumination is already being provided through natural sources. When sunlight comes through windows or skylights, these specialized sensors can detect the level of natural illumination and dim or even turn off lights in the area. As the natural light fades, lights can automatically illuminate back up to the appropriate level. This helps not only to conserve lighting energy, but also to reduce the amount of heat being emitted by the electric lights, which in turn can help save money on air conditioning costs.

- *Movement sensors.* In nonlinear activity areas (squares, car parks, residential streets, and places with some nocturnal activity), lighting can be dimmed to a minimum most of the time. By using movement sensors, illumination levels can be raised as soon as a pedestrian or a slow moving vehicle is detected in the area. This light-on-demand capability enhances the safety and the well-being of the users while saving energy.

- *Speed and direction sensors.* Compared to movement sensors, a speed and direction sensor works with a wider detection area to classify the identified moving item following its speed and its direction. This classification provides the correct response according to predefined lighting scenarios. Solutions fitted with speed and direction sensors operate in large areas to ensure safety and well-being in the most sustainable way.

- *Presence sensors.* Today it is becoming prevalent as well as pragmatic to leverage presence sensors inside buildings to switch lights on and off, thereby saving a great deal of power and energy for a better future.

Different situations and applications are emerging wherein such kinds of lighting control provide further advantages.

- *Task tuning.* Traditional lighting systems were often designed to maintain a consistent level of illumination across all areas all the time. This results in overprovisioning of lighting for many users and their tasks. Therefore task tuning is an essential characteristic that allows facility managers, building owners, knowledge workers, and individuals to tune lighting levels in each area of a building via dimmable lights based on their requirements.

- *Global as well as local control.* In the previous setup, every room in a building or house has separate switches for its lighting and hence it requires someone to visit the place physically and operate those switches on and off. The recent lighting control systems can change this equation forever. That is, light control systems have decisive and delicate control over the entire building and are capable of controlling light settings collectively as well as individually. A single light or multiple lights within a room, flat, floor, several floors, or the entire building can be simultaneously and remotely operated with just a click. This vastly improves management cost and complexity. Lighting flexibility, controllability, visibility, modifiability, maintainability, manageability, and sustainability are the hallmarks of next-generation control systems.

- *Energy monitoring.* Monitoring and measurement lead to better management. With advanced lighting control systems, facility managers can access real-time and historical information about the usage of energy by light, room, zone, building, and more. This provides them with a set of tools for better decision making, as well as the ability to test new strategies, verify results, and make changes over time to get the most energy savings out of their system. As real-time analytical systems are quickly maturing, the extraction of real-time and actionable insights and the subsequent dissemination of comprehensive insights in time are laying a stimulating and sophisticated foundation for smart lighting environments.

- *Demand management.* Increasingly, utilities are offering tremendous incentives for buildings to go beyond simple energy efficiency and reduce their demand for energy at peak times. Lighting control systems can tie into utility demand management and peak-day pricing parameters to temporarily reduce lighting usage.

9.3.2 Wireless Lighting Control Systems

This is the talk of the town. Although the current lighting control systems have been of tremendous help in energy saving, the capital, deployment, and operational and management complexities and costs are consistently on the rise. Therefore by leveraging the noteworthy advancements in wireless communication technologies, next-generation wireless lighting control systems are being designed and deployed devoid of wires. The wireless nature completely eliminates the need for wiring, eases installation and use, enhances extensibility, and so on.

Wireless lighting control systems utilize the powerful wireless technology to communicate commands between endpoints such as sensors, switches, and the stabilizers or LED drivers connected to lights. Whereas traditional lighting control systems utilize a controller that is hard wired to each device, a wireless system uses a controller with an antenna that communicates wirelessly between a set of devices. Each endpoint is wirelessly enabled, either directly by the device manufacturer or through an external wireless adapter. A software system provides managers or individuals with access to manage the system and change settings and policies, which are then routed through a controller to the individual endpoints. Wireless systems are often organized using the proven and potential "mesh" architecture. That is, the unshakable power of the mesh network is that each device can talk to others in the network through a controller, and if there is a device failure or weakness, then alternative paths can be chosen cognitively to route all incoming messages to the correct destination without any delay. The built-in redundancy of having multiple pathways available helps to make the mesh network robust and reliable.

In summary, the next-generation solutions for smart lighting have the following functionalities and features.

1. *Huge energy savings through a smart combination.* Several praiseworthy smart lighting technologies are forthcoming to make lighting robust, reliable, and rewarding. Lighting-specific software services are being widely conceptualized and deployed in remote clouds to be publicly discoverable, network-accessible, composable, and usable. On the other hand, the lighting hardware goes through a series of wonderful transformations,

miniaturizations, and so on. Instrumentation, integration, and intelligence have acquired special significance these days in designing personal as well as commercial devices, machines, and so on. Similarly there are enticing improvisations in antenna, sensing, and actuation technologies. Communication has simply become wireless and hence vendors are highly optimistic about the grand success of wireless control systems in meeting head-on all the existing and emerging challenges in the lighting segment. In short, technology-inspired solutions for smart energy are gaining momentum in the market. By smartly combining all the intrinsic innovations, future lighting solutions promise to offer huge energy savings of up to 85% and radically reduce the time to pay back the cost of a new installation.

2. *Remote management and repair.* As lighting solutions are becoming more pervasive and attaining primacy, the management complexity is bound to increase remarkably. There are several cases and scenarios wherein remote operation of lighting arrangements is being insisted on. For example, diversions and the closure of roads during maintenance bring in a whole series of inconveniences such as loss of money and time, increase in distances traveled, difficulties for residents, avoidable greenhouse gas emissions, and so on. Therefore lighting solutions providers have expanded their solutions portfolio to monitor and access light installations independently and remotely to get the correct need and usage of lights and to proactively plan ahead to reduce all sorts of inconveniences to people as much as possible.

3. *Lighting on-demand.* The concept of on-demand lighting is on a fast track as it has the wherewithal to decrease energy expenditure considerably. When the usage is at a low level, lighting at full illumination is a sheer waste of energy, which is incidentally becoming scarce, counterproductive, and expensive. There are occasions and opportunities wherein dimming of lights is expected. Any competent lighting solution with light-on-demand capability that can adapt the lighting to the real-time and real-world needs of the place, time, and users is definitely a boon for society. Each luminaire level ought to be

configured individually with several parameters such as minimum and maximum light output, delay times from minimum to maximum, and the duration of ON/OFF times.

4. *Reliability*. By monitoring every single lighting point, advanced solutions proactively prevent failure by detecting operating issues (broken lamps, device temperature, power surges, etc.). Such preemptive measures go a long way in positioning and prescribing control systems for massive adoption. If problems arise, the system switches to a default program ensuring that the lighting installation does not turn off.

Indisputably lighting is one of the largest energy guzzlers on the planet. The most effective and easily attainable way to reduce energy use is by turning off lights or making them dim at every opportune time. Lighting control systems can take multiple factors such as occupancy level, available daylight, time of the day, and so on into account to decide the power needs. This sort of data-driven control provides significant energy and cost savings, a great level of flexibility and control for building owners and administrators, and above all, added comfort for occupants.

Finally, the traditional wired control systems have been limited by cost and complexity. Removing cluttering wires delivers on the promise of lighting control by providing even greater benefits at a lower cost, and to a much broader set of potential customers. In short, wireless networking is bringing intelligence to a new generation of lighting control systems—helping companies take simple steps to save money and make our planet greener.

9.4 Smart Transport

Smart transport is another inclusive ingredient of smart cities. Travel for personal as well as professional purposes is very common, and is getting costly these days. All kinds of transportation vehicles are being prepared from the ground up or improved to make driving simple and smooth while ensuring a safe and useful journey for the occupants by externally as well as internally incorporating all the correct and relevant technological sophistication. Vehicles are increasingly becoming a tantalizing and trendsetting platform for ubiquitous infotainment, edutainment, and entertainment. Today's automobiles and their important components are being sensor attached, facilitating their remote monitoring, diagnosis, control, repair, and maintenance. Sensors themselves are smart and are capable of forming ad hoc networks with one another on an as-needed basis (sensors are cooperative objects) to accomplish composite tasks that in turn automate one or more processes directly and fully. The underlying sensor-filled infrastructures, high-speed telecommunication networks, a bevy of enabling technologies, a growing range of sleek and handy gadgets, and a growing repository of cyber systems are being suitably readied to contribute individually as well as collaboratively to make all kinds of trips smooth, smart, safe, and secure. The persistent obligation is for travel infrastructures and systems to have a very negligible impact on the environment.

Smart transports are gaining a great deal of market and intellectual share these days. Automobile companies, product vendors, and research labs across the globe are gearing up to bring in disruptive and transformative blueprints for next-generation smart vehicles that have less of a carbon footprint. Connected, sensor-laden, and insights-driven transports are the latest buzzes in the automobile sector. As automobiles are the main culprit in consuming a great deal of precious energy (more than 70% of the total oil being produced) and in releasing a great deal of carbon into our environment, vehicle manufacturers are seriously thinking of alternative fuels and vehicles. Electric vehicles are one important option, described in detail in the next section.

9.4.1 Electric Vehicles

Economic and environmental pressures are continuously driving countries worldwide to electrify transportation. There are plenty of electric cars on the roads these days, together with some practical constrictions that get in the way of widespread usage. Technologies are forthcoming to overcome those barriers so that electric vehicles (EVs) will be more pervasive and persuasive for both the general public as well as for governments in the years to come. EVs are more favorable for the environment and less expensive also. There will be more telling impacts as electric vehicles fundamentally change the way electric utilities function. There will be more intensive strains on electric utility infrastructures. Utilities need to have highly synchronized and competent solutions for facilitating the success of EVs while minimizing all kinds of risks and vulnerabilities. In short, the transportation becoming electrified will have a series of influences as well as implications. The surging popularity of electric cars has already rekindled organizations to show more focused interest and investment in EVs. The main drawbacks and issues are being consciously identified and addressed through collaborative research initiatives and technology-inspired solutions.

There are some valid concerns regarding EVs. For example, the main customer complaint is that EVs need frequent charging. Other important pain points are that certain limitations are imposed on car speed and size. Further, it takes a considerable time to get fully charged. On the other hand, for electric utility service providers, infrastructure is the main stumbling block. Electricity charging stations and their associated infrastructures need to be in several places to facilitate the smooth passage of vehicles. Business models for utilities providing charging services need to be worked out to a win–win situation for both users as well as providers. The infrastructural considerations are very important. A single EV plugged into a fast charger can double a home's peak electricity demand and hence it is very important to have a smart grid to effectively and efficiently manage EV charging.

A smart grid, the prime infrastructure for utilities, has the inherent capability of providing the much-needed visibility and power to protect components such as transformers of distribution networks from being overloaded by EVs through continuous monitoring, measurement, and management. With a smart grid, utilities can fully adhere to customers' expectations while managing EV charging, collecting EV-specific metering data, applying customer- and time-specific rates for EV charging, engaging consumers with information on EV charging, and finally collecting data for greenhouse gas abatement credits. Smart grids are therefore being positioned and prescribed as the silver bullet for all the ills of electricity management.

As the number of EVs is constantly growing, utilities can maximize the utilization of their infrastructure, create fruitful relationships with customers, and leverage EV communications investments for other energy initiatives. By bringing these transitions, there are better days ahead for transportation electrification that can benefit all stakeholders including consumers, automakers, utilities, and the environment. Electronic transportation through smart grids and EVs will grow in the years ahead because it is conducive to the comfort and efficiency of human society.

9.4.2 Smarter Vehicles

As indicated earlier, transportation is a crucial cog in realizing smart cities. A cornucopia of novelties and ingenuities is being investigated in the ever-growing transport sector. As discussed in the previous section, electrification of vehicles is one prominent aspect gaining a great deal of market and intellectual share. On the functional side, a variety of improvisations are being brought in, as detailed in the following text. Vehicles are increasingly connected, sensor laden, and extremely digitalized through the lavish and illuminating usage of IT. Hundreds of microcontrollers are being packed into advanced cars. All kinds of safety, security, simplicity, and smartness are being carefully embedded in modern-day vehicles to sharply enhance people's comfort, convenience, choice, and care.

A new-generation in-vehicle infotainment system in sync with an eye-catching and multipurpose dashboard has become the most indispensable module in any car. Automobiles are empowered through innumerable specialized sensors and actuators. A number of strategically sound advancements are occurring silently to realize highly advanced and automated vehicles. Sensor-attached vehicle components send out their latest status update to the centralized infotainment systems for preemptive diagnosis and correction of components. Application developmental platforms, scores of enabling tools, and execution containers are very promising these days to orchestrate sophisticated applications for vehicles and their users. Cloud-based application stores are being formulated to store and maintain hundreds of vehicle-specific services and applications for vehicles throughout the world.

People spend more time commuting to their offices, shopping malls, recreation facilities, and back to their homes. People use vehicles for many purposes other than just pleasurable driving. Every moment of travel therefore has become precise. The point here is to ensure occupants are wirelessly connected with the outside world at vehicular speed and entertained and informed. Vehicles emerge as the next-generation platform for ubiquitous learning, fruitful interactions, remote dictation, and purpose-specific collaborations. Vehicles are fast becoming software-intensive; sensor-, microcontroller-, and actuator-laden; connected (locally as well as remotely); highly digitalized; and continuously empowered by a growing array of cloud-based vehicle-specific services. The in-vehicle infotainment system is being positioned as the core and central gateway for realizing smarter vehicles.

Luminaries and visionaries foresee a bright future for creative thinkers and software engineers in flawlessly conceiving innumerable smart services exclusively for the transportation sector. There are many game-changing initiatives such as autonomous driving, vehicle-to-vehicle communication, vehicle-to-cloud integration, and so on. There are specialized software solutions for on-demand assistance to drivers while driving, parking, looking for landmarks, fuel stations, food establishments, and so on. Natural interfaces are being made available for drivers for hands-free interactions.

9.4.3 Technological Implications for Vehicles

It is very clear that several technologies are emerging to ensure and sustain a number of notable disruptions and transformations in our life journey. By carefully embracing these versatile technological developments, every business vertical is preparing for hitherto unheard of and unforeseen acceleration, augmentation, and automation in their service deployment, delivery, and usage models in the days ahead. Product vendors are envisaging a series of smarter environments and establishments as a direct outcome of the undiminished stream of insightful and impactful technologies. Every organization is bound to be smarter in its cost optimization through resources rationalization, customer-centricity, fresh revenue generation, dynamic capacity addition, and conceptualization of multifaceted services to retain its customers and attract new clients and consumers. In this section, we discuss the possible and pragmatic derivatives in the fast-expanding transport sector.

9.4.3.1 Insights-Driven Connected Vehicles The first and foremost outcome of these promising and potential technologies is connected vehicles. The second is vehicles empowered with timely, context-aware, and data-driven insights. There is a consistent increase in the number of diverse and distributed data sources pumping data from all directions that can be smartly captured and subjected to deeper and decisive analysis to extract all sorts of hidden patterns, tips, alerts, opportunities, associations, and so on for vehicle owners, operators, and so on to formulate both short-term as well as long-term plans. There are two predominant ways in which vehicles can be connected.

9.4.3.2 Vehicle-to-Vehicle (V2V) Connectivity This is the real-time exchange of decision-enabling data among vehicles. Such dynamic data exchange at a critical point offers ample opportunities for significant improvements especially on the vehicle safety aspect. By interchanging valuable vehicle data regarding its speed, direction, position, and location dynamically, the much-anticipated V2V communication capability enables vehicles to sense any impending threats and hazards with a 360-degree view and visualization of vehicles in synchronization with other vehicles' positions. This vehicular interaction results in issuing appropriate advisories to drivers to proactively take countermeasures to avoid or mitigate the intensity of crashes. There are specific sensors and GPS systems collaboratively working to arrive at accurate data (latitude, longitude, etc.) to make cars self-, surroundings-, and situation-aware.

The vision for V2V connectivity is that eventually all vehicles (sports cars, multiutility vehicles, buses, container trucks, goods wagons, etc.) on the road will be able to connect and communicate with one another beneficially. The data that are being generated and transmitted in time facilitate the production and delivery of next-generation applications for enhanced safety. The much-anticipated V2V communications will significantly reduce accidents on the road.

9.4.3.3 Vehicle-to-Cloud (V2C) Connectivity Clouds are being positioned as the best-in-class infrastructure (servers, storage arrays, and network modules) for effectively and efficiently hosting a variety of platforms. Integrated development environments (IDEs) and rapid application development (RAD) tools for application and service design, development, debugging, deployment, delivery, and decommissioning (end-to-end software lifecycle tasks) are increasingly finding a residence in clouds. Further, advanced platforms comprising standards-based service integration, orchestration, management, governance, monitoring and billing, resource provisioning, capability planning and scaling, and enhancement capabilities are being migrated to cloud environments. Not only generic but also specific service implementation platforms are found to be efficient in clouds. Platforms for building, deploying, and delivering social, cloud, mobile, embedded, analytics, and even vehicle-specific applications are becoming very popular these days owing to the unprecedented maturity and stability of the respective technologies.

Not only platforms, but also an increasing number of service registry repositories reside in clouds. These multidevice services are opening up fresh opportunities for a bevy of everyday environments such as homes, hospitals, offices, vehicles, and so on. Thus the raging cloud idea is bringing real sophistication for humans. For example, Ericsson's Multiservice Delivery Platform provides infotainment, applications, and communication services in Volvo's new models. Drivers and passengers are bound to benefit from a growing array of cloud-enabled services and applications. This platform enables drivers, passengers, and the car to connect, access, and leverage all kinds of services (navigation, driving assistance, parking management, edutainment, and entertainment) being made available in the cloud. Content providers will have agreements with vehicle owners and other ecosystem partners such as Internet radio providers, road authorities, traffic patrols, ambulances, insurance providers, emergency services and cities' governments, toll-road operators, and so on in the near future.

Today's smart phones are loaded with many unique and universal applications that help accomplish a number of personal needs on-the-go at vehicular speed. Similarly all kinds of in-vehicle infotainment systems and dashboards are being provided with a growing set of new-generation applications to significantly empower car drivers as well as occupants to be productive. With the increased push for more electric cars, car manufacturers will offer more digital and connected services such as the ability to warm up the car remotely or to manage the charging time of the battery. In short, driving will be made safer and more secure, enjoyable, and informative. Whether it is a ride for pleasure, reaching a destination, or transport of goods, future vehicles will be supplied and supplanted with converged, cognizant, and cognitive services. Insights-driven driving will become a common occurrence. The in-car infotainment system connects with Google Maps and Places to guide the driver appropriately to reach the destination in a risk-free fashion on time. Car care can go to the next level with applications allowing users to check vehicle diagnostics, status, maintenance schedules, and driving behavior on a home computer or smart phone.

9.4.4 *Vehicle Connectivity Platforms, Tools, and Applications*

Developmental platforms for producing a variety of applications (generic as well as purpose-specific) are found aplenty in the IT world. With connected vehicles being realized, integrated platforms play a vital role in producing newer applications and enabling them to run efficiently.

Sprint Velocity Connect opens the way for automakers to explore innovative ways to serve their customers.

- *Fleet management.* Vehicle manufacturers could help fleet operators easily adopt value-added services provided by the manufacturer at any time after the vehicles are purchased. This includes applications that track and monitor vehicle locations, improve dispatch and routing, evaluate driving behaviors, and more efficiently manage vehicle maintenance.
- *Rental car features.* Automakers might offer rental car companies the opportunity to learn more about the status of their cars, such as distance traveled and vehicle maintenance needs.
- *Dealership sales.* Auto manufacturers could consider using Sprint Velocity Connect to add services for its dealership network, including new ways to differentiate previously owned vehicles with connected services.

Airbiquity's Choreo Service Delivery Platform is a global, open, and scalable cloud platform that is designed for automotive manufacturers, wireless carriers, tier 1 suppliers, and third party app developers to deliver connected services to a better connected customer and driver. Choreo can be modularized for numerous applications including mobile integration, embedded connectivity in a vehicle's head unit, EV optimization, and fleet management. Airbiquity's smart phone application integration platform links vehicles to a range of mobile applications and cloud-based services delivered via Airbiquity's private cloud platform, delivering third-party applications such as Yelp and Trip Advisor in addition to popular infotainment applications. Drivers will be able to download the applications to their smart phones and tether them to select vehicles via Bluetooth or USB using the Airbiquity platform, with in-built support for a range of popular music, social media, and navigation applications.

SiriusXM's in-vehicle telematics solution will provide vehicle owners 24/7 emergency support for accidents, stolen vehicle tracking, and roadside assistance, along with a host of additional services to be announced at a later date.

9.4.5 Use Cases of Technology-Inspired Vehicles

It is expected that there will be more internal as well as external systems voluntarily collaborating and contributing toward the risk-free provision of enhanced care, choice, convenience, and comfort especially to car users. The prominent components in next-generation cars could be smart phones, in-vehicle infotainment systems, remote clouds and a repository of car-specific services, and all kinds of tangible car parts. There will be a greater number of elements in future cars for accurately providing precise and perfect automation. These modules can be interconnected among themselves as well as with the centralized car infotainment module inside the car and also with any remote cloud servers over the Internet. The infotainment system inside will be multifunctional and have multichannel communication capability with a comprehensive yet compact dashboard.

It is logical to expect every worthwhile part of vehicles to be self-, surroundings-, and situations-aware. Vehicle components can find other related entities within the car dynamically on an as-needed basis and network with them in ad hoc mode to enable seamless cooperation and coordination for producing specific and emergent functionality. In short, the extreme connectivity capability of service-enabled vehicle modules, infotainment system, car users' smart phones, and a growing collection of specific as well as generic applications on on-demand, online, and off-premise cloud platforms enables them to have fruitful interactions. Precisely speaking, futuristic cars emerge as the most elegant and evolving platform for ambient entertainment and remote monitoring besides facilitating business transactions with those empowered elements that find, bind, and leverage each other's unique capabilities and competencies in runtime.

9.4.6 An Assortment of Vehicle–Centric Applications

Owing to the positive uptake in the eccentric connectivity and service-enablement aspects, there arise a series of nimbler services for vehicle users: information, knowledge, and transaction and physical services. These days a growing collection of travel-centric services (location maps, driving and parking assistance, fuel station identification, automated toll collection, road and traffic details, edutainment, entertainment, and context-aware services and applications are being developed and hosted in geographically distributed clouds for ubiquitous access and leverage. Car maintenance and repair, post-sale support, insurance, and so on are the leading services being facilitated with spectacular advancements in the vehicle technology. Today, mobile users are bombarded with a number of mind-boggling mobile technologies (HTML 5) and services. Similarly for vehicle users, owners, manufacturers, insurers, and service providers, there are specific platforms such as vehicle application development and service delivery platforms (SDPs) for simplifying service conceptualization, concretization, registration, discovery, accessibility, subscription, usage, billing, delivery, management, and enhancement.

9.4.6.1 Knowledge Services
Knowledge engineering through the fast-maturing discipline of big data analytics is on the rise. There are big data analytics platforms (on-premise as well as cloud-based) to efficiently perform data analysis. There are different visualization tools for the presentation of actionable insights. All kinds of data originating from vehicles on the road and their body parts are being collected and streamed to real-time data analytics platforms wirelessly for generating real-time insights that enable drivers, manufacturers, insurance companies, and other stakeholders to confidently consider and perform preemptive measures. The vehicle infotainment system

will evolve as the centralized data gathering, aggregation, and transmission engine. Any brewing problem in any part of the vehicle can be preemptively identified and users are accordingly notified to act on the identified needs instantly and insightfully. Car security, integrity, and safety are fully guaranteed with the technological advancements.

There are newer in-vehicle systems and connectivity solutions for next-generation vehicles for activating and augmenting all the electronic devices and vehicle components within. The decision-enabling data include tire air pressure, engine alerts, lubrication, temperature alert, and so on. The latest cars are being fitted with automatic emergency braking systems (AEBS), air-bag systems (ABS), multifaceted sensors, and disposable as well as replaceable body parts (wheels, lights, brake shoes, wipers, windshield, tires, bumpers, wheel alignment, etc.) to significantly enhance the production and delivery of smart and sophisticated telematics applications.

Finally, all kinds of fake components can be stopped from being incorporated in vehicles by unscrupulous mechanics and repair persons in place of original components. All kinds of impending risks and existing problems can be immediately communicated to the right owner at the right time to attend to them in a timely way. The energy efficiency of vehicles can be measured and managed automatically so that cleaner and greener vehicles will become a reality sooner.

9.4.6.2 Big Data Analytics for Smarter Transports As vehicles become networked devices, automakers and wireless telecommunication carriers are able to collect different kinds of data, especially driver-generated data such as automotive performance and driving patterns. Further, hundreds of sensors embodied in every advanced vehicle produce a large amount of tactical as well as strategic data to be carefully collected and subjected to a stream of polished investigations that ultimately assist handsomely to finalize viable means of bringing in more assuaging automations. In a nutshell, the amount of data generated by smart cars is expected to grow dramatically over the coming years. This emphasizes the need for high-performance data analytics solutions to conceptualize cognitive services for next-generation vehicles. The combination of a significant rise in the production of connected car sales and a growing amount of information coming from the connected cars will result in the collection of some

11.1 petabytes of connected car data by 2020 according to a new IHS Automotive study. Today, auto manufacturers are systematically using the data they collect from connected cars for such things as internal diagnostics, location, and vehicle status. Thus the real-time analytics of vehicles' data will breed innovations for car makers, owners, and occupants.

With the faster proliferation and penetration of promising connectivity technologies, vehicles are being empowered to have newer capabilities through seamless and spontaneous interactions with other vehicles on the road, vehicle manufacturers and mechanics, insurance providers, product vendors, and so on. With cloud connectivity, a bevy of nimbler services and applications can be made available to drivers and occupants. Besides making driving simpler, safer, and more satisfying, those inside vehicles could be more productive through e-learning, e-commerce, entertainment, gaming, and infotainment. Application platforms are emerging and inspiring worldwide software developers to conceptualize and concretize sophisticated services for vehicles and their users. The platform features include data and application integration, data-driven knowledge discovery and dissemination, information visualization, and so on. Through these vehicle-specific and cloud-based application development platforms, a growing array of next-generation vehicle-enablement services and applications are being created and deposited in cloud application stores to be accessed and used by smart phones and in-vehicle infotainment systems and dashboards to substantially elevate the comfort, care, choice, and convenience levels of vehicle owners, drivers, and occupants.

9.5 Approaches for Smarter Transportation

As discussed previously, having a smart transportation is essential for all cities across the world to facilitate a smooth and safe movement of people and goods, as it has been solidly proven that a well-developed and maintained traffic takes the city toward its economic prosperity and provides a better quality of life for city dwellers. Any badly managed traffic clogs the system and brings it to an unpalatable halt.

With the brimming population, the city transport system has to be well oiled through the adoption of resilient technologies. In recent decades, significant increases in urbanization have placed an unbearable burden on most traffic systems around the world. Clogged traffic systems deter economic activity as well as drain resources. They also waste energy and release significant amounts of carbon dioxide (CO_2) into the atmosphere. The traditional approach to solving the perpetual traffic problems has been to increase the capacity of the underlying infrastructure by building more roads and bridges and to increase the number of vehicles providing transportation services such as more public buses and trains.

These initiatives have visibly reached their limits in existing cities. Cities need an altogether new approach to tackle these perennial challenges. There are smart city solutions and service providers, and IBM is prominent among them. IBM's smarter traffic solution enables the following:

- Predict demand and optimizing capacity, assets, and infrastructure
- Improve the end-to-end experience for travelers
- Increase operational efficiency while reducing environmental impact
- Ensure safety and security

9.5.1 Predict Demand and Optimizing Capacity, Assets, and Infrastructure

A smarter traffic goal is to improve capacity utilization and make better use of existing investments in assets and infrastructure. This goal is accomplished by using the following methods.

- Collecting data on real-time network conditions
- Identifying mobility and usage patterns
- Predicting demand
- Encouraging a balanced use of available infrastructure and capacity

This goal is accomplished by using both near real-time analytics and historical data analysis on the data that are being captured from roadside sensors and on-board equipment. This is supplemented by data obtained from other agencies. Analysis helps traffic management centers and transit service providers make well-informed decisions about the use and optimization of transportation resources. The data collected can also be used to provide value-added services and propose new methods for funding road use and maintenance such as through congestion charges. These methods can be used to shape travelers' behavior to aid the environment.

9.5.2 *Improve the End-to-End Experience for Travelers*

Smarter traffic seeks to improve the traveler's experience. For example, the solution can provide driving directions, inform travelers of route changes because of an accident or traffic congestion, and suggest various public transit options. The solution can also offer incentives to travelers to balance the use of public versus private transportation systems. The data being collected from distributed and difference sources are being smartly leveraged to give a newer experience to travelers. There will be close collaborations between traffic monitoring centers and ground-level traffic.

9.5.3 *Increase Operational Efficiency While Reducing the Environmental Impact*

Smarter traffic will enhance the operational efficiencies of individual transportation agencies, transit operators, and commercial fleet operators. Through tracking of assets, optimizing equipment availability, and ensuring maintenance effectiveness, smarter traffic techniques reduce waste, improve reliability, and remove operational costs for transportation operators.

Smarter traffic is bound to provide visibility of agency operations to other participants in the value chain. Included in this group are parts suppliers and maintenance crew contractors, enabling more effective collaboration. In addition, smarter traffic aids planning and decision making, resulting in significantly enhanced operational efficiencies throughout the system.

9.5.4 *Ensure Safety and Security*

To ensure the safety of citizens, information from on-board vehicle-equipped sensors is integrated with information from sensors on-board other vehicles and from infrastructure sensors on roads, curbs, and rail tracks. This technique improves the range of warnings that the vehicle driver receives, such as wrong lane entry, slippery road, and proximity alarms. Moreover, sensors that monitor conditions on infrastructure such as roads or tracks help to detect hazardous conditions so that maintenance crews can respond effectively. Through smart surveillance systems, rail lines, airports, and roadways can be constantly scanned to detect suspicious activities.

Road safety has been a tricky issue for governments, city officials, and car manufacturers. There are promising vehicular technologies toward achieving that goal. The latest wireless communication technologies facilitate the formation and firming up of vehicle ad hoc networks (VANETs) that ensure wireless intravehicular interactions and interactions between vehicles and infrastructures. VANETs are attracting growing attention as a result of the promising important applications from road safety to traffic control, infotainment, and entertainment for passengers. Car accident prevention, safer roads, and pollution and congestion reduction are some goals of VANETs. The deployment of an efficient system to manage warning messages in VANETs has important benefits, from the perspective of both the road operators and the drivers. Efficient traffic alerts and updated information about traffic incidents will reduce traffic jams, increase road safety, and improve driving in the city. Further, from the sustainable and economic perspective, real-time traffic alerting will reduce the transit time and fuel consumption and therefore decrease the amount of CO_2 emissions. Traffic software systems are extensively deployed to make and manage traffic intelligently. Vehicles, traffic servers, and road infrastructures are interconnected on-demand to guarantee road safety. Smart traffic is an indispensable component of smart cities.

9.5.5 Intelligent Transport Systems

Intelligent transport systems have been around for a while now. But in the context of smart cities and with the availability of several competent technologies such as cloud, mobility, machine-to-machine (M2M) communication, and real-time analytics, new-generation intelligent transport systems are emerging with additional capabilities:

- Integrated fare management
- Enhanced transit/customer relationship management
- Traffic prediction

- Improved transport and traffic management
- Traveler information and advisory services
- Road user charging
- Variable parking pricing

In short, cloud-based software services for the transport sector; the power of doing real-time analytics out of heterogeneous data gleaned from different sources; the consistent growth of device ecosystem for drivers, vehicle users and operators, police officials, traffic monitoring personnel, and so on; the ad hoc nature of purpose-specific smart sensor/actuator networks; and so on are laying a sustainable platform for the next-generation smarter transports.

9.6 Smart Utilities

As we know, there are several social utilities such as gas, water, electricity, mobile communication, and Internet connectivity. Even computing is all set to become a social utility with the unprecedented maturity of cloud computing. The face of the energy and utility industries has changed dramatically over the years as customer-centricity is being prescribed as the most important aspect for providers to survive the heat and to surge ahead. Increasing scrutiny from investors and regulators, the insistence on strict policy compliance, corporate social responsibility (CSR) and sustainability requirements, the demand to lower capital and operational expenditure, the proactive design and release of premium services for customers, and so on are the key drivers for utility service providers to be intrinsically innovative. All providers in this highly competitive environment are forced to ascertain and adopt smart technologies to be ahead of their competitors and to continuously serve their customers with full ingenuity. These technologies ultimately help to simplify and streamline utilities' everyday operations, shore up the sagging delivery system to keep their customers happy, and enhance efficiency through an assiduous management of strategic resources when applied properly.

9.6.1 Smart Metering

The metering domain has been growing steadily on several fronts, especially in ascertaining and absorbing promising technologies. Utility providers are increasingly leaning on advanced meters to accurately monitor, measure, and bill usage. The field of advanced metering infrastructure (AMI) is definitely acquiring special significance for utilities providers. Typically AMI supports multi-vendor meter environments with different wired or wireless communication technologies. AMI is generally equipped with a high-performance integrated management system that enables seamless and efficient network operation.

Smart metering, the latest incarnation in the ever-evolving metering field, is being widely used to facilitate a wide range of applications across multiple fields. Remote meter reading is one distinct aspect of smart metering, and this special capability facilitates a stream of newer applications in the fields of customer relationship management (CRM), demand-supply management, and so on. Further, smart metering is the undisputed fountainhead for conceptualizing and concretizing flexible value-added services for people.

The first and foremost benefit of smart metering is the ability by utilities providers to provide energy bills based on the actual usage to their customers (commercial buildings, residential apartments, educational campuses, industrial parks, homes, shopping complexes, manufacturing plants, etc.). All noteworthy improvisations contribute to improved cash flow, less bad debt, and fewer complaints and inquiries; above all, customer satisfaction is being accomplished. Smart meters enable the establishment of new prepaid services that can be offered to those customers who lack the funds for an upfront deposit or high prepayments. In a nutshell, smart meters are empowering utility companies to efficiently collect meter data, facilitate two-way communication, and leverage the data gleaned to cognitively tailor newer and specific offerings to different customers. Fundamentally smart metering enables less energy usage, resulting in less heat dissipation into our fragile environment and ensuring sustainability. Smart meters play a very life-critical role in reaching the national goals of less global warming and the slowdown of climate change.

Smart utility suites are available from worldwide software product vendors for automating many of the routine tasks of utility services providers. These suites are mainly for increasing operational efficiency, reducing carbon emissions, and suggesting nimbler ways of utilities management. This kind of software significantly helps utilities providers reduce energy consumption, greenhouse gas emissions, and capital investment, and to explore newer opportunities.

The key attributes of ST Electronics' Smart Utilities Suite include

1. Provides flexible and secure advanced metering infrastructure
2. Supports multi-utility applications (integrated electricity, water, and gas)
3. Supports seamless integration to smart facilities such as homes, building, factories, and schools
4. Supports electric vehicle integration
5. Supports integration of a microgrid
6. Supports a control and management center

Such software-intensive integrated suites help utility service providers retain their existing customers and attract new ones by providing both basic as well as advanced services with all the nonfunctional attributes embedded.

In the recent past, a new kind of information value chain has emerged where meters are the gateway and infrastructure for enabling deeper customer engagement. Whereas the traditional value chain stopped at the meter to the premises, the new value chain will integrate devices beyond the meter and the actions of customers themselves. In the expanded value chain, the customer has more to offer power providers and other participants than just payment for energy. At the same time, customers are becoming more demanding; they actually have much more to offer in reciprocal value to energy and other product/service providers.

9.7 Conclusion

It is a simple truth that everything is transitioning to be smart in its operations, offerings, and outputs with the seamless addition of proven technologies such as cloud integration, mobility, ultrahigh broadband connectivity, analytics attachment, extreme connectivity, service-enablement, and so on. Functional as well as nonfunctional capabilities increase remarkably through the smart leverage of proven, potential, and promising technologies. For example, with cloud-based home-specific software services, ordinary homes are slated to become smart in their articulations and activities. Here too with the incorporation of analytics, any transportation system is bound to be smart in its contributions and cognitions.

Typically smart cities are the sum of many important systems. In this chapter, we specifically focused on some of those subsystems such as smart energy, transportation, and utilities. Why smartness is needed; how it is being embedded; the immediate implications of those technology-inspired transitions; and the various business, user, and technical cases have been depicted in this chapter.

References

1. Gerhard P. Hancke, Bruno de Carvalho e Silva, and Gerhard P. Hancke Jr. (2013). The Role of Advanced Sensing in Smart Cities. *Sensors*, 13(1):393–425.
2. Stamatis Karnouskos (2014). The Cloud of Things Empowered Smart Grid Cities. Karlsruhe, Germany: SAP Research.

10
INTELLIGENT AIRPORTS

Abstract

The aviation industry has always been a forerunner in the field of technological innovation and its application in various airports for the benefit of air travel passengers. Airports are continuously catering to the ever increasing and ever changing demands of air travel passengers. It is predicted that by 2020, the number of travelers worldwide who use airports will be roughly around 10 million. But present-day airports do not have the capacity to accommodate and serve this huge number of passengers. This calls for devising intelligent processes, technologies, and revenue strategies to use the existing airport infrastructure to accommodate passengers and also ensure a pleasurable travel experience for them. This chapter covers all of these aspects that are required to convert existing airports into intelligent airports that will scale dynamically according to passenger requirements. An airport is not a single entity; rather, it is a conglomerate of various components that form a part of the airport ecosystem. Each of these components needs to function intelligently to fulfill the true promise of intelligent airports. The various components that form part of the airport ecosystem are discussed in the first section of the chapter. Next, for ease of classification, airports have been split into three different categories: (1) *Airport 1.0* (C-airport)—This depicts the first-generation airports where basic airport operations were done in silos with no interaction between the various components of the airport ecosystem. (2) *Airport 2.0* (E-airport)—Many airports of today fall under this category. However, some of the technologies that are described for this class of airports will continue to be used for Airport 3.0. (3) *Airport 3.0* (U-airport)—This depicts the concept of airports of the future that will come into existence in the next four or five years. The true concept of intelligent airports and the various aspects such as conceptual models, technological models, and revenue-generating models for these airports are examined in detail in this section.

10.1 Introduction

The aviation industry has always been a forerunner in the usage of cutting-edge technologies and innovation. There has been a stupendous growth in the aviation industry, which can be attributed to the various players who are part of the airport ecosystem. These players have contributed immensely to the ever changing requirements of diverse types of travelers by providing them low-cost, affordable travel with all the benefits and facilities required to make travel a memorable and pleasurable experience. In the last few years, these players in the airport ecosystem have realized the importance of coexistence with various players of the airport ecosystem and the role it plays in their survival and proficiency. The next few years are expected to propel stupendous growth in the airport space and the aviation industry as a whole because of the emergence of cutting-edge technologies such as mobile, social, cloud, and analytics. Adoption of these technologies is the need of the day to keep up with the ever increasing pace at which the entire technology ecosystem is growing.

Some of the key challenges faced by the airport industry are ever increasing fuel prices, continuous pressure to improve the airport infrastructure, and assets with restricted budgets and ever increasing demands from customers for more facilities without increasing travel fares. These challenges have forced the airport ecosystem and industry to adapt techniques to deliver more value to travelers at lower cost. The various components of the airport ecosystem are summarized in the following diagram:

Among these components of the airport ecosystem, it is essential to focus on certain key parameters that govern the business of the entire aviation industry and also examine the various components that are likely to have an adverse effect on those parameters. Some of the key challenges that need immediate attention by the airport industry are explained in the following paragraphs.

10.1.1 Inadequate Capacity

There is an ever increasing demand for aviation services across the world. Every year on average, about 2 million passengers use aviation services. This is roughly depicted in the graph below. It is estimated that by the year 2020, the number of travelers who use the airports worldwide for travel will be around 10 million.

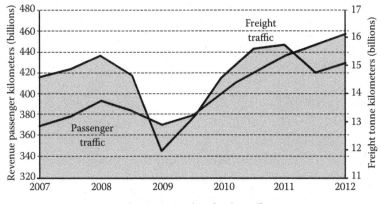

Total passenger and air freight traffic,
seasonally adjusted (Source: IATA)

But the present-day airport infrastructure does not have the capacity to support this huge number of passengers. So the need of the day is to expand the airport infrastructure to accommodate this soaring rise in the number of passengers.

10.1.2 Dissatisfied Passengers

Passengers who travel via airways can be highly dissatisfied with their travel experience because of diverse factors such as lost baggage, delayed flights, and insufficient transit facilities at airports. Passengers expect many features for a good traveling experience such as easy guidance of relevant routes within the airports, quick check-in of their baggage, and minimal waiting time for flights. Apart from these travel-related parameters, many passengers also desire a high-end shopping and entertainment experience in the airport. Inability to provide these facilities within airports has adversely impacted the revenue generated by the aviation sector in recent years. So it has become a necessity for airports to embrace the new technologies and look at ways to integrate them with the existing airport infrastructure to improve the travel experience of passengers.

10.1.3 Increased Regulatory Requirements

Diverse types of regulatory requirements from the various government bodies (both national and international) and various aviation bodies across the world are imposing a great deal of pressure in the functioning of the airport ecosystem. These regulatory requirements impose various types of constraints on existing passenger and cargo handling processes. This in turn will increase the operating costs of the airport ecosystem. In addition, environmental regulations are expected to change various components of airport operation radically so that airports will be able to limit various unfavorable parameters such as noise, toxic air pollutants, and carbon emissions, thereby making the airport infrastructure more ecofriendly.

These diverse challenges have spurred the mandate for an immediate change in the airport ecosystem. In the next few sections, we examine the different types of airports that exist across the world and the technological changes that need to be adopted by them to transform themselves to intelligent airports.

RADICALLY CHANGING THE AIRPORT ECOSYSTEM TO ATTRACT MORE PASSENGERS—INCHEON AIRPORT

To keep up pace with the ever increasing demands of passengers, Seoul's Incheon airport is planning to have a $3 billion resort to attract more tourists from China to the area. Incheon Airport, which is located 50 kilometers (31 miles) west of Seoul, also has plans to set up high-end medical centers, malls, and other entertainment facilities to impress and attract more passengers. These measures have helped Incheon airport to surpass Dubai and London's Heathrow airports to grab the position of the world's biggest airport in terms of duty-free sales in 2011. The airport operator of Incheon airport generates more than half of the revenue from sales at various outlets in the airport and from other business activities that are related to flying. This has helped the airport operator to reduce landing fees, which in turn has helped to attract more flights and passengers to this airport.

10.2 Evolution of Airport Infrastructure

Airport infrastructure has continuously been in an evolutionary phase. The first phase of airport infrastructure had the necessary amenities to ensure safety and security of passengers and also provided the features required for basic airport operations. For these airports, the land was typically provided by some real estate owner or agency and all other components of the airport ecosystem were set up by the respective business environments. The various components of the airport ecosystem operated in silos with limited or no interaction with one another. The technologies that were used for the operation of airport infrastructure worked in a stovepipe fashion with no provisions for centralized monitoring and management. This airport could be referred to as the first phase in the evolution of airport infrastructure. In this chapter, we refer to this type of airport as Airport 1.0.

Based on the maturity of the airport infrastructure, the various types of airports can be classified as shown in the following diagram:

Step 1 of airport evolution

- Airport 1.0 (Conventional airports or C-airports)
- Basic airport operations in silos with no interaction between the various components of the airport ecosystems

Step 2 of airport evolution

- Airport 2.0 (E-airports)
- Limited technology integration, intelligence, and collaboration among the various components of the airport ecosystem

Step 3 of airport evolution

- Airport 3.0 (Ubiquitous or intelligent, I-airport)
- Cutting-edge technology innovations and all the features required for anytime, anywhere collaboration between various components of the airport ecosystem

10.3 Airport 1.0

Airport 1.0 refers to the conventional airport that existed in the initial stages of evolution of airports in the early 1980s when airline travel was becoming prominent. These airports had the necessary infrastructure to ensure safety and security of the passengers and aircraft. But the focus was solely on the safety aspects and no specific attention was given to facilities given to the passengers to improve their travel experience. Some of the typical characteristics of Airport 1.0 are summarized in Table 10.1 (these are based on the parameters that form the major components of the airport ecosystem).

Most present-day airports do not fall under this category, but instead under the category of Airport 2.0. It is anticipated that many existing airports will transform to Airport 3.0 models by 2015 or later.

10.4 Airport 2.0

In Airport 2.0, much information technology (IT)-enabled infrastructure is already in place and the need for collaboration among the various components and the business units of the airport ecosystem has been acknowledged. The passenger travel experience has also been given much focus by these airport models. These airports use a converged network architecture that will help them to offer a set of common shared services to passengers. This is in contrast to the stovepipe

Table 10.1 Characteristics of Airport 1.0

SERIAL NUMBER	PARAMETER THAT IS EXAMINED	DESCRIPTION
1	People and processes	Minimal automation and a great deal of manual work was involved. Information technology was used only for critical processes such as details of passenger entry and tracking. There were numerous forms that had to be completed manually by passengers and the airport staff. This manual data entry introduced significant delays in the system as well as many errors. A large number of staff was required, as there was limited automation.
2	Assets and real estate	Real estate was typically provided by an owner or an agency under a rental agreement. Any additional infrastructural components were set up individually and there was limited or no interaction between these components that operated in the airport.
3	Operations	• Operations to ensure safety of passengers and aircrafts were in place though they were limited. • There was no system in place for energy consumption monitoring and tracking. This led to a waste of utilities such as power and water. • There was absolutely no focus on the travel experience of the passengers. They had to wait in long queues to check in their baggage and also wait for several hours to board their flights only to be informed at the last moment that their aircraft are further delayed. There was no concept of malls or other shopping outlets to improve the travel experience. Only some limited stores/retail outlets for essential commodities were present in the airport.
4	External components	There were very limited rules and regulations that governed the functioning of airports.

model used by Airport 1.0. Some of the key technologies that have found their way to Airport 2.0 are wireless broadband, video surveillance, and various types of mobile applications and other social media applications that are capable of providing an improved travel experience to the passengers. In this section, we examine the various technologies and the process improvements in place in Airport 2.0. We group these technologies and process improvements into four categories:

- Personal technology/processes for passengers
- Technology/processes to streamline the passenger journey

- Technology/processes to enhance the passenger experience
- Information technology/processes for the benefit of passengers

We will handle each of these topics separately. It is important to understand that there are no metrics available for the exact classification of airports. The airport classification is purely based on the hypothetical assumption of the authors. Hence some of the technologies of Airport 2.0 may be widely used only in Airport 3.0. In that perspective, Airports 2.0 and 3.0 carry equal importance, though attempts have been made to differentiate the two types of airports to the best possible extent.

10.4.1 Personal Technology/Processes

The personal technology or processes comprise the components shown in the following diagram:

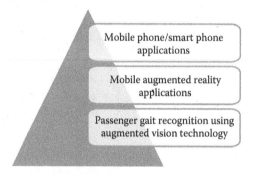

10.4.1.1 Mobile Applications for Airports
With the ever increasing use of mobile applications by human beings, mobile devices and applications have found their way into every stream of our life and activities. When it comes to airports, this is never an exception, with a host of mobile applications devised exclusively to provide various kinds of applications. We discuss some of those applications in this section.

- *Skyscanner.* This mobile application proves to be very useful if a scheduled flight gets canceled and it becomes necessary to look for alternate flights that operate along the same routes. This mobile application works on Android™, iPhone®, and Windows® mobile phones. It provides information on the alternate flights that are available based on the required search criteria. The cost of the flight ticket is also displayed in this mobile application.

- *Flight predictor.* This mobile application is very useful to predict whether a specific flight will arrive on time. The flight's time is predicted based on various factors such as the statistics of the flight over a period of time, delays at other airports, and so on. This application works on Web OS devices, Windows Phone, and Android. This application also has the location map of many other airports. These location maps provide a layout of the entire airport and the various aspects of the airport such as restaurants and retail outlets.
- *Flight status.* This mobile application provides the various types of status information pertaining to the flight such as arrival and departure times and the specific gate-related information through which the boarding needs to be done. This application works only on Windows Phone 7 devices.
- *Car locator.* All airports provide car parking facilities for flight passengers. However, after the return journey, passengers sometimes tend to forget the location of their parked cars. This is the exact situation in which the Car Locator application comes into picture. It helps passengers mark their car's parking location using GPS and this will guide them back to the correct parking location. This works on Windows Phone 7 devices.
- *Airport codes.* This application provides codes of all the airports in the world and is very helpful for airline travelers. Airport codes are added by the airport authorities to the check in baggage tags of the airline passengers. If the passengers know the airport codes, they can double check to ensure that their baggage is being sent to the correct destination. Airport code application is available for mobile Windows 7 version at present.

MOBILE AUGMENTED REALITY APPLICATION FOR AIRPORTS

Mobile augmented reality applications are available in some airports such as Malaysian Airport and Copenhagen airport. Some of the features provided by these applications are a list of the fares offered by different airlines to different destinations, as well as the locations of restaurants, retail outlets, check in baggage counters, and so on.

10.4.1.2 Passenger Gait Mapping Using Augmented Vision Technology The long queue check points at the screening area of the airport counters are frustrating experiences for most passengers. Here is where augmented vision technology can help. Many airports offer this feature and the passengers who want to derive benefits of this technology should opt for the Screening Program. At the time of enrollment for this program, passengers are assigned a unique Passenger Identification Number (PIN) that correlates with their gait.

The airport security authorities have glasses that support augmented vision technology. These glasses identify various parameters of the passengers such as their speed, stride, and kinematic movement and match the passenger's gait to their unique PIN and overlay the passenger's PIN to the security operator's field of vision. The security operator then compares that information about the passengers with the PIN information from the ticket codes to verify each passenger's identity. This technology, along with advanced explosive trace detection sensors and other X-ray cameras fitted along the sidewalk area, allows the traveler to move through the gate area within a few seconds.

10.4.1.3 Social Media Applications in Airports The results of the most recent social media usage according to Amadeus are as follows [1]:

- 72% of Internet users now actively use social media networks.
- 18- to 29-year-olds have an 89% usage of social media networks.
- 30- to 49-year-olds have a social media usage of 72%.
- 60% of people between 50 and 60 years of age are active on social media.
- In the 65 plus age group, 43% are using social media.
- The top three countries in terms of time spent on Facebook per hour spent online are the United States at 16 minutes, followed by Australia at 14 minutes, and Great Britain at 13 minutes.
- 71% of users access social media networks from a mobile device.

These statistics clearly illustrate the potential for social media usage in airports to foster improved communication between passengers and various components of airport ecosystem. The survey results regarding the use of social media in airports are summarized in the following graph:

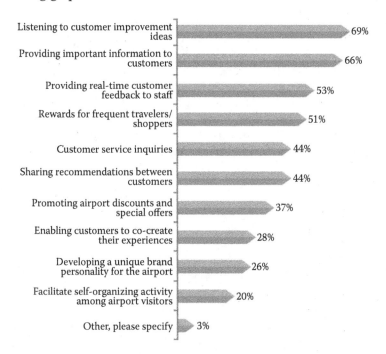

Listening to customer improvement ideas — 69%
Providing important information to customers — 66%
Providing real-time customer feedback to staff — 53%
Rewards for frequent travelers/shoppers — 51%
Customer service inquiries — 44%
Sharing recommendations between customers — 44%
Promoting airport discounts and special offers — 37%
Enabling customers to co-create their experiences — 28%
Developing a unique brand personality for the airport — 26%
Facilitate self-organizing activity among airport visitors — 20%
Other, please specify — 3%

Many airports and airlines have realized the tremendous potential that lies in the usage of social media networks and they are using social media networks extensively to sell travel tickets and also interact with passengers to understand their feedback and the various pain points experienced by them. Some of the key aspects in which social media is used by some of the present day airports and airline services are

- Selecting co-passengers based on their social media profiles
- Providing key flight details such as timings, delayed flights, and so on through social media networks
- Comparing the services offered by various airports/airline service providers using surveys that are conducted using social media networks
- Advertising special promotional offers for air travel using social media networks
- Using social media to provide communication between passenger and crew

USE OF SOCIAL MEDIA PROFILES
FOR CHOICE OF PASSENGERS

KLM provides a feature called KLM Meet & Seat. Using this feature, it is possible for passengers to know various types of information about the other passengers in the same flight by accessing their social media profiles. Using these profiles, the passengers also have the option to reserve their seats so that they can travel with like-minded people or people who are traveling to attend a similar event, and so on.

Social media networks are also used by various airports and airlines as a means to enhance their brand value in the market by advertising the various value-added features offered by them in the social media networks so that it will reach huge masses of people. The most recent statistics regarding the use of social media networks by airports is given below:

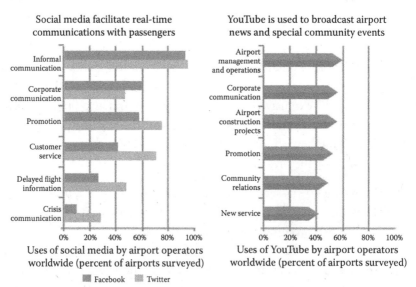

Social media facilitate real-time communications with passengers

Uses of social media by airport operators worldwide (percent of airports surveyed)

■ Facebook ■ Twitter

YouTube is used to broadcast airport news and special community events

Uses of YouTube by airport operators worldwide (percent of airports surveyed)

10.4.2 Technology/Processes to Streamline the Passenger Journey

The technology/processes that are used to streamline passenger journey are summarized in the following diagram:

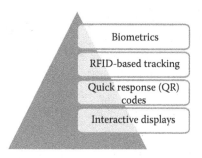

10.4.2.1 Use of Biometrics in Airports

10.4.2.1.1 Biometric Passports Traditional document-based methods for verification of passengers that are used in airports are error prone and time consuming. They rely on the photographs of the passengers for verification of their identity and many times the photograph can be forged or duplicated. In addition, information about criminals resides in multiple databases and systems without any integration or communication. Identity verification of passengers is a crucial task when it comes to the security of airports, flights, and countries on the whole.

To ensure accurate and appropriate verification of passengers, many countries are currently adopting the concept of biometric passports. These biometric passports, also called e-passports, contain a smart card with biometric information about the passenger and are provided along with the traditional paper-based passports. The passenger's biometric information is validated against the biometric information that is present in the smart cards of the passports and this provides an efficient and reliable mechanism to verify the identity of the passengers.

SINGAPORE—THE FIRST TO IMPLEMENT BIOMETRIC PASSPORTS

The Immigration & Checkpoints Authority of Singapore (ICA) was one of the first organizations in the world to adopt and implement the concept of e-passports. They adopted this technique to ensure secure immigration at their various borders and checkpoints. The ICA uses a combination of smartcard and fingerprint matching to help them validate the identities of passengers who are traveling through automated lanes. This biometric-based authentication process is completed in less than 12 seconds.

10.4.2.1.2 Other Biometric Applications in Airports Early detection of suspicious people/passengers is key to the safety and security of airports. This task becomes much more difficult and challenging in a huge and high-traffic airport until and unless appropriate tracking and verification mechanisms for passengers are present at each and every point within the airport. Typically, the passenger flow begins at airport check-in counters where passengers check in their baggage and receive their boarding pass. At this stage, security can be integrated into the system by using the concept of e-boarding. E-boarding provides self-service kiosks that have fingerprint readers and cameras for facial authentication of the passengers. In some cases, this can also be done with the help of smart cards that are attached to the biometric passports. This process ensures that the passenger's identity is verified at the starting point of entry into the airport itself.

Apart from this, facial recognition and fingerprint reading systems can be deployed near the airport gates to ensure that only authorized people are walking around the gates of the airports. Such systems can also be used in aerobridge and other security areas around the airport to detect any suspicious individuals of vehicles. These biometric-based authentication systems are a reliable and trustworthy way to ensure safety of airports. The various ways in which biometric systems can be integrated with the airport infrastructure are summarized in the following figure:

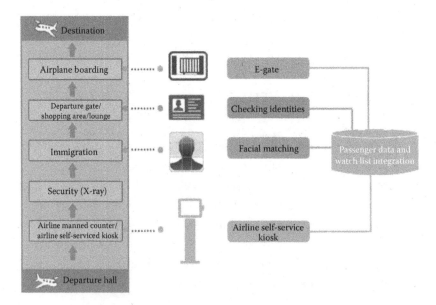

10.4.2.2 RFID-Based Tracking of Baggage in Airports   Radio frequency identification (RFID) technology is used extensively across the world for tracking in the supply chain industry. It uses radio waves for tracking and hence does not require line-of-sight. Hence it is very beneficial when compared to the bar code technology that was traditionally used in airports for baggage tracking.

RFID-based tracking of baggage offers the following benefits to the airport when compared to the conventional bar code–based tracking of baggage.

- Reduce instances of baggage loss and baggage theft as RFID tags can be tracked from a distance also using RFID readers. This in turn reduces the amount paid by airport authorities for lost and stolen baggage.
- RFID-based tracking of baggage also increases customer satisfaction as a result of a reduction in the number of instances of lost or stolen baggage. This is because the baggage can be tracked continuously from the entry point until it is loaded into the appropriate aircraft.
- RFID also reduces the staffing cost for baggage handling in airports because of the nature of technology and the benefit it offers.

10.4.2.3 Quick Response Codes in Airports for Mobile Check-In   Quick response (QR) code is a two-dimensional bar code that is machine readable and can be used to gather more information about the item to which it is attached. One recent trend that has emerged is the use of QR code for mobile check-in to the airports. This is done in the following manner.

- The airline authorities will send a boarding pass to the passenger with a link to the QR code assigned to the passenger. This information is typically sent in an e-mail that can be accessed using a smart mobile phone.
- The passenger will click the link and obtain the QR code assigned to him or her and store the code in the mobile device as well.
- Any time the passenger needs to present the boarding pass, he or she instead presents the QR code stored in the mobile phone to the scanner, which reads the information.

- The QR code also acts as a unique link to all of the flight-related information of the passenger such as the seat details and so on. In case of changes to any of these details, the QR codes can be refreshed to display the updated or new information.

The use of QR codes for mobile check-in saves a great deal of time and goes a long way to improve the travel experience of passengers. This is already used in many prominent airports across the world. However, in some other airports, it is yet to be introduced and used.

10.4.2.4 Interactive Displays and Billboards in Airports   Interactive touch displays are useful in any real-life situation, more so when it comes to airports. Many airports across the world have interactive maps. These maps can be used by passengers to view the route information about their favorite spot within the airport such as a restaurant or the gate to which a passenger needs to go to board a specific flight.

Today many leading players in the IT industry are trying out new innovative approaches for the use of interactive displays in airports. One such interesting approach is an interactive billboard in airports designed by Google. These interactive billboards from Google use Red Crystal software to stream the required content onto users' smart phones. The users can select the type of content they want to be displayed on the advertising displays. Apart from this, users can also download movies, games, or anything of interest from the Google Play Store to their smart phones.

10.4.3 Technology/Processes to Enhance Passenger Experience

The various technologies or processes to enhance passenger experience are summarized in the following diagram:

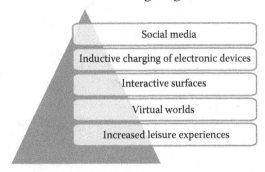

10.4.3.1 Inductive Charging of Electronic Devices One of the main pain points for passengers in airports is the lack of availability of charging points for their electronic devices. Though most airports have charging points, they are insufficient to meet the demands of the ever increasing number of passengers. This is where inductive charging technology comes in as a handy option.

Inductive charging technology consists of a main charging station. From the charging station, energy is transferred to other devices through an electromagnetic field. The electromagnetic field consists of a primary inductive coil that transfers energy to a secondary coil that is present in the device to be charged. The secondary coil in the device can transfer the charge to batteries and other components of the device that need to be charged. This solves the passenger concern about the reduced availability of charging points in airports. However, for this technology to be successful, it needs to be present on both ends: charging station and on the electronic devices that are carried by the passengers.

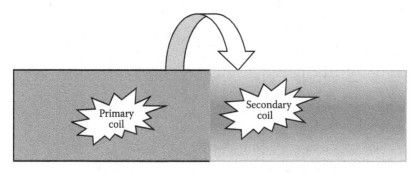

Charging station/coil   Devices to be charged

Many leading international airports have adopted inductive charging. There are two modes in which inductive charging can occur:

- *Physical contact–based inductive charging*: In this mode, there should be physical contact between the charging plate and the device to be charged so that transfer of charge can happen between the coils that are present in the two devices. This method is constrained by the physical proximity requirements between the devices. However, in places such as airports, this can happen by placing multiple charging plates in rooms/ tables.

- *Wireless inductive charging*: In this mode, no physical contact is required between the charging plate and the device to be charged. This mode works on the basis of resonant inductive coupling. Resonant inductive coupling uses the principle of near-field wireless transmission of electrical energy between two devices that are tuned to resonate at the same frequency. This approach is very popular and is widely used in airports and other public venues such as conference halls that require facilities to provide mass charging of electronic devices.

10.4.3.2 Virtual Worlds and Interactive Surfaces

10.4.3.2.1 Virtual Reality Systems for Tracking Ground Movement   Virtual reality systems in airports for tracking ground movements of aircrafts is an application that allows airport supervisors to have a three-dimensional display of actual ground movements of aircrafts in real time. These systems can be used to provide enhanced terminal operation movement capabilities to airport supervisors and operators. These systems can integrate with airport databases to provide real-time information that can be combined with graphical and other 3D models to provide a very clear and comprehensive picture to airport authorities.

10.4.3.2.2 Remote and Virtual Towers   Remote and virtual tower (RVT) is a concept that could be considered an aftermath of the virtual reality concept. With the help of this technology, the air traffic service (ATS) at an airport is performed at a remote location other than the local control tower. RVT technology is aimed at providing the following key features for airports:

- Monitoring, controlling, and management of air traffic services from a remote tower by staff who operate from a remote tower center that is not located locally within the airport premises.
- Emergency services at airports in case of events such as fire can happen from a remote location. This way the contingency facility will not be impacted by events that occur at a local airport location.
- Clear visibility of airport premises without any impact caused by fog, mist, and other environmental conditions that may affect the local airport premises.

RVT technology uses optical sensors and cameras that provide a high-quality real-time image of the runway. These images are typically displayed at large monitors. In addition to the live video feeds from the airport, air traffic management systems, voice communication systems, meteorological systems, and surveillance display systems are all present in RVTs. The key benefits of RVT are the following:

- No necessity to maintain and operate control towers at local airport buildings
- Possibility of monitoring multiple small and medium airports from a single centralized location
- Lower human resource requirement by providing features to monitor multiple airports from a single centralized location

EXTENSION OF VIRTUAL REALITY TO 6D CINEMAS AT SCHIPHOL, AMSTERDAM

Schiphol airport at Amsterdam has a 6D XD cinema theatre in the airport. This theatre provides passengers special motion-based seats that offer "rides" that includes sound, wind, and lighting effects that are synchronized with the cinema to provide a 6D effect.

10.4.3.3 Interactive Surfaces Interactive screens/displays that respond to gestures of people by providing different types of multimedia content are used in many airports across the world. The main objective of using such components in airports is to provide an enhanced traveling experience to passengers. The underlying technology used is the gesture recognition technology where the system is equipped with technology that can examine the surrounding area and respond to the movement of the people around by displaying various types of content that are preloaded and preconfigured into the system.

These interactive surfaces can also be used to display logos and brand messages of various organizations. The interactive screen content can be designed in such a way as to offer a simple transition from one brand image to another along with 3D and other visual effects, audio and video.

Apart from interactive screens, it is also possible to have interactive floors that respond to gesture recognition technology and provide a fully immersive traveling experience for the passengers. In the context of airports, apart from using these interactive surfaces as advertising media, it is also possible to use these interactive surfaces to provide valuable insights to travelers about their destination locations and the various points of interest that are located in a specific destination location.

INTERACTIVE SURFACES IN ACTION AT UNITED ARAB EMIRATES AIRPORT

United Arab Emirates airport has unveiled its dedicated technology-based entertainment corner called e-zone. This entertainment zone is located in the Business Class Lounge at Terminal 3. e-zone has several games and interactive components that are suitable for all ages. e-zone uses several different technologies that include the latest Microsoft Surface™ computers. Microsoft Surface provides a true experience of intuitive computing by eliminating components such as mice and keyboards. It has the capability to recognize objects that are placed on it. Objects could vary from digital cameras to wireless phones and even "tagged" glasses. These objects are recognized and treated as objects of communication with the user. Use of these cutting edge technologies in the airport marks the beginning of a new era in human–computer interaction. Some of the applications that come as a part of this entertainment component are the following:

- Attract—This application provides a water pond that allows passengers to touch and feel the pond using the features offered by Microsoft Surface.
- Destination Guide—This application allows customers to interact with a moving 3D globe. It is built using a Microsoft Virtual Earth platform and allows customers to zoom into any location on Earth. After zoom in, it helps the passengers to view general information about the destination location and also provides photos of specific photos. The 3D globe also provides extensive information about the various holiday destinations for travelers in the United Arab Emirates.

- Photo Album—This application provides a collection of photos of the various holiday destinations in the United Arab Emirates. It is possible for people to view, touch, move, zoom in/out, and share photographs.
- Paint—This application allows children to use their hands to paint as per their desire. Once a painting is completed, there are options to convert the painting into a postcard. This postcard can later be e-mailed as a souvenir.

10.4.4 Processes for Increased Leisure Experience

Air travel passengers have expressed a strong opinion that they would like to have some leisure activities as part of their travel experience. This is more prominent when additional time is available between connecting flights. The limited support available in various airports for virtual reality, multimedia, and other entertainment technologies is also a reason for the rise in passenger demand for leisure facilities in airports. Some of the leisure facilities available in various airports are explained below.

10.4.4.1 Finnish Sauna at Helsinki Airport
The national airlines of Finland (Fin air) that operates flights between Helsinki and Singapore airport has introduced a spa and sauna offer for transit passengers at Helsinki [2]. The facility is being offered at the Finnair lounge in the single terminal building. The lounge is available to passengers on production of a business class ticket, oneworld Emerald/Sapphire card, or €45. The spa alone costs €45 for access to various spa pools, saunas, and baths, while treatments range from €51 to €141. Combined lounge-spa access costs €70. With the direct Finnair flight from Helsinki to Singapore, business travelers will find Helsinki a geographically convenient connection to many European cities that are not directly served by a one-stop flight from Australia. Singapore's Changi airport is renowned as a thoroughly enjoyable place to transit, so adding Helsinki to the mix will make for a thoroughly enjoyable experience [2].

10.4.4.2 Free Sightseeing Tour at Changi Airport, Singapore
If there is any possibility of spending more than a couple of hours in transit at

Changi Airport, there is a free guided tour service for the passengers. Passengers are provided a bus and then a ride along the Singapore River to get a view of the entire city of Singapore. This feature has become such a great success that many passengers traveling via Changi Airport opt for a forced delay in their transit to enjoy the free city tour.

10.4.4.3 Free Cooking Classes at Paris Orly Airport   Passengers in transit through Orly Airport in Paris get a chance to attend free cooking classes. In these cooking classes, French chefs teach passengers how to prepare French culinary specialties. The passengers also have an option to try the recipes and carry them back to their destinations if they opt for this.

10.4.4.4 Traditional Culture Workshops at Incheon Airport, South Korea Traditional culture workshops are organized at Incheon International Airport for the passengers who are in transit and also for those who are flying to various destinations across the world. In these culture workshops, activities that have a deep linkage to the culture of Korea are exhibited in the workshops. As of now, the workshops cover more than 70 art and craft themes that span various aspects of Korean culture such as Korean ceramic ware, clothing, and accessories.

Apart from the aforementioned leisure activities, many present-day airports also have facilities such as spas, art zones, Christmas markets, movie theaters, and so on.

GAMING ZONE IN HONG KONG INTERNATIONAL AIRPORT FOR PASSENGER ENTERTAINMENT

Hong Kong International Airport is one of the world's busiest airports and ranks fourth in terms of international air traffic. This airport introduced a game zone that includes 14 Play Station 3 (PS3) kiosks that can be used by passengers free of cost. PS3 kiosks contain the following games:

- Uncharted 2
- Assassin's Creed 2
- Final Fantasy XIII
- James Cameron's Avatar: The Game

ENHANCED DINING EXPERIENCE USING TOUCH SCREEN MONITORS AT JOHN F. KENNEDY INTERNATIONAL AIRPORT, NEW YORK

The JetBlue Terminal 5 experience in John F. Kennedy airport, New York is the result of a partnership between some of New York's exclusive restaurants and expert chefs from the area. The JetBlue Terminal 5 experience includes the following aspects:

- Nine full-service restaurants
- Bars and cafes
- A gourmet food hall with eight quick-serve eateries
- Gourmet markets/grab-and-go
- Three coffee bars
- Six bars/lounges
- Innovative gate area program

The innovative gate area program allows passengers to order their meals using a touch screen monitor. These meals will then be delivered to the dining tables in the gate area of the airport. This is a niche dining experience that is made available to air travel passengers.

10.4.5 IT for the Benefits of Passengers

The IT components for the benefits of passengers are summarized in the following diagram:

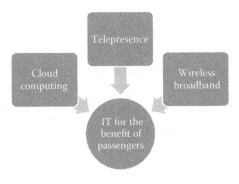

10.4.5.1 Cloud Computing Present-day airports across the world are embracing cloud computing because of the immense cost benefits offered by it. The main crux of cloud computing is anytime, anywhere access to all types of resources that are included as part of the IT ecosystem when the user requires it. The cost benefit part of it stems from the fact that the user needs to pay only per usage.

The following are the main benefits offered by cloud computing to airports.

- The infrastructural components that are required for maintaining the entire IT infrastructure of the airports are provided and maintained by the cloud service provider. This removes the capital expenditure component from the airport infrastructure management, which in turn provides huge cost benefits for the airport authorities.
- From an environmental perspective, as cloud-based solutions typically use only pooled hardware resources; there is less energy consumption, which helps reduce carbon emissions. In addition, through the use of shared resources, e-waste can be reduced by a substantial margin.

Apart from the airport authorities, the facility to use cloud computing services at airports becomes a very handy option for many air travel passengers to store and access data created by them while in transit at airports and access high-end applications that are hosted in the cloud infrastructure without any infrastructure limitations.

10.4.5.2 Telepresence Telepresence refers to a group of technologies that provide a feeling of being present in a location other than the actual one. The major application of telepresence is for video conferencing. Most present-day organizations follow a borderless concept, meaning that organizations that are split across different parts of the world function as a single entity despite time zone and all other types of differences. There is support for telepresence in many present-day airports. This technology helps employees to attend important official meetings via video conferencing and allows them to be productive even during transit at airports.

10.4.5.3 Wireless Broadband   Wireless broadband access is provided in most present-day airports. Some airports have imposed a restriction on the duration for which wireless broadband could be used free of charge. After a specific duration, the wireless broadband becomes a paid service. Apart from wireless broadband service, many airports offer PCs with pay-as-you-go Internet service for the benefit of air travel passengers. These facilities are widely used and appreciated by air travel passengers for official work and entertainment purposes.

10.5 Envisioning Airports of the Future (Airport 3.0)

Next-generation airports will be a conglomeration of all the new and evolving next-generation technologies. Next generation in this context refers to the airports in the time frame of 2018 or 2020, when many nascent technologies of the present day would have evolved into fully mature ones. How do you expect the airports to be in the next 5- to 10-year time frame? This question harbors much uncertainty because of the continuously evolving and radically changing nature of the business ecosystem and the technology ecosystem. People's attitudes are also constantly changing. When there is an astonishing idea about the intelligent airports of the future, there are many more aspects to be considered apart from the technological backbone. Some of these aspects are the infrastructure model, revenue-generating model, and the various conceptual models that are revolving around the intelligent airports of the future. We cover all of these aspects in this section. This section contains the coverage of the intelligent airports from the following dimensions:

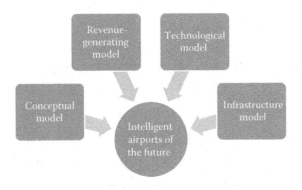

10.5.1 Conceptual Models

Multitudes of concepts are evolving around the airports of future. Each of them has a diverse landscape and thought process that bundles around the expectations of the air travel passengers.

The following are some of the prominent conceptual models.

10.5.1.1 Independent City Model

In this model, the airport is visualized as a fully self-sustaining and independent entity that caters to all types of requirements of its customers (air travel passengers) by providing them food, accommodation, entertainment, and retail outlets. Airports could reach such a level of independence that it would generate the energy required for its functioning using in-house energy generation options. In short, an airport would be a city in itself with all the components required for its efficient functioning.

10.5.1.2 Extended City Model

In this model, the airport is tightly integrated with the surrounding city and is influenced by various aspects of the city such as culture, history, and food habits. The airport will be treated as an important arm for the economic growth of the city. The city government and the citizens will have a strong say in running the airport and in deciding the practices to be adopted by the airport. Some airports, such as Dubai International Airport, follow a concept that closely resembles the extended city model.

10.5.1.3 Transit Point Model

In this model, passengers perform all of their travel-related tasks remotely with the help of sophisticated technologies and they consider the airport only as a short transit location to board their flights, similar to the situation in a bus station or railway station. This model will reduce the cost involved in the maintenance of airports, as the expectations of the passengers from the airports will be minimal.

Among all the conceptual models discussed earlier, the one that is most popular among present-day passengers is the Independent City model.

10.5.2 Infrastructure Models

A number of models are being proposed for the construction and maintenance of airport infrastructure and are discussed in this section.

10.5.2.1 Rented Assets Model In this model, the airport operator does not buy or own any assets. The assets are rented as a service based on some rental charges. These rental charges can be agreed on by the parties involved in terms of an agreement. The greatest benefit of this model is that no capital cost is involved.

In this model, only during some peak times when a large crowd is expected at a destination, for example, during an event such as the World Cup or other sporting events, the assets are rented and used as an airport terminal to accommodate the huge inflow of air travel passengers. After the peak season, the temporary terminals are no longer used.

10.5.2.2 Modular Model In this model, terminals are built as prefabricated modules that can be assembled and used when required at relatively low cost.

10.5.3 Revenue-Generating Models

10.5.3.1 Generation of New Income Avenues The objective of this model is to increase the revenue generation from nonaeronautical sources. Some of the revenue sources that are used now are retail outlets, temporarily renting a portion of the airports for fairs and other events, and so on. Apart from the existing ones, new avenues should be explored and added to increase the revenue of the airports, such as making specific organizations sponsor the maintenance of specific utility services that are used in airports in return for their brand advertisement, making organizations provide some equipment and utilities that are required for the airport in return for their brand advertising, and so on.

10.5.3.2 Profit Redistribution A profit redistribution model should be in place between the nonaeronautical revenue-generating sources present in the airport and the airport authorities. Nonaeronautical revenue-generating sources could include restaurants and other retail outlets that are present in the airports. Some such schemes currently exist in selected airports. Efforts should be made to spread this model to all other airports. In return for revenue sharing, the revenue-generating sources may expect something in return. These could be reductions in rental charges, providing free avenues for advertisements, and so on.

PROFIT REDISTRIBUTION IN ACTION AT AIRPORTS

Since October 2008, JetBlue has exclusively owned and operated Terminal 5 at New York's John F. Kennedy International Airport. The Port Authority of New York and New Jersey provided the $800 million funding for the terminal. JetBlue pays the Port Authority a per-enplanement fee to help recover terminal infrastructure costs over a 30-year term. JetBlue is also the landlord for retail areas, sub-leasing space to concessionaires and sharing a percentage of total revenue with the Port Authority, and captures the in-terminal advertising revenues, which are shared with the Port Authority and the advertising agency [3].

10.5.3.3 Ecosystem Funding   In this model, some or all the players of the airport ecosystem are allowed to participate in new development activities of the airports that may require additional funds. These players are allowed to fund airport development activities in return for equity shares or membership on the airport's key decision-making team.

10.5.4 Public–Private Partnerships

In the present business situation, where there is an acute shortage of funds for airports, it is necessary to find new innovative ways of creating partnerships between the airport authorities and private parties or organizations that are interested in funding. One example of this type of partnership is the agreement between Dallas Airport and Southwest Airlines for the modernization of the airport. It has seen tremendous success and such models should be adopted by more and more airports across the world.

10.5.5 Technological Models

In the emerging technology ecosystem, some of the technologies that could serve as the key technological backbone of the intelligent airport infrastructure in the future to serve air travel passengers are

- Big data and analytics
- Internet of Things
- Genetic profiling
- Biomimicry

10.5.5.1 Big Data and Predictive Analytics Big data analytics is emerging as a hot technology. Its usage in the context of airports to serve air travel passengers is a topic that has gained a great deal of traction recently. In the context of the airline industry, big data refers to the huge amount of customer and transactional data that are generated daily by airports across the world. These data could serve as storehouses of valuable information that could predict unravel and various patterns of customer behavior. Many tools to manipulate and handle these large datasets are available in the market now, but there are no specific tools that are custom made for the airline industry. However, efforts are being made to develop big data analytics tools that are specific to domains so that the patterns that are derived could be directly used by the respective authorities without any further customization.

There are plans to create data warehouses in airports to capture all types of information regarding a customer that may involve travel, shopping, and food preferences. This will enable creation of value-added service packages that are specific to the choices of each customer. This will go a long way in enhancing the travel experiences of air travel passengers.

10.5.5.2 Internet of Things Intelligent airports of the future will be data rich, with thousands of devices that are communicating with one another. This huge network of communicating devices constitutes the Internet of Things (IoT) concept. In the context of airports, this huge network of communicating objects will help people to communicate with each passenger within the airport. This in turn will generate huge amounts of information that can serve as useful inputs for the big data analytics concept described in the previous section. However, to exploit fully the benefits provided by these data, the existing IT infrastructure in airports should scale up in terms of storage capacity and support for advanced and evolving networking technologies that will help to capture and store vast amounts of these data to convert them into knowledge that can be used for the benefit of air travel passengers.

10.5.5.3 Genetic Profiling   Genetic profiling is the technology of mapping a person's genome to delineate his or her DNA make-up. This is used extensively to assess various health parameters such as disease risk and possibility of allergic reactions to various medicines, and also presents the possibility of detecting the presence or absence of various traits in an individual. This technology can be used in airports to develop medical tourism that can be customized and offered to air travel passengers. Another major application of genetic profiling is for identification of individuals. At present, this technology is still in its nascent stages of evolution. However, in the future, it is expected to be widely adopted and used in airports by embedding genetic information of individuals in intelligent smart cards that are carried by passengers.

10.5.5.4 Biomimicry   Biomimicry is the imitation of nature's design in human engineering to solve the problems that occur as a result of flaws in human engineering. Some applications of biomimicry in the aviation sector are discussed in the following paragraphs.

10.5.5.4.1 Lotus Effect   A lotus leaf is designed in such a way that it sheds the water that falls on it, which helps to keep the surface of the lotus leaf clean as well. This technique, called the lotus effect, is starting to be used for the design of airbus cabinets with coatings that are capable of throwing off water. The lotus effect technique, when used in the design of cabinets, improves hygiene and drastically reduces the water requirement. This in turn reduces the overall weight of the aircraft, which reduces fuel consumption and carbon emissions of the aircraft.

10.5.5.4.2 Moveable Wing Surfaces   Sea birds have the capability to sense gust loads in air with the help of their beaks and accordingly shape the feathers in their wings to suppress lift. The noses of aircrafts can be designed using this technology to detect gust and use moveable wing surfaces for more efficient flight. This reduces the overall fuel consumption of the aircrafts as well.

10.5.5.4.3 Bionics   Many creatures use an active lightweight skeletal structure for a variety of purposes. These examples have inspired

Airbus to consider the use of such "bionic structures" as part of future aircraft structures. If the aerodynamic surfaces could be made lighter or more adaptive to the local environment, the weight of the aircraft could be reduced, which would result in reduced emissions [4].

10.5.5.4.4 Formation flying In nature, large birds sometimes fly together to save energy and to enable them to travel farther. When flying in formation—as seen with migrating geese or ducks—the leading bird's wings generate whirling masses of air. The following birds benefit from this air current to obtain extra lift, meaning they need to use less energy to fly. Aircraft wings create the same effect, known as a trailing vortex. Military pilots often use the same formation flying techniques to reduce the amount of energy—fuel burn—that the aircraft use. At the moment, passenger jetliners do not use this technique because of safety concerns. However, Airbus is working with some of its partners to explore the idea as a way to reduce both fuel consumption and emissions on long-distance flights [4].

These are only a very few examples of the use of biomimicry technology for efficient design of aircrafts. Apart from the examples quoted, there are a wide variety of use cases of biomimicry technology in the aviation sector.

Apart from these technologies, mobile and social media technologies will also find increased usage in the intelligent airports of the future. Mobile technologies such as near-field communication are predicted to replace all physical components of air travel such as boarding passes and passports. Existing manual baggage handling systems in airports would be replaced by robotic or fully automated systems. In addition to these key technology trends, intelligent virtual assistants that are capable of using social media network data and work schedules to plan and organize complete tailored journeys on request for individuals or groups will soon be a reality in airports.

10.6 Conclusion

A near "perfect storm" of influencing factors is dramatically driving the need for a radical rethinking of the concept of the airport ecosystem. The entire chapter revolved around this concept. The various components that are part of the airport ecosystem were discussed at the beginning of the chapter. The various challenges faced by the airport ecosystem were examined in detail and used as a starting point for the infrastructure evolution models of the airports that are proposed by the authors.

Airports were grouped into three different classes based on various factors and each category of airport was examined in detail, with an increased focus on Airport 2.0 and Airport 3.0 as they are more relevant to the context of our intelligent city discussion. The chapter concluded with the description of various aspects of future intelligent airports, or Airport 3.0. The various dimensions of Airport 3.0 such as conceptual models, technological models, revenue-generating models, and infrastructure models were discussed in detail to give a bird's eye view of the proposed intelligent airport concept. Ample examples are included throughout the chapter to give a more realistic perspective for readers.

References

1. Jeff Bullas (2014). 22 Social Media Facts and Statistics You Should Know in 2014. http://www.jeffbullas.com/2014/01/17/20-social-media-facts-and-statistics-you-should-know-in-2014/.
2. Brien Posey (2012). Five airport survival apps. http://www.techrepublic.com/blog/five-apps/five-airport-survival-apps/.
3. Reinventing the Airport Ecosystem. Amadeus report on airport ecosystem.
4. http://www.airbus.com/innovation/eco-efficiency/design/biomimicry/?contentId=[_TABLE%3Att_content%3B_FIELD%3Auid]%2C&cHash=22935adfac92fcbbd4ba4e1441d13383.

11

Next-Generation Healthcare Systems

Abstract

The healthcare sector is in the midst of a technological revolution in an attempt to overcome the issues it faces as a result of various aspects such as aging infrastructure and lack of adoption of appropriate technologies at correct points in time in the past. Another critical problem faced by the healthcare sector is the huge number of large datasets generated by them. Traditional storage infrastructure and technologies are not adequately efficient to handle these large amounts of data. To add to this array of problems is the change in the attitude and mindset of present-day patients. Patients today are not willing to compromise on the quality of their experience with their healthcare service providers. Patients no longer accept extended waiting times due to unavailability of various infrastructure components. Cloud computing service providers can offer promising benefits to healthcare organizations. The following are some of the key benefits they offer. (1) Drastic reduction in the infrastructure cost of healthcare organizations. (2) Scalable infrastructure that can store the huge amounts of data generated by the healthcare sector. (3) 24/7 availability of the infrastructure components, which can offer an enhanced experience for patients. The various healthcare use cases of cloud computing are discussed in detail in the first section of this chapter. Big data analytics can revolutionize the healthcare industry by offering a diverse range of benefits to patients such as early detection of disease symptoms and timely advice to patients by using real-time parameters that are gathered from them using various mobile applications. The various use cases of big data analytics in the healthcare sector are also discussed in detail in the second section of this chapter.

11.1 Introduction

Huge mountains of digital information are being created on a daily basis. These include diverse forms of data such as text, audio, video, and images. The proliferation of mobile devices into people's daily lives has in fact created a data deluge. It is very surprising to note that the majority of digital data has been created only in the last two years. This is the information landscape in general. If we look at healthcare specifically, in 2012, the worldwide healthcare data was 500 petabytes. By 2020, the healthcare data are expected to multiply by 50 times and will be approximately 25,000 petabytes. The graph given below shows the amount of data generated by various industry sectors. It is clearly evident that the healthcare sector is in the forefront of data generation.

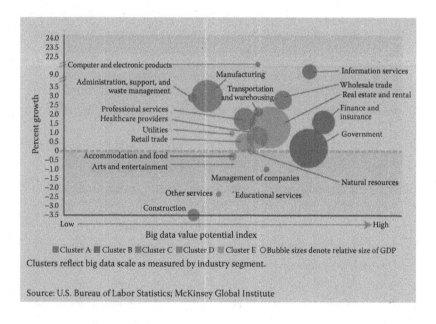

Legacy storage systems and conventional technologies are not equipped to store and manipulate this massive amount of data. Hence it is the need of the day to devise specialized mechanisms to store and handle these huge piles of data cost effectively. In addition, the healthcare sector is under a great deal of pressure to lower infrastructure costs by embracing new systems that provide good and secure data sharing features for storing electronic medical records (EMRs). Traditionally, the healthcare sector has been very slow to adopt new technologies and many hospitals retain their information technology (IT) infrastructure longer than the defined time span of this equipment. The need to adopt EMRs and the pressure to adopt cutting edge technologies have led to an increased interest and activity in the adoption of cloud-based service options for the healthcare sector around the world. In the first part of this chapter, we focus on cloud-based use cases that are available for the healthcare sector.

Big data analytics is of immense value in the healthcare sector because of the huge amount of large datasets generated by the healthcare sector. In the second half of this chapter, we focus on use cases of big data analytics in the healthcare sector.

The chapter is organized as follows:

11.2 Cloud Services in the Healthcare Sector

Present-day healthcare organizations are under tremendous pressure to lower infrastructure costs and replace their existing aging infrastructure. In addition, the healthcare sector generates huge amounts of data on a continuous basis such as EMRs and other patient-related data such as scanning reports that have huge sizes. For storing and managing such enormous amounts of data, significant investment is required by the healthcare organizations.

Cloud computing provides lucrative options for healthcare organizations to implement new technologies for diverse aspects such as electronic management of healthcare records that otherwise requires significant infrastructure investments. Healthcare organizations can utilize the services offered by cloud service providers to replace their aging infrastructure with new applications and solutions that offer more flexibility.

The main use cases of cloud computing in the healthcare sector are summarized in the following diagram:

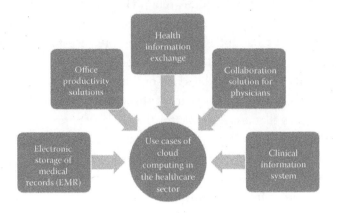

11.2.1 Electronic Storage of Medical Records

Diverse types of health records are maintained by healthcare organizations, and most of them require enormous storage space. In addition, there are many compliance controls imposed by the legislatures of various countries across the globe. These aspects also need to be followed by healthcare organizations while maintaining healthcare records. EMR service offerings by cloud service providers come as a boon to many healthcare organizations and provide the following benefits to them:

- No capital expenditure and only operating expenditure
- Compliance-related aspects taken care of by the cloud service provider as a part of the service level agreement
- High levels of scalability to store huge amounts of healthcare data

11.2.2 Office Productivity Solutions

Most organizations invest heavily in the infrastructure that is required for storing emails and other office-related documents. In many cases, because of legal restrictions, emails of employees need to be maintained for extended durations even after they leave the organization. This would further add to the infrastructure cost incurred by healthcare organizations. A cost-effective solution adopted by healthcare organizations to solve this problem is to store old emails and documents in low-cost storage options, a process called archiving. Many cloud service providers offer archive as a service without any additional investment. In the context of healthcare organizations, records of patients who have not visited them for a long time can be archived and stored as a service with the cloud service providers.

11.2.3 Health Information Exchange

Many cloud service providers are in the process of building health information exchanges. These are portals for exchange of useful healthcare-related information by various healthcare organizations for the benefit of the public and other stakeholders in the healthcare sector. This is an arduous task, as it requires bringing together many organizations in a common forum to share and collaborate with one another for their mutual benefit on a nonprofit basis.

11.2.4 Collaboration Solution for Physicians

There is a shortage of expert physicians across the world. To overcome this shortage, telemedicine is used widely by healthcare providers. By means of telemedicine, doctors share their expertise using video conferencing to, for example, perform complex surgeries and help in the diagnosis of rare diseases. Many cloud service providers have started offering services that could be used to host video conferences that are required for telemedicine. This service comes as a boon in making telemedicine available in remote and disaster-prone areas.

11.2.5 Clinical Information System

Clinical information systems are required by healthcare providers to maintain the notes of doctors, keep track of laboratory tests prescribed to the patients, and ensure that the appointment slots of various patients are maintained accurately to ensure that patients have a seamless healthcare experience. Clinical information systems that are maintained locally by healthcare providers often run into problems, making them unavailable for use for extended durations. This will incur significant delays in the treatment of patients. Today many cloud service providers offer a clinical information system as a service, which ensures that the systems are available for use 24/7 and results in zero waiting time for patients, thereby enhancing their experience with the healthcare providers.

11.3 Big Data Analytics in Healthcare Sector

Different types of data get into healthcare systems from a wide range of devices such as fitness devices, genomics research, social media networks, and a variety of other sources. Most of these data are huge files in different formats that include both structured and unstructured types of data. Hence big data analytics has also found much traction in the healthcare sector of late. If big data analytics is used effectively in the healthcare sector, it can provide numerous benefits such as

- Detection and prevention of infections at an early stage
- Provision of the right kind of treatment based on the correct identification of disease symptoms
- Early identification of new types of pathogens
- Development of new drug mechanisms against the new types of pathogens

There are different stakeholders for the application of big data analytics in the healthcare sector, each with a different expectation about the outcome of big data analytics. The different stakeholders are summarized in the following diagram:

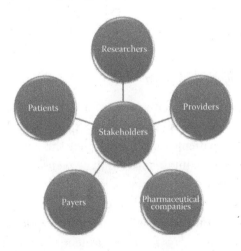

- *Patients* want an application that would provide them a dashboard to compare the services and the associated costs of the various healthcare providers. This would help them choose the most cost-effective healthcare provider for them.
- *Researchers* want to use big data analytical tools to perform predictive modeling and other types of sophisticated statistical analyses to derive valuable insights and find ways to solve unsolved problems that exist in the healthcare sector.
- *Pharmaceutical companies* want to use big data analytics to identify the causes of diseases quickly, identify candidates for specific types of drugs, and design efficient clinical trials to prevent failures. Pharmaceutical companies are also interested in using big data analytics to predict future disease trends so that they channel their drug discovery attempts in those directions.
- *Providers* want to use big data tools and technologies to get quick and real-time access to patient information. This will help them in their decision-making process and will in turn go a long way in providing timely and quick medical care to patients.
- *Payers* want to use big data to help them stratify population risk and guide them to adopt more sustainable business models that would promote their growth and development.

The different use cases for big data analytics in healthcare are the following:

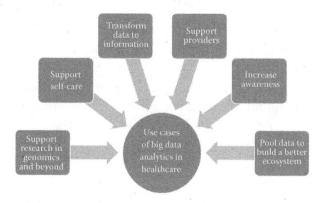

11.3.1 Support Research in Genomics and Other Healthcare Projects

Genomics is the branch of genetics that uses a combination of DNA sequencing methods and bioinformatics to analyze the structure and function of genomes. Genomics has been the starting point of the big data revolution in the healthcare sector and holds much promise to facilitate personalized medicine. Many healthcare organizations today are using big data analytics for genomics, but each of them is using a different approach. Some of the approaches adopted by a number of leading healthcare organizations are discussed in the following paragraphs.

Genome Health Solutions (GHS) uses its expertise in the area of genomics to create a network of doctors and technology providers who can use genomics to devise a new standard of healthcare to treat patients who are suffering from cancer and other diseases. The following are the approaches used by GHS to facilitate this.

- Designs and uses genomics oncology workflows that have the capability to guide patients to the appropriate doctors at the right time. The workflows are also designed in such a way that they will also provide correct diagnosis and treatment options for the patient.
- Develops educational resources and decision support systems that can be used by patients and healthcare professionals on diverse genomics topics.
- Provides consulting on genomic medicine and also develops diverse types of solutions for healthcare organizations.

GNS Healthcare uses REFS™ (Reverse Engineering Forward Simulation) to build mathematical cause-and-effect models. REFS is a scalable framework that uses supercomputers to construct causal models. These models are built from observational data and form the basis for the creation of visual interactive simulations. This framework also helps researchers to obtain information on outcomes for different types of interventions. The different steps of the process used by GNS Healthcare are summarized in the following diagram:

Step 1	• Input patient data
Step 2	• Data conversion
Step 3	• Enumeration
Step 4	• Optimization
Step 5	• Simulation
Step 6	• Visualization outputs using advanced analytics and recommendations to the patient based on that

NextBio combines large public with private datasets to enable new genomics discoveries [1].

- Assembles vast amounts of curated and annotated clinical and molecular data enabling clients to make unique discoveries that would not be possible with their own private datasets alone.
- Uses big data technology to make correlations between the billions of data points from the public domain with private genomic and clinical data sets.
- Delivered as Software as a Service (SaaS).
- A rich set of application programming interfaces (APIs) enables clients to integrate NextBio within their workflows.
- Current clients include pharmaceutical Research & Development and academic medical centers.
- The initial focus is on oncology, now expanding into metabolic and autoimmune diseases.

11.3.2 Transform Data from Information

The most important requirement in the healthcare industry or any other industry is to transform data into useful information. This task becomes all the more complicated if the data that come in are unstructured data. Converting the unstructured data into a machine understandable and manageable format is the key to enable data-driven decision management in the healthcare sector. Explanatory analytics is a variant of analytics that uses a collection of tools that are based on data mining, cluster analysis, statistics, machine learning, text analytics, and natural language processing (NLP) to mine data for patterns and meaning [1].

11.3.2.1 Use of Explanatory Analytics by Predixion Software Predixion software is a healthcare organization that uses predictive analytic software hosted in the cloud to uncover patterns that are present in hospital datasets. These patterns are used mainly to prevent patient readmissions. The analytic software used by Predixion works in the following manner.

- Pulls data from a wide variety of sources. Uses a combination of data mining and machine learning algorithm based analytical tools to generate predictions.
- Uses a predictive analytics algorithm to assign a risk score to the patients that helps them to identify patients who have a risk of readmission. The results are about 86% accurate.

11.3.2.2 Use of Big Data by Health Fidelity Health Fidelity uses NLP to convert unstructured data into information that is later used as inputs by analytical and compliance applications.

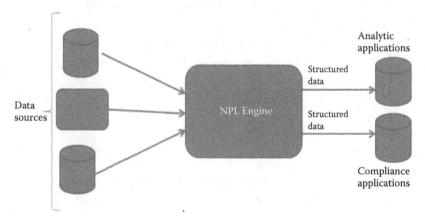

11.3.3 Supporting Self-Care

Another interesting use case of big data analytics in healthcare is helping patients to understand and keep track of their health parameters. This is done with the help of mobile applications that are equipped to track certain physiological parameters of an individual. The individual will also have options to enter additional health-related information. This information is transferred to an external healthcare service provider (with the individual's permission) who will use analytics to predict the onset of diseases and recommend appropriate corrective and preventive measures to the individual.

Numerous mobile applications are available for tracking healthcare parameters. Some of the applications are platform specific and available as free downloads from the application store. Some other applications require a fee to be remitted to the service provider before downloading and installing the application. Some examples of mobile healthcare applications were discussed in the previous chapter on mobile devices. Some other mobile application examples that are specific to cloud and big data are discussed in the following paragraphs.

Ginger.io is a cloud platform that offers healthcare-based services by collecting real-time active and passive data from patients through their mobile phones. These collected data are used by doctors, family members, and caretakers to monitor and manage the health of patients. The novel approach used by this healthcare service provider uses a combination of machine learning and predictive modeling techniques to identify changes in normal behavior and lifestyle patterns that could predict the onset of some diseases or the possibilities of a disease getting worse.

11.3.4 Support for Providers

Providing support to the healthcare providers is one of the most interesting use cases of big data in the healthcare sector. Providers always have less time, money, and information and they face immense competition in the healthcare sector. Many applications are being developed by the various service providers to help providers in the healthcare sector. The main challenge in dealing with providers in the healthcare sector is their lack of flexibility to user interface changes and resistance to adopt new technology changes. However, with the increasing pressure in the healthcare provider ecosystem, present-day healthcare service providers are embracing new technologies and applications to better support their customers (patients).

One Health Solutions uses a combination of social media and hospital data to create and update health records in real time. It is one of the first health platforms to do this, with the help of flexible APIs that can pull data from both sources. It also has the necessary security measures to protect the privacy of the data. This platform also supports following some addiction-related disorders such as smoking, alcohol, and drugs. It includes features for chronic disease management, overall wellness, stress management, and patient care advice for specific diseases. One Health Solutions has several customers at present, including healthcare providers.

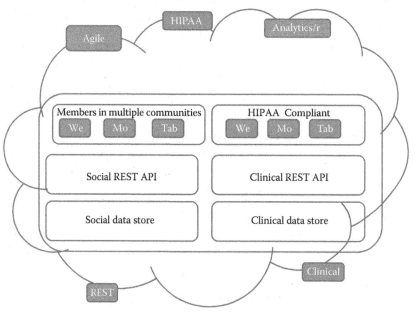

11.3.5 Increase Awareness

Big data is providing increased awareness that helps to solve a wide arena of problems. Some of the common problems widely prevalent today include

- Presence of counterfeit drugs in the market and lack of techniques to differentiate original and counterfeit drugs
- Lack of techniques to predict outbreak of epidemics or other diseases
- Lack of systems that provide proper preventive healthcare advice

Big data platforms and solutions for the healthcare industry help to remediate all of the aforementioned problems because of their capability to assimilate data from a large number of data sources and run predictive calculations on the data.

11.3.5.1 Sproxil Uses Big Data to Identify Counterfeit Drugs   Sproxil is a healthcare application that uses big data to identify counterfeit drugs. This is done by attaching PIN codes to drug packages. These PIN codes can be queried with the help of the service provided by Sproxil to differentiate between real and counterfeit drugs.

11.3.5.2 Sickweather LLC Uses Social Media to Track Disease Outbreaks Sickweather LLC uses posts on social media networks to predict outbreaks of specific diseases in specific areas. It also offers disease forecasts to its users that are very similar to weather forecasts. The following are the key benefits of this service:

- Keeps residents aware of disease outbreaks in their areas so that they can take appropriate precautions to safeguard themselves.
- Provides features that will help residents add disease-related information pertaining to their areas.
- Offers advice to residents about the various medication options that are available to handle diseases.

11.3.6 Pool Data to Build a Better Ecosystem

Big data platforms help combine data from several sources to derive valuable insights about various aspects related to the healthcare sector that was never possible before because of the presence of disparate data sources. One typical example is IBM Watson™, which is known to be the most advanced processor for natural languages on earth, a capability that was demonstrated during its participation in a *Jeopardy!* competition.

IBM Watson comprises 21 supercomputer subsystems. The following capabilities of Watson facilitate very quick and accurate diagnostics and decision making:

- Deep content analysis
- Evidence-based reasoning
- Natural language processing

IBM Watson has 16 TB of memory to store huge amounts of data. These data include patient-related information and all types of documents pertaining to different aspects of healthcare. IBM Watson has the capability to read 200 million pages of text in just 3 seconds and it can also recall each and every word when required later on. Watson will pool data from diverse sources such as family history, patient history, disease symptoms, and so on to help doctors in their diagnostics and treatment.

11.4 Conclusion

The healthcare industry is facing a myriad of problems due to an aging infrastructure that is incapable of handling the huge volume of data generated in the healthcare sector. Apart from that, healthcare organizations have not been in the forefront for new technology adoption because of cost concerns, adding to the multitude of problems they face. Today patients are very demanding in terms of the quality of healthcare they receive and also in terms of their experience with healthcare providers. Patients are no longer ready to accept delay caused by situations such as unavailability of clinical information applications, incorrect appointment schedules with physicians, and so on. This has further added to the pressure experienced by organizations in the healthcare sector.

Because of a wide range of problems, present-day healthcare organizations have started embracing recent technologies such as cloud computing and big data analytics. Cloud computing provides numerous cost benefits for healthcare organizations. Use cases of cloud computing for healthcare organizations were discussed in detail in the first section of this chapter.

The majority of the data generated by the healthcare sector are good candidates to be treated as big data because of the huge size of the patient documents. If analytics is applied to this big data, very useful insights can be derived from them that can offer a wide range of health benefits to patients by detecting outbreak of diseases at an early stage, offering expert medical advice to patients based on the real-time monitoring of their physiological parameters, and so on. Use cases of big data analytics in the healthcare sector were discussed in detail in the second half of this chapter.

Reference

1. Bonnie Feldman, Ellen M. Martin, and Tobi Skotnes (2012). Big Data in Healthcare Hype and Hope (white paper).

12

SECURITY MANAGEMENT OF INTELLIGENT CITIES

Abstract

The key enabler of an intelligent city is the underlying information technology (IT) infrastructure. However, the IT infrastructure of an intelligent city contains a wide gamut of technologies such as cloud, big data, mobile devices, and Internet of Things (IoT). Each of these technological components is susceptible to various types of security vulnerabilities and threats that can render it ineffective. For an intelligent city to do due diligence to the expectation of its citizens, it is very important to ensure that the IT infrastructure components are adequately safeguarded from various security breaches. The crux of the lesson is the techniques to be adopted for securing the IT platforms and technologies that form a part of the IT ecosystem of intelligent cities. The first section of the chapter examines the various security requirements for the IT infrastructure of an intelligent city. From the next section of the chapter onward, we focus on the security threats that exist in each IT platform of an intelligent city. Starting with the cloud platform, the threats that exist for each underlying platform of an intelligent city such as big data, mobile devices, and IoT are examined in detail. The various ways and means to tackle the security challenges are also discussed in detail in the chapter. The different types of applications that form part of an intelligent city ecosystem are intelligent buildings, intelligent transportation systems, intelligent water systems, intelligent grids, and so on. The security threats for some of these applications and the techniques to safeguard them are also discussed in this chapter. The chapter concludes with a framework that can be adopted by intelligent cities to build and maintain a safe and secure IT framework.

12.1 Introduction

Information and communication technology (ICT) will be the key foundational component for intelligent cities of the future. These ICT components will be closely interconnected with one another to facilitate efficient coordination among the various city agencies in real time. However, for this to happen, it is critical to ensure the safety and security of the underlying information technology (IT) infrastructure. "According to 2013 Symantec Security threat report, 22% of the targeted security attacks to aimed at governments and energy or utilities companies, while governments and healthcare institutions are the target of 24% identity breaches" [1]. This fact sheds light on the importance of security for the IT infrastructure of intelligent cities.

In this chapter we identify the security challenges and requirements to be kept in mind for the design of intelligent IT infrastructure for intelligent cities. We identify security threats based on the four key platforms and technologies that are used by the IT infrastructure of intelligent cities. They are summarized in the following diagram:

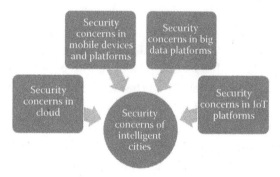

We also examine some of the techniques to be used by intelligent cities to leverage the underlying technological resources in a smart manner by ensuring that there is no unintentional or malicious access to city data that are stored and accessed in the underlying IT components of an intelligent city.

12.2 Security Requirements of an Intelligent City

The key security aspects that need to be kept in mind for the security of IT components that are applicable to an intelligent city are discussed in this section.

12.2.1 Confidentiality, Integrity, and Availability Triad

The security architecture of an intelligent city should fulfill three fundamental requirements, commonly referred to as the CIA triad, that need to be kept in mind during the design and development phase of the underlying IT infrastructure, as depicted in the following diagram:

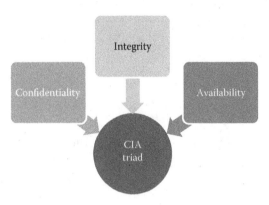

- *Confidentiality* ensures privacy by allowing only authorized users to have access to the underlying information that is stored and transmitted using the IT infrastructure of intelligent cities.
- *Integrity* ensures that only authorized users are allowed to modify the underlying information. Unauthorized users will not be able to alter the information in any manner by writing, deleting, or updating operations.
- *Availability* ensures that authorized users have access to the underlying information when it is required. This includes ensuring that the IT infrastructure of intelligent cities has inbuilt fault tolerance capabilities. Fault tolerance can be built into the IT infrastructure by ensuring that backup components are present for each of the IT infrastructure components—servers, storage, and networks. Server backup can be ensured by clustering the servers to provide a high-availability environment. It is also important to ensure that the backup server is an identical copy of the primary server and can take over the role of the primary server immediately if the latter experiences failure. Storage backup can

be ensured by using the highly scalable RAID (redundant array of inexpensive [or independent] disks) architecture for hard disks in which the same data are striped and mirrored across multiple hard disks so that even if one hard disk fails, data will not be lost as they will be stored in the other disks of the array. Fault tolerance in networks can be ensured by providing multiple switches, ports, and cables between the two connecting endpoints to ensure that the failure of any network component will not hamper the transfer of data through the network.

12.2.2 Authentication, Authorization, and Audit Trial Framework

The Authentication, Authorization, and Audit (AAA) framework is a security requirement that is of paramount importance for the IT infrastructure of intelligent cities. The various components of the framework are

- *Authentication.* This process checks that a user's credentials are valid so that users with invalid credentials will not be allowed to access the underlying information. The simplest way to use authentication is with the help of user names and passwords. But as hacking techniques are evolving day by day, it is very important to ensure that sophisticated authentication techniques are in place. One such authentication mechanism that is used is called multifactor authentication. Multifactor authentication is a special authentication technique that uses a combination of a parameters to verify a user's credentials. An example of a multifactor authentication mechanism is described below.
  - A *first factor* is a user name and password that will be unique for the specific user and sometimes may be unique for the specific session as well.
  - A *second factor* is a secret key that is generated by a random number generator or a secret key phrase that is known only to the user or an answer to a secret question that is specific to a particular user.

- A *third factor* could be any biometric parameter of the user that could be used as his or her biometric signature. This could include aspects such as iris recognition, fingerprint recognition, and so on.
- Multifactor authentication uses a combination of all of the parameters mentioned previously to verify a user's credentials. In some cases only two of the factors mentioned may be used for authentication, and this is called two-factor authentication.

- *Authorization* is a process that ensures that a specific user has rights to perform specific operations on a specific object. This generally involves granting different types of permissions to different types of users based on their role in a city government. For example, a fire station executive may be able to read only the data pertaining to other city departments such as water but not to edit it. Editing permission may be given only to the city supervisors or executives who are part of the water department of the city. The different types of permissions for different users on different objects are mapped and stored in a table called the Access Control List (ACL). The different types of permissions that are given for users are classified as
  - *Read Only.* The user has permission only to read the object. The user cannot delete or edit the object. This type of permission is granted to staff members who perform day-to-day city operations and are not required to perform any alteration on the data.
  - *Read and Write.* The user has permission to read and alter the object. This type of permission is granted to city administrators and city supervisors who have the overall authority and discretion to validate the rights and access permissions of other city officials.

- *Audit trial* is an activity conducted periodically to assess the effectiveness of the security measures that are implemented in the IT infrastructure of an intelligent city. An audit trial is performed with the help of audit logs that track the operations performed by different users.

12.2.3 Defense-in-Depth

Defense-in-depth is a mechanism that should be used to provide a high level of security to the IT infrastructure of an intelligent city. It ensures that multiple levels or layers of security are present within an IT infrastructure to ensure that even if security at one level is compromised for some reason, security at other levels should be able to safeguard the underlying IT infrastructure. As multiple levels of security are provided in this approach, it is also called a layered approach to security implementation. It offers enhanced security to the IT infrastructure by providing multiple layers of security and more time for city officials to react to a security breach that has occurred in one layer because the security measures in the other layers will be working to protect it. A high-level architecture of the defense-in-depth approach is given below:

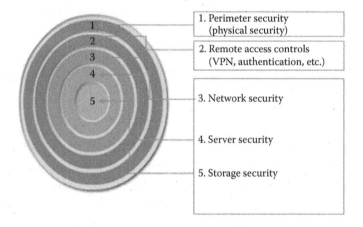

12.2.4 Trusted Computing Base

The trusted computing base (TCB) defines the boundary for the critical information components that form part of the IT infrastructure of intelligent cities. Any security breaches that occur within the TCB boundary will affect the entire IT infrastructure in an adverse manner. This helps to establish a clear definition between the critical and noncritical components of the IT infrastructure of the city. For example, if we take an example of a PC or tablet, the operating system (OS) and configuration files will be a part of the TCB, as any security breaches to the OS will corrupt the entire PC. It is very important for TCB to be defined for the IT infrastructure of an intelligent city. It helps to provide multiple additional levels of security for the components that fall under the TCB of the IT infrastructure.

12.2.5 Encryption

Encryption is the process of converting data into a format that cannot be interpreted easily and directly by unauthorized users. It is very important to ensure that data stored in the IT infrastructure of the intelligent city and the data that are transmitted via the networks are in encrypted form. This is very helpful to prevent unauthorized deception of data by third-party agents. The process of converting the data back to their original form is called decryption. Several encryption software are available in the market.

Pretty Good Privacy (PGP) is a strong data encryption and decryption program that is widely used by the federal government for protecting all types of government data such as email, files, and entire disk partitions of computers.

Apart from the security requirements mentioned earlier, an additional security requirement of the IT infrastructure of an intelligent city is resilience. Resilience is the capability of an IT infrastructure to return to its original state after it is disturbed by some internal or external factors.

The majority of the intelligent city applications will be built and deployed on cloud platforms. Hence all security concerns of cloud platforms will pose security threats for intelligent cities as well. In the next section, we examine some of the security concerns of cloud platforms.

12.3 Security Concerns of Cloud Platforms

Cloud security architecture has three different layers: software applications, platform, and infrastructure layers. Each layer has its own set of security concerns. We discuss some of them in the context of intelligent cities that would rely mainly on the public cloud for its IT requirements.

One of the main concerns related to the cloud is multitenancy. Multitenancy refers to the fact that the cloud infrastructure, because of the underlying virtualization platform, provides features to serve multiple independent clients (tenants) using the same set of resources. This consequently increases the risks to data confidentiality and integrity. These risks are especially severe in the public cloud environment because in the public cloud services can be used by competing clients as compared to private clouds; in addition, the number of cloud users is much higher in public clouds.

Some of the ways to overcome the concerns due to multitenancy are

- Virtual machine segmentation
- Database segmentation
- Virtual machine introspection

12.3.1 Virtual Machine Segmentation

Virtualization forms the basis of most of Infrastructure as a Service (IaaS) offerings. There are many types of virtualization softwares available in the market. These softwares provide the capability to convert a physical machine into multiple virtual machines (VMs). These VMs are provided to customers as part of IaaS; they run on virtual platforms and serve as databases, Web servers, and file servers. The main component of a virtualization platform is a hypervisor that acts as an OS for the VMs and provisions all the resources required for the operation of VMs. The major security concern in a virtualized infrastructure arises from the fact that VMs owned by multiple customers reside on the same physical machine. This aspect places the VMs in a privileged position with respect to one another and can introduce several types of security risks such as unauthorized connection, monitoring, and malware induction. To prevent such security threats, it is very important to ensure that VMs that contain confidential customer data are segmented and isolated from one another, a process called VM segmentation.

12.3.2 Database Segmentation

In IaaS, infrastructure resources are offered as a service. In SaaS, apart from software applications, a database is also offered as a service. This will introduce a scenario in which multiple customers will store their data in the same database as multiple rows that are differentiated based on assigned customer IDs. In some situations such as application code errors or access control list errors, there is much risk to customer data. For controlling access to database data, quite a few tools and technologies are available. To prevent the occurrence of such situations, many tools are available in the market. These tools work on the basis of a system for authentication and authorization that ensure that only some rows are modifiable based on certain predefined security policies that ensure that access to data is warranted. Another technique that could be used to reduce security threats in this situation is the encryption of data stored in the database. This ensures that even if the security of the data is compromised, it would be difficult to decrypt it.

12.3.3 VM Introspection

Another important technique that could be used to eliminate the risks of multitenancy is VM introspection. VM introspection is a service that is provided by the hypervisor. It examines the internal state of each VM that runs on top of the hypervisor. Many tools are available in the market that leverage the benefits of this service to provide VM segmentation and isolation. VM introspection provides the following details of each VM.

- Applications and services that are present
- Configuration details

With the help of these details of VMs, it is possible to create and implement custom security policies on each VM. An example of such a policy could be to ensure that no other VM should join a specific VM group until it has some matching OS configuration parameters. This ensures that in a multitenant environment, VMs remain segmented and isolated.

12.3.4 *Distributed Denial of Service*

In a cloud system, if a host of messages attack all nodes of the cloud system and overutilize the server resources, making the resources unavailable for actual requirements, it is called a distributed denial of service (DDoS) attack. There are two primary versions of DDoS attacks that can occur: simple and complex. Examples of simple DDoS attack tools are X-Dos (XML-based denial of service) as well as H-Dos (HTTP-based denial of service). Example of complex DDoS attack tools are Agobot, Mstream, and Trinoo. H-DoS are used by attackers who are interested in using less complex Web-based tools for attack. One additional advantage of these simple tools is the ease of implementation of attacks. DX-DoS occurs when XML-based messages are sent to a Web server in such a way that they will use up all the server's resources. Coercive parsing attack is an X-Dos attack in which Web content is parsed using Simple Object Access Protocol (SOAP) to transform it into an application. A series of open tags are used by a coercive parsing attack to exhaust the central processing unit (CPU) resources on the Web server. In case of an H-DoS attack, a series of about 1000 plus threads are started to create HTTP simultaneous random requests to exhaust all the resources. Several tools are available in the market to detect and eliminate DDoS attacks. Cloud service providers can use these tools at their discretion. One such example is discussed in the following paragraph.

12.3.4.1 Real-Life Example of DDoS Attack Bloomberg News reported that hackers used AWS's EC2 cloud computing unit to launch an attack against Sony's PlayStation Network and Qriocity entertainment networks. The attack reportedly compromised the personal accounts of more than 100 million Sony customers.

12.3.4.2 Imperva SecureSphere Web Application Firewall to Prevent DDoS Attacks The Imperva SecureSphere Web Application Firewall is a security appliance that is capable of preventing DDoS attacks in a cloud infrastructure. In addition to DDoS, this software also has the capability to prevent several types of Web attacks such as Structured Query Language (SQL) injection.

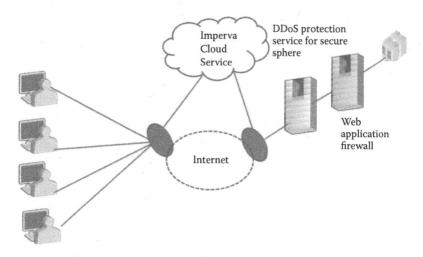

The tool uses the following features to prevent DDoS attacks on the cloud infrastructure:

- *ThreatRadar Reputation.* This service keeps track of users who are attacking other websites. By using this information, it will filter off any request from those users and prevent them from getting into the cloud system.
- *Up-to-Date Web Attack Signatures.* This service helps to monitor and keep track of bot user agents and DDoS attacks vectors.
- *DDoS Policy Templates.* This service helps to detect users who have the pattern of generating and sending HTTP requests with long response times.
- *Bot Mitigation Policies.* This service has the capability to send a JavaScript challenge to users' browsers. This JavaScript challenge has the capacity to detect and block bots.
- *HTTP Protocol Validation.* This service monitors and records buffer overflow attempts and other intrusion techniques.

12.3.5 VM/Hypervisor-Based Security Threats

The VMs, which form the basis of the cloud infrastructure, are also subjected to various types of vulnerabilities that pose severe threats to the cloud infrastructure. Some of them are shown in the following:

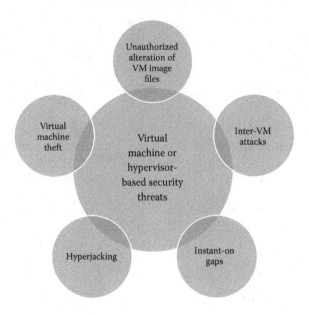

12.3.6 Unauthorized Alteration of VM Image Files

VMs are susceptible to security threats when they are running as well as when they are powered off. When a VM is powered off, it is available as a VM image file. This image file is exposed to several security threats such as malware infections. Apart from that, if appropriate security measures are not in place, VM image files can be used by hackers to create new unauthorized VMs. It is also possible to patch these VM image files so as to infect the VMs that are created using these image files. VM security can be compromised even during VM migration. At the time of VM migration, the VMs are exposed to several types of network attacks such as eavesdropping and unauthorized modification. One technique that could be used to protect the VM image files is to encrypt them when they are powered off or being migrated.

12.3.7 VM Theft

VM theft enables a hacker or attacker to copy or move a VM in an unauthorized manner. This is made possible mainly because of the presence of inadequate controls on VM files. These inadequate controls will allow the unauthorized copy or movement of VM files. VM theft could prove to be fatal if the VM that is stolen contains confidential customer data.

One way to restrict VM theft is to impose a required level of copy and move restrictions on VMs. Such restrictions effectively bind a VM to a specific physical machine in such a way that even if there is a forceful copy of the VM, it will not operate on any other physical machine. A VM with required level of copy and move restrictions cannot run on a hypervisor installed on any other physical machine.

Apart from VM theft, another threat that can happen at the VM level is known as "VM escape." Normally, VMs are encapsulated and isolated from each other and from the underlying parent hypervisor. In normal scenarios, there is no mechanism available for a guest OS and the applications running on it to break out of the VM boundary and directly interact with the hypervisor. The process of breaking out and interacting with the hypervisor is called a VM escape. Because the hypervisor controls the execution of all VMs, due to VM escape, an attacker can gain control over every other VM running on it by bypassing security controls that are placed on those VMs.

12.3.8 Inter-VM Attacks

Multiple VMs run on the same physical machine. So if the security of one VM is compromised, there is a very easy possibility for the security of other VMs running on the same physical machine to be compromised. In one scenario, it is possible for an attacker to compromise one guest VM that can then get passed on to the other VMs running on the same physical machine. To prevent the occurrence of such scenarios, it is very important to have firewalls and intrusion detection systems that have the capability to detect and prevent malicious activity at the VM level.

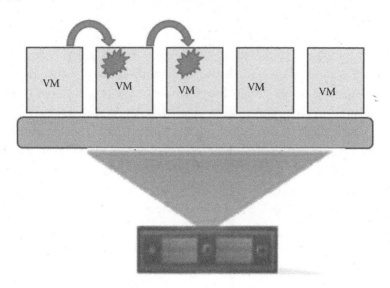

12.3.9 *Instant-On Gaps*

VMs have some vulnerabilities that are not present in physical machines. This is mainly due to the techniques that are used to provision, use, and de-provision them. Sometimes these cycles are repeated very frequently. This frequent activation and deactivation of VMs can pose challenges to ascertain that their security systems are constantly updated.

After some time, these VMs can automatically deviate from their defined security baselines and this in turn can introduce significant levels of security threats. This will give many options to attackers to access them. There is also a possibility that new VMs could be cloned and created from these VMs that have vulnerabilities. If this is done, the security threats will be passed on to the newly created VMs, which will increase the area of the attack surface. It is very important to ensure that VMs possess a security agent that has all the latest security configuration updates.

When a VM is not online during an antivirus update, that VM will have vulnerabilities when it comes online, as it would not have received the latest security updates. One solution to this problem could be to have a dedicated security VM in each physical machine to automatically update all VMs running in that physical machine with all the latest security updates.

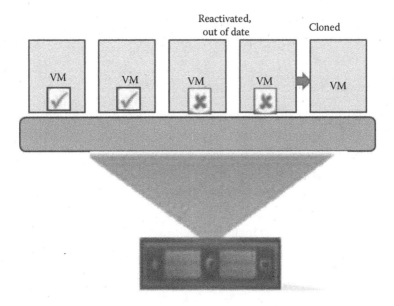

12.3.10 Hyperjacking

Hyperjacking enables an attacker to install a rogue hypervisor that has the capability to take complete control of the underlying physical server. This is a rootkit level vulnerability. A rootkit is a malicious program that is installed before a hypervisor fully boots on a physical server. In this manner, the rootkit is able to run in the server with privileged access and remains invisible to the system administrators. Once a rootkit is installed, it gives permission to an attacker to mask the ongoing intrusion and maintain privileged access to the physical server by bypassing the normal authentication and authorization mechanisms that are employed by an OS.

Using such a rogue hypervisor, an attacker can run unauthorized applications on a guest OS without the OS realizing the presence of such an application. With hyperjacking, an attacker could control the interaction between the VMs and the underlying physical server. Regular security measures are ineffective against this rogue hypervisor because

- The guest OS is unaware of the fact that the underlying server has been attacked.

- Antivirus and firewall applications cannot detect the presence of the rogue hypervisor, as it is installed directly over the server itself.

Measures against hyperjacking include

- Hardware-assisted secure launching of the hypervisor so that rootkit level malicious programs cannot launch. This would involve designing and using a TCB for the hypervisor getting support at the hardware level.
- Scanning hardware level details to assess the integrity of the hypervisor and locate the presence of the rogue hypervisor. This scanning may include checking the state of the memory as well as registering in the CPU.

12.4 Security Threats to Big Data

Big data is huge volumes of constantly changing data that come in from a variety of different sources. The constantly changing nature of big data introduces a variety of security threats for big data platforms. Some of the key challenges are summarized in the following diagram:

12.4.1 Distributed Programming Frameworks

Many programming frameworks that process big data use parallel computation to process huge amounts of data quickly. One such example is the MapReduce framework that is used for processing big data. This framework splits the data into multiple chunks. The mapper then works on each chunk of data and generates key/value pairs for each chunk. In the next step, the reducer component combines values that belong to each key and then generates a final output. In this framework, the main security threat is with regard to mappers. Mappers can be hacked and made to generate incorrect key value pairs. This in turn will lead to the generation of incorrect final results. Owing to vast amounts of big data, it is impossible to detect the mapper that generated the incorrect value. This in turn can affect the accuracy of data, which may adversely affect data-rich computations. The main solution to this problem is to secure mappers using various algorithms that are available.

12.4.2 Use of NoSQL Databases

NoSQL databases that are designed to store big data scale well to store huge amounts of data. But they do not have any security controls/policies embedded in them. The security controls are designed and incorporated into the middleware by the database programmers. There is no provision to include security practices as part of NoSQL database design. This poses a significant threat to the big data stored in the NoSQL databases. A solution to this problem is for organizations to review their security policies thoroughly and ensure that appropriate levels of security controls are incorporated into their middleware.

12.4.3 Storage Tiering

Most present-day organizations have a tiered approach to store data. The tiered approach consists of multiple tiers of heterogeneous storage devices that vary in terms of cost, performance, storage capacity, and security policies that are enforced. In normal scenarios, data are stored in different tiers based on their frequency of access, cost, volume, or any other parameter that is important for the organization. The tiering of data is done manually. However, with the ever increasing volumes of big data, it is becoming very difficult for storage administrators to do tiering of such huge amounts of data manually. Hence many organizations now have automatic storage tiering that is done with the help of some preconfigured policies. This might ensure that some data such as Research & Development data that are not frequently used as per the policy may be stored in the lowest tier. But it might be an important data from the context of organizations and storing such data in the lowest tier that has less data security may expose the data to security threats.

12.4.4 Data Source Validation

As per the 3V's of big data—Volume, Velocity, and Variety—input data can be collected from diverse kinds of sources. Some sources may have data validation techniques in place and others may not. This is more prominent when the input comes in from mobile devices such as tablets and cell phones. Because many present-day organizations are promoting the Bring Your Own Device concept (BYOD), the possibility of threats that are likely to creep in from the mobile devices is still higher. Some examples of mobile device threats are spoofed cell phone IDs.

12.4.5 Privacy Concerns

In an attempt to perform analytics to derive insights, many activities of the users are being tracked without their knowledge. These data, which are tracked by organizations for deriving various types of insights, could prove to be extremely harmful for the users if they are passed on to some untrusted third party.

12.4.5.1 Privacy Concern of Big Data Analytics   A recent event reported in the news is an eye opener on how big data analytics could compromise the privacy of an individual. An analysis that was done by a retail organization for marketing purposes was able to inform a father about his teenage daughter's pregnancy.

12.5 Requirements of the Security Management Framework for Big Data

Big data involves data of huge sizes and different types that are constantly changing in nature. To design a security management framework for big data, the three key parameters to be kept in mind are summarized in the following diagram:

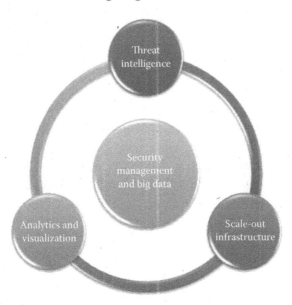

12.5.1 Agile Scale-Out Infrastructure

To manage huge amounts of constantly changing data, the IT infrastructure of organizations should have agility and scale-out capabilities. Apart from storing and managing huge amounts of big data, organizations also use these data to support a plethora of new delivery models such as cloud computing, mobility, outsourcing, and so on. The security management infrastructure should have the capability to adapt quickly to collect and secure this type of data. The underlying security infrastructure should be able to expand and adapt easily to facilitate easy identification of new threats that evolve continually with each new type of data and the associated delivery mechanism.

12.5.2 Security Analytics

Many data analytics and visualization tools exist in the market. They support analytics for a wide range of activities and device types. But the number of tools in the market that provide security analytics capabilities is limited. Security management officials require many types of sophisticated analytical tools that can provide them with diverse kinds of security analysis insights and visualization capabilities. Security management in enterprises covers a wide range of functions including security analysis of networks, security analysis of databases, and so on. Each type of security analysis requires different types of data. For example, to perform security analysis of networks, logs and network information pertaining to specific sessions of activity are required. Software that supports the analytical and visualization requirements of diverse types of security personnel in an organization should be present in the organization. For example, to perform security analysis of log information, a separate category of tools is available that comes under the broad umbrella called machine-to-machine (M2M) analytics.

12.5.2.1 IBM Accelerator for Machine Data Analytics Machines produce large amounts of data. These data contain a wealth of actionable insights. However, to extract and perform analysis on such a huge amount of data, tools with large-scale data extraction, transformation, and analysis capabilities are required. IBM® Accelerator for Machine Data Analytics provides a set of diverse applications that helps to import, transform, and analyze these machine data for the purpose of identifying event and pattern correlations and use them to make informed decisions based on the data present in the log and data files.

IBM Accelerator for Machine Data Analytics provides the following key capabilities [2]:

- Search within and across multiple log entries using text search, faceted search, or a timeline-based search to find specific patterns or events of interest
- Enrich the context of log data by adding and extracting log types into the existing repository
- Link and correlate events across systems

12.6 Threat Monitoring and Intelligence

Diverse types of threats for data exist within an organization and outside as well. To add to this, new types of threats are evolving every day. It is very important for organizations to stay updated on the threat environment so that the security analysts can get a clear picture of the various types of threat indicators and the security compromises inflicted by them.

All the mobile applications and use cases of intelligent cities discussed in the previous section are designed with respect to smart phones. In the next section, we examine some of the security threats to smart phones and also some mechanisms that can be used to secure smart phones.

12.7 Security Threats in Smart Phones

Smart phones have the capability to connect to various types of external systems such as Internet, GPS, and other different types of mobile devices using wireless networking technology. This is the key feature of smart phones that makes them one of the most widely used and popular devices. Residents of intelligent cities use smart phones to store much of their personal data such as address book, bank account details, meeting and appointment details, and so on. Proliferation of technologies such as near-field communication for various purposes in an intelligent city makes it critical to ensure security of the smart phone and the data stored there. A smart phone is exposed to numerous vulnerabilities that can compromise its security. In an intelligent city, it is inevitable to devise security measures for the security of smart phones.

The vulnerabilities in smart phones can be classified into two broad categories: internal and external. Internal vulnerabilities exist within the smart phone and external vulnerabilities creep into smart phones from the external systems to which they are connected. Some of the internal vulnerabilities are

- *Operating system implementation error.* This error will occur due to the presence of some erroneous code in the OS of mobile devices. Usually these types of errors are not introduced by the end-users and they creep into the mobile devices as a result of lapses in the mobile OS-owning organizations. It is very common to have such errors in the new version or version upgrades of a mobile OS. These OS errors can easily provide many options to the attackers to hack the OS and gain illegitimate access to the smart phone or install rogue applications that can track and retrieve the details of the user from the smart phone. One way to avoid this could be by installing only version upgrades that have been fully tested and corrected and to refrain from installing beta versions of operating systems.

- *End-user unawareness error.* The smart phone end-user can compromise the security by one or all of the following actions that are mainly due to the lack of awareness of the end-user.
  - Using untrusted wireless networks to connect to Internet
  - Installing mobile application from untrusted sources
  - Connecting to untrusted websites using mobile phones that can inject some malware into the device
  - Improper configuration settings in the mobile device browser
  - Loss of mobile devices, which can pose a serious security threat to the user's personal information stored in the mobile device

The following are some of the external vulnerabilities.

- *Wireless network threats.* The attacker could hack the wireless network to which the smart phone is connected and thereby gain access to the mobile device of the user.
- *External websites.* If the external website to which an end-user is connected is hacked by an attacker, it is also possible for the attacker to gain access to the mobile device of the user with the help of the details that are gathered from that specific website. It is also possible that a malware that is present in an external website can get automatically installed in the mobile device if security mechanisms in the mobile device are not properly configured, such as unavailability of antivirus software in the mobile devices.
- *Other wireless devices.* Smart phones have the capability to connect and communicate with a wide range of other wireless devices. If any of those wireless devices have a malicious component, then there is a possibility of smart phones to be attacked by those malicious components as well.

12.8 Security Solutions for Mobile Devices

Many measures can be adopted by the user to enhance the security of the mobile devices. But none of these measures will offer complete security to mobile devices, as threats are being added day by day and it is impossible to devise solutions at the pace at which threats are being created. Some of the possible security solutions that can be adopted by the users are

- *System add-on.* This refers to system updates that are periodically made available to the smart phones. They include platform updates that will provide enhanced features and in some cases enhanced security as well. It is the responsibility of the user to ensure that the system updates are installed periodically.
- *System configuration.* This is a very expensive and time-consuming process, as it involves modification of the mobile OS code to add enhanced security features at the kernel level. This approach is rarely adopted by the users because of the enormous cost and time involved.
- *Antivirus, spam filter.* To protect smart phones from virus attacks, antivirus software is available for specific mobile OS. Some attacks from rogue websites can also be prevented by turning on the spam filter in smart phones.
- *Cryptographic security mechanisms.* Cryptographic techniques are available to ensure confidentiality and integrity of the data that are stored in the smart phone. Cryptography can be implemented in smart phones in two ways: mobile applications and mobile platform application programming interfaces (APIs). Cryptographic techniques use various mechanisms to ensure security of data that are stored in the smart phone. One such mechanism is to encrypt the data stored in the smart phone so that even if it is hacked by a third party, the information cannot be deciphered without the availability of the key, which is known only to the smart phone user. Most mobile platforms make several APIs for use by the developers. Some of these APIs can be used to access the mobile OS-specific security library. This way, the developers can develop specialized mobile security applications for various mobile platforms.

Apart from these methods, several mobile security applications are available in the mobile application store. It is the responsibility of the user to check and install the appropriate applications. In addition, to protect the information stored in the mobile devices, users can lock the mobile phones using strong passwords. Another option is to make a note of the International Mobile Equipment Identity (IMEA) number of the mobile device so that if the mobile device is lost/stolen, the IMEA number can be deactivated, which will disable all the functionalities of the mobile device automatically.

12.9 Security Concerns in the Internet of Things Platform

An Internet of Things (IoT) platform will contain hundreds of sensors and other different types of devices that are sending data to a public or private cloud or some big data platform using a wired or wireless network through a gateway as shown in the diagram below. The gateway for some devices will be present within the device itself, and for some other devices it will be present externally.

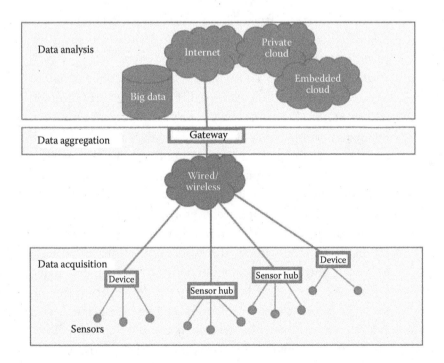

In IoT platforms, all types of platforms and technologies that were discussed previously in this chapter are used. So the security concerns present in each of them are applicable to the IoT platform as well. In addition, because of huge numbers and types of devices and the plethora of technologies used by them for communication, it is necessary to adopt a multifaceted and multilayered approach to ensure appropriate security for all components that are part of the IoT platform. The diverse aspects of this multifaceted approach should start right from the booting of the devices and should continue at each phase of the device lifecycle to build an IoT ecosystem that cannot be tampered with. Some of these security measures are discussed in the following paragraphs.

12.10 Security Measures for IoT Platforms/Devices

To ensure security of various devices and platforms that are part of the IoT network, it is essential to adopt a holistic mechanism that spans all the phases of a device's lifecycle. Some such mechanisms are discussed in the following paragraphs.

12.10.1 Secure Booting

When a device powers on, there should be an authentication mechanism to verify that the software that runs on the device is a legitimate one. This is done with the help of cryptographically generated digital signatures. This process ensures that only authentic software designed to run on the devices by the concerned parties will run on the devices. This establishes a trusted computing base for the devices upfront. But the devices still need to be protected from various kinds of runtime threats.

12.10.2 Mandatory Access Control Mechanisms

Mandatory access control mechanisms should be built into the operating system of the devices to ensure that the various applications and components will have access only to those resources that they need for their functioning. This will ensure that if an attacker is able to gain access to any of those components/applications, the attacker will be able to gain access only to very limited resources. This significantly reduces the attack surface.

12.10.3 Device Authentication for Networks

A device should get connected to some kind of a wired or wireless network to begin transmission of data. When a device is connected to a network, it should authenticate itself before it starts data transmission. For some types of embedded devices (which operate without manual intervention), the authentication can be done with the help of credentials that are maintained in a secured storage area of the device.

12.10.4 Device-Specific Firewalls

For each device, there should be some kind of firewall that will filter and examine the data that are specifically sent to that device. It is not mandatory for the devices to examine all types of traffic that traverse through the network, as that will be taken care of by the network security appliances. This is required also because of the fact that some specific types of embedded devices have custom-made protocols that are different from the common IT protocols that are used by organizations for data transmission. One classic example is the smart grid, which has its own set of protocols for communication. Hence it is essential for the device to have firewalls or some such mechanism in place to filter the traffic that is intended specifically for that device.

12.10.5 Controlled Mechanism to Ensure Application of Security Patches and Upgrades

Once devices are connected to the networks, they start receiving security patches and upgrades. It so happens that in some situations these patches and upgrades consume a great deal of network bandwidth, making it unavailable for other devices or applications that are part of the network. Operators need to ensure that patches, upgrades, and authentication of the devices should be planned in such a way that they involve minimum bandwidth consumption and do not impact the functional safety of the device.

In short, for an IoT network's security, the traditional safety measures that are typically adopted are not sufficient. It is mandatory to install security measures starting from the operating system of the participating devices.

12.11 Security Threats to Different IT-Based Infrastructure Components of an Intelligent City

An intelligent city will have many IT-based infrastructure components, each of which is subjected to some kind of security threat. Apart from the ones listed in the diagram below, additional IT-based applications might be present in an intelligent city. Some of the key components are summarized in the following diagram.

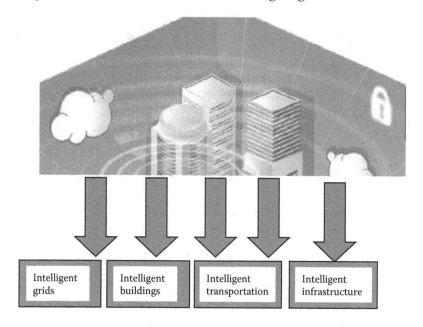

| Intelligent grids | Intelligent buildings | Intelligent transportation | Intelligent infrastructure |

Next we identify key security threats that are present in these IT infrastructure components along with some measures to curb them.

12.11.1 Security Threats in Intelligent Transportation Systems

Intelligent transportation systems enhance the quality of life of residents by tracking and monitoring the transportation services across the city. Sensors can capture data about the real-time status of transportation services and send the data to a centralized control center or dashboard that can then use the data to coordinate transport services across the city. Tracking and monitoring of transportation services requires a highly sophisticated IT infrastructure and close coordination between the various components to avoid disruptions. The different types of security threats that are possible in an intelligent transportation system are the following:

- The travel navigation systems may be hacked to misguide vehicle drivers into wrong routes by providing erroneous information about the traffic volume at various routes.
- The data transmitted to or from mobile devices may be subjected to spoofing.
- Unencrypted traffic reports can be attacked by hackers who can inject incorrect or false traffic-related data or reports into satellite-based navigation devices.

12.11.1.1 Attack of a Public Transport System in Europe   A teenager in Europe was able to attack the public transport systems with the help of a modified television remote control. He was able to cause severe traffic disruption in the city and was even able to cause a tram derailment by forcing a vehicle to take an abrupt turn when it was traveling at high speed.

12.11.2 Security Threats in Intelligent/Smart Grids and Other Infrastructure Components of an Intelligent City

The different components of intelligent grids are the following:

- Smart meters—digital meters that can track user consumption in real time and provide alerts to user end point devices
- Networks with two-way communication capabilities
- Meter data acquisition and management systems—software that collects data from the smart meters, calculates bill value, and analyzes usage metrics.

The security of each of these components can be compromised. Smart meters may be hacked to steal energy or to tamper with consumption data. Meter data acquisition and management systems can be hacked by the attackers using some of the vulnerabilities that may be present in the system, and this can severely hamper the transmission of data to the end-users. White listing techniques that can ensure that only certain applications or processes are active at specific points in time are effective in some situations. However, there are no solutions to zero-day vulnerabilities. Zero-day vulnerabilities are those for which no security patches are available.

Networks used by smart grids and other infrastructure components can be hacked by the attackers by installing some malwares that are capable of tracking sensitive network-related information. This sensitive information can be used by the attackers later to create denial-of-service attacks. These network-related threats can be eliminated to a great extent by using intrusion prevention techniques combined with some robust security practices to handle aspects such as browser patches, end-user awareness creation, and network usage tracking.

One of the best possible ways to prevent tampering of smart meters and meter data acquisition and management systems is the use of public key infrastructure (PKI). PKIs can be directly implemented on smart meters. This will ensure authentication and validation of meters in a connected network. It is also important to ensure that keys and certificates pertaining to a PKI environment are guarded appropriately using an appropriate management solution.

12.12 Best Practices to Be Adopted for a Secure Intelligent City

Some of the best practices that can be kept in mind for building and sustaining a safe and secure intelligent city are summarized in the following diagram:

Establish an appropriate governance framework

Fulfill governance, risk, and compliance

Maintain continuity of services

Protect information adequately

Adopt threat intelligence mechanisms as a part of security framework

Secure IT infrastructure components

Develop a robust Information Management strategy

Give adequate attention to the security of various city services

12.13 Conclusion

The IT infrastructure of an intelligent city is a conglomeration of technologies such as cloud, big data, mobile devices, and IoT. It is essential to ensure that each of these components is safe and secure to ensure continuous availability of services to citizens. The security requirements of the IT infrastructure components of an intelligent city were examined in detail in the first section of the chapter.

Each component of the IT infrastructure of an intelligent city is subjected to diverse types of vulnerabilities and threats. The vulnerabilities and threats that exist in each of these platforms were examined in detail. The techniques to safeguard the IT infrastructure components from these threats and vulnerabilities were also discussed in this chapter.

The different intelligent applications that are present in an intelligent city are intelligent grids, intelligent transport systems, intelligent water systems, intelligent buildings, and so on. The security concerns of these applications and the different ways to tackle them were also discussed. This chapter concludes with a set of best practices that can be adopted by cities to ensure safety and security of their IT infrastructure.

References

1. http://www.symantec.com/security_response/publications/threatreport.jsp?inid=us_ghp_thumbnail1_istr-2013.
2. Giampiero Nanni (2013). Transformational 'smart cities': Cyber security and resilience. http://www-01.ibm.com/support/knowledgecenter/SSPT3X_2.0.0/com.ibm.swg.im.infosphere.biginsights.product.doc/doc/acc_mda.html.

Index